IDLY SCRIBBLING RHYMERS

Studies of the Weatherhead East Asian Institute
Columbia University

STUDIES OF THE WEATHERHEAD EAST ASIAN INSTITUTE, COLUMBIA UNIVERSITY

The Studies of the Weatherhead East Asian Institute of Columbia University were inaugurated in 1962 to bring to a wider public the results of significant new research on modern and contemporary East Asia.

Idly Scribbling Rhymers

*Poetry, Print, and Community
in Nineteenth-Century Japan*

Robert Tuck

Columbia University Press   *New York*

Columbia University Press wishes to express its appreciation for assistance given by the Wm. Theodore de Bary Fund in the publication of this book.

Columbia University Press wishes to express its appreciation for assistance given by the Association for Asian Studies toward the cost of publishing this book.

Columbia University Press
Publishers Since 1893
New York   Chichester, West Sussex
cup.columbia.edu

Cataloging-in-Publication Data available from the Library of Congress
ISBN 978-0-231-18734-3 (cloth)
ISBN 978-0-231-54722-2 (ebook)

Cover design: Milenda Nan Ok Lee
Cover image: Paul Fearn / © Alamy

To Kate

Contents

Acknowledgments

Many people contributed to this project over the nearly ten years leading up to its publication. Thanks are due first of all to Haruo Shirane, whose guidance, good advice, and unflagging support laid the foundations not only for this book but also for a number of other subsequent projects. Tomi Suzuki pushed me to push myself throughout my time as a graduate student, helped me to develop as a scholar, and provided much useful advice on how to structure the book. David Lurie was always available and eager to bat ideas around and was a never-ending source of encouragement, particularly when I happened to stumble across something cool. Wiebke Denecke, while at Barnard, made me a better reader of *kanbun* and *kanshi* and introduced me to a number of both new ideas and people that helped my career immensely. Paul Anderer broadened my horizons in modern Japanese literature and film and trained me to think about texts in ways I had never previously considered.

While at Waseda from 2008 to 2010, Munakata Kazushige and Toeda Hirokazu helped me not only to find my feet in Tokyo but also to make sense of the unwieldy project I had brought to Japan and to take it in a more manageable direction. Fellowship support from the Japan Foundation and from Shinchōsha also provided invaluable time and freedom to do the archival work, particularly in terms of Meiji-era newspapers and periodicals, that underpins the book. I extend my sincere thanks to both organizations: the book would not have been possible without their generous support.

In June 2017, the Weatherhead East Asian Institute at Columbia University selected *Idly Scribbling Rhymers* as a recipient of its First Book Prize, a major honor and real vote of confidence in the project. My thanks to the selection committee and also to Ross Yelsey at the institute for all of his hard work, which helped to make the path to publication immeasurably smoother. I also would like to express my thanks to the Association of Asian Studies for providing subvention support through the AAS First Book Subvention Program.

I have been lucky enough to have a wonderful and supportive set of colleagues at the University of Montana. Judith Rabinovitch was, simply, the best mentor a junior scholar could wish for, helping me to get myself up and running (and to figure out how to teach effectively), and was always willing to chat about *kanshi*, the tenure track, or life in general. With Tim Bradstock, too, I spent many enjoyable hours discussing innumerable aspects of Chinese and Japanese literature, filling in the (many) gaps in my own understanding. Tim and Judith both took the time to read early drafts of a number of articles and of the chapters of this book; I owe them both a great deal. Brian Dowdle was (and is) a great source of support, good advice, and an all-around wonderful colleague. My new colleagues Michihiro Ama and Eric Schluessel took the time, despite being in their first year at the University of Montana, to read my lengthier chapters and provide insightful comments. I also received grant support for research and travel to Japan from the Yamaguchi Opportunity Fund and University Grants Program at the University of Montana, as well as from the Northeast Asia Council of the Association of Asian Studies, all of which enabled me to gather additional archival materials on a second trip to Japan in 2013.

Many others played important roles. Matthew Fraleigh provided helpful criticism and a second pair of eyes early on, and he continues to be extremely generous with his time and advice. Paul Rouzer read over the Kegon Falls poems and helped point out things I had overlooked. Machi Senjurō, Matthew Mewhinney, Ted Mack, and Tom Gaubatz all helped me access vital primary sources when I was unable to go to Japan or lay hands on them myself. I would also like to thank Janine Beichman, Emmanuel Lozerand, and Keith Vincent for support and encouragement throughout the past few years. I also extend my thanks to the two anonymous readers for Columbia University Press, whose careful reading of and perceptive comments on the manuscript improved it beyond measure.

Finally, thanks are due to my family, on both sides of the Atlantic, for their love and belief in me: my mother and father, Amanda and Anthony Tuck, and my brother Mike and his family; and, in the United States, my gratitude to Jack, Victoria, Dan, Joan, Anita, and David. Last, but not least, thanks to my wife, Kate, and to our two children, Alex and Zoë, who make life worthwhile.

Introduction

In February and March of 2006, the haiku poet and critic Fukunaga Norihiro published a two-part piece in the journal *Haiku*, one that was strikingly pessimistic about what the internet would do for—or rather, to—haiku in Japan. Although Fukunaga recognized that the internet offered haiku certain benefits, such as allowing "mothers with children, very busy salarymen, and people living overseas" to participate in haiku gatherings remotely, he also saw a number of dangers.[1] Noting that the internet had been developed by the U.S. military and was originally configured for writing in English, he expressed alarm that internet haiku would therefore be written horizontally rather than vertically as they should be. That the internet was not configured for the proper Japanese way of writing haiku was not a minor point; those who thought this unimportant were, he suggested, unqualified to "become intimate with haiku" (*haiku ni shitashimu*). A further concern was what he called haiku's "dilution" (*kihakuka*).[2] Fukunaga had been appalled to hear a haiku poet boast of how he could now use a computer to copy and paste haiku's characteristic seasonal words (*kigo*) and produce hundreds of verses very quickly. If haiku could be composed this easily, there would be no incentive for anyone to work at their verse, and standards would plummet.[3] Likewise, now that anyone could publish their haiku online at the click of a mouse, there could be no effective quality control. Already,

Fukunaga railed, "imitation haiku [*haiku modoki*], very low-level stuff, which really doesn't deserve the name of haiku, has begun to flood the net." Given this ease of production and publication, many promising poets who might otherwise have made something of themselves would not strive for greatness, and he feared that "they will end up never knowing true haiku" (*shin no haiku o shiranai mama ni owatte shimau koto de aru*). In closing, Fukunaga proclaimed, "I shall defend to the death the position that haiku is something you *write vertically*, not something you *type horizontally*."[4]

Fukunaga's piece drew a number of rebuttals. Critic Takayanagi Katsuhiro, writing in the same journal in 2010, noted that advances in coding in the intervening four years had made it easy to write haiku vertically online if one chose.[5] More substantively, though, Takayanagi suggested that Fukunaga had construed the range of abstract and physical social spaces in which haiku was practiced—the *za*, or "parlor"—too narrowly. For Takayanagi, the spirit of the *za* lay in the people behind it, not the technology itself. In fact, as he went on to observe, much of pioneering poet Masaoka Shiki's 正岡子規 (Tsunenori 常規, 1867–1902) project to fashion a new and consciously modern haiku during the Meiji period (1867–1912) had taken advantage of the new media spaces and communication technologies of that time, particularly newspapers, literary journals, trains, and a nationwide postal system.[6]

As Takayanagi's invocation of Shiki suggests, the issues with which Fukunaga was concerned—literary quality versus broad participation, concerns over new media technology and the boundaries of literary community, the question of elite versus popular genres—were not new ones in Japanese poetic history. In fact, Fukunaga's reflections, in the aftermath of a shift in media technology, on haiku's value as a popular genre would not have been out of place in the Meiji era itself; in some ways, they sound remarkably similar to Shiki's own writings on the subject. At the root of Fukunaga's concerns appears to be a simple question: if anyone can do it, what is the value of being a poet? Or, stated in more concise terms: who can, or should, be a poet?

This question was equally pressing in Japan during the period 1870–1900, the main focus of this book. These years were a crucial period of modernization that also saw the creation of many of the ideological underpinnings of the modern Japanese nation-state, and in what follows, my main area of interest is the role that the three traditional poetic genres of haiku, *kanshi* (Sinitic poetry), and *waka* (classical Japanese poetry) played in the Meiji state's programs of nation building and national subject formation.[7] The book is particularly concerned with intellectual debates over what I term a national-poetic community. This can be defined most simply as a community, real or imagined, made up exclusively of poets of a particular nationality. In the case of Meiji Japan, a series of assumptions underpinned the idea of a national-poetic community: that a given poetic genre had a special connection to national identity; that to compose in that genre was to express that identity; and that poets therefore composed both as individuals and as actors within a greater national project. The ongoing process of poetic creation was not fully separable from the work of strengthening and representing the nation; as such, the community was thus both national and poetic.

The idea of a national-poetic community was closely connected to intellectual discourse on "national poetry" (*kokushi*), a term that begins to appear most frequently in the early 1890s, after many of the structures of the Meiji state had been put in place and just as the academic field of "national literature" (*kokubungaku*) was beginning to emerge. Many Meiji poets and critics during this period argued that there was a very close overlap between national-poetic community and national community, or that they were in fact the same thing. Discussing *haikai*'s future in modern Japan, one critic wrote in 1890 that "everyone among the people of our land, even at the lowest levels of society, possesses a certain amount of artistic spirit."[8] Because all Japanese people were endowed with poetic ability, every member of the nation could and should compose the national poetry of haiku. We see here a vision of haiku as a common cultural inheritance, the actual or potential composition of haiku a bond uniting all Japanese subjects. Much the same applied with *waka*; as one prominent *waka* reformer wrote in 1892, the genre should be the property of "every member of the nation" (*kokujin oshinabete*).[9] In a striking public affirmation of the unity of national and poetic communities, in the late 1870s the Meiji government initiated a New Year's tradition of the emperor composing in *waka*, in response to which the common people were invited to send in their contributions. Through this, the entire nation, people and sovereign, would be united in the common act of composing *waka* poetry.

On this point, the notion of national-poetic community might seem as if it were largely an extension of previous narratives of the relationship between literary genres, print media, and the national imagination, most notably those advanced in Benedict Anderson's well-known 1983 *Imagined Communities*. This book, however, aims to complicate existing narratives of literature, nationalism, and modernity by showing that the imagined boundaries of the Meiji national-poetic community were frequently unstable and often exclusive, emphatically not the "deep, horizontal comradeship" of which Anderson spoke.[10] One of the most important questions in this book is how, precisely, the Meiji national-poetic community came to be defined. There were indeed Meiji-era poets and critics who spoke of an inclusive national-poetic community, even to the point of arguing that all Japanese subjects could or should be potential members therein. But others—among them many of the figures conventionally credited with modernizing their respective genres—argued more in terms of exclusion and hierarchy, the national-poetic community given shape and meaning by who should *not* be included. Even as it emerged at the beginning of the 1890s, then, the idea of a national-poetic community was defined by internal hierarchies and strategies of differentiation. Playing out in terms of gender (especially masculinity), social class, and political affiliation, these internal hierarchies and distinctions largely faded from view as the idea of an inclusive national-poetic community gathered strength during the early twentieth century, particularly after the 1904–1905 Russo-Japanese War. Yet insofar as the communities and intellectuals discussed in this book shaped the terms of "reform" and modernization discourses across multiple poetic genres, these fault lines of gender, class, and politics are critical to understanding how modern Japanese poetry came into being.

PRINT, POETRY, AND IMAGINING COMMUNITY

In discussing poetry in Meiji Japan, this book contributes to an extensive body of scholarship focusing on the roles literary genres play in modern nation-states. Following Anderson's *Imagined Communities*, scholars focusing on Japan have generally argued that both print media and literary genres were important institutional spaces within which the modern Japanese nation-state imagined itself. As Anderson famously claimed, "print capitalism," especially the daily newspaper, unifies and connects formerly disparate groups by making visible a shared language, culture, and set of experiences.[11] Literary genres also play an important role as a stage on which to present a national imagination and sense of community, particularly the novel, a genre that is itself often serialized in the newspaper.[12]

Scholarship on Japan's experience of modernization has found much in the Meiji period's novels and newspapers that is consistent with Anderson's arguments. James Huffman's study of Meiji print media, for instance, argues that newspapers of this period had the effect of "creating a public"—that is, a self-aware national community that understood itself clearly as Japanese—through their reporting of events deemed significant to the national interest.[13] In terms of literary studies, too, much scholarly attention has been devoted to the role of prose fiction in fashioning a national consciousness. John Pierre Mertz's study of early Meiji narrative fiction, particularly the political novels (*seiji shōsetsu*) of the period, finds that the characters in these works articulate a new, cohesive Japanese national identity—though at this comparatively early stage in Meiji, he suggests, the process is at least partly unintentional.[14] Analyzing later Meiji works, scholars such as Ken K. Ito, Karatani Kōjin, and Satoru Saito have identified a wide array of ideological roles that prose fiction can play in promoting and reflecting ideas of national subjecthood and state ideology.[15] The nation, it seems, is both reflected in and created by its novels.

The great majority of studies of the relationship between the national imagination and literary genres in the modern period have, however, overlooked poetry. Japanese critic Suga Hidemi has criticized *Imagined Communities* itself for having little to say about what Suga calls "the easily discernible connection between poetry and nationalism,"[16] with the result that, in Suga's view, Anderson's model cannot fully explain the emphasis on the sublime and the aestheticization of politics that Suga sees as key to both nationalism and fascism.[17] In the field of literary studies as a whole, modern Japanese poetry is a comparatively neglected area especially in English-language scholarship,[18] and more specifically no study in Japanese or English has attempted an extended investigation into how modern poetry and print media intersect, or what that intersection might mean for ideas of nationalism and national literary identity.[19] The near-total absence of poetry from critical discussions of Japanese modernity has implications beyond simply our understanding of the development of modern poetic genres; as this book shows, the study of poetry can make a material contribution to our understanding of the formation of national imaginations in Japan, of modes of literary reading and writing, and, because poetry was an important form of public discourse in Meiji print media, the relationship between press and public. The present study thus fills a significant gap in literary, media, and social history.

Applying the term "poetry" to Meiji requires a certain degree of care, since the idea of a holistic, overarching notion of poetry did not come to be firmly established in Japan until even as late as the mid-1890s, nor was there a stable terminology to go with it. In early Meiji, depending on the journal, *kanshi* and *waka* might appear together under the heading *shiika*, a term that in present-day usage denotes poetry in general; but until the mid-1890s, *shiika* did not include *haikai*, which rarely if ever appeared alongside the other two poetic genres. Other terms, such as *shifu*, might occasionally be used to denote poetry writ large, while another common present-day term, *shi*, was usually understood until the mid-1880s as denoting specifically Sinitic poetry, not poetry in general. These distinctions were maintained for so long in part because throughout the Edo period and well into Meiji, *haikai*, *kanshi*, and *waka* all had quite different practitioner demographics and degrees of cultural prestige; as we shall see in discussions on Meiji *waka* reform, the idea that *waka* could even be classed as "literature" in the same way as the other two genres was a matter of heated debate. Of the three poetic genres, *kanshi* was probably the most highly esteemed, with *waka* a close second, and *haikai* a distant third, in part on account of its large number of commoner practitioners. This division was often reflected in the structure of Meiji poetry periodicals; during early Meiji in particular, newspapers and literary journals would almost never feature all three poetic genres in the same space. If *haikai* was featured, it was often in a column separate from *kanshi* and *waka*.

Differences of prestige aside, the three traditional poetic genres were hugely important during Meiji because they were so widespread. Almost every newspaper during the Meiji period published poetry, and many ran a regular poetry column. In addition to newspapers, a number of important literary journals devoted largely or exclusively to poetic genres arose during early Meiji, especially those focusing on Sinitic poetry, such as Mori Shuntō's 森春濤 (Rochoku 魯直, 1819–1889) pioneering *Shin-bunshi* (1875–1884) and Narushima Ryūhoku's 成島柳北 (Korehiro 惟弘, 1837–1884) *Kagetsu shinshi* (1877–1884), both of which attracted widespread notice in Tokyo. Usually overseen by a well-known poet or group of poets, most such columns and periodicals accepted and encouraged reader submissions as well.

Poetic genres were, then, just as common as serialized prose fiction in Meiji Japan's print media, perhaps even more so; and yet the role that they played in such media has received little or no attention to date.[20] In what follows, I have elected to focus on poetic genres not only to rectify this oversight but also because poetic genres were written, consumed, and published in a way that was markedly different from prose fiction and that therefore requires us to rethink certain prose-based assumptions about how literary genres are written, consumed, and published. One important point is the sheer number of people involved in their creation; where only a tiny handful of people in Meiji Japan might ever manage to have a novel set before the reading public in serialization or book form, literally millions could (and did) publish poetry. Instead of the relatively top-down approach of a few creators and millions of (largely anonymous) consumers that the novel obliges us to take, study of poetic genres and the groups and media associated with them allows us to explore the creation and definition of imagined national communities at something much closer to ground level.

A related point is that poetic genres were usually interactive. The newspaper novel, for instance, generally performed its ideological work simply by being read; the reader of a serialized novel in a newspaper would not be expected to respond by producing a novel him- or herself and submitting it to the paper for publication. By contrast, the idea that most or all of its members would write poetry was crucial to Meiji ideas of national-poetic community. As one (male) critic urging elite women to study *waka* wrote in 1893, "I do not say to you, ladies . . . that you should produce something like the *Tale of Genji*; rather, I simply ask that you learn something through which you can express your heaven-endowed emotions."[21] In this conception, *waka*'s benefits for Japanese women lay not only in passive appreciation; it was essential that they write their own verse as well. Much the same idea held with both *kanshi* and haiku; one read poetry collections not simply to appreciate the works therein but as a preparation to learn to write poetry oneself, and the poetry columns of Meiji newspapers and journals usually assumed that readers would not only read what was published but also send in their own verses as a matter of course. As such, especially in early Meiji, the dividing line between reader and writer in a poetry column was seldom clear-cut. A column on any given day might well have been written entirely by its ostensible readers, and an aspiring poet who proved particularly skilled might be hired to write for the publication on a formal basis. The Meiji poetry column was a dynamic and interactive space, one defined as much by its "writership" as by its readership. This kind of dynamic reader participation is unique to poetic genres during Meiji, and its implications for our understanding of both print media and literary genres have received little critical attention.

Poetry as practiced in Meiji Japan was thus active, dialogic, and above all social. For the most part, it was also a group activity, with many practices and mechanisms of poetic composition predicated upon social interaction among individuals. Among these practices, which I classify under the term "poetic sociality," were the tendency to practice poetry as a group activity, pedagogical practices such as mutual critique and the master-disciple relationship, and the exchange between individual poets of textually linked forms of verse. As a defining element of poetic practice, poetic sociality allows the book to ground its discussion of national-poetic community in highly specific terms, in interactions between specific groups and named individuals. In approaching national-poetic discourse in culturally specific, ground-level terms, I aim to supplement and expand the largely top-down, abstract Andersonian model.[22]

Poetic sociality was in no way an exclusively modern phenomenon; throughout much of the Edo period, *haikai*, *waka*, and *kanshi* alike were usually practiced as a group-based activity. A poet would almost always belong to one or more poetic societies and attend regular meetings at which he (or, occasionally, she) would compose poetry and receive comments and criticism from a master or senior poets, and often enjoy food and drink. Though precise figures are hard to come by for Edo-period groups, some early Meiji *haikai* societies claimed memberships in the thousands, with one, Mimori Mikio's 三森幹雄 (1829–1910) Meirin Kōsha, at one point claiming ten thousand members.[23] Although early modern *waka* groups were not as widespread as *haikai* ones, they were far from rare, with particularly strong representation from Shinto priests, National Learning scholars (*kokugakusha*), and certain court nobles.[24] Much the same model of social organization applied in the case of *kanshi* poets, though their overall numbers were somewhat smaller than with the other two genres. The *kanshi* society (*ginsha* or *shisha*) begins to appear as a distinct social phenomenon in the mid-eighteenth century and remained the basic unit of social organization for the *kanshi* world well into the twentieth century.[25]

The social bonds of the poetic society were reinforced by a series of textual practices that emphasized interaction among individual poets. What we now think of as the modern haiku, for instance, derives from the *hokku*, or "opening verse," in a communally-composed linked-verse sequence. The initial *hokku*, in 5-7-5 syllabic pattern, would be followed by a response from another poet in a 7-7 syllabic pattern, then another 5-7-5 verse, and so on, for a total sequence of thirty-six iterations (or, more rarely, one hundred). Possessed of complex rules and relatively time-consuming, linked verse gradually dropped out of favor over the course of the Edo period and was superseded by practices of "point-scoring *haikai*" (*tentori haikai*). Initially developed as a pedagogical tool and understandable as a shortened form of linked verse, point-scoring *haikai* involved a master providing the first part of a verse sequence, to which students would then respond.[26] The master would award points based on the quality of each student's response.

Point-scoring *haikai* was a divisive topic in both the early modern and modern *haikai* world because it was easily adapted into a lucrative business for many *haikai* masters. Using a go-between or printed pamphlets to distribute the first part of the verse or sequence, a master could charge a fee for grading entries and award a material prize to a set number of winners. Point-scoring *haikai* devolved as a result into essentially a form of gambling, and although reform-minded masters periodically attacked it as immoral and the Tokugawa government banned certain forms of *haikai*-based gambling on a number of occasions, it was still being practiced well into the Meiji period.[27] This commercialization and the resulting degradation of literary value was an area that Shiki in particular singled out for criticism as part of his later reform movement.

Monetary issues aside, the basic notion of soliciting verses on set themes from poets across a wide geographical area was already well established by mid-Edo, and a number of major Meiji newspapers in fact continued the spirit of these activities into the spaces of modern periodical media, running prize-haiku (*kenshō haiku*) competitions in their pages that featured cash prizes for the best entries. Though it rarely had this openly mercenary aspect, *waka* was also often composed at poetry parties (*utakai*), at which one would compose and recite poems or compare the work of one team of poets with that of another in a formal competition (*utaawase*) presided over by a judge, a practice still in use well into Meiji.

Kanshi, too, had its own mechanisms of social and dialogic composition, and one that was particularly popular among Japanese poets was rhyme matching (Ch. *heyun*, J. *wain*) or rhyme following (Ch. *ciyun*, J. *jiin*). In a matched-rhyme poem, one would retain the rhyme graphs, located at the end of specific lines of another poet's existing work, and use the graphs as a structure around which to build a responding poem. The responding poem thus retained part of the language, imagery, and structure of the original while usually adding a new twist. A sequence of rhyme-matching *kanshi* can be viewed as a kind of poetic conversation, in which poets emphasize their shared experiences and values through the lexical link of the matched rhymes and the handling of similar themes back and forth from one poem to another. Matched-rhyme poems were frequently composed as a way of expressing friendship with or admiration for another poet, and the sequence of poems could be extended, via iterations of the same rhymes, for as long as the poets involved could sustain their interest. Capable in this way of generating a theoretically infinite chain of poetic discourse, the practice of rhyme matching meant that any given *kanshi* verse was never a completed, closed work; it would always be possible for another poet to use it as a starting point for a subsequent series.[28]

What I term poetic sociality, therefore, extends beyond the single, finished poetic work to encompass a wide range of compositional, dialogic, and pedagogical practices through which individual works come into being and further poetic production is encouraged. Virtually all these practices and mechanisms of composition were equally effective (perhaps even more so) within the abstract space of periodical print media. The idea of poetic sociality in Meiji print media owes a considerable debt to Ogata Tsutomu's idea of the *za*, or the "parlor," the social space in which poetry is composed. In his influential *Literature of the Parlor* (*Za no bungaku*, 1973), Ogata suggests understanding the parlor in both a physical sense, as the actual face-to-face space of a literary gathering, and in a broader sense, as a series of conceptual bonds linking a larger community of poets across space and even across time.[29] In arguing that the modern spaces of the Meiji print media functioned as an extended parlor, however, I am applying Ogata's ideas beyond their original scope, for as Ogata sees it, modern Japanese literature is concerned primarily with individual rather than communal production.[30]

THE FRACTURED NATIONAL IMAGINATION

Given the preceding, it would seem tempting to point to Edo-period Japan's various poetic groups as potential precursors for the emergence of a national-poetic community. After all, by the coming of Meiji, poets already practiced their work in well-defined communities, with textual practices that articulated a common cultural identity across both time and space, and so it should have been only a small step from poetic community to national community. Eiko Ikegami, for example, has made a similar argument, suggesting that the bonds of community that structured Edo-period artistic and aesthetic practices (including *haikai* poetry) play an important role in laying the groundwork for an aesthetically based conception of nationalism in modern Japan.[31] More broadly, it has generally been taken as read that poetic genres played an important role in the Meiji nation-building project. Joshua Mostow has written that both *waka* and haiku "were intimately implicated in the construction of the new modern imperial Japanese nation-state,"[32] and Michael Bourdaghs, discussing Shimazaki Tōson 島崎藤村 (1872–1943), has highlighted poetry's importance to the national imagination: "Nationalist critics in the 1890s explicitly called for a new national poetry to become the voice of the national people." Among the ranks of critics calling for this new poetry was Shiki, whom Bourdaghs terms "explicitly nationalistic."[33]

Rather less attention has been paid, however, to the precise mechanisms linking poetry to the Meiji nation-state, or to the different ways in which Meiji critics drew the boundaries of the national-poetic community that was a necessary corollary for a national poetry. As I show throughout this study, the process of integrating poetic communities and genres with national imaginations was contentious and divisive. The nation, as community, must necessarily construe itself exclusively, as "us" and "them," and similar processes of exclusion were also replicated on a smaller, internal scale in many visions of national-poetic community. The national-poetic community was usually not coterminous with the nation itself; frequently the groups and reformers I discuss in this book predicate national-poetic community on the exclusion or marginalization of one or more other groups in Japan. In certain cases, even where poetic groups may deploy rhetoric of inclusivity and shared values, this rhetoric can run parallel to and conceal more subtle discourses of hierarchy and internal differentiation. In highlighting hierarchy and differentiation rather than cohesion, I draw on the work of a number of scholars who have criticized Anderson's "imagined communities" model. Among these is Prasenjit Duara, who has noted that "the nation is . . . hardly realization of an original essence, but a historical configuration designed to include certain groups and exclude or marginalize others—often violently."[34] Likewise, Partha Chatterjee has pointed to the important role played in Bengal by structures of caste, social class, language, and religion in fashioning what he calls "numerous fragmented resistances to [the] normalizing project" of nationalist modernity.[35] Addressing gender specifically, Tamar Mayer has noted that "because nationalism is about difference—and imagined communities can therefore not be inclusive—internal hierarchies often occur along lines of gender, race, class, and sexuality."[36] In the specific context of Japan, Michael Bourdaghs has also observed that "there is not one national body, national family, or national space, but several—and they overlap, fall apart, and cohere, all at once."[37]

One of this book's main critical contributions is applying these insights to the role of print media in Meiji Japan, arguing in the case of Japanese poetic groups modern print media divides and fragments as much as it unites. One reason for this is that the impact of modern print media is never uniform among different groups. Poetry columns in newspapers and literary journals do indeed make other poets and their work visible, encourage interaction, and thereby give a certain concrete reality to ideas of national-poetic community. At the same time, though, the availability of a diverse array of new media technologies provides opportunities for previously marginalized or peripheral groups to assert their own visions of poetic community. Newcomers given voice by access to their own media pulpit often question the claims to authority of previously dominant poetic groups with a view to displacing or replacing them, and in turn these established groups try to find ways to limit the challenge that new groups pose. One concrete result of this is to drive new discussions of poetic qualification, authority, and identity—that is, who should be a poet—and these inevitably play out in the language of hierarchy and differentiation. The nature of Meiji poetic sociality—its processes of reciprocal critique, the insistence that poets should not simply read but also write, and the new range of media venues opened to greater numbers of people than ever before—helped to catalyze such discussions. In this sense, Fukunaga's concerns in 2006 about "dilution"— that is to say, about new poets entering the haiku world in a manner that its existing establishment could not control—had plenty of historical precedent. Shiki's pulpit at the newspaper *Nippon* (1889–1906) and, later on, the literary journal *Hototogisu*, was crucial to his challenging the previously dominant "old school" (*kyūha*) *haikai* masters. Likewise, Yosano Tekkan 与謝野鉄幹 (Hiroshi 寛, 1873–1935), who launched a famous broadside against the Bureau of Poetry (Outadokoro) poets in 1894 as part of a project of *waka* reform, greatly magnified his reach by writing in the *Niroku shinpō* newspaper at which he had recently been hired.

This study's discussion of poetic authority and identity in Meiji focuses on three main lines of hierarchy and differentiation—specifically gender, social class, and political affiliation. Although print media may have rendered these tensions more visible, they were always there to some degree. For instance, issues of social class had often been present around the edges of even the theoretically egalitarian social spaces of premodern poetry. One of the main attractions of premodern *haikai* and *waka* groups was that they allowed people from different class backgrounds to mingle; but this demographic diversity had also to be balanced with the dilution of a poetic genre's value as cultural capital. One village headman, writing in the late seventeenth century, complained that his beloved *haikai* had come to the point where "everyone in the country was playing at it—women, children, even mountain bandits." Taking up *waka* poetry instead, in time he found to his dismay that this too "spread to the lower levels of villages."[38]

Such concerns were also in the background with Meiji poetry reform groups, especially in haiku and *waka*, for their members were almost always men who had made it to the pinnacle of Japan's state educational system, studying at institutions such as the Imperial University or one of the elite higher schools around Japan. They therefore possessed a sense of themselves as an intellectual elite that, they believed, gave them the authority to enact poetic reform, along with a frank disdain for poetic practitioners who were not part of this world.[39] The so-called old school poets who were the objects of their attacks understood the class distinctions at work here quite clearly, painting their antagonists in return as overeducated students and overbearing college professors.

If there is an apparent class divide running through a great deal of poetic reform, there is also a significant political divide. Many, if not most, of the poets and journalists who were at the forefront of poetic reform came from domains that had opposed the Satsuma-Chōshū coalition that overthrew the Tokugawa *bakufu* in 1867 and that had then assumed control of Japan. Some, like *waka* poet Ochiai Naobumi 落合直文 (1861–1903), had been old enough to actually remember the fighting; others, like Shiki, grew up in domains that remembered their treatment at the hands of what became the new government with considerable bitterness. Many such domains were receptive to the message of the Freedom and Popular Rights Movement (Jiyū Minken Undō; hereafter abbreviated to FPRM) early in Meiji, and though that movement petered out in the late 1880s, many of its sympathizers continued to find ways to assail the Meiji government, particularly on the thorny topic of foreign relations. For many of the poets discussed in this study, the nation of which they considered themselves part was often at odds with the apparatus and institutions of the Meiji state.

The issue of gender—more specifically, masculinity—is also connected with the two aforementioned factors and is a recurrent note in discourse on *kanshi* and *waka* in particular. Many poets, most famously Tekkan, framed their criticism of contemporary poetry in gendered terms, arguing that it was insufficiently bold or manly, and that the poets they sought to marginalize were weak and feminized. Developing at the same time as national literature ideologues were also grappling with the idea of two women, Murasaki Shikibu 紫式部 (ca. 973–ca. 1020) and Sei Shōnagon 清少納言(ca. 966–ca. 1025), as the authors of the greatest prose works of Japanese literature, this insistence on poetic manliness worked to gender the national poetic imagination; while revealing unease with the presence of women in the poetic sphere (in both *kanshi* and *waka*), it simultaneously created a hierarchical vision of male Japanese poets, drawing distinctions between those who were sufficiently masculine to represent the nation and those who were not.

NATIONAL POETRY AND NATIONAL LITERATURE

The idea of a national-poetic community has a strong connection to, and emerged at around the same time as, the articulation of a "national literature" (*kokubungaku*) beginning in 1890 by a group of literary historians at Tokyo Imperial University. These were, primarily, Mikami Sanji 三上参次 (1865–1939), Takatsu Kuwasaburō 高津鍬三郎 (1864–1922), Haga Yaichi 芳賀矢一 (1867–1927), and Ueda Kazutoshi 上田万年 (1867–1937). Influenced by European models of literary history, notably the work of French literary historian Hippolyte Taine (1828–1893), these scholars made a wide-ranging argument for literary works as a reflection and articulation of a country's national essence. Showcasing the nation's literary history would, they hoped, help the Japanese people to understand the "development of the mentality of the nation" and to "deepen their love for the nation" so that the "national spirit would be elevated."[40]

What role poetry might play in this was also a major issue, though a surprisingly thorny one. Regardless of the precise genre under discussion, critics rarely agreed on the who, what, or how of national poetry. Where one critic might see *haikai* as a national poetry because it was distinctly Japanese and every Japanese subject could compose it, another might see it as unsuitable because it was irredeemably plebeian. *Haikai* seemed an obvious candidate for a national poetry; it had the largest practitioner base of any major traditional genre, and as early as 1873 the Meiji government had enlisted a group of *haikai* masters to help promote its moral and cultural reform programs, on account of *haikai*'s supposed connection to the common people.[41] For many intellectuals during the 1890s, however, that connection was precisely the problem: *haikai* could not be serious literature because it was practiced primarily by commoners. *Waka*, with its associations with the imperial court and nativist groups, was also a strong candidate for a national poetry. However, as with *haikai*, some critics wondered if *waka* was too short to be serious poetry, and others, such as Ochiai Naobumi and Yosano Tekkan, felt that *waka*'s elegant language and tradition of poems depicting wistful love made it insufficiently masculine, unsuited to a nation that would need to be both vigorous and martially minded.

Kanshi poets, too, had to grapple with the question of how their art positioned them with regard to ideas of national community. Here, though, the relationship between *kanshi*, the modern nation-state, and ideas of national literature is a more complex one, recently addressed by a number of scholars including Saitō Mareshi and Matthew Fraleigh.[42] To oversimplify, *kanshi* is poetry written in a language that very closely approximates classical Chinese and is in many cases indistinguishable from it. Many of its practitioners in Japan considered themselves part of a great, transnational tradition of Sinitic verse, heirs to the work of both their Japanese predecessors and Chinese master poets such as Du Fu 杜甫 (712–770) and Li Bai 李白 (701–762). The term *kanshi* (literally, "poems of the Han") is itself a mid-Meiji neologism; before that point, the genre was generally known simply as *shi* and had a distinguished tradition of composition in Japan stretching back to the earliest days of the Heian court.[43] Particularly from 1890 onward, however, the ethnocentric and linguistically exclusive paradigm of national literature painted both *kanshi* and *kanbun* (Sinitic prose) as being written in a foreign language. Both *kanshi* and *kanbun* therefore occupied an uncertain position in terms of expressing national identity, something that was a key requirement of a putative national poetry. For example, Mikami Sanji argued that the practice of writing histories of Japan in Sinitic prose, common in the Heian period and still discussed as a possible option in early Meiji, would be as incongruous as "building the Ise Grand Shrine out of bricks and mortar."[44] But *kanshi*'s role was not always as a negative exemplar of nonnational poetry. In 1893, for instance, Shiki declared *kanshi* to be more advanced than other traditional poetic genres in Japan, despite its being "foreign gibberish" (*gaikokugo no chinpunkanteki kanshi*).[45] In 1895, as Japan was concluding its war with China, another critic acknowledged *kanshi*'s important role in Japanese literary history even as he argued for its abandonment. Naming several prominent Edo-era *kanshi* poets, he suggested that "perhaps in this sense, *kanshi* wears the laurels of our national poetry [*kokushi*], and its writers enjoy the esteem of being national poets." But, he continued, *kanshi*'s days were likely numbered, for "this awakening island empire ultimately has need of a national poetry in its national language."[46]

It would be a mistake to exclude *kanshi* from discussions of national-poetic community in Japan, for even if it did not fit the strict definition of "national language," the very act of writing *kanshi* required the poet to take a position in relation to both the institutional structures of the Meiji state and the nation as idealized or imagined entity. To an extent not generally true with *waka* or *haikai*, for a certain class of men in nineteenth-century Japan, "the production of poetry in Chinese was co-extensive with their identity as earnest and upright men who were committed to the service of the state."[47] In Meiji, this could play out in a variety of ways. During early Meiji in particular, *kanshi* strengthened its traditional associations with government service; many ministries viewed training in the Chinese classics favorably in potential new recruits, and substantial numbers of government employees practiced *kanshi* themselves.[48] Poetry manuals in early Meiji presented the study of *kanshi* as something that could potentially lead to government employment; yet *kanshi* also had a notable antiauthoritarian streak. In particular, the "men of high purpose" (*shishi*) during the mid-nineteenth century evoked righteous exemplars from Chinese history in their *kanshi* as a method of protest against the Tokugawa *bakufu*, and for certain highly educated members of the FPRM throughout the 1880s *kanshi* remained the premier literary vehicle for criticizing what they saw as an oppressive government. Even after the failure of that movement, politically focused *kanshi* continued to be a staple of a number of newspapers—notably *Nippon*, at which Shiki spent most of his career.

THE CUCKOO'S NEST: SHIKI AND
THE NEWSPAPER *NIPPON*

This book is structured around the life and work of one man, Masaoka Shiki. Shiki is a towering figure of modern Japanese literature; although known first and foremost as probably the greatest haiku poet of the modern era, he was also a prolific literary critic, occasional novelist, and writer of *waka* and *kanshi*. His direct disciples numbered in the dozens, most famous among them Kawahigashi Hekigotō 河東碧悟桐 (Heigōrō 秉五郎, 1873–1937) and Takahama Kyoshi 高浜虚子 (Kiyoshi 清, 1874–1959), who became the two dominant figures in Japan's haiku world in the first half of the twentieth century. Scholars generally credit Shiki's haiku reform movement, which took off after he joined the newspaper *Nippon* in late 1892, with raising the haiku to the level of modern literature via an emphasis on simple, direct observation of the natural world. In the process, the standard narrative has it, Shiki "rescued" *haikai* from the degenerate state it had fallen into in the hands of the old-school masters. For these masters, *haikai* was about abstruse, riddle-like imagery, wordplay, puns, and vulgarity, or else it was a means to make a living through verse-grading fees, point-scoring *haikai*, selling verses written on hanging scrolls, or other mercantile practices. One of the major concepts Shiki used to differentiate himself from these old-school masters, and perhaps his most important contribution to Japanese literature, was the idea of *shasei*, or "sketch from life." Developed initially through conversations with the Western-style painter Nakamura Fusetsu 中村不折 (Sakutarō 鈼太郎, 1866–1943) as a compositional method in haiku that emphasized direct, objective description, it later proved influential not only in *waka* but in prose as well, the concept of *shaseibun* (sketch prose) influencing prose authors such as Shiga Naoya 志賀直哉 (1883–1971).

Shiki's career was also distinguished by his pugnacious and polemical critical writings, the source of many of the pronouncements for which he is best known. Early in his critical career, for instance, he would famously declare that nine-tenths of the work of Matsuo Bashō 松尾芭蕉 (1644–1694), *haikai*'s greatest poet of all time and worshipped as a literal god during Meiji, was made up of "bad, awful poems" (*akku daku*).[49] In another well-known moment of literary iconoclasm, he would state in his 1898 discussion of *waka* that the legendary Ki no Tsurayuki 紀貫之 (872–945) "was a terrible poet [*heta na utayomi*], and [his anthology] the *Kokinshū* is a collection of garbage" (*kudaranu shū ni te arisōrō*).[50] Shiki was a little less outspoken in the field of *kanshi* criticism, but he still had his moments, at one point terming the respected contemporary poet Mori Kainan 森槐南 (Kimiyasu 公泰, 1863–1911) an "idly scribbling rhymer [*itazura ni moji o tsuranuru hyōsokuya*] who does not understand true poetic beauty."[51]

With such a long list of achievements and notorious pronouncements to Shiki's credit, there is a vast array of both scholarly and popular literature on him in Japanese, though substantially less in English. The main English-language studies are two critical biographies, by Janine Beichman and Donald Keene, as well as Mark Morris's two articles on the relationship between Shiki and the Edo-period poet Yosa Buson 与謝蕪村 (1716–1784).[52] Although Shiki is its main figure, this study differs from previous biographical treatments in that it uses Shiki as a central site to discuss broader issues of poetic genres and print media. Shiki is a particularly good figure for this purpose because he not only wrote in all three major traditional poetic genres but also spent the last decade of his life writing for *Nippon*, one of Japan's most important Tokyo newspapers. A highbrow newspaper with strong political views and a highly educated readership, *Nippon* occupies an important place in Japanese literary history on the grounds that virtually every major poet of the Meiji period worked or published there. Aside from Shiki himself, *Nippon* also employed Kokubu Seigai 国分青厓 (Takatane 高胤, 1857–1944), a veritable titan of the Meiji *kanshi* world, and Honda Shuchiku 本田種竹 (Kōnosuke 幸之助, 1862–1907); together with Mori Kainan, these three were ranked as the three greats of mid-Meiji *kanshi*. *Nippon* also had a significant role in the development of *waka* into the modern tanka; it played host to Ochiai Naobumi and the Asakasha, an early *waka* reform group from which emerged Tekkan and a number of other important poets. Attesting to *Nippon*'s broad sway in matters poetic, Tekkan's more famous wife, Yosano Akiko 与謝野晶子 (1878–1942), recalled being inspired by reading Shiki's criticism on haiku and *waka* in *Nippon* as she developed her own poetic voice.[53]

Besides Shiki, the book's focus on *Nippon* allows it to discuss a number of other important Meiji poets who worked or published there, notably Seigai and the father-and-son team of Mori Shuntō and Mori Kainan, who have received little coverage in English. Seigai in particular was a literary megastar during Meiji, and it is perplexing that he has received so little attention in either English or Japanese. As a newspaper, *Nippon* itself is also an excellent venue from which to consider issues of social class, gender, and political affiliation in Meiji poetry. *Nippon* was quite unusual among Meiji newspapers in its highly educated audience, deliberately elitist attitude, and strong engagement with politics. In this last aspect, it was best known for being staunchly opposed to most of the policies of the Meiji government, something that colored much of its poetic content. A large part of the reason for this was that *Nippon*'s editor and main editorial writer, Kuga Katsunan 陸羯南 (Minoru 実, 1857–1907), and its star poet, Seigai, were from northern Japan, an area that had fought to the bitter end against the Satsuma-Chōshū coalition that led the Meiji Restoration. Similarly, Shiki came from Matsuyama on the island of Shikoku, a town located in the Iyo domain, which had been forced to submit to the anti-*bakufu* forces. If Shiki's recollections and those of his friends are to be believed, Matsuyama's experience of defeat and submission during the Restoration disturbances had not been completely forgotten even decades later.[54]

STRUCTURE OF THE BOOK

The book consists of five chapters in roughly chronological order, two devoted to *kanshi*, two to haiku, and the final chapter discussing *waka*. Chapter 1 traces the development from the early nineteenth century of a series of materials such as poetic lexicons, rhyming dictionaries, and composition manuals for beginners. Using Shiki's experience learning Sinitic verse as a representative example, the chapter shows how this "textual infrastructure" removed potential linguistic barriers to *kanshi* composition and fashioned a standardized, accessible poetic curriculum. The result was *kanshi*'s rise as a popular genre, and the new media spaces of early Meiji, as well as the link between *kanshi* and a career in the new government, drove a further boom in demand for *kanshi* instruction. Drawing attention to the role of poetic lexicons and similar materials in promoting *kanshi* literacy, the chapter also highlights their role in cultural reproduction. At the same time as they imparted practical knowledge of *kanshi*'s idiom, structures, and genres, in their selections of topics and available poetic language, poetic lexicons also shaped what could be said on topics such as government service, the FPRM, and modernity in general. As these texts expanded access to *kanshi* literacy, they also reflected and created fundamental divides as to the purpose of the genre and who should be composing it.

Chapter 2 explores critical debates over the so-called fragrant style (Ch. *xianglianti*, J. *kōrentai*) of Sinitic poetry during the Meiji period and the role that these debates played in creating hierarchies of poetic masculinity and moral seriousness in the *kanshi* world. Defenders of this style, which took as its main concern the depiction of the sexualized feminine form and which attained a peak in popularity in the late 1870s, argued for its value as expressing the emotional truth of sexual desire; detractors, by contrast, assailed both the poems and the poets who wrote them as frivolous and weak, the style's fascination with the female figure evidence of feminization in the poet himself. Since many of the most prominent advocates of the fragrant style, notably Kainan and Shuntō, either enjoyed government patronage or worked directly for the Meiji government, these debates feature a strong partisan political subtext, some critics holding that feminized poetry constituted evidence of being unfit to serve the nation. These issues came to a head in a marathon exchange of *kanshi* through the pages of *Nippon* in the autumn of 1890 between Kokubu Seigai, Mori Kainan, and the eminent politician Soejima Taneomi 副島種臣 (1828–1905), in which Seigai assailed Kainan as effeminate and offered a competing model of vigorous and masculine poetry. As a national-poetic community of *kanshi* poets emerged in the context of the modern Meiji state, this chapter shows, this community was riven by strategies of internal differentiation and competition that centered on hierarchical conceptions of masculinity.

The subsequent two chapters turn to haiku, discussing the themes of political affiliation and social class as they apply to Shiki's reform movement during the 1890s. Chapter 3 focuses on newspaper haiku during the 1890s, the decade in which it emerged as a modern genre. It makes the provocative argument that, contrary to the conventional understanding of the modern haiku as centered on the seasons and the natural world, explicitly partisan "topical haiku" (*jiji haiku*) commenting on social and political affairs were extremely common and may even have been the dominant use of the genre as a whole in the print media of this period. Although not unique to *Nippon*, such verses were common at the newspaper throughout the early 1890s, Shiki himself composing a substantial number early in his career there. Shiki was not especially enthusiastic about verse with a political bent, but they played a major role in establishing haiku as a serious literary genre in Japan's more highbrow newspapers and helped gather a core readership that would serve as a base for Shiki's reform movement. As the chapter also shows, the exclusion of political commentary from haiku's bailiwick, in favor of the more ideologically neutral focus on the natural world, was a move that came only after Shiki and his fledgling reform group had secured their position, a move necessary to the formulation of the category of literature (*bungaku*) as a focus for national identity.

Chapter 4 locates Shiki's early critical writings in a series of 1890s debates over haiku's status as "commoner literature" (*heimin bungaku*) and its suitability as a national poetry. Noting that Shiki disdained the proposition that haiku could be a genre for commoners and criticized the idea that it was a literature of the nation's people (*kokumin bungaku*), the chapter offers an alternative, revisionist view of Shiki's haiku reform movement. Through demographic and discourse analysis of the *Nippon* Group (*Nippon*-ha) and two of its competitors, the Autumn Winds Society (Shūseikai) and the so-called old school, the chapter shows the *Nippon* Group's vision of haiku to be based on an exclusionary, class-based discourse in which the main problem with the genre was that too many commoners were composing it. Introducing the hitherto neglected writings of the old-school poets themselves to highlight the importance of social class and educational background to haiku "reform," the chapter shows the intellectual underpinnings and social organization of the modern haiku to be socially fragmented from its very inception. The idea of a close overlap between poetic community and national community that "commoner literature" implied came to be understood as a positive only in the early twentieth century.

Chapter 5 covers *waka*'s role in discussions of national-poetic community. Introducing Ochiai Naobumi and his Asakasha group, who published much of their early work in *Nippon*, the chapter first considers Yosano Tekkan's 1894 manifesto for *waka* reform, "Sounds of the Nation's Ruin" (Bōkoku no on), and its attack on the Outadokoro poets. Characterizing Tekkan's call in "Sounds of the Nation's Ruin" for vigorous, masculine poetry as exclusive and gender hierarchical, the chapter shows how his arguments and vision of national-poetic community emerge from an earlier, largely unstudied critical essay titled "Women and National Literature" ("Joshi to kokubun," published in *Fujo zasshi* in 1893), which was highly critical of both contemporary female poets and the perceived feminization of male poets. This essay in turn speaks to contemporary anxieties over the gendering of the national literary imagination implied by the developing canon of a Japanese national literature, particularly the valorization of female-authored Heian prose works such as the *Pillow Book* and *Tale of Genji*. Concluding with Shiki's famous series of "Letters to a *Waka* Poet" ("Utayomi ni atōru sho," published in *Nippon* in 1898), the chapter explores how Shiki adopts a different yet equally hierarchical vision of poetic community, placing *waka* within a quasi-universal notion of "literature" (*bungaku*) and aiming to sever the seemingly obvious connections between *waka* and Japanese national identity. As in chapter 4, this chapter provides an alternative to conventional narratives of poetic reform, showing how Shiki's idea of *waka* reform (and of literature itself) was predicated on discourses of exclusion that worked to the benefit of university-educated "men of literature" (*bungakusha*).

Fukunaga's piece, quoted at the beginning of this introduction, shows that the issues discussed in these five chapters are not simply matters of historical interest; rather, what the rise of new media technologies does to a country's national imagination, and particularly the hidden fault lines of gender, class, and politics, are concerns equally pressing in the present day. My aim in the book is, therefore, not only to explore poetry in Meiji Japan but also to offer a close, ground-level account of the interaction of poetry and print media with a view to providing greater nuance to existing models of the media-driven emergence of modern nationalism and national imaginations.

IDLY SCRIBBLING RHYMERS

↓

CHAPTER ONE

Climbing the Stairs of Poetry

Kanshi, *Print, and Writership in Nineteenth-Century Japan*

This chapter is structured around one relatively simple question: how did one learn to write *kanshi* in nineteenth-century Japan? Suppose that you are a young man in a provincial part of Japan during the middle years of the nineteenth century—rather like, say, Masaoka Shiki—and you decide, for any of a variety of reasons, that you want to learn to write Sinitic verse. You have little previous background in literary Sinitic, maybe a basic grounding in reading certain canonical texts aloud (*sodoku*), but this is not enough to allow you to dive straight into reading anthologies of *kanshi* verse, and certainly not enough to start writing *kanshi* by yourself. What should you do?

One option might be to enroll in a private academy of Chinese studies (*kangaku juku*), an institution that proliferated from the middle years of the nineteenth century onward. Though one would certainly thereby improve one's knowledge of the classical Chinese canon, a *kangaku juku* was not always the best option for a budding poet; depending on the institution, poetic composition as a specific subject was often peripheral to the curriculum at such academies.[1] If *kanshi* composition and appreciation were the aims, rather than a broad grounding in the Chinese classics as a whole, in many cases the best option would be to find and join a local poetic group, if one existed. There, one could work with more experienced poets and have one's poetry readings and verse composition supervised by a recognized, professional *kanshi* master, assuming one was available locally. An oversupply of professional teachers in the main urban areas of Edo, Kyoto, and Osaka during the mid-nineteenth century meant that a number of famous *kanshi* poets made a living traveling around Japan as itinerant instructors, and so the availability of such teachers would vary depending on the area. For his part, however, Shiki had no need to enroll in a private academy or seek a local master since he had a highly qualified teacher in his very family. His maternal grandfather, Ōhara Kanzan 大原観山 (1817–1875), an adviser to the fourteenth daimyo of the Iyo domain, was a scholar of some renown and had taught at the Meikyōkan, the official Matsuyama domain Confucian academy. Although Kanzan resigned his official duties in Meiji 4 (1871), he taught privately thereafter and, as Shiki recalls, took a keen interest in his grandson's education in the Chinese textual canon:[2]

> I think it was around the time when I was about eight or nine years old and going to my maternal grandfather Kanzan's home for *sodoku* instruction. One morning I went into his entrance hall, and off to one side were two or three of his students with their desks side by side, and I saw that one of them had a pocketbook in which there was some writing in black ink with writing in red ink in among it. I asked what it was, and they said it was a Sinitic poem [*shi*]. Obviously I knew nothing about writing in red ink [to correct and comment on poems] or what sort of thing a Sinitic poem might be. . . . I probably just thought that the red and black mixed together looked very attractive. I thought, "I want to grow up as soon as I can and write Sinitic poetry."[3]

Though Kanzan normally delegated the teaching of *sodoku* to the senior students at his private academy, he elected to personally supervise the instruction of his first grandson, giving lessons to both Shiki and the latter's first cousin Minami Hajime 三並良 (1864–1940) early in the morning, sometimes before it was fully light.[4] Unfortunately, Kanzan did not live to see either boy finish his studies, since he passed away in 1875. After this, Shiki continued his studies with another local teacher: "Kanzan died shortly after that, but we continued by going to Tsuchiya Hisaaki's home for *sodoku*, and so finally it was the summer of Meiji 10 [1877] when

I learned how to compose Sinitic poetry from him—that is to say, I went off carrying my *Handbook for Beginning Learners* and learned how to arrange tonal prosody. After that I composed one pentasyllabic quatrain [Ch. *wuyan jueju*, J. *gogon zekku*] each day and had him look at it."[5]

Although we know almost nothing about Tsuchiya Hisaaki, the details in this short passage show that his *kanshi* pedagogy conformed largely to the standard practice of the time. First, like most other novice poets of the period, Shiki started by composing quatrains (Ch. *jueju*, J. *zekku*), a four-line form of Sinitic verse. Over the course of the nineteenth century in Japan, the quatrain had come to be viewed as the first form that novice learners should attempt, and its prominent place in entry-level *kanshi* pedagogy meant that it was also well represented in contemporary print media. Second, Shiki mentions making use of what he calls a *Handbook for Beginning Learners* (*Yōgaku benran*). By 1877, the year of which Shiki was writing, "handbook for beginning learners" had come to be used as a generic term for a wide range of entry-level instructional manuals aimed at helping novice poets learn *kanshi*'s structures and vocabulary. While they varied slightly in form and content, virtually all such manuals featured a lexicon of preprepared poetic vocabulary, divided by topic, on which the novice poet could draw while learning composition. Later manuals also provided more explicit, step-by-step instruction in how to write *kanshi*, usually beginning from the quatrain form. In Shiki's specific case, it seems that he also made use of such a manual in learning tonal prosody (Ch. *pingze*, J. *hyōsoku*), probably under Tsuchiya's close supervision; tonal prosody was an important formal feature of *kanshi* writing and one that entry-level materials consistently emphasized as very important.[6]

Shiki's recollections therefore point us in the direction of a number of answers to the basic question of how one might take one's first steps in learning to write *kanshi* in nineteenth-century Japan. His mention of using an instructional manual highlights the important relationship throughout the nineteenth century between *kanshi* learning and print capitalism; as I show later, the broad expansion of *kanshi* producers and consumers in nineteenth-century Japan owes much to the development of what I term a textual infrastructure for *kanshi*. By "textual infrastructure," I mean primarily instructional materials such as poetic lexicons, composition guides, rhyming dictionaries, and the like, by means of which the reader could acquire a basic functional knowledge of how to read and compose *kanshi*, without necessarily needing a background in the Chinese classics or to receive instruction from a teacher. *Kanshi* publishing as a whole, including anthologies of verse by both Japanese and Chinese poets and "poetic talks" (*shiwa*), flourished during the nineteenth century, but seemingly one of the most widely published—and therefore lucrative—categories was guides for beginning learners with little or no previous background in Sinitic poetry. Producing entry-level materials was, of course, in a publisher's long-term interest, since it broadened the potential readership for other such materials, and as a poet progressed he (or occasionally she) would presumably need to lay hands on more advanced materials such as poetic collections and treatises.

It should be emphasized that materials such as the poetic lexicons were very much entry-level materials, particularly helpful to those who did not have access to (or were not interested in) a more traditional course of study in the Chinese classics. In practice, all indications are that their use dropped away rapidly as the poet progressed; Shiki himself seems to have discarded the lexicon-based "cut-and-paste" approach within a couple of years of the time of the previously quoted passage. Albeit probably intended for novice poets almost exclusively, these materials are nevertheless important, for several reasons. One is that entry-level *kanshi* materials over the course of the nineteenth century not only show a remarkable degree of standardization but also seem to have been used almost universally among beginning poets, making it easier to draw some broader conclusions about the mechanisms through which *kanshi* literacy was initially acquired. Furthermore, as I subsequently argue, because the poetic manual was often a novice learner's first point of contact with the genre, a given manual's content and cultural assumptions shaped ideas of what *kanshi* was for and who should compose it.

One of the main reasons why printed *kanshi* manuals (particularly the specific genre of the poetic lexicon, which I discuss extensively later in this chapter) were so important was that they made possible a major expansion of *kanshi* practice in Japan during the latter half of the Edo period, both in terms of practitioner demographics and thematic scope. They did this by helping aspiring learners to manage the linguistic and technical challenges that *kanshi* presented. One obvious challenge was that literary Sinitic was a nonvernacular language for Japanese poets and so required concentrated study to master.[7] Likewise, the composition of *kanshi* required understanding certain formal and technical structures, particularly tonal prosody and rhyme (Ch. *ya yun*, J. *ōin*), which were not found in either vernacular or classical Japanese, both of which are nontonal.[8]

On the basis of these factors, it seems fair to conclude that, for most novice Japanese poets, *kanshi* was relatively challenging, certainly more so than the other two main poetic genres of *haikai* and *waka*, and it was in response to this need that the *kanshi* manual arose. Whether in tandem with in-person instruction or used on its own, the *kanshi* manual usually provided clear and accessible explanations of *kanshi*'s technical and formal requirements. Many manuals, poetic lexicons in particular, also provided either classical or vernacular Japanese glosses (sometimes both) of specific words and phrases, thereby bridging the potential linguistic gaps between literary Sinitic, classical Japanese, and vernacular spoken Japanese.

The Edo-period expansion of *kanshi* practice and its connection to print capitalism have usually been understood in the framework of modernization theory, with growing literacy allowing *kanshi* to become a genre that spanned the country and in which people from all walks of life might participate, addressing their distinctive personal concerns as they saw fit. There has, however, been rather less attention to the development of *kanshi* literacy and the conceptual scope of the genre during the ensuing Meiji period. It is indeed true that, overall, the trend of growth continued, to the point that by the coming of Meiji *kanshi* was being practiced in Japan to an unprecedented extent. Demand for instructional materials boomed through mid-Meiji, driven by the appearance of new, nationally circulated media venues in which to potentially publish one's work and by an explicit association between *kanshi* learning and the possibility of a prestigious job in the government bureaucracy.

However, if the narrative of late Edo *kanshi* can be said to be an expansion of the concerns and expressive scope of *kanshi*, by contrast the narrative of early Meiji is one of narrowing and of the emergence of discourses of differentiation and hierarchy in the way the genre was represented. As *kanshi*'s practitioner base expanded, so its value as social and cultural capital was called into question (or, following the terminology mentioned in the introduction, we might say "diluted"). The vision of the genre we see in early Meiji print media and *kanshi* manuals stresses its connections to the world of elite male intellectuals, especially civil servants and those members of the educated elite who might aspire to a government career. At the same time as print capitalism thus expanded the boundaries, real and imagined, of the *kanshi* community throughout Japan, it also created and reinforced mechanisms of hierarchy and differentiation that were essential to how such communities were envisioned. Meiji *kanshi* pedagogy, as reflected in manuals for novice poets, acted as a major mechanism of cultural reproduction for the genre: following an increasingly standardized pattern, during early Meiji *kanshi* manuals and *kanshi* media created, reflected, and reinforced a series of cultural, literary, and political assumptions that spoke to who could be a poet, what one could say through the medium of *kanshi*, and why one would want to do either in the first place. Produced in vast numbers throughout the nineteenth century, these manuals have generally been of limited interest to literary scholars and occupy at best a peripheral place in discussions of *kanshi* practice.[9] Yet because of their apparently near-universal adoption, these manuals shaped the discursive boundaries of *kanshi*—not only what could be said through poetry but also how and by whom.

KANSHI LITERACY BEFORE MEIJI: JOTEI AND THE LIANZHU SHIGE

Scholarly narratives of *kanshi* during the latter half of the Edo period have been virtually unanimous in describing the expansion of the genre in both thematic and demographic terms. One important example of thematic expansion comes at the end of the eighteenth century as the prevailing poetic orthodoxy in Japan began to shift away from the faux-Tang style of Ogyū Sorai 荻生徂徠 (1666–1728) and his followers Dazai Shundai 太宰春台 (1680–1747) and Hattori Nankaku 服部南郭 (1683–1759). Adapting the views of the Ming Archaists (Kobunji-ha), which stressed the poetry of the High Tang as superior to all other periods, Sorai and his disciples emphasized Li Panlong's 李攀龍 (1514–1570) *Selections of Tang Poetry* (Ch. *Tang shixuan*, J. *Tōshisen*) as a textual and thematic model. The poems in this collection should, per the Japanese Archaists' views, be imitated as closely as possible in diction and theme, even if many of the themes therein (such as failure by a scholar-literatus to pass the selection exam for the Chinese civil service) were often alien to the actual experiences of Japanese poets.

From the early 1780s, this emphasis on *Selections of Tang Poetry* as a specific textual model, as well as the narrowly circumscribed range of subject matter it allowed, came under attack on the grounds that it encouraged poets to compose on matters of which they had no direct experience and resulted in poetry that was insincere or even plagiarized. Among the most prominent of such critics was Yamamoto Hokuzan 山本北山 (1752–1812), who in his 1783 *Sakushi shikō* (Thoughts on the composition of poetry) assailed those who "discard the true poetry within themselves and imitate and plagiarize the works of others."[10] Hokuzan singled out Li Panlong and his followers in Japan in particular: "From Panlong and the 'Seven Masters' onward, including the poems of Nankaku and [Takano] Rantei [高野蘭亭, 1704–1757] and the rest of them in Japan, everything has been plagiarism and imitation, and this does great harm to the way of poetry . . . the choice of poems in *Selections of Tang Poetry* and the like is extremely unsatisfactory . . . there is not a single work that reflects the true essence of its composer."[11]

Hokuzan later became a key member of the Kōko Shisha (Rivers and Lakes Poetic Society), a group formed in 1787 in Edo by the Confucian scholar Ichikawa Kansai 市川寛齋 (1749–1820) after his resignation from the Shōheikō shogunal academy. Formed with opposition to Sorai's poetics as one of its major aims, Kōko Shisha went on to become one of the most influential poetic societies of the early nineteenth century and counted many of the future celebrities of the Edo *kanshi* world among its members, particularly Kikuchi Gozan 菊池五山 (1769–1849), Kashiwagi Jotei 柏木如亭 (1763–1819), and Ōkubo Shibutsu 大窪詩仏 (1767–1837). Initially espousing the poetics of the Song dynasty (960–1276) as an antidote to Sorai's Tang-focused orthodoxy, by the early nineteenth century the group had also begun to show an interest in more recent Qing poetry. Its members had also begun to compose on topics such as the licensed quarters that were outside the scholar-literatus's traditional focus but that were nevertheless a part of everyday urban life. In assessing this transition, Ibi Takashi has argued that this expansion of poetic scope, especially the discovery of new poetic material in the urban environment, was "a necessary first step" for *kanshi* to make the transition from "a literature of the cultured scholar-official" (*shidaifu bungaku*) to become "a literature of the citizenry" (*shimin bungaku*).[12]

In order for *kanshi* to truly become a literature of the citizenry during the Edo period, it would also be necessary for the genre to undergo a major demographic expansion—in other words to be practiced by the citizenry at large. Such a demographic expansion does indeed appear to have taken place, scholars generally agreeing that the nineteenth century in Japan saw Sinitic poetry being written and read on an unprecedented scale. Marius Jansen, for instance, has noted that during the Tokugawa period "the tide of poetry in Chinese . . . may have exceeded what was being written in Japanese,"[13] while Burton Watson has observed that *kanshi* "came to rival native verse forms such as the *tanka* and haiku in the literary excitement it generated and the widespread popularity it enjoyed."[14] Not only did the numbers of *kanshi* poets increase but also their social diversity. For much of the first half of the Edo period, Sinitic poetry had been the primary preserve of court nobles or those at centers of Confucian or monastic learning, yet the latter half of the period saw what Judith Rabinovitch and Timothy Bradstock have referred to as a "widening of the social spectrum of *kanshi* poets to include members of the peasant, artisan, and merchant classes."[15] Ibi Takashi likewise has argued for the genre's "popularization" (*taishūka*); what this meant, in his view, was that *kanshi* became "a poetry that anyone could compose [*dare demo ga tsukureru shi*], so long as they had a certain degree of literacy in Sinitic graphs and a grounding in rhyme and tonal prosody."[16]

In common with an expansion in the practice of both *haikai* and *waka* during the same period, this broadening of *kanshi* practice is usually attributed to a growth in commoner literacy.[17] But in the specific case of *kanshi*, growth in general literacy provides only a partial explanation. As J. Marshall Unger has noted, "literacy" in the context of nineteenth-century Japan could span everything from "a bare knowledge of the elements of the *kana* syllabaries to productive facility in several socially prestigious and functionally distinct styles of Japanese and Sino-Japanese writing."[18] What we might term *kanshi* literacy was toward the far end of the scale Unger describes; "productive facility"—that is, the ability not only to read poetry but also to write it—required one to grapple with the technical and linguistic issues discussed in the preceding. As Ibi's qualification to the notion of "poetry anyone could compose" points out, production of *kanshi* required understanding aspects of the genre such as rhyme, tone, and tonal prosody.

This was the need that the poetic manual aimed to address. Although the precise coverage provided by each kind of manual could vary considerably, over time these manuals became increasingly standardized on four main points: (1) the provision of a ready-made bank of words and phrases on which one could draw in composition; (2) contemporary vernacular explanations of specific phrases; (3) annotation of tonal prosody for each phrase, to help with composition; and (4) clear explanations of the tonal patterns and rhyme scheme of (predominantly) the quatrain form. This accessible and relatively standardized manual-based pedagogy contrasts with the wide range of texts that had been used in *kanshi* instruction in Japan until the end of the eighteenth century. Before this time, most texts used in poetic education were copies or reproductions of works originally produced in China, and they rarely catered to the novice learner by addressing specific formal features in a systematic manner. Discussing Matsuo Bashō's use of Chinese sources, Peipei Qiu has listed a number of texts known to have been in common use in poetic instruction in Japan by the late seventeenth century: among the most popular were *Yuanji huofa shixue quanshu* (J. *Enki kappō shigaku zensho* [Practical knacks and workable methods: An encyclopedia of poetics], ca. 1697), *Shiren yuxie* (J. *Shijin gyokusetsu* [The gemlike words of poets], ca. 1244), *Santishi* (J. *Santaishi* [Poems in three styles]), *Guwen zhenbao* (J. *Kobun shinpō* [True treasures of ancient literature], ca. thirteenth century), and *Tang Song qian jia lianzhu shige* (J. *Tō Sō senka renju shikaku* [A string of jewels of poetic form from the Tang and Song periods], ca.1300).[19] Also popular was *Kinshūdan* (Collections of brocade pieces, ca. fifteenth century), a collection of poems by Chinese poets spanning the Tang through Ming dynasties compiled by Japanese Zen monk Ten'in Ryūtaku 天隠龍澤 (1422–1500).

Each of these texts varies somewhat in scope and composition; *Kinshūdan* and *Santishi*, for instance, are primarily poetic anthologies, from which the student of poetry is expected to learn by reading and drawing certain intuitive lessons from the poems themselves; the collection does not pretend to offer a step-by-step guide to composition. Likewise, *Shiren yuxie* consists of a summary of critical discussions of various poets from Chinese history and, though it does outline various principles for composition, would likely have been intimidating or even baffling to someone not already familiar with *kanshi* composition. The preface of *An Introduction to the Study of Poetry* (*Shigaku shōsei*), an instructional text of 1769 by Chiba Unkaku 千葉芸閣 (1727–1792), suggests that eighteenth-century instructional texts often assumed a certain baseline of previous knowledge. In the preface, Unkaku suggests that his text would be best suited for those who had finished their instruction in *sodoku* reading (in most cases, children from around the age of ten or so) and so had a basic grounding in the grammar of literary Sinitic by the time they attempted poetic composition.[20] Texts such as the aforementioned were not supplanted with the later development of a standardized elementary pedagogy; in fact, most continued to be used and printed into Meiji. Rather, these texts probably came to be the preserve of more advanced learners. An 1883–1884 edition of the poetic lexicon *Enki kappō shigaku zensho*, for example, does not provide any Japanese-language gloss for its featured vocabulary, nor does it explicitly mark tonal prosody, presumably working on the assumption that a reader of the manual would already be advanced enough to know about these aspects.

Where standard poetic pedagogy in the first half of the Edo period centered on Chinese-derived collections, to be used by a reader with some previous exposure to literary Sinitic, by the end of the Edo period there existed a standardized, step-by-step poetic curriculum centered on purpose-built educational manuals that made extensive use of vernacular Japanese to explain their contents and that even a complete novice might profitably use. One example as a midpoint in this overall transition, and an interesting case study in *kanshi* groups in general, is Kashiwagi Jotei's reissuing of the late Song poetic collection *A String of Jewels of Poetic Form* (Ch. *Lianzhu shige*, J. *Renju shikaku*) to help in teaching *kanshi* to members of Bansei Ginsha (Clear Evening Skies Poetic Society), a poetry group in the provincial town of Nakano in present-day Nagano Prefecture.[21]

Jotei, a member of the Kōkō Shisha and something of a rising star among Edo *kanshi* poets, found himself in Nakano after electing to leave Edo and spend much of his thirties traveling throughout Japan. In part this was to look for work, a response to the oversupply of *kanshi* teachers in urban areas; it was also because he had spent a lot of time carousing in the licensed quarters, and acquaintances felt that leaving the city might help him to straighten out. One of his first ports of call was Nakano, which was a major supply depot for the *bakufu* on the Tōkaidō highway. It was also, therefore, exactly the kind of provincial economic center where demand for *kanshi* instruction was likely to be high, since wealthy local notables sought to add cultural achievements to their economic success.[22] Jotei probably arrived in Nakano in 1795 at the age of thirty-three and found that the town already hosted the amateur Bansei Ginsha group, made up primarily of merchants and artisans who drew their living from the local economy. One of the group's more prominent members, Kishiku Hyakunen 木敷百年 (1768–1821), was a local notable who came from a family of carpenters and engineers in the service of the *bakufu* and served both as a village headman (*shōya*) and calligraphy instructor.[23] Though well-to-do, the members were not the domain scholars and elite samurai who would have had access to an in-depth education in the Chinese textual canon, and Jotei therefore needed to instruct these enthusiastic amateurs largely from first principles.

One of the ways in which he did this was to reannotate the *Lianzhu shige* so as to make it more accessible for his poetic charges. Jotei was not the first poet to adapt Chinese poetic collections in order to make them more accessible to nonspecialist readers—Bashō's disciple Morikawa Kyoriku 森川許六 (1656–1715) was responsible for issuing *Poems in Three Styles with Japanese Glosses* (*Wakun santaishi*), a version of the *Santishi* that rendered the poems therein into classical Japanese—but Jotei's *Annotated "Lianzhu shige"* (*Yakuchū Renju shikaku*) was quite unusual in providing not only *kundoku* glosses (notation allowing the poems to be read in classical Japanese syntax and word order) for the poems but also full glosses in contemporary vernacular Japanese, something very few collections or manuals had attempted to this point. One example of Jotei's glosses can be seen in his reading of a famous poem by Tang poet Li Bai:

答山中人	Answering a Question from Someone Amid the Mountains
問余何意棲碧山	You ask me why I dwell in green mountains;
笑而不答心自閑	I laugh and do not answer, heart naturally at peace.
桃花流水杳然去	Peach blossoms depart on flowing waters, leaving not a trace;
別有天地非人間	There is yet another world, one that is not of men.[24]

Jotei renders the literary Sinitic of the first two lines, 問余何意棲碧山 / 笑而不答心自閑, into classical Japanese as *yo ni tou, nan no i zo heki-zan ni sumu to / waraite kotaezu, kokoro onozukara hima nari*. Along with this *kundoku*-style reading of the text, Jotei also provides a separate gloss in contemporary vernacular Japanese, the first two lines being given as *dō iu ki de yamaoku ni sumu to ore ni kiku kara / nikoniko mono de aisatsu mo senu, nugurumi kokoro ga shizen to hima da*.[25] Apparently based on notes taken by Bansei Ginsha members themselves in response to Jotei's lectures on *kanshi* composition, the vernacular renderings provide a more beginner-friendly stage ahead of the usual practice of rendering the poem into classical Japanese through *kundoku* reading practices.[26] There are here effectively three layers of reading possible with the poem: the original literary Sinitic, the classical Japanese rendering, and the vernacular Japanese version, the last being the easiest for a beginner to grasp. In addition to the vernacular glosses for the poems themselves, many of the poems Jotei chose from the collection also showcase specific rhetorical or structural features. The Li Bai poem cited in the preceding, for example, which opens with an imagined question being posed to the speaker, is presented as an example of "using question and answer in the first two lines" (*mae no ni ku mondō no kaku*). The specific lesson that the learner is intended to absorb from a study of the poem is therefore made entirely explicit.

Jotei's instructional model and use of the *Lianzhu shige* seems to have been quite effective, since the indications are that Bansei Ginsha members made fairly rapid progress under his tutelage. In 1800, the group published a small collection of members' work titled simply

Bansei Ginsha Poems (*Bansei ginsha shi*), and the group and its major members also merited a mention in Kikuchi Gozan's long-running yearly roundup of Japan's *kanshi* world, *Gozan's Talks on Poetry* (*Gozandō shiwa*, 1807–1832).[27] Perhaps realizing that he had devised a successful instructional formula, Jotei also moved to publish his annotated *Lianzhu shige* for broader consumption, releasing it in four volumes from an Edo publisher in 1801.

The *Lianzhu shige* continued to be widely used in poetic instruction in Japan for most of the rest of the century, even if it was not necessarily Jotei's precise annotated version. An 1804 edition, reedited by Jotei's colleague in the Kōko Shisha Ōkubo Shibutsu and featuring prefaces from fellow poets and scholars Yamamoto Hokuzan and Satō Issai 佐藤一斎 (1772–1859), gives some sense of how and why the collection might have seemed so useful. It seems, according to Satō's preface, to have been valued for providing both lexical examples (*jirei*)—that is, words and phrases a beginning poet might wish to make use of in their own poetry— and examples of poetic form in an integrated and gradated fashion:

> This volume is, of course, set up for young learners to study Sinitic poetry. When studying Sinitic poetry, one must begin from lexical examples. Once one has a mature grasp of lexical examples, poetic form will take shape. To seek poetic form without going through lexical examples is like seeking to ascend to a great hall without the use of stairs; it can never be achieved. Therefore these lexical examples are the stairs to poetic form. Who can say that this is without benefit in learning Sinitic poetry?[28]

Satō's point here is that the learner of Sinitic poetry must develop a broad vocabulary bank upon which to draw before understanding the structural and rhetorical features of poetry, and the *Lianzhu shige* provides both aspects.

GOLD DUST, POETIC RHYMES, AND HANDY GUIDES: EDO-ERA POETIC LEXICONS

Jotei's annotated *Lianzhu shige* thus offered a number of advantages to the less-experienced poet: it confined itself to the relatively short quatrain form, provided clear examples of structural and rhetorical features, and included vernacular glosses so that almost any speaker of Japanese could understand the poems, regardless of training in literary Sinitic or classical Japanese. Attesting to its widespread dissemination, Shiki himself seems to have made use of the *Lianzhu shige* at some point during his studies, since a hand-copied version of the text is among his papers held by the National Diet Library.

Jotei's decision to annotate and reissue an extant Chinese text was, however, the exception rather than the rule in terms of poetic instructional materials during the first half of the nineteenth century. Far more widespread was the specific format of the poetic lexicon, which experienced tremendous popularity throughout the century. Essentially, the poetic lexicon was a vocabulary bank for the novice poet, which could be used to supply part or the whole of a composition. A lexicon usually contained a range of ready-made two- or three-graph phrases, grouped together by topic; the tone of each graph, whether level or oblique, was also usually marked, with a black dot indicating an oblique tone and a white dot (or sometimes the absence of a mark) indicating a level tone. Fitting each compound's tone pattern to the required tonal prosody for the poem he wished to compose, the novice poet could thus essentially "paint by numbers"—that is, select such two- and three-graph compounds as would meet the required number of five or seven graphs, arrange them according to the required tonal prosody and rhyme, and then repeat the process for each line until the poem was complete.

Comprehension of the words presented in the lexicon was aided by both classical Japanese glosses, to indicate how a phrase should be read, and vernacular explanations of what the phrase meant, the latter often providing additional contextual information. So, for instance, under the overall poetic topic of "Celebrating the New Year" (祝新年) one might find the two-graph compound 嘉辰 (happy morning) given the reading of *kashin* and its meaning explained as *medetaki hi* (an auspicious day); or, under the same topic, the three-graph phrase 萬戸煙 ("smoke from every hearth," an auspicious image of a prosperous realm) glossed as *banko no kemuri* and explained as *yutaka naru keshiki* (a vista of prosperity).[29]

Armed with clearly explained, ready-made vocabulary, poetic lexicons thus made it relatively easy to compose rudimentary *kanshi*. An example, using vocabulary from a manual published in 1878, will illustrate briefly how this "cut-and-paste" approach to *kanshi* composition worked in practice. We can imagine a hypothetical student electing to compose on the topic of "Reading a Book on a Snowy Night" (雪夜読書) and then turning to the appropriate page in the manual to find possible phrases to use. Deciding to compose a pentasyllabic quatrain, requiring five graphs for each line, our student checks the tonal prosody required for the first line and selects graphs that match the required order of level and oblique tones. The student chooses one two-graph phrase, "a cold night" (寒宵, which the manual glosses as *kanshō* and explains as *samuki yoi*), and one three-graph phrase, "sleep yet eludes me" (猶未寐, glossed as *nao imada nemurazu*, explained as *mada ne mo senu*).[30] Putting these five graphs together, the poem thus has its complete opening line:

雪夜読書   *Reading a Book on a Snowy Night*[31]

寒宵猶未寐   A cold night, sleep yet eludes me.

With the lexicon providing an ample supply of vocabulary to draw on, our novice poet could therefore repeat the process three more times to complete the remaining three lines, using only the language in the lexicon or perhaps adding some phrases of his own devising. The end product would, therefore, be a formally and tonally correct Sinitic verse, albeit probably a rather uninspiring one.

As a pedagogical practice, assembling a poem by drawing on extant vocabulary likely antedates the emergence of the poetic lexicon as a publishing phenomenon; probably the earliest known such lexicon, the 1768 *Shigo saikin* (A patchwork brocade treasury of poetic words), features a preface by Confucian scholar Hattori Somon 服部蘇門 (1724–1769) that claims the practice was widespread among the students of Takano Rantei, a blind scholar who was one of Ogyū Sorai's disciples.[32] Somon had also been a disciple of Sorai's, although he had later rejected his master's Archaist poetics, and his views of the cut-and-paste approach seem to echo the standard criticism of the latter group's excessively formalistic approach; later in his preface, Somon points out that the cut-and-paste approach could lead to students' composing a poem they themselves did not understand:

These days, when a learner sets to choosing topics and selecting words, these books order the words for use as necessary, but when a learner gets one of these books, it is as if he had "entered a Persian shop";[33] he selects and adopts without rhyme or reason, and, because he views every single word as rare and wonderful, what happens is that though the learner does not yet understand what the words mean, he may still unknowingly bring everything together in harmony. So the learner ends up succeeding without really knowing what he is doing, and it is this so-called diligent instruction that has brought him to this point.[34]

In common with the lexicon's compiler, Nagata Kanga 永田観鵞 (1738–1792), Somon apparently believed that the lexicon-centered approach should be treated as a pedagogical expedient, which the learner should set aside as soon as possible. In the closing lines of his preface, Somon quotes Kanga as likening the lexicon to "merely a grass dog, there being no need to go back to using it" once the student had attained a certain level of proficiency.[35]

Somon's mild disapproval notwithstanding, poetic lexicons rapidly became the established method for elementary *kanshi* instruction during the nineteenth century. Bibliographic surveys by Suzuki Toshiyuki and Higuchi Motomi show that three main titles claimed perhaps the majority of market share during the first half of the nineteenth century: *Shigo saikin* (Gold dust treasury of poetic words—note that this is a different work from the 1768 *Shigo saikin* discussed in the preceding),[36] *Yōgaku shiin* (Poetic rhymes for beginning learners), and the slightly later *Yōgaku benran* (Handbook for beginning learners).[37] While the origin of each title can be traced back to a specific lexicon, by late Edo, over the course of subsequent reprintings and the production of various "sequels" by other scholars not associated with the original, the titles seem to have been used more in the sense of generic brand names for entry-level lexicons, in much the same way that Xerox or Kodak came to be used as general referents for photocopiers or cameras in twentieth-century America. When Shiki spoke of taking his *Yōgaku benran* to his *kanshi* lessons in the passage cited at the beginning of this chapter, then, he was probably not referring to a manual with that specific title but rather to beginners' manuals as a generic category. The longevity and continued use of these poetic lexicons is attested to by a remark in a more advanced manual from Meiji 12 (1879), which notes that "though there are various books on poetry for beginning learners, none surpass the *Shigo saikin* and *Yōgaku shiin*. . . . You should use this volume after having first become thoroughly acquainted with the above."[38] As this suggests, the elementary-level pedagogical practice of having the novice poet assemble a *kanshi* from a bank of ready-made poetic vocabulary persisted well into Meiji, and so, too, did the basic format of the manuals that sprung up to meet this need.

Tracing the development and reception of the two specific titles mentioned in the preceding, as well as their later amalgamation in the *Yōgaku benran*, makes clear two main trends over time. First, such lexicons provide increasingly detailed and explicit explanations of both individual phrases and poetic forms, suggesting that poetic lexicons were gradually refined so as to appeal to an audience with little previous exposure to literary Sinitic. Second, the sheer numbers in which these lexicons were produced and printed attests to an enthusiastic reception, particularly in the three main cities of Edo, Osaka, and Kyoto, and to their continued impact over the course of the century. Nagata Kanga's 1768 *Shigo saikin*, for instance, proved enough of a success that it remained in print for another seventy years, almost certainly continuing to be widely used for some time thereafter,[39] and the same was also true of a number of other such lexicons.

One example, named in the aforementioned Meiji manual, is another manual also named *Shigo saikin* (the title was written using slightly different graphs, and the manual featured different content), which appeared at the end of the eighteenth century and would become perhaps the most widely used poetic manual in Japan over the next fifty years.[40] Following the format of arranging two-graph compounds by topic, this manual was compiled by a pair of largely obscure scholars, Izumi Kaname 泉要 (dates unknown) and Ishizukuri Jō 石作貞 (dates unknown), at the request of their colleague, the rather better-known Confucian scholar Nangū Taishū 南宮大湫 (1728–1778). Highlighting the connection between Edo print capitalism and *kanshi* literacy, the project was apparently suggested to Nangū by a Kyoto bookseller, who had requested the compilation of a lexicon accessible to novice poets.[41] Published first in 1776, Izumi and Ishizukuri's *Shigo saikin* follows the same basic format as its similarly named predecessor, though it went a step further in terms of accessibility by providing not only vernacular explanations of the compounds themselves but also classical Japanese glosses, something that Nagata Kanga's *Shigo saikin* had lacked.

The success of Izumi and Ishizukuri's manual can be judged by the fact that it was continuously in print over virtually the whole of the next century. Subsequent editions appeared in 1778, 1792, 1810, 1812, 1834, 1842, 1845, during the Bunkyū 文久 era (1861–1864), and in 1866;[42] and, as seems to have happened frequently with popular manuals, there also appeared a "sequel" compiled by other parties, *Zoku Shigo saikin* (*Shigo saikin* continued, 1817). The other major best-selling lexicon mentioned earlier was the *Yōgaku shiin*, compiled by Hinoki Nagahiro 桧長裕 (dates unknown) and Naritoku Rin 成徳隣 (dates unknown), and first published in 1802. This manual followed in most respects the format of its predecessors, although it differed slightly in providing only three-graph compounds, rather than the two-graph compounds featured in the two *Shigo saikin* titles. *Yōgaku shiin* also saw numerous reprintings and spin-off editions, most notably the 1814 *Yōgaku shiin zokuhen* (*Yōgaku shiin* continued).[43]

These two major lexicons, the *Shigo saikin* and the *Yōgaku shiin*, were subsequently amalgamated midcentury into a comprehensive volume featuring both two- and three-graph compounds. This was, to give it its full title, *Shiin saikin yōgaku benran* (Gold dust treasury of poetic rhymes: A handbook for beginning learners, usually referred to simply as *Yōgaku benran*), compiled in 1842 by itinerant Confucian scholar Itō Hōzan 伊藤鳳山 (Kaoru 馨, 1806–1870). Originally from the city of Sakata in what is now Yamagata Prefecture, Hōzan twice served as an adviser to the Tahara fiefdom (now Aichi Prefecture), as well as establishing his own academy in Edo, and he seems to have assigned the task of editing and compiling his new manual to the students at this academy. Conceived explicitly as an amalgamation of the two previous lexicons with the aim of allowing learners to look up words more rapidly,[44] Hōzan's manual featured two-graph compounds along the top half of the page and three-graph compounds on the bottom half, thus allowing a novice learner to compile an entire poem from the vocabulary provided. The lexicon proved popular, reprinted in 1847, 1850, 1851, 1852, 1865, and 1870, and was still being used well into Meiji, both in itself and as a template for new manuals; the new format of presenting both two- and three-graph compounds on the same page subsequently became virtually universal.[45] Much like the previous lexicons on which it was based, Hōzan's work was almost continually added to, reedited, and reissued by any number of other subsequent publishers.

NEW WORDS FOR NEW TIMES: EARLY MEIJI POETIC LEXICONS

Both Hōzan, who lived until 1870, and the lexicon that he had supervised and edited would therefore survive to see the upheaval of the Boshin War and the establishment of the new era of Meiji. A new age demanded a new poetic vocabulary, and the market for poetic primers was happy to oblige. As the preface to one Meiji manual argued, "Though we have the *Shigo saikin* and the *Yōgaku shiin*, neither of these is suited to the human emotions of Meiji onward."[46] Accordingly, the first fifteen years or so of the Meiji period saw a surge in newly published and reedited poetic manuals that took account of the era's new realities, some of which extended into unexpected areas. One necessary adjustment was that the adoption of the solar calendar in 1874 had made obsolete a number of seasonal poetic expressions tied to specific months, which thus needed to be adjusted to fit the new calendar. Likewise, a whole range of new Meiji cultural phenomena, such as newspapers, the postal service, and military conscription, all required the addition of new poetic vocabulary. Particularly in early Meiji, when demand seems to have been highest and the market was flooded with these manuals, many handbooks therefore distinguished themselves by prefacing their titles with "newly selected" (*shinsen*), "Meiji," or "for our times" (*kinsei* or *konse*). More broadly speaking, even production and publishing practices for poetic lexicons had to adjust to certain new Meiji realities; with the coming of new concepts of copyright and intellectual property, what had been a widespread practice of adaptation and amalgamation of previous lexicons could be legally problematic. One publisher found this out to his cost in July 1878, when the Osaka district court imposed a fine of fifteen yen for publishing a new lexicon that used Hōzan's work without explicit attribution or explanation that this book was an expansion of his.[47]

One notable difference between late Edo and early Meiji *kanshi* manuals is the introduction of visual aids explaining the required tonal prosody for pentasyllabic and heptasyllabic quatrains, the two main *kan-shi* forms widely considered most suitable for the beginner. Throughout the course of the nineteenth century, *kanshi* pedagogy as a whole tended to emphasize these two forms, seemingly because, at only four lines, their relative brevity meant that, in terms of form at least, they were considered to be the easiest for a novice poet to read and compose. The quatrain accordingly remained the first form in the *kanshi* curriculum well into Meiji.[48] As late as 1895, a poetry manual for beginners enjoined readers to "start to compose first of all from quatrains" (*mazu zekku yori tsukurihajimeyo*):

> Start to compose first of all from quatrains . . . a quatrain's lines are short and its words few, and so it is easy for early learners to grasp; therefore it is good to start composing from there. But on the other hand, concerning the quatrain's merits, it is also more difficult than other kinds of forms where one has several hundred graphs to string together. This is because it demands that one's words are short and one's intent long. . . . But for beginners, putting aside the issue of a verse's quality or lack thereof, the quatrain is the easiest to put together, and thus I recommend one start from there.[49]

The implication of this commentary, then, was that while a quatrain was easy to compose and thus suited for beginners, true mastery of the form was significantly harder. Not all teachers necessarily adopted a quatrain-first curriculum; Miura Kanō records that Ōnuma Chinzan 大沼枕山 (1818–1891), one of the *éminences grises* of the early Meiji *kanshi* world, often had new students start by composing more technically demanding "old-style" (Ch. *gushi*, J. *koshi*) poems, reasoning that other forms would seem easier thereafter.[50] During late Edo, at least one prominent educator, the Kyushu-based Hirose Tansō 広瀬淡窓 (1782–1856), also felt that a greater focus on the quatrain represented the "dumbing down" of *kanshi* practice. In an undated piece, Tansō complained that "these days no form enjoys such popularity in the three cities as the heptasyllabic quatrain. This is a strategy that nobles or the wealthy adopt in order to entice townsmen to join their poetic societies. This sort of people get to the level of being able to read the Chinese classics aloud [*sodoku*], and then they want to become poets, and for this reason they are not capable of doing anything other than composing quatrains . . . one has to say that this is all very vulgar in its import."[51]

Tansō's complaint seems to suggest a sense of frustration at the prospect of *kanshi*'s dilution as cultural capital, with those who do not have the proper background composing in only the simplest form. Nevertheless, the quatrain's perceived accessibility and its position as the first step in the *kanshi* curriculum meant that there was a strong incentive for publishers, who naturally wished to reach as wide an audience as possible, to favor it as well. From the late 1820s until well into Meiji, many nationally circulated collections of *kanshi* featured quatrains exclusively, for precisely this reason.[52] Gōyama Rintarō has noted that one of these collections, the 1848 *Quatrains by Twenty-Five Poets of the Kaei Era* (*Kaei nijūgoka zekku*), sold as many as two thousand copies, an impressive number by the standards of the time, and proved highly profitable for its publisher.[53]

The first pages of a Meiji lexicon would almost invariably begin by explaining the proper tonal prosody sequence for each quatrain, usually using white circles to depict level tones and black circles to depict oblique ones.[54] This seems to have been an early Meiji innovation, since earlier lexicons generally did not feature this device; its addition was apparently welcomed, as suggested by a copy of an 1856 edition of the *Zoku Yōgaku shiin* held by Gifu Prefectural Library. To this, a later owner added the standard black-and-white dot pattern in a blank space after the lexicon's table of contents, for his or her own reference. Almost all manuals went

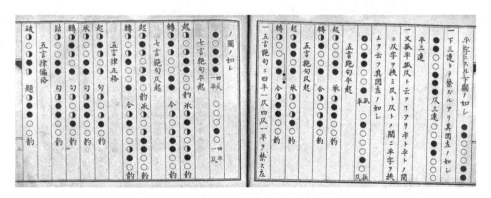

FIGURE 1.1 An early Meiji *kanshi* manual illustrates tonal prosody using black and white circles.

out of their way to stress the importance of correct tonal prosody for the novice poet, and Shiki's own experience suggests this may have been a necessary admonishment. As a beginner, he seems to have been quite sloppy in his observance of tonal prosody, being repeatedly scolded for his lack of care by one of his later teachers of *kanshi* in Matsuyama, Kawahigashi Seikei 河東静渓 (1829–1894).[55]

I have already noted Shiki's reminiscences about using compositional manuals early in his *kanshi* career, and his actual poems would seem to provide further evidence. Analyzing Shiki's earliest *kanshi*, Shimizu Fusao has convincingly demonstrated that Shiki composed his first ever such poem using precisely this lexicon-based cut-and-paste method:

聞子規   *On Hearing the Cuckoo*

[Note:] 余作詩以此為始 (The first Sinitic poem I ever composed)

一声 ｜ 孤月下	A single cry under the lonely moon,
啼血 ｜ 不堪聞	Coughing up blood, I cannot bear the sound.
半夜 ｜ 空欹枕	Midnight, in vain I lie awake and listen—
故郷 ｜ 万里雲	My hometown, ten thousand leagues of cloud away.[56]

Shimizu shows that each of the two- and three-graph phrases that make up this poem can be found in one of Hōzan's primers, the evidence therefore suggesting that this was indeed the method that Shiki, along with countless other novice poets at the time, used in his early experiments with *kanshi*.[57]

We might say, therefore, that Shiki's poem was not so much composed as it was assembled. This rather mechanical method of composition would certainly seem to run counter to more Romantic ideas of poetry as deriving from emotional inspiration, favoring an idea of poetry—at the beginning stages, at least—as more craft than art, something with a standardized curriculum that anyone might master who was willing to work at it. A number of poets explicitly rejected the lexicon-centered method or commented on it with scorn later in their careers; Shiki's disciple and friend Naitō Meisetsu 内藤鳴雪 (Nariyuki

素行, 1847–1926), for instance, wrote of his dissatisfaction at being instructed to learn through poetic manuals:[58]

> Back when I was attending the private academy of Master Takechi [Junnosuke 武智隼之助, dates unknown] to learn calligraphy, I was told, "It would be good if you could compose Sinitic poetry a bit, and to do that it would be a good idea to look at the *Handbook for Beginning Learners*," so I had my father buy me a copy, but it wasn't interesting, so I left it at that. . . . Obviously, a lot of beginners would stick the two- and three-graph phrases found in the *Handbook* alongside one another and thereby create a pentasyllabic or heptasyllabic poem, but I felt that if I sewed together a lot of preexisting words, it wouldn't really be my own work, so I decided to compose by using my own language to say something that I myself felt I wanted to say, having made sure to check the tonal prosody. Obviously I was quite well read in the Chinese classics and knew how to use literary Sinitic, but the language of Sinitic poetry is quite another matter, and so from the point of view of those who were skilled in poetry, even if you had the right number of five or seven graphs, that clearly didn't mean that what you had was actually a poem.[59]

Similarly, Shiki wrote in 1896 that he ultimately found that the lexicon-centered approach was "formalistic" (*keishikiteki*) and did not allow him to express himself as he would wish.[60] Shiki's own *kanshi* suggest that he moved on from using the *Handbook*-type vocabulary and compositional methods relatively quickly, in favor of vocabulary and broader poetic themes from other, more advanced sources. Katō Kuniyasu's exhaustive study of Shiki's personal library and the likely sources of inspiration for many of his poems finds, for example, that by 1884 Shiki was likely reading the *Guwen zhenbao* and the work of Japanese *kanshi* poet Kan Chazan 官茶山 (1748–1827) for inspiration, as in the following poem:

題画四首　其四	*Four Poems Composed on a Painting (No. 4)*
黃鸝飛織柳	Oriole's flight weaves through willows,
蛺蝶舞縫花	Butterfly's dance threads through flowers.

| 公子尋春去 | The young master has gone in search of spring, |
| 紫騮独車護 | Majestic steed left alone to guard his carriage. |

The precise painting on which this poem is based is not clear, but the poem itself is easy to follow: in a spring garden flourishing with signs of life and energy, a young nobleman has gone off in "search of spring"—the question of whether this search is aesthetic or (perhaps) romantic is left to the reader's imagination. Katō finds that very similar conceits of birds and butterflies "weaving" amid flowers and trees can be found in the work of eighteenth-century Japanese poets Chiba Unkaku and Ryū Sōro 龍草廬 (1714–1792); moreover, the specific term "majestic steed" (Ch. *ziliu*, J. *shiryū*) and its connection to the imagery of flowers likely come from a poem by Li Bai included in the *Guwen zhenbao*, which Shiki is known to have copied out by hand. Likewise, while the phrase "in search of spring" (Ch. *xun chun*, J. *jinshun*) is not uncommon in Sinitic poetry as a whole, Katō suggests that Shiki may have learned the phrase from a line in a poem in Kan Chazan's *Yellow Leaf Sunset Lodge Collection* (*Kōyō sekiyō sonsha shishū*), sections of which Shiki is known to have copied out by hand.[61] In short, like most serious *kanshi* poets, Shiki quickly moved beyond the cut-and-paste methods recommended for elementary learners and immersed himself in both more advanced manuals and in Sinitic poetry collections in general.

DRINKING COFFEE AND WALKING WITH WESTERNERS: *KANSHI* AS ASPIRATIONAL GENRE DURING MEIJI

Over time, invoking the *Handbook for Beginning Learners* seems to have become a kind of self-deprecating way to refer to one's own poetry; in a 1908 letter to journalist and author Tokutomi Sohō 徳富蘇峰 (Iichirō 猪一郎, 1863–1957), for instance, politician Gotō Shinpei 後藤新平 (1857–1929) includes a *kanshi* verse about which he comments, "As per usual, I've been fiddling around with the *Handbook for Beginning Learners*. I enclose the verse for your amusement."[62] Though Shiki and Meisetsu may have chafed against it, the lexicon-centered approach to composition seems to have been extremely common among beginner-level Meiji *kanshi* poets. Future luminaries of the Japanese cultural world such as novelist Nagai Kafū 永井荷風 (1879–1959) and ethnographer and author Yanagida Kunio 柳田國男 (1875–1962), for example, both record having studied *kanshi* using lexicons of this type during their youth.[63] My own bibliographic survey of manuals published during the first two decades of Meiji in particular also attests both to the popularity of the lexicon composition method and to the surge in interest in *kanshi* composition. Between the years 1877 and 1884, for instance, at least fifty new or reissued *Handbooks* for aspiring poets appeared on the market.

What was behind this surge in enthusiasm for *kanshi* composition? Part of the explanation lies in the advent in the mid-1870s of a variety of nationally circulated media venues specializing in part or in whole in publishing *kanshi*. The attraction of seeing one's name in print before a national audience was a major motivating factor for many younger poets and drove the considerable success of the *New Journal for Splendid Talents* (*Eisai shinshi*, 1877–1899). Founded as a sideline for a paper manufacturer, *Eisai shinshi* became an early Meiji publishing phenomenon as a venue for prose and poetry in various genres, written almost exclusively by middle- and higher-school students. In this student milieu, *Eisai shinshi* was extremely prestigious; the novelist Tayama Katai 田山花袋 (1871–1930) recalled that even though he could not always afford to buy the journal, he would hike over to the booksellers in Yotsuya in Tokyo every time it came out and flip through its pages to see if his work had been published. When it had, he noted, he felt "as happy as if I had ascended to the heavens" (*ten ni demo nobotta yō ni yorokonde iru*).[64] Even down in Matsuyama, Shiki and his friends also seem to have read *Eisai shinshi* and may also have sent in their work for consideration.[65]

In addition to *Eisai shinshi*, one other major force in the market for *kanshi* media was the learner's journal *Kokon shibun shōkai* (1880–1887). Publishing on the fifth, fifteenth, and twenty-fifth days of each month, this journal carried prose and poetry by the major figures of the Tokyo *kanshi* and *kanbun* worlds, along with copious headnotes that explained and glossed specific phrases and rhetorical features for inexperienced readers. It also featured a vibrant question-and-answer (*bengi*) section in which readers could submit and have answered their questions on Sinitic poetry and prose in general; requests for explanation of allusions and the meaning of specific passages by both contemporary Japanese and famous Chinese poets were particularly common. As might be expected, *Kokon shibun shōkai* carried advertisements for poetic manuals and lexicons of the kind discussed in virtually every issue; it also carried advertisements from enterprising masters around the country, taking advantage of the new nationwide postal system to offer to read and grade students' prose and poetic compositions for a fixed fee.[66]

Rintaro Goyama's analysis of circulation figures from the early 1880s shows that *Kokon shibun shōkai* was hugely popular in its day, its yearly circulation reaching a peak of one hundred twenty-four thousand copies in 1884—an average monthly readership of around ten thousand. For context, this was at a time when most metropolitan newspapers had a daily circulation of only a few thousand at most.[67] The success of *Kokon shibun shōkai*, a journal explicitly aimed at less-experienced but aspiring poets and writers in Sinitic genres, strongly suggests that what Suzuki Toshiyuki has called a "fever for *kanshi* composition among common people [*minkan*], heightening in the run-up to the last days of the *bakufu*" was sustained and even grew during the first two decades of the Meiji era.[68] Yet Suzuki's rhetoric of "common people" surely requires some qualification; even with growing access to entry-level materials such as those discussed in the preceding, there remained significant differentials in background and experience among *kanshi* poets throughout the country. Perhaps as a direct result of the expansion in the sheer numbers of poets practicing the genre, we can find in Meiji poetic lexicons a narrowing of *kanshi*'s conceptual scope, as well as a privileging therein of the specific identity of the government employee. Rather than continuing its Edo trajectory as a "literature of the citizenry," *kanshi* took on a new quality as public performance of either the possession of, or aspiration toward, elite status. It is here that a discernible divide begins to emerge between aspiring amateur poets and their metropolitan, professional, and government-connected counterparts.

At the center of this early Meiji shift in visions of what and who *kanshi* was for is the specific figure of the government official, and the extent to which early Meiji's textual infrastructure seemed to rearrange itself around this figure's concerns and putative experiences is quite striking. We can see this stratification begin to emerge in two of the better-known early Meiji *kanshi* journals, Mori Shuntō's *Shinbunshi* and Narushima Ryūhoku's *Kagetsu shinshi.* These journals were among modern Japan's very first dedicated literary periodicals of any kind, and both featured the work of the best *kanshi* poets Tokyo had to offer. Though an important and prestigious venue for *kanshi* poets to publish, both were quite far from the open forum model adopted by publications such as *Eisai shinshi* and, to an extent, *Kokon shibun shōkai.* For its part, *Kagetsu shinshi* seems to have circulated quite widely throughout Japan; Shiki probably read it while he was living in Matsuyama, since he apparently copied out certain poems from it as calligraphy practice.[69] It is not known whether he ever submitted his poems for publication to *Kagetsu shinshi* as he did with *Eisai shinshi,* but if he did they were never published. If Shiki did indeed have work rejected by *Kagetsu shinshi,* this would not have been at all unusual, because in practice it was very difficult for an unknown amateur poet to have his work published in Ryūhoku's journal. A little under half of all the poems that appeared in *Kagetsu shinshi* during its print run were produced by just ten poets, and fully a quarter by only three men, Ono Kozan 小野湖山 (1814–1910), Mori Shuntō, and Suzuki Shōtō 鱸松塘 (1824–1898).[70] *Shinbunshi* was even more notorious for being a closed shop, in the sense that it gave favorable treatment to poems by government employees and officials. This tendency was pronounced enough to prompt Narushima Ryūhoku, editor of the rival *Kagetsu shinshi,* to grumble that "it seems that there are submissions [to *Shinbunshi*] that are quite inferior and don't deserve to be recorded. If the works of the great and the good get in regardless of quality, then change the title to 'Government Poetry' or 'The Corridors of Power,' or something like that, and nobody will have any objections."[71] Ryūhoku's complaint was largely justified, since *Shinbunshi* in its time published works by such luminaries of the Meiji political world as Yamagata Aritomo 山県有朋 (1838–1922) and Itō Hirobumi 伊藤博文 (1841–1909).

Whereas seeing their work appear in its pages may not have been a realistic ambition for most aspiring poets, it seems likely that for many aspiring poets *Shinbunshi* did much to cement an association between *kanshi* practice and government employment. Where late Edo manuals had often favored poems by Chinese poets or Japanese masters such as Rai San'yō 頼山陽 (Noboru 襄, 1780–1832) and Kan Chazan as model compositions, a number of early Meiji poetic manuals, such as the 1878

Yōgaku hikkei konsei shisaku shinpen (Beginning learners' essential handbook in poetic composition in our time: New edition), made use of poems by high-ranking contemporary politicians such Kido Takayoshi 木戸孝允 (1833–1877), one of the key architects of the Meiji state.[72] The effect of this was to communicate not only that high officials studied and wrote *kanshi* but also by further implication that, for ambitious young men, learning *kanshi* would be worthwhile. The reason for this was that, in addition to its artistic value and cultural prestige, *kanshi* could also be a means of communicating and socializing with high-ranking officials—and it offered the tantalizing possibility that the poet might in time count himself among their number.

Unsurprisingly, the topics and suggested vocabulary in many early Meiji poetic lexicons reflect this; although for the most part there is a consistency in suggested topics and vocabulary from late Edo to early Meiji, many of the new topics distinctive to Meiji manuals have to do with government employment in some capacity. Many such lexicons seemed to assume that the prospective poet would move in a social milieu in which he was likely to meet officials and government elites; most also hailed government employment as a desirable outcome and alluded to the various privileges that might come with the job, particularly the possibility of studying in another country. For example, one 1878 lexicon, *Kaika shigo saikin* (Gold dust treasury of poetic words for enlightened times), had among its suggested topics "Viewing Government Officials as They Attend Morning Ceremonies at Court" (一日観百官入朝 *ichinichi hyakkan no nyūchō o miru*, explained as *yakunin no sandai suru o miru koto*). Suggested vocabulary for composing on this topic included "harmony among the people" (人和, explained as *yoku osamarishi koto*, "the realm being well governed") and "the waves stilled" (波静, *nami shizuka nari*, explained as *shizuka naru miyo*, "the tranquil realm").[73] Rather more direct in encouraging the flattering of government officials was another heading, "[A Poem] Sent to a Prefectural Official" (贈懸官), for which the possible phrases included "unparalleled virtue" (至潔, explained as *kiyoki yakunin*, "pure official") and "man of righteousness and virtue" (仁人, explained as *yoki yakunin*, "good official").[74]

Kaika shigo saikin's envisioned linkage between *kanshi* and aspirations to a career in the Meiji bureaucracy is rather confirmed by another suggested topic, "On Duty on a Spring Night in the Imperial Palace"

(春夜禁中寓直), a role in which the manual's readers were thereby invited to imagine themselves, even as all but the tiniest minority would never actually be in such a position.[75] As we have seen, the late eighteenth century, during which the lexicon genre arose, had seen *kanshi* practice move away from *Selection of Tang Poetry*–inspired poems composed on the concerns of the scholar-official, and which were removed from the direct experiences of the poets themselves. Yet during early Meiji, it seems, the pendulum had swung back the other way, novice poets being encouraged to compose after first imagining themselves to be representatives of the Meiji government, or about to be. A different manual, *Shinsen shiin yōgaku benran* (Newly chosen poetic rhymes: A handbook for beginning learners, 1878) contains the suggested topic "Congratulating Someone on Being Appointed to an Official Post" (賀拜官人, explained as *hito no kan ni tsukitaru o iwaite tsukuru*, "composed to celebrate someone getting an official job"). Suggested vocabulary for this topic includes "confrere" (同僚, explained as *nakama*, "buddy") and "to be envious" (仰羨, explained as *urayamu*, "to be jealous").[76] Another, slightly later, lexicon from 1883 echoes the idea of government employment as desirable and virtuous, suggesting that the reader respond to a friend who has left an official job to return to his hometown (辞官帰家) by imploring, "Resign not your post" (君莫辞, explained as *jitai suru na*, "don't quit!") and stating that "I cannot bear my sadness" (不勝悲, explained as *kanashisa kotaegatashi*, "I am so sad I cannot bear it").[77] The same lexicon also contained the topic "On an Autumn Day, Sending Off a Certain Official Traveling to a Certain Country" (秋日送某官使某國); suggested vocabulary for this purpose included "valued tool of the state" (國器, explained as *kuni no takara*, "treasure of the nation") and the three-graph phrase "I envy those of high official status" (羨高官).[78]

Even where not explicitly referring to the specific jobs of the government official, many topics in Meiji poetic lexicons suggest that both their publishers and their authors saw their target audience as being less the population at large, as is usually argued in narratives of the Edo-period expansion, and more the country's educated elite, as well as those who believed they would shortly join that elite. In other words, after having moved toward a "citizen literature" during late Edo, Meiji *kanshi* was beginning to move back again to a literature of the "cultured official," though the Meiji understanding of the role and allure of the "official" was rather different. In addition to providing its readers with ways to congratulate a newly appointed official, one of the manuals discussed in the previous paragraph, *Shinsen shiin yōgaku benran*, also contained a number of topics that suggested the reader would likely be interacting with the wealthy and powerful, and even with foreigners. Among these were, for instance, the startlingly specific "On an Autumn Day, Meeting a Friend Who Has Come Back from Great Britain" (秋日遇友人歸自英国) and "On a Spring Day, Sending Off a Friend Who Is Going to the World's Fair in France" (春日送人赴佛國博覧會).[79] Salutations addressed to people departing for foreign pastures, such as France, Great Britain, and the United States, were common topics across a variety of manuals, as in, for example, "Sending Off a School Friend Who Is Traveling by Boat to the West" (送学友洋航), under which the composing poet was invited to hail his friend as acting "for the sake of the nation" (為国).[80] Very few novice *kanshi* poets would be likely to interact with those who had the financial resources (or official sponsorship) to travel internationally; on the other side of the coin, however, several of this lexicon's topics also suggested that the aspiring poet might find himself in a position to interact with foreign visitors on Japanese soil. Among these were "Accompanying a Westerner to See the Flowers at Arashiyama" (拉洋人嵐山観花)[81] and "On a Spring Day, Watching Westerners at Horse Racing" (春日観洋人競馬), the latter given an explanatory note that "this happens in Yokohama and Kobe" (*kore wa Yokohama Kōbe nite aru nari*).[82] Even if not actually interacting with foreigners, knowledge of their ways would still be necessary for the newly envisioned Meiji elite; yet another suggested topic, "Thanking Someone for a Gift of Coffee" (謝人恵珈琲), featured an explanatory note to the effect that "coffee holds a similar place to tea in our country. In the West, they partake of it all the time" (*kohī [sic] wa wagakuni de ieba cha no gotoki mono nari, Seiyō ni wa tsune ni mochiyu*).[83]

THE POLITICS OF MEIJI *KANSHI* LEXICONS

Although the majority of early Meiji poetic lexicons surveyed thus held government employment up as glamorous, desirable, and honorable, there are exceptions to this trend. *Kanshi* had, after all, been a major vehicle for antigovernment protest throughout the nineteenth century, first in the hands of the "men of high purpose" (*shishi*) of the *bakumatsu* era and then later for a number of prominent members of the FPRM. For FPRM members, the government official was, so to speak, a natural enemy, and there are a few examples of poetic lexicons providing their readers with what appears to be a ready-made vocabulary of political protest. Under the heading "Reading a Newspaper on a Cold Night" (寒夜讀新聞), the 1878 *Shinsen yōgaku benran* appears to envision the novice poet moved to take up his pen in response to newspaper reportage of unsavory events, providing the expressions "swelling anger" (発憤), "violating the ways of morality" (乱大倫), and "Alone, I lament" (獨長嘆). As to why the reader might wish to express anger, the same manual also provides suggestive examples: "courtesans" (倡伎) and "sexual immorality" (淫奔) seem to encourage critical commentary on politicians' sexual peccadilloes, and "loans" (負債) on their underhand financial dealings. In a similar vein in the same section, the lexicon offers "rights of the people" (民権), "freedom" (自由), "autonomy" (自主), and "the people of the realm" (天下民), all of which would seem to echo the concerns and language of the major representatives of the FPRM. As if to confirm that much of this vocabulary was to be understood as directed against the government in general, the same section suggests a three-graph compound that could be read almost as a direct rebuke to a number of other contemporary manuals vaunting the figure of the government employee— namely, "Why should I envy the official?" (豈羨官). Lest the lexicon's reader miss the point of this particular phrase, the manual explains its meaning as "I don't want to become an official" (*kannin ni naritaku wa nai*).[84]

The critical, antigovernment impulses on display in this manual are, in the grand scheme of Meiji lexicons, relatively unusual; for the most part, the genre was structured around an official position as something to which one might aspire. In that sense, the lexicons are symptomatic not necessarily of a unified *kanshi* world but of stratification and differentiation therein, in terms of both success and failure in securing government employment and pro- or antigovernment views. Shiki, for his part, likely fell into the latter camp for much of his early *kanshi* days; caught up in the FPRM fever that surrounded Matsuyama during the mid-1880s, he apparently produced a number of political speeches echoing the movement's rhetoric and calling for political freedom (*jiyū*). This fever, seemingly, passed when he reached Tokyo, the mutual aid association to which he belonged desiring that the students they sponsored not get caught up in political factionalism that might jeopardize their chances of future employment.

It is, therefore, wise to avoid assuming a process of linear development from the demographic expansion of *kanshi* from Edo into the Meiji period; the change in nature, during early Meiji, of the textual infrastructure that made an expansion in numbers possible throughout the nineteenth century means that we cannot necessarily posit a trajectory of *kanshi* poets developing a shared, unified identity structured around the imagined construct of the nation. Rather, the social parameters of *kanshi* practice become increasingly narrower, focused on and structured around the concerns of those in Japan who belonged to the social, cultural, and economic stratum that could realistically aspire to a career in government. It may be worth noting, in light of the frequently suggested topic of sending a friend overseas, that Shiki's own experience would have allowed him use of just such a topic. Although far from materially wealthy, Shiki's upbringing in a well-educated family of warrior descent placed a considerable premium on intellectual development, and his maternal uncle, Katō Takusen 加藤拓川 (Tsunetada 恒忠, 1859–1923), was in fact dispatched to France by the Meiji government in a diplomatic capacity while Shiki was studying in Tokyo.

The poetic lexicon as genre seemingly continued to hold an important place in *kanshi* education throughout Meiji, though the numbers of new manuals being printed slowed to a trickle from the flood of the 1870s and early 1880s. Some shift in topics is discernible in later versions, as in an 1895 manual titled *Shigaku shōkei*, which encouraged its readers to compose on the recently concluded Sino-Japanese War; under the topic "Reading Accounts of the Battle of Weihaiwei" (讀威海衛戦記), this manual included the suggested phrase "to think little of sacrificing one's life" (甘殉難).[85] Unlike with the 1878 *Shinsen yōgaku benran*, the conceptual landscape of *kanshi* in 1895 allowed for no ambiguity or dissent: to write *kanshi* was, in the vision provided by this manual, necessarily to express accord with the aims and ideology of Japan as a modern imperialist state.

Yet as this chapter has argued, and subsequent chapters support, this conception of *kanshi* in 1895 as apparently encouraging novice poets to speak in the language of a unified nationalism could emerge only after eliding and covering up a wide variety of divisions in the ranks of poets across the country. Precisely because *kanshi* was a literary genre closely tied to the possibility of socioeconomic advancement and prestigious status in government, it necessarily promoted anxieties and strategies of differentiation among individual poets. I have focused in this chapter largely on *kanshi* as aspirational genre, concentrating on the priorities of an educated elite; in the next chapter, I explore some of the same issues, of the importance of government employment, as they relate to ideas of masculinity and gender in the field of *kanshi* practice.

CHAPTER TWO

Not the Kind of Poetry Men Write

"Fragrant-Style" Kanshi *and Poetic Masculinity in Meiji Japan*

An otherwise unremarkable passage in Mori Ōgai's 森鴎外 (1862–1922) semiautobiographical *Wild Geese* (*Gan*, 1911–1913) finds the narrator recalling his days as a student in late 1870s Tokyo and mentioning, in passing, the kind of *kanshi* he used to enjoy: "In terms of lyrical poetry, this was before Shiki's haiku and Tekkan's tanka had come about, so everyone read journals like *Kagetsu shinshi*, which was printed on Chinese-style paper, or *Keirin isshi*, printed on plain white paper, and thought that [Mori] Kainan and [Ue] Mukō's 'fragrant-style' poems were the height of sophistication."[1]

Ōgai's narrator, who goes by the name of Okada, does not explain what the "fragrant style" (Ch. *xianglian ti*, J. *kōrentai*) actually was or why it was so memorable, and so this passage is easily skipped over in the larger flow of the story.[2] To anyone who had had even a casual interest in *kanshi* during the Meiji period, however, the term "fragrant style" would have been very familiar. In a Meiji context, "fragrant style" functioned as an umbrella term for Sinitic poetry depicting the sexualized female figure.[3] Among the most common topics and themes in this category were the "boudoir lament" (Ch. *guiyuan*, J. *keien*), featuring an abandoned woman languishing in her bedchamber or other private, intimate space; portrayals of courtesans and their clients in the licensed quarters; and remembrances of famous beauties from Chinese or Japanese history.[4] Meiji critics also grouped these topics together under the term "alluring style" (Ch. *yanti*, J. *entai*), a description that could apply both to the content and to the style and tone of the poem.

In this chapter, I focus on the frequently controversial reception of fragrant-style poetics in Japan during the latter half of the nineteenth century. At issue, fundamentally, was a question of poetic morality: was it appropriate for a poet to produce poems that centered on romantic love and the sexualized feminine? And more broadly, what was the place of the feminine—whether in the shape of depictions of women or of female poets—in *kanshi* as a whole? The chapter points to the late 1870s and early 1880s as a final flourish in a nearly century-long process of expansion of subject matter and inclusion of female poets. Beginning in the mid-1880s, the period of popularity for fragrant-style poetics that Ōgai describes would give way to a backlash as numerous poets and critics assailed the fragrant style as not only immoral but also as corrosive to proper masculinity. Although both male and female poets made use of the style, the primary focus in Meiji debates on the fragrant style was its alleged effect on male poets. Male fragrant-style poets found themselves being accused of lacking moral seriousness, of damaging the way of *kanshi* by focusing on immoral subject matter, and of becoming weak and feminized themselves, their interest in the sexualized feminine indicative of a lack of proper masculine vigor.

My argument throughout the chapter is that debates over fragrant-style poetics, particularly the insistent emphasis on performances of masculinity, reflect a reconfiguring and shifting conception of the national-poetic community of *kanshi* poets. With vigorous, upright masculinity increasingly valorized as a mechanism of differentiation and hierarchy, allegedly weak and feminized male poets had their poetic qualifications called into question. This question of weak and feminized versus strong and vigorous *kanshi* poets was rarely a matter of personal ethical failings on the part of the individual poet; rather, enemies of the fragrant style framed the alleged spinelessness or feminization of its proponents as damaging to the national-poetic community as a whole. While women's *kanshi* practice was rarely problematized in and of itself in these debates, this insistent emphasis on masculinity as an important qualification to be a "proper" poet was hardly likely to encourage female *kanshi* poets. Hierarchical conceptions of poetic masculinity thus defined the ways in which male *kanshi* poets thought about themselves and others as actors in an explicitly national community; and as chapter 5 makes clear, the discussions in this chapter also resonate with Ochiai Naobumi's and Yosano Tekkan's later attacks on purportedly "feminized" *waka* poetry as harming the moral fabric of the nation.

Usually, the working assumption in these debates was that the poem was the poet; in other words, a poem was a performance and index of masculinity and revealed the character of the man who wrote it. A man who composed poems showing weak, languid women revealed his own character to be weak, languid, and feminized, at least according to opponents of the fragrant style. For male poets, the expression of heterosexual desire was thus understood as inimical to true masculinity. A truly masculine poet would be serious of purpose and concerned with the state of the nation rather than frivolous; bold and heroic, not languid; and vigorous and martial in his outlook, never feminized. Beginning in the mid-1880s, then, an emergent Meiji national-poetic community of male *kanshi* poets was defined in part by one crucial question: who was a real man, and who was not.

EROTIC POEMS AND MORAL SERIOUSNESS: HAN WO'S *FRAGRANT TOILETTE COLLECTION*

Although a number of different kinds of poems could theoretically be grouped under the umbrella term "fragrant style," probably the majority of poems so labeled during Meiji were of the subgenre of the boudoir lament, sometimes also termed emotions of the boudoir (Ch. *guiqing*, J. *keijō*). A couple of examples, both from Meiji poets, will give some idea of the style's main tropes and themes:

無題	*Untitled*
粉愁香恨両凄迷	Grief in powder, regret in fragrance; both bring only misery.
手剥青苔認舊題	Her hands peel back green moss, to find old inscriptions.[5]

| 春色満庭不見人 | Spring colors fill the garden, but no one is seen; |
| 海棠枝上画眉啼 | In the branches of the aronia tree, a laughing thrush sings.[6] |

Written by Mori Shuntō, this poem is a fairly typical boudoir lament, focusing on the physical surroundings and mental state of a highborn woman who has been abandoned by her lover. Within the intimate space of the woman's private garden, the poem makes extensive use of pathetic fallacy and imagery of the natural world to portray the woman's emotional state. In the first line, powder and fragrance are ironic reminders of past dalliances; where they might once have been used to enhance her physical charms, they bring only sadness now that her lover does not come. Visual puns and allusive references to birds and trees underpin the mood of frustrated desire; the final line's reference to the aronia tree (Ch. *haitang*, J. *kaidō*) evokes the doomed love between Emperor Xuanzong 玄宗 (685–762, r. 712–756) and the Prized Consort Yang Guifei 楊貴妃 (719–756), whose beauty Xuanzong likened to that of the aronia.[7] Similarly, the laughing thrush (*Garrulax canorus*; Ch. *huamei niao*, J. *gabichō*, aka Chinese hwamei) carries painful associations; the bird's name (literally, "painted-eyebrow bird") derives from markings around its eyes that resemble eye makeup. As the poem's emphasis on eye makeup suggests, cosmetics, conventionally rouge (脂, Ch. *zhi*, J. *shi*), powder (粉, Ch. *fen*, J. *fun*), and perfumes (香, Ch. *xiang*, J. *kō*), also play an important role in the imaginative landscape of the fragrant-style poem; they function as signifiers of feminine allure, and the term "rouge and powder" (Ch. *zhifen*, J. *shibun*) was also used as a metonymical way of referring to women and the feminine in general. The resonances of these terms were not always positive; Xiaorong Li has noted, for instance, that in China "male critics often used [the term 'rouge and powder'] to characterize trivial feminine qualities, including the writing of poetry by women."[8]

Structured thus around frustrated female desire and deploying what Paul Rouzer has termed the erotics of pity, boudoir poems may be narrated from the point of view of a hypothetical (usually male) observer, or sometimes in the voice of the woman herself.[9] Albeit common elements, regret and pain were not essential, and in some cases the erotic potential of the boudoir came to the fore, as in this 1878 poem by Ue Mukō 上夢香 (Sanemichi 真行, 1851–1937), whom Ōgai mentions in the earlier quote:

春暁	*Spring Dawn*
脉々輕寒透洞房	A slight chill keeps making its way into the bedroom,
半簾殘月白微茫	Shades half up, the waning moon white and slightly hazy.
流鶯一囀不知處	A drifting oriole chirps, from where one cannot tell.
帳裏梅花春夢香	Behind the screens, fragrant are plum flowers and dreams of spring.[10]

The "drifting oriole" (*liu ying*) in the third line signals to the reader that this is a courtesan's bedchamber, since the bird bears a traditional association with women who "drift" among many possible clients. Hidden behind screens, the woman herself is never described or seen, but the reference to "dreams of spring" suggests that she is just awakening from a night either of lovemaking or from an erotic dream. This boudoir, at least, would seem to be very much in use.

Though it was controversial in its Meiji heyday, the overt sexuality of the fragrant style was hardly a recent addition to the field of Sinitic poetics. In fact, the so-called fragrant style took its name from an anthology of quasi-erotic verse, the *Fragrant Toilette Collection* (Ch. *Xiangli-anji*, J. *Kōrenshū*),[11] that had been written in late Tang China by (most likely) the scholar-official Han Wo 韓偓 (J. Kan Aku, 842–923?, also known as Donglang 冬郎).[12] Han Wo had held high official rank in the turbulent last days of the Tang empire, remaining staunchly loyal to his sovereign amid a variety of court intrigues before finally being sent into exile in the quasi-autonomous region of Min (present-day Fujian). Here, he spent the last fourteen years of his life, and here, too, he apparently wrote and compiled the *Fragrant Toilette Collection*. As might be expected, many of the verses in the *Collection* were sufficiently racy to earn it subsequent notoriety:

詠浴	*On Taking a Bath*
再整魚犀攏翠簪	She adjusts her fish rhino horn again, pulls together jade hairpins,[13]
解衣先覺冷森森	Takes off her robe, a foretaste of the cold's chill,
教移蘭燭頻羞影	Asks that the orchid candle be moved, for she's skittish at its shadows,
自試香湯更怕深	Tests the fragrant waters herself, though she's even more scared by their depth.
初似洗花難抑按	To begin with, she's as difficult to get a hold of as if one were washing a blossom,
終憂沃雪不勝任	By the end, she is pitiably delicate and fragile, hot water poured onto snow.
豈知侍女簾帷外	How could she know that her servant girls, beyond the screens and curtains,
賸取君王幾餅金	Gather any number of her lord and master's many pieces of gold?[14]

This unabashedly voyeuristic verse depicts a high-class woman taking a bath while waited on by female attendants. Lines 3 and 4 show the woman as shy and vulnerable, hesitant at the shadows cast by the candle and intimidated by the depth of the bathing tub. Lines 5 and 6 describe the slipperiness of her naked body as her attendants wash her, likening the white tenderness of her skin to snow melting in hot water. The final two lines confirm the sense of voyeurism by revealing that the woman's lord and master has bribed her servant girls to allow him to spy on her as she bathes.[15] The reader is implicitly invited to gaze on the woman's naked body, before learning in the final lines that the woman's state of undress is also being observed by her lover within the poem itself.

As might be expected, one enduring topic of debate on the fragrant style, both during Meiji and in the case of the *Fragrant Toilette Collection*, was the propriety of writing such verse in the first place. As the *Collection* circulated in China in the centuries after Han Wo's death, for instance, many scholar-literati found themselves grappling with the question of how Han Wo, in most other respects an exemplar of loyalty and public service, could have written such thoroughly improper poetry. A number of later versions of the *Collection* text contain a (possibly inauthentic) preface in which Han Wo seems to apologize for his own poems: "I am truly aware that this is not the kind of thing a man should do. Yet to be unable to forget one's own emotion is a gift bestowed by Heaven" (誠知非士大夫所為、不能忘情、天所賦也).[16] The preface thus anticipates possible criticism of erotic poetry as incompatible with the specific male identity of *shidaifu*, the cultured scholar-official, defending the collection by arguing that its focus on love and sex expresses human emotional truth. This line of argument seems to have been only partially effective, since judged by what Nanxiu Qian has called "mainstream male poetics" in China, much of the content of the *Fragrant Toilette Collection* was consistently viewed as objectionable.[17] Yuan-dynasty poet Fang Hui 方回 (1227–1306), for example, found it odd that so resolute a poet-official as Han Wo should have written erotic verse; as he wrote, "[Han Wo was] virtuous in his affairs and extreme in his loyal indignation, yet the works of the *Fragrant Toilette Collection* have refined phrases but vulgar tastes; was this not because, with matters already impossible to rectify, he chose to dwell in debauchery as a way of assuaging his grief?" (善用事、極忠憤、惟香奩之作詞工格卑、豈非世事已不可救、姑留連荒亡以紓其憂乎).[18] More vociferously, Qing poet Chu Renhu 褚人護 (fl. 1681) attacked the collection as "unrepentant in its wicked licentiousness; to read it is necessarily to promote thoughts of lustfulness" (淫惡不悛也。閱之必增益淫邪之念).[19]

As its alleged preface suggested, emotional truth was one possible defense of the *Fragrant Toilette Collection*; another was to argue that the apparent eroticism of the collection was in fact nothing of the sort. In an argument often made in China to explain seemingly erotic poems of various periods, some critics held that the apparent sexual desire depicted therein was actually an allegory for the scholar-official's desire to render loyal service to the sovereign and assist in the good governance of the realm. This argument was clearly familiar to Meiji *kanshi* poets, since it was deployed in 1883, around the time a backlash against the style's popularity was gathering steam. A headnote to a piece by Confucian scholar Kawada Ōkō 川田甕江 (Takeshi 剛, 1830–1896) published in 1883 in the *kanshi* learners' journal *Kokon shibun shōkai* in memory of the deceased poet Niwa Kanan 丹羽花南 (Ken 賢, 1846–1878) explains a passing reference by Ōkō to Kanan's liking for fragrant-style poems as follows: "The *Fragrant Toilette Collection* consists of poems authored by Han Wo of the Tang, and many of these express the emotions of the boudoir, so some say it has a feminine air. Yet it is said that Han Wo was a man of loyal virtue and one who truly revered his lord and sovereign, because he used these poems as an allegory for his love for his lord. Though Mr. Niwa favored the fragrant, he, too, was possessed of the great virtue of patriotism."[20]

Ōkō's headnote is evidence that the loyal service allegory within the fragrant style was clearly understood by Meiji poets; the headnote uses this to anticipate and rebut the criticism that erotic poetry might be incompatible with patriotism and doing one's duty for the nation (*hōkoku*). At issue, then, was not simply masculinity for its own sake but also displaying proper, loyal, and vigorous masculinity as a qualification for a privileged position within a broader imagined national community of *kanshi* poets.

Within the early and mid-Meiji debates that are the subject of this chapter, there were therefore multiple possible avenues of attack for detractors of the style. One was, simply, that erotic poems were immoral; another, related argument was that erotic poems weakened and feminized the men who composed them and must therefore be avoided. This line of argument, of the debilitating effects of proximity to the feminine, seems to echo both contemporary and Edo-period gender ideals of the Japanese warrior class in particular. It is probably no coincidence that Mori Shuntō, one of the fragrant style's main advocates, was unusual among prominent mid-nineteenth century *kanshi* poets in not coming from a warrior background.[21] The basic idea of poets as being strong or weak depending on their attitude toward the feminine also resonates with the paradigmatic division of "hard" and "soft" that Jim Reichert has identified as a key element in both aesthetics and discourse on male sexuality in Meiji Japan. Where Reichert's discussion of this binary in prose fiction is interested in its role in normalizing heterosexuality, as it appears in *kanshi* the "hard-soft" juxtaposition mitigates *against* the expression of heterosexual desire and does not juxtapose it with homosexuality, at least explicitly.[22] That the fragrant-style debates were in large part about competing understandings of masculinity is further confirmed by terminology in later narratives of the Meiji *kanshi* world. Scholars both sympathetic to and disdainful of Mori Kainan, one of the fragrant style's most visible exponents, have suggested that his critics effectively accused him of being a "softie" (*nanpa*).[23] As Gregory Pflugfelder has pointed out, the distinction between "softies" (or "smoothies," in Pflugfelder's translation), who displayed a strong interest in male-female eroticism, and "roughnecks" (*kōha*), who spurned romantic interest in women as beneath their dignity, was at the heart of competing models of masculinity during the Meiji period.[24]

Further complicating debates over the fragrant style was the style's entanglement in Meiji-era political factionalism; divisions between advocates and detractors tended to follow the partisan political lines of the Meiji *kanshi* world. Although Mori Shuntō never held government office himself, he acquired a largely deserved reputation for using his poetic skills to curry favor with officials.[25] As one important example, Shuntō used the contacts he cultivated through his poetic associations to get his son Kainan a job, albeit a low-ranking one, in the government bureaucracy. Kainan's position would subsequently improve dramatically when his own poetic skills prompted Itō Hirobumi, a keen *kanshi* poet, to appoint him as his personal secretary.[26] This was only the most high-profile example of the benefits of courting official favor; in addition, Shuntō counted among his poetic disciples a number of judges, bureaucrats, and various other functionaries in the Meiji apparatus of state. When Shiki wrote in *Nippon* in 1896 that one of the main faults of contemporary *kanshi* poets was "latching on to government ministers and wealthy men in the manner of a male geisha" (*hōkanteki ni daijin chōja o torikomu*), he may well have had Kainan in mind.[27]

Since Mori *père et fils* both owed much to open patronage from elements in the Meiji government, those who bore little love for that government were unlikely to welcome their fragrant-style poetics. This was certainly true of Kokubu Seigai, Kainan's chief rival and antagonist during the 1890s. Born and raised in Sendai, a domain that had been on the losing side in the Meiji Restoration, Seigai had won admission to the highly competitive Ministry of Justice Law School in his youth, only to be expelled for dissent, with the result that he was barred from attending any other official training schools and thus effectively from government employment in toto.[28] Embarking on a literary career as poet in residence for the newspapers *Tōkyō denpō* in 1888 and *Nippon* in 1889,

Seigai made a name for himself for both a ceaseless flow of *kanshi* attacking the Meiji government and a perceived vigorous and masculine style in his poetry as a whole. Though they were initially able to work together in the formation of Seisha, late Meiji's most prominent *kanshi* society, Seigai had little time for Kainan or for his poetics, and in the pages of *Nippon* during the autumn of 1890, he launched a sustained and public attack on him. Polarizing as they were, Seigai's and Kainan's very different models of poetic composition ushered in a divide in the Tokyo *kanshi* world that would endure well into the twentieth century, and the echoes of their dispute would continue into the postwar era.

THE FRAGRANT STYLE FROM EDO TO EARLY MEIJI: *XINGLING* TO SHUNTŌ

Although Shuntō and Kainan were closely identified with the fragrant style, they were not responsible for its introduction to Japan. The *Fragrant Toilette Collection* reached Japan in 1811, before Shuntō was born, as part of a volume of Han Wo's works edited by the scholar Tate Ryūwan 館柳灣 (1762–1844) and calligrapher Maki Ryōko 巻菱湖 (1777–1834), a book that Shiki himself apparently owned.[29] As such, the fragrant style's popularity during the late 1870s and early 1880s can be understood as part of a nearly century-long process of Japanese adoption and adaptation of Ming and Qing poetics. Particularly influential here, and explicitly mentioned by a number of Meiji poets as a justification for fragrant-style compositions, is the poetics of "innate sensibility" (Ch. *xingling*, J. *seirei*). Innate sensibility poetics had grown in popularity in late eighteenth-century Japan as part of the move away from the faux-Tang style of the Ming Archaists. Beginning in the 1780s, the Archaists' insistence on adherence to the themes and language of the *Selections of Tang Poetry* came under attack as encouraging poets to compose on matters of which they had no direct experience, resulting in insincere poetry or even plagiarism. Among the most prominent of such critics was Yamamoto Hokuzan, who, as mentioned in the previous chapter, wrote the preface to Kashiwagi Jotei's *Lianzhu shige*. An advocate of innate sensibility as espoused by the Ming poet Yuan Hongdao 袁宏道 (1568–1610), Hokuzan had argued that a poet should spurn imitation of others and aim for emotional authenticity by tapping into his or her own inner nature.[30]

A full discussion of the differing understandings of innate sensibility in Japan is beyond the scope of this chapter, but one result of the embrace of such poetics in Japan was a broadening of subject matter beyond the archetypal concerns of the scholar-literatus to include the concerns of daily urban life—which included sexual activity in all its various forms. One example of this trend was Ichikawa Kansai's *Songs of the Northern Quarters* (*Hokurika*). Published in 1787, while Kansai was still an instructor at the Shōheikō shogunal academy, this work consisted of thirty thematically linked quatrains depicting scenes from Edo's Yoshiwara licensed quarters. Given the shogunate's disapproval of the licensed quarters, the subject matter was rather daring for someone in Kansai's position and may be why he published the work pseudonymously. Nevertheless, the impact of the *Songs of the Northern Quarters* can be gauged from a comment by Ōkubo Shibutsu, one of Kansai's most successful disciples and a founding member of the Kōko Shisha. In Shibutsu's view, Kansai had illustrated with the *Songs of the Northern Quarters* that "there was nothing on which one could not compose a poem" (*shi tsukuru bekarazaru mono nashi*).[31]

Kansai's *Songs of the Northern Quarters* can also be viewed as a revival of the "bamboo-branch ballad" (Ch. *zhuzhi ci*, J. *chikushi shi*), a genre of poetry that dated back to the mid-Tang poet Liu Yuxi 劉禹錫 (772–842). Much as was the case with Kansai's *Songs of the Northern Quarters*, the bamboo-branch ballad tended to focus on scenes from a city's licensed quarters, often serving a dual function of a kind of travelogue or ethnography and a vehicle for portraying male-female sexual relations. The popularity of the bamboo-branch ballad grew over the course of the nineteenth century as Kansai's disciples, notably Shibutsu and Kashiwagi Jotei, followed their senior colleague in producing a number of such works on Edo's Yoshiwara and other areas. Showcasing the bamboo-branch ballad's travelogue function, Japanese men of letters traveling abroad after the end of the ban on foreign travel often wrote bamboo-branch ballads on what they saw and experienced overseas.[32] Shuntō, for his part, was well known as an exponent of the bamboo-branch ballad, with verses describing the cities of Gifu and Niigata Prefectures among his most famous works.[33]

This seemingly greater prominence of the feminine in *kanshi* during the first half of the nineteenth century was not limited to imagery and compositional topics in the poems themselves. The late Edo *kanshi* world also saw an apparent increase in the numbers—and certainly in the visibility—of female *kanshi* poets, such as Ema Saikō 江馬細香 (Tao 多保, 1787–1861), Hara Saihin 原采蘋 (Michi 猷, 1798–1859), and Kamei Shōkin 亀井少琴 (Yū 友, 1793–1857). A number of female poets who gained prominence during the last days of the Tokugawa shogunate also continued to write poetry well into Meiji, notably Yanagawa Kōran 梁川紅蘭 (Kei 景, 1804–1879) and Shinoda Unpō 篠田雲鳳 (Nori 儀, 1810–1883).[34] One factor driving the greater prominence of female *kanshi* poets during the early nineteenth century was the enthusiastic reception in Japan of the work of the Qing poet and scholar Yuan Mei 袁枚 (J. En Bai, 1716–1797). An advocate of innate sensibility poetics, Yuan Mei's writings and poetry reached Japan during his lifetime, through the port of Nagasaki,[35] and the reputation that the Qing poet enjoyed as both an enthusiastic advocate of women's poetry writing and mentor to a large number of female disciples also made an impression on many Japanese poets.[36] Ōkubo Shibutsu, for instance, reedited and rereleased a work by Yuan Mei, *Selected Poems by My Female Disciples* (*Suiyuan nüdizi shixuan*, completed in 1796), to produce his own text, *Selections from "Selected Poems by My Female Disciples"* (*Zuien onna deshi shisen sen*), which was published in 1830.[37] In a similar vein, late Edo poet Nakajima Sōin 中島棕隠 (Yoshinori 徳規, 1779–1855) alluded to Yuan Mei's famous group of female disciples in a poem of 1826 describing the pleasures of reading the Qing poet's work: "Even if I do not have a great coterie of beauties to call my disciples / Still I can be proud of my meetings with many great talents" (縦缺名娃稱弟子 / 猶誇群彦辱相知).[38] Rai San'yō, one of the most distinguished poets of the nineteenth century and a mentor to Ema Saikō, likewise invoked Yuan Mei in describing his relationship with Saikō as being like that of Yuan Mei and the latter's favored female disciple, Jin Yi 金逸 (1770–1794).[39]

To a limited but nevertheless significant extent during the first half of the nineteenth century, *kanshi* by women also began to feature in the popular print media of the time. Kikuchi Gozan's *Gozandō shiwa*, one of the most significant windows onto the late Edo *kanshi* world, featured thirty-seven verses by fifteen separate female poets during its twenty-five-year print run, and Gozan himself commented that "whenever I encounter a poem by a female poet, I make sure to excerpt it and circulate it widely."[40] A decade or so later, Shōheikō scholar Tomono Kashū 友野 霞舟 (1791–1849) continued this focus in his collection *Kichō shiwai* (Abundant poetry for a flourishing age, 1847) by including a volume devoted to seventy-seven poems by twenty-three female poets.

Despite the upheavals of the Boshin War, this late Edo interest in the fragrant style and the feminine continued largely unaltered into early Meiji. One can find work in the fragrant style even among that most quintessentially vigorous, spirited, and masculine group of *kanshi* poets, the "men of high purpose" of the final years of the Tokugawa shogunate.[41] Not only was there apparently little contradiction as yet between writing in the fragrant style and displaying bold masculinity; if anything, the evidence from the early Meiji *kanshi* publishing world suggests that interest in the fragrant style experienced something of a boom. In 1878, for example, Shuntō and Kainan published a collection titled *Quatrains by Three Qing Poets* (*Shin sanka zekku*) consisting of works by three near-contemporary Qing poets who were as yet largely unknown in Japan: Zhang Chuanshan 張船山 (1764–1814, aka Zhang Wentao 張問陶), Chen Bicheng 陳碧城 (1771–1843, aka Chen Wenshu 陳文述), and Guo Pinqie 郭頻伽 (1767–1831, aka Guo Lin 郭麟).[42] The preface to this collection, penned by Iwaya Kobai 巌谷古梅 (Ichiroku 一六, 1834–1905), drew parallels between Shuntō and the Kōko Shisha and located the poems in the anthology within the tradition of innate sensibility poetics:

> Master Shuntō has chosen quatrains by the three poets Zhang Chuanshan, Chen Bicheng, and Guo Pinqie and published this collection with its elegant and wondrous allure. If one reads it, then one will be able to bring out one's innate sensibility. Previously, the old masters of the Kōko Shisha advocated Song poems and published a book of the works of the three poets Fan [Chengda 范成大, 1126–1193], Yang [Wanli 楊萬里, 1127–1206], and Lu [You 陸游, 1125–1210]. Styles of poetry in the realm changed completely. Now this collection is published in our times. I am sure that those later talents of the poetic world will find much that interests them, and there will emerge poems of true innate sensibility.[43]

Many (though by no means all) of the poems in *Quatrains by Three Qing Poets* were in the fragrant style, as in the following quatrain by Guo Pinqie:

繡毬花	*Hydrangea Flowers*
梅天香潤試羅衣	Rainy season, sleek and fragrant, she tries on a silk robe;
緑繡毬花開已稀	The green hydrangea flowers bloom but rarely now.
簾裡美人春夢斷	Behind the shades, a beauty's dreams of spring are over,
不知蝴蜨作團飛	No one knows when the butterflies will take wing together.[44]

Literally "embroidered-ball flower," the hydrangea flower (*xiu qiu hua*) in China is associated with a folk ritual in which maidens throw embroidered balls in the hope that prospective male lovers will catch them; these flowers, by contrast, have ceased to bloom.

Evidence from other publications supports the notion of an early Meiji surge in the popularity of the fragrant style. The sixteenth *kanshi* Shiki recorded, of 1881, is a boudoir lament, for instance, and he was still writing works in a similar vein as late as 1888.[45] Possibly Shiki gained inspiration from his poetic manuals, since poetic composition manuals from the late 1870s often suggested bamboo-branch ballads or fragrant style as a variety of *kanshi* the beginner might want to compose and provided the vocabulary and themes to do so. One 1878 *kanshi* manual, grouping together the topics "Boudoir Lament," "Bamboo-Branch Ballad," and "Composing on a Picture of a Beautiful Woman" (*bijin zu ni daisu*), provided an extensive list of possible words to form such poems. Among the words suggested were "ruby lips" (*shushin* 朱唇), "yet unwed" (*imada ka sezaru toki* 未嫁時, glossed as *imada yomeiri senu toki*), "hair tousled" (*bin midaru* 鬢乱, glossed as *kami ga midareru*), and "the marital bed" (*gōkanshō* 合歓床, glossed as *fūbu* [sic] *no toko* and readable literally as "joint pleasure bed")—all perfect for erotic poetry.[46]

Such was the early Meiji fascination with the fragrant style that even Chinese visitors to Japan, taking advantage of the new freedom to travel, found themselves pressed into service to help Japanese poets get to grips with it. The written "brush talks" (Ch. *bitan*, J. *hitsudan*) among Sinophile former daimyo Ōkōchi Teruna 大河内輝聲 (pen name Keikaku 桂閣, 1848–1882) and members of the 1877 Qing diplomatic legation dispatched to Tokyo, for instance, have Ōkōchi asking embassy attaché Shen Meishi 沈梅史 (Wenrong 文榮, dates unknown) how to compose fragrant-style poems. Shen suggests that Ōkōchi should read Han Wo but avoid later Ming works such as the *Hint of Rain Collection* (*Yiyuji*) by Wang Yanhong 王彦泓 (Cihui 次回, 1593–1642) lest Ōkōchi's "tone become low and vulgar." Shen stresses that when writing in the fragrant style, one "should have elegant language and profound emotion and not cross over into obscenity—then it is at its best. This is what is called romantic, yet not licentious."[47] Though helpful in practical terms, Shen Meishi's reply to Ōkōchi sounds a note of caution. There is, Shen suggests, both a "good" and a "bad" fragrant style; one must take care to select the correct models and avoid poets whose work is "low and vulgar" or "licentious" so as not to succumb to the style's inherent dangers.

THE TALENT OF WILLOW CATKINS: THE BOUDOIR TOPOS AND MEIJI WOMEN *KANSHI* POETS

As had been the case in the late Edo *kanshi* publishing world, early Meiji also saw significant attention paid in print media to female poets. As noted in the previous chapter, quatrain anthologies with verse by Japan's leading poets were a common feature of mid-nineteenth century *kanshi* publishing; and, in 1869, one of the first such quatrain anthologies to appear after the Restoration, *Quatrains by Thirty-Eight Poets of the Meiji Era* (*Meiji sanjūhakka zekku*), broke new ground by including a verse by Yanagawa Kōran, widow of the celebrated poet Yanagawa Seigan 梁川星巌 (1789–1858). The apex of this trend came with two additional collections, *Quatrains by Female Poets of the Nanamagari Poetic Society* (*Nanamagari ginsha keien zekku*, 1877) and *Collected Poems of Japan's Female Poets* (*Nihon keien ginsō*, 1880), both of which showcased works by exclusively female poets. The Nanamagari Ginsha, a *kanshi* group based in Tokyo and run by prominent poet Suzuki Shōtō, seems to have been particularly invested in female poets; Shōtō himself edited the 1877 collection that bore his society's name and wrote a foreword for the 1880 collection. Not only that, but no fewer than ten of the female poets listed in *Nihon keien ginsō* were, as a note in the collection makes clear, his direct disciples. *Dongying shixuan* (Collection of poetry from the eastern ocean, 1883), a collection of *kanshi* by Japanese poets brought together by the Qing official and scholar Yu Yue 俞樾 (1821–1907) and published in China, not only featured a number of the *Nihon keien ginsō* poems but also contained a remark by Yu Yue that Suzuki "has a great many female pupils in his school; he has the air of Yuan Mei about him" (松塘門下女弟子甚多有隨園之風矣).[48]

Nihon keien ginsō, which featured works by fifty-four individual female *kanshi* poets, was almost certainly the largest collection of women's *kanshi* verse to be compiled to that point. Its opening pages suggest that it could, perhaps, have been larger still; a short introduction (*shogen*) observes that "there are many talented ladies the length and breadth of the land, so this volume cannot truly claim that it has left no precious stone unturned. One looks forward to the day sometime in the future when one may cover each and every one" (全國之廣。才媛之多。此編豈云無遺珠。余欲竢他日而網羅之).[49] The fifty-four poets in question were divided into two volumes, the majority of the former being made up of poets who had been active before the Meiji Restoration, such as Ema Saikō, Tsuda Ranchō 津田蘭蝶 (1795–1815), and Ōta Rankō 太田蘭香 (1798–1856).[50] The second volume, by contrast, featured contemporary female poets. Of these, ten were disciples of Suzuki Shōtō, while a further eight were students at Atomi Women's School (Atomi Jogakkō, later to become Atomi University). The school's head, Atomi Kakei 跡見花蹊 (1840–1926), was herself featured in the collection.[51]

Nihon keien ginsō is of interest in the present context not only because of its presentation of female poets but also because a number of the poems featured therein are very obviously in the fragrant style, almost exclusively in the boudoir lament subgenre. In her study of late imperial Chinese women's poetry, Xiaorong Li notes the importance of the *gui*, the "boudoir," as a widely used and clearly recognized signifier of femininity, one used in a variety of ways by different women poets. The idea of the *gui*, she writes, became a "recognized discursive field . . . for reiterating gender boundaries and constructing female subjectivity."[52]

A number of the poems in *Nihon keien ginsō* follow the classical contours of the boudoir lament, as in this verse by Suzuki Keien 鱸蕙畹 (Rei 禮, dates unknown), another of Shōtō's daughters:[53]

春寒	*Spring Chill*
睡起春寒入翠蛾	On waking from sleep, a spring chill grips her,
峭風吹雨卷簾波	Harsh winds driving rain, waves on the roll blinds.
落花寂寂人無語	Fallen flowers sad and still, no one says a word;[54]
蝶怨鶯愁奈汝何	Butterfly's anger, warbler's sadness: "What am I to do with you?"[55]

The setting is, once again, a woman who has been abandoned by her lover; she wakes from sleep to find her lover absent, and the natural world, of flowers, rain, butterflies, and warblers, reflects her inner emotional state. Though the fragrant style as a whole could span a wide range of topics and degrees of eroticism, as Han Wo's poetry showed, the inevitably erotic overtones of the boudoir space made the subject matter potentially problematic for men and women alike. In several of the boudoir poems in *Nihon keien ginsō*, there seems to be an effort at preemptive justification, with the poets taking pains to ground the topos and subject matter in an orthodox, canonical (and above all morally respectable) poetic lineage. In Keien's poem, for instance, the final two lines contain textual allusions to Chinese poetic greats Wang Wei 王維 (699–759) and Du Fu, both unimpeachable in their poetic qualifications and moral respectability.

Another poet in *Nihon keien ginsō*, Shirakawa Kinsui 白川琴水 (Sachi 幸, 1856–1890), addresses the issues of women's poetry, and more specifically women's writing in the fragrant style, in more overt fashion. From Hida in central Japan, and a student of both Narushima Ryūhoku and Kikuchi Sankei 菊池三渓 (1819–1891), Kinsui contributes a total of eleven verses, several of which seem to address the specific position of women poets:

清少納言搴簾圖	On a Picture of Sei Shōnagon Rolling Up the Blinds
曾聞永筵宮中多佳人	I have heard that there were many great beauties in the palace, with its eternal feasts,
六宮才藻孰絶倫	But which of the talents of the Rear Palace was truly the cream of the crop?
瑤階雪滿曉如玉	Snow covered the jade terrace; at dawn, it looked like jewels,
翠簾未搴映紅旭	And green bamboo jade blinds, not yet rolled up, glowed scarlet in the rising sun;
誰奉詔者清氏姫	And then, who followed imperial command better than Lady Sei?
才名一朝驚凡俗	Her talent and fame instantly astonished the mediocre and vulgar.
嗚呼女徳不在才須在貞	Alas, though, women's virtue lies not in literary talent but must lie in chastity and propriety;
嫌他小慧愆半生	Shunning all other small shrewdness and half a life spent in error.[56]
別有紫氏君知否	And there was also Lady Murasaki; I wonder if you know her?
三寸彤管能摸寫曲	With her three-inch woman's brush, she could carry on the tune,
盡古今世態人情	Capturing all the ways and emotions of the world, old and new.[57]

Kinsui's poem situates itself in a famous episode involving the Heian court lady, poet, and diarist Sei Shōnagon, in which she subtly displayed her knowledge of the poetry of Bai Juyi 白居易 (772–846) by raising a set of window blinds.[58] In the following lines, though, Kinsui suggests that too overt a display of literary talent can be problematic for a woman, and that, no matter how great a woman's skill, she is still expected to observe "chastity and propriety." Kinsui's sense of walking a tightrope as a female poet was not without good reason; Narushima Ryūhoku wrote of Kinsui that "in times both ancient and modern, when a woman has some literary talent, she tends to become arrogant and impertinent, losing much of her womanly virtue. But Kinsui alone is modest and respectful. I find much to applaud."[59] In a headnote to two poems in the boudoir style (of which the second is quoted here), Kinsui sounds a similar note of caution and ambivalence; almost as a preemptive justification, she alludes to the canonical Chinese text *Classic of Poetry*'s (Ch. *Shi jing*, J. *Shikyō*) depictions of women and romantic love in the "Airs of the States," as well as the example of celebrated Chinese poetess Xie Daoyun 謝道韞 (b ca. 376):

| 紅絃餘唱 | Echoing Harmonies from Scarlet Strings |

Chirp, chirp go the yellow orioles, singing of the spring; chirrup, chirrup go the crickets as they tell of autumn. I have studied a little the poems bequeathed to us in the "Airs of the States," and so I play around with the "brightness of the red tube."[60] Though I may be bereft of the talent and skill to compose poems of "willow catkins,"[61] at times my verse conveys the emotions of the scarlet boudoir. But they lack any sense of charming gaiety, so inevitably they may seem like mockery.

妾思　黒髪／	*The Thoughts of a Mistress (After "Black Hair")*[62]
妾思紛紜如髪亂	Her thoughts are in turmoil, disordered like her hair,
髪亂尚可理	Her hair may yet be put back in place,
妾思紛紜不可断	But the turmoil of her thoughts, she cannot quell;
相見多則別亦多	Many meetings mean many partings, too.
雙枕雙枕如汝何	"Alas, you twin pillows; what am I to do with you?"[63]
孤衾擁来聊相伴	She draws the lonely quilt to her, finding a little companionship.

無情鐘聲半夜過	The heartless bell sounds! The night is half over.
昨夢今朝再難結	"Last night I dreamt; now it is morning, will I ever be with those dreams again?
唯恐昨日鬢上雪	I fear, just yesterday: snowy flecks of gray upon my hair."[64]

Despite the disclaimer in the headnote, Kinsui's verse here seems to differ little from the boudoir poems by male poets discussed previously. In particular, images such as twin pillows or a woman embracing a quilt charged with memories of past lovemaking inevitably convey notes of subtle eroticism, mitigated perhaps by the "snowy flecks of gray," which add an element of pathos by highlighting the woman's awareness of the fading of her beauty.[65]

BOUDOIR BACKLASH: MORI SHUNTŌ, "DEMON OF POETRY"

The late 1870s were in most respects the high point of the popularity of the fragrant style and of female *kanshi* poets as a high-profile presence in Japan's poetic world; despite the claim in the preface to *Nihon keien ginsō* that a future time would see a volume covering all of Japan's female poets, such a project seems never to have actually happened. One reason for this may have been a growing disquiet among many of Japan's major *kanshi* poets about the fragrant style's popularity and, from the early 1880s, a series of vociferous attacks on both the style itself and its practitioners. One of the earliest examples of pushback came in 1879, when, at the age of sixteen, Mori Kainan published an original drama in literary Sinitic titled *Restoring Spring Sunlight: A Romance* (*Hoshunten denki*), centering on a quest to repair the neglected graves of three famous beauties from Chinese history. Published with forewords by Yoda Gakkai 依田学海 (1833–1909) and Qing diplomat Huang Zunxian 黄遵憲 (1848–1905), this earned the young Kainan both attention and public criticism. In March 1879, one anonymous critic (possibly Narushima Ryūhoku) penned an attack in the *Chōya shinbun* newspaper on those who "idly read a few romances and long for a beauty already dead and buried" or who "fall in love with stunning beauties whose face they've never actually seen." This kind of writing was, the author of the piece charged, "fake passion and borrowed wistful nostalgia."[66] Though it apparently annoyed Kainan, this allegation of emotional inauthenticity does not seem to have deterred him from continuing to explore the fragrant style over the next few years.[67] One 1881 collection showcasing his work, for instance, bore the suggestive title *Collection of Tender Feelings for Pretty Girls* (*Rinkō sekigyoku shū*).

Whoever the author of the *Chōya shinbun* criticism of Kainan may have been, he was far from unusual in harboring reservations about the fragrant style. There is little doubt that a number of the senior figures of the Meiji *kanshi* world, most of whom had been active before the Restoration and continued to enjoy the respect of their fellow poets, were uncomfortable with Shuntō's favored style, although they varied in their degree of willingness to confront Shuntō directly. Kikuchi Sankei, for his part, had no hesitation in using Shuntō's preference for the fragrant style to insult him to his face. After several rounds of drinking at a poetic gathering, Shuntō apparently annoyed Sankei by butting in to answer a question originally directed to Ōnuma Chinzan over the provenance of a specific poetic term: "Shuntō spoke up from the sidelines and said, 'It's in such and such a book. Didn't you know that, Sankei?' Sankei immediately became flushed and said, 'No, it's not that, I just didn't want to ask someone like you who spends his time composing nothing but fragrant poems.' Shuntō was greatly embarrassed and dropped the matter. This was told by someone who had attended the gathering at the time ([as told by] Komiyama Nanryō [小宮山南梁, 1829–1896])."[68]

Less overtly confrontational but equally critical was Okamoto Kōseki 岡本黄石 (1822–1898). When asked whether he, too, might try writing fragrant poems, Kōseki, who ran the Kikubō Ginsha (Kōjimachi Poetic Society) in Tokyo's Kōjimachi and was, like Shuntō, a former pupil of Yanagawa Seigan's, responded that Shuntō's poems were not without their attraction but that they were not decent or virtuous and could be termed the path of immorality. Word of this remark apparently got back to Shuntō, who responded frostily the next time he encountered Kōseki.[69]

It may also have been Kōseki who was responsible for terming Shuntō the demon of poetry (*shima*); presumably intended as an unflattering epithet that suggested his negative influence on poetry, Shuntō responded to this particular jibe with humor, penning a series of eight quatrains in rebuttal:

The nodding heads make me out to be a "demon of poetry."[70] In times past, Wang Yi made Yang Tieya out to be the "devil of literature," largely because he wrote bamboo-branch ballads and fragrant-style works. I am one who takes pleasure in fragrant-style works and bamboo-branch ballads, and it has been my lifelong desire to receive someday the appellations of both "demon of poetry" and "devil of literature." And so if those worthy masters wish to accuse me of being such, then of course I shall not turn away from it.

[First of Eight]

空中之語写魂銷	Words in the empty air, depicting sadness and disappointment,
可見才人結習饒	You can clearly see the man of talent's usual loquaciousness.
永劫不磨脂粉気	I shall never scrape off the fragrance of rouge and powder,
詩魔賴得並文妖	This poetic demon quite happy to rank alongside the devils of literature.

[Eighth of Eight]

小詩何敵大文章	How is it that my little verses are enemies to Great Works of Literature?
吟諷聊供歡一場	My compositions are only to provide a little cheer to a gathering;
貶處瓣香褒處酒	They denounce correctness and piety, sing the praises of drink,
祇應醺徹老魔王	Yes indeed, the stink of booze hangs around this old demon king.[71]

Shuntō's comparison of himself to the Yuan-dynasty poet and painter Yang Tieya 楊鐵崖 (Weizhen 維楨, ca. 1296–ca. 1370) is a humorous and provocative response to the accusation of immorality; Tieya was famous for his dissolution, in particular his practice of drinking wine from the shoes of courtesans.[72] Equally, in the poems themselves Shuntō appears to embrace the accusations leveled at him. Line 3 of his poem plays on the possible literal and metonymical meanings of the expression "fragrance of rouge and powder" (Ch. *zhifen qi*, J. *shibun ki*), used to denote both the actual fragrance of cosmetics and, by extension, an air of femininity. Shuntō's refusal here to "scrape it off" could equally be read as saying that he will never stop composing such poems, or as suggesting that he himself is the one wearing the cosmetics—and in either case, he cares little what other people may think about it.

While Shuntō's response was archly humorous, there were also more serious attempts made to justify fragrant-style poetics. Among the main defenders of Shuntō was Ono Kozan, who, though expressing concern about the wisdom of one as young as Kainan working in the style, published a series of poems in *Shinbunshi* titled "Song of the Demon of Poetry" (Shima uta) that were supportive of Shuntō.[73] Likewise, Yoda Gakkai, translator of a number of quasi-erotic vernacular Chinese novels, penned a vigorous defense of Shuntō in a letter from around July of 1881 that was published in the pages of *Shinbunshi*:

> You are skilled in various styles of poetry, yet it is through your "alluring style" that you have gained the most fame. Truly, Li Yuxi [Li Shangyin 李商隱, 812?–858] and Wen Feiqing [Wen Tingyun 温庭筠, 812–872] are your fellows, and you are among the brothers of Chen Bicheng and Guo Pinqie. Some might suspect that this flashy and decadent style is frivolous and not proper, but I do not consider it so. Poetry is about emotion. "The Ospreys Cry" is the beginning of the "Airs of the States"; is this not entirely proper in its grasping of emotion?[74]

Much as the female poets discussed earlier had done, Gakkai here emphasizes fragrant-style poetry as belonging within an orthodox, canonical Chinese tradition, traceable back even to the very first poem of the *Classic of Poetry*. Gakkai goes further, with mentions of the Tang poets Wen Tingyun and Li Shangyin, both of whom were known for writing poems that could be classified as fragrant style. In Gakkai's understanding, the depiction of human emotions such as sexual desire is entirely within the descriptive ken of Sinitic poetry, and criticism based on a narrow, prescriptive moral understanding of poetic history is therefore misdirected.

Those who defended fragrant-style poetry often did so on the grounds of emotional truth, especially as part of the innate sensibility tradition. The umbrella of emotional truth and innate sensibility poetics could, however, stretch only so far; one notable strain in the range of poetic practice grouped as fragrant style in Meiji was the depiction of general carousing in the licensed quarters, scenes that had little to do with true emotion and more with projecting the author as a *tsū*, the connoisseur of the licensed quarters. Rather more in keeping with the mood of "charming gaiety" that Shirakawa Kinsui declared to be lacking in her own poems, this can be seen in a poem by another well-known fragrant-style exponent, Kanda Kōgan 神田香巖 (1854–1918), the grandfather of the celebrated Japanese Sinologist Kanda Kiichirō 神田喜一郎 (1897–1984), addressing Ue Mukō. Neither Kōgan nor Ue Mukō were direct disciples of Mori Shuntō, but both became noted for their work in the fragrant style, drawing inspiration from the elder poet indirectly. Both poets display a tendency, more pronounced than in Shuntō or Kainan's work, to interpret the remit of fragrant-style poetry as license to celebrate the nightlife of the licensed quarters in general:

寄懷上夢香	*Sending My Thoughts to Ue Mukō*
紙醉金迷詠彼姝	Dazzlingly disporting, singing songs of those female beauties,
舊歡剩有十眉圖	Past loves, we have plenty, and "Ten Pictures of Beauties" too.[75]
不多親友頭難聚	With few close friends, it's hard to get together,
如此春宵夢亦孤	So that is why I am lonely in my spring-night dreams.
璧月華燈新北里	Jade moon, colored lanterns in the new Northern Quarter,
嫣花媚柳小西湖	Coyly smiling flowers, seductive willows, in "little West Lake."[76]
若逢阿軟煩傳語	And if you run across A Ruan,[77] then I'll trouble you to pass on a few words—
記得吾儂故態無	Does she still remember how I was in the old days—or not?

Kōgan paints himself here as a semiretired playboy recalling his heyday in the licensed quarters; though no longer active, his memories of
the old days of courtesans as "coyly smiling flowers" and "seductive willows" are still worth sharing with his friend Mukō. The journal that
published this poem, *Azuma shinshi* (1883–1886), often celebrated the
lifestyle of the patron of the licensed quarters; serialized for several issues
before and after the this poem appeared, for instance, was a guide
to purchasing the services of courtesans. Commenting on the poetic
exchange here between Kōgan and Mukō, journalist and fellow aficio-
nado Miki Aika 三木愛花 (1861–1933) observed, "These two gentlemen
Kōgan and Mukō are both unsurpassed in the fragrant style. However,
Kōgan pays more attention to ensuring that his poems are deeply alluring; he is very much like the courtesans of Kyoto. Mukō's poems are
lighter and wittier, just like the courtesans of Tokyo. Truly, they are like
two precious stones, impossible to rank one above the other."[78]

In celebrating a lifestyle of dissipation in the licensed quarters,
this interpretation of the fragrant style was more open to criticism for
immorality than the depiction of imaginary beauties. One early critic
of the style, Inoue Tetsujirō 井上哲次郎 (1855–1944), provided a verse
and exchange of commentary addressing exactly this point in dialogue with educator and poet Nanma Uhō 南摩羽峯 (Tsunanori 綱紀,
1823–1909):

論詩	*Discussing Poetry*
小技観詩眼缺明	Those who view poetry as a lesser accom-plishment, their eyes lack clear judgment,
長章短句寫眞情	For whether long passages or short verses, it depicts true emotion.
矧乎裨教其功大	All the more, then, should we promote and teach of poetry's great merits,
不啻多知草木名	Which are much more than simply knowing the names of lots of trees and flowers.[79]

[Nanma] Uhō comments: Indeed. I would add that what I say when
discussing poetry is that a true poem is one that is flowing in tone,
elegant and pristine in its bearing, short on words but long on intent,

and the more one chants it, the more one appreciates its lasting depths. But to speak now of that which is skillfully intricate and daintily wrought, cramped in tone and vulgar in bearing, which uses elegant words and embroidered stanzas to dazzle people, and which on the first read delights but on rereading repulses—this is something in which one should not engage. Nonetheless, all have their own individual tastes as to sweet or sour, light or dense, and I would not presume to tell another to have his face be like mine. I wonder what you, my brother, make of this.

[Inoue] Tetsu[jirō] comments: My usual position is as follows: what indeed is the point of taking up elegant words and embroidered stanzas to dazzle people? But then, of late we have a lot of these kinds of poems, using words like "green wine," "red lanterns," "drunk on flowers," "composing on the moon" in each and every line. They're frivolous and weak, truly to be despised. I myself term this the playboy style—haha![80]

Although the older Uhō expresses dislike of the fragrant style, he allows that others' tastes may be different. Inoue, by contrast, is much less forgiving; for him, such poems reflect languid weakness, a style fit only for effete young men who chase women in the licensed quarters.

TO DIE OF SHAME: KOKUBU SEIGAI AND THE KEGON FALLS POEMS

Inoue's comments here represent one of relatively few examples before around 1885 of overt written criticism of the fragrant style and its practitioners. Much of the evidence of discomfort with the style on the part of senior members of the *kanshidan* in particular comes less in the shape of direct, written criticisms and more from anecdotes and recorded gossip. This may have been partly a wish to maintain a degree of cordiality in the Meiji *kanshi* world; or it may have reflected a desire to keep on the right side of Shuntō, a powerful figure in Tokyo poetic circles. After Shuntō's death in 1889, however, a growing body of open criticism of fragrant-style poetics and of Kainan personally can be seen in both newspapers and literary journals. By this point the style may have lost some of its initial freshness and appeal—Gōyama has suggested that Kainan and Mukō distanced themselves from such poetry as they grew older and assumed greater responsibility in their government jobs—but the issue of poetic masculinity clearly remained on many poets' minds.[81]

As an indication of the shift in reception of the style, one 1893 guide to *kanshi* composition for novice poets provided its readers with a warning concerning such verse. Under the heading "Fragrant Style," the manual commented, "Describes the sensual emotions of a woman in her chambers. Many such poems have a tone that is weak and feeble and language about skirts, rouge, and powder. Named for Han Wo's *Fragrant Toilette Collection*."[82] The contrast with the 1878 manual cited earlier is striking, and the subtext of this warning seems obvious: a proper poet should avoid that which is weak and languid in tone.

One of the catalytic moments in this move toward more open criticism of the fragrant style came in the autumn of 1890 with a marathon exchange of *kanshi* in the pages of *Nippon*. Starting out as an exchange between *Nippon*'s resident *kanshi* poet Kokubu Seigai and the prominent Meiji statesman Soejima Taneomi 副島種臣 (pen names Sōkai 蒼海 and Ichiichi Gakunin 一一学人, 1828–1905), this sequence eventually spanned nineteen separate poems over nearly two months and also featured works from Kainan and his allies Yazuchi Kinzan 矢土錦山 (1849–1920) and Iwaya Kobai. The latter two apparently chimed in both out of a desire to exchange poems with the distinguished statesman Soejima and to rebut Seigai's criticisms of Kainan and his poetics.

The poem that served as the template for the entire exchange originated in the summer of 1890, when Kainan, Seigai, Kinzan, and Kobai had been invited to visit the villa of court noble Sanjō Sanetomi 三条実美 (1837–1891) in the Nikkō area, about a hundred miles north of Tokyo. A keen *kanshi* poet who signed himself with the pen name Ridō 梨堂, Sanetomi was a supporter of Shuntō and Kainan's poetic activities and until 1885 had served as grand minister of state (*daijō daijin*). At the villa, perhaps because Sanetomi had not met him before, Seigai was apparently seated as guest of honor and offered drink by his host, while Kainan, the youngest in years and junior in government rank to both Kobai and Kinzan, was relegated to the lowest seat.[83] Kainan may have been unhappy at Seigai's being so honored while he himself was overlooked; certainly a drinking poem from the gathering suggests he found

Seigai's presence at the very least surprising, referring to him as an "unexpected [or perhaps 'unwelcome'] guest" (Ch. *bu su* [*zhi*] *ke*, J. *fusoku* [*no*] *kyaku*).[84] Though penned during a presumably convivial drinking party, it is hard to read Kainan's description of Seigai as friendly, especially given the favorable treatment Sanetomi provided to Seigai. During their stay at Sanetomi's villa, the group also visited Kegon Falls near Lake Chūzenji, a major attraction of the Nikkō area that provided an opportunity for the group to compose additional verse on their surroundings. Kainan himself did not take part in the trip to the falls, since he had to return to Tokyo.

The gathering in Nikkō proved to be the starting point for an extended exchange of poetry among the four poets who had been present, and several others who had not. From early September, *Nippon*'s literary column began to feature a number of the verses the poets had composed in Nikkō, the first of these a verse Seigai composed on the grandeur of Kegon Falls and their mountain surroundings, which appeared on *Nippon*'s front page on September 9, 1890. Seigai had a fondness for composing poems on mountain scenery, and some of his earliest verse to appear in print had been on the experience of climbing Mount Fuji in 1882. The venue for their publication was Shuntō's *Shinbunshi*, which featured them along with a laudatory critique from Shuntō that likened Seigai to the mid-Tang poet Meng Jiao 孟郊 (751–814), renowned for the harsh and forceful nature of his poems.[85] Based on the tone of the poems and exchange that followed, Seigai seems to have understood the soaring, grand scale and martial imagery of his poems as offering an aesthetic antidote to the intimate, private, and above all feminized aesthetics of the fragrant-style poem.

Seigai's verse on Kegon Falls, a heptasyllabic old-style poem in forty lines, appeared on September 9, a date that was entirely appropriate: the ninth day of the ninth month was the "Double Ninth" (Ch. *chongyang*, J. *chōyō*) in the Chinese literary tradition, an auspicious occasion to climb mountains and drink wine. Seigai's poem describes the falls as awe-inspiring in their power and scale, their grandeur enhanced by the experience of seeing a summer lightning storm in the mountains. He goes on to describe how seeing the falls reminded him of famous battles from Chinese history, and he hails the mountain scenery as a place apart from the human realm, a world of gods, immortals, and otherworldly spirits:

風雨観華嚴瀑歌　　　*A Song of Kegon Falls Amid the Storm*[86]

黒髪之山高入空　　　The black-haired mountain thrusts high into the sky,[87]

百靈呵護青龍慫　　　Mountain spirits stand guard over the towering green peak.[88]

絶頂滙碧三萬頃　　　At the summit, whirling emerald waters span thirty thousand *qing*;[89]

溢為巨瀑專其雄　　　The runoff forms a vast waterfall, to it alone belongs magnificence.

遠望匹練掛林末　　　Seen far off, it is as white silk blanketing tree tips;　　　5

近疑河漢橫蒼穹　　　Close up, is this the Milky Way across the great blue sky?

一落為霰再落霧　　　Here it falls as hail, there it falls as mist—

霧飛霰迸林生風　　　The mist flies, the hail spatters as the wind arises from the woods.

三落而下不見水　　　Another drop falls, down into unseen waters.

俯観一白雲濛濛　　　I look up and see a white cloud, drizzly and indistinct—　　　10

驪珠飜倒百千斛　　　As if one had knocked over a million bushels of dragon pearls,[90]

老精夜哭鮫人宮　　　Or aged spirits were weeping by night in the shark-men's palace.[91]

我来正遇熱如燬　　　Coming here, truly I encounter heat like a furnace,

火雲硨兀奇峰重　　　Red summer clouds, jagged and wondrous peaks redoubled.

隆隆之雷起岳頂　　　Crashing thunder springs up around the highest peak,　　　15

颯然飛雨吹萬松　　　A stiff breeze sends rain blowing through myriad pines.

紫光礛潭閃眉睫　　　A flash of purple lightning dazzles right before my eyes,[92]

一聲霹靂双耳聾	Then a single word of crashing thunder leaves me deaf in both ears,
泉聲風聲不可別	Unable to discern roaring spring waters and roaring winds.
林木訇礚濤崩洶	In the trees of the wood echoes a great crash, wave smashing into wave. 20
莫是雷雨助真主	Is this not the lightning and rain that aided the true ruler?[93]
虎豹犀象爭奔衝	Or tigers, leopards, rhinos, elephants, clashing and colliding?
不然大風撼赤壁	Or else it is the great gale that shook Red Cliff,[94]
龍蛇駭逸摧艨艟	Great dragons roaring forth to smash the enemy fleet.
粉紜鬭亂不可亂	Amid the turmoil and tumult of battle, they seemed disordered, yet were in perfect order.[95] 25
奇正百出交相攻	Direct and indirect forces striking at one another, a hundred interlocking interactions.
飛廉鞭叱天馬走	The wind god whips and spurs his heavenly horse to a gallop,
馮夷擊皷聲鼕鼕	The river god strikes his drum, the beat a resounding boom,
陰晴倏忽幾變幻	Sun and shadow pass in an instant, so quickly changing,
風雲奇譎誰能窮	Wind and clouds are most mysterious; who can fathom them? 30
乃知精靈逞狡獪	Now I have come to know mountain spirits, steeped in trickery,
戲與詞客爭神工	They playfully tease the poet, competing among themselves to show off their mystical handiwork.
須臾雨歇夕陽出	In an instant, the rain yields, the evening sun emerges,
一條飲澗垂彩虹	A thin valley stream trickles down in the colors of the rainbow.

層巖蘿薜露痕湿	Layered crags, tangled vines, slick with remaining moisture,[96]	35
殘霞掩映紛青紅	A veil of lingering mist conceals, then reveals motes of green and red plants.	
晚投湖棲独呼酒	Tonight I shall repair to my lakeside tower, call for wine and drink alone,	
驚魄未定神怕怕	My affrighted spirit not yet settled down, my heart filled with fear.	
青蓮千歳不可起	For a thousand years, no one has been able to raise up the Green Lotus;[97]	
詩成欲舞潭中龍	My poem complete, I will dance with the dragon in the depths.[98]	40

Seigai's "Song of Kegon Falls" is a study on the power and scale of the falls themselves, the momentum of the falling water and the later storm inspiring musings on great sea battles and a string of images such as horses galloping, boats charging, and drums beating. Seigai's language in lines 20–26 is consciously martial, with words such as "striking," "smashing," "colliding," "clashing," and "shaking," and lines 25 and 26 directly echoing descriptions of battle from Sunzi's *The Art of War*. Seigai's reference to *The Art of War*, a highly unusual text to use as a source for poetic allusions, seems to neatly encapsulate his determination to create a martial, hypermasculine mood. As the storm continues and finally abates, the poet envisions himself as a Daoist immortal, leaving the human world to commune with the gods and spirits that dwell in this remote and mystical place before returning to the human world. As his closing reference to Li Bai in line 39 makes clear, Seigai's invocations of the grandeur and mystical qualities of mountain spaces are in part modeled on the Tang poet's depictions of the otherworldly majesty of China's great mountain spaces; for Seigai, the Japanese mountains of Nikkō are an equally good venue in which to let the imagination roam.

Once published in the pages of *Nippon*, Seigai's poem attracted attention from a number of other poets. In the recollections of Seigai's contemporaries, this poem and the subsequent exchanges with other poets did much to raise his reputation as a skilled poet whose forceful works could offer an alternative to the allegedly effeminate style of Mori Kainan.[99] Most notable among the poets responding to Seigai was the politician Soejima Taneomi, who was so impressed with Seigai's poem that he sent in to *Nippon* no fewer than five separate rhyme-matching responses over the following month. Known to be a fan of *Nippon*'s poetry column, Soejima had similar tastes to Seigai's, favoring the poetry of the Tang dynasty over more recent Ming and Qing poetics; Soejima's collected works contain poems modeled on such luminaries as Tao Yuanming 陶淵明 (365–427) and Li Bai and Zhang Jiuling 張九齡 (678–740) of the Tang. At sixty-three years of age, Soejima was thirty-five years Seigai's senior and a former holder of the prestigious position of imperial adviser (*sūmitsu komon*). For him to express his admiration by matching rhymes with Seigai was a great honor for the younger poet, especially considering they had yet to meet in person.[100] Soejima's first response, published on September 14, five days after Seigai's first poem, contained a number of lines highly complimentary of Seigai's work:[101]

. . .	
青崖居士胡為者	O Master Green Cliff, how is it that you[102]
欲與白也爭英風	Might match Li Bai in bold, heroic style?
今誦華嚴瀑布歌	For now you sing a song of Kegon Falls,
陸離文情晴兼濛	Your talent dazzling with bright light and dark shadow.
. . .	
以為君句今驚人	I hold that your verses now astonish people.
衰年膽悸多畏恟	In my declining years, courage fails, fear often fills my heart,[103]
借問天下若君有幾人	And so I ask: how many like you are there in the realm,
是皆文中虎與人中龍	Who are all tigers of letters and dragons among men?

When reading poems produced in Meiji print media, it is often helpful to also consult the responding critiques that tended to appear alongside them (and which are usually omitted when the poem is subsequently reproduced or anthologized). Locating the poem within a broader social and critical context, the responding critique helps the reader to understand how other poets interpreted the poem. All the verses published in the Kegon Falls exchange featured such critiques, and, as it happened,

Soejima's poem featured comments from both Kainan and Seigai. Kainan's critique was featured first and praised Soejima's work lavishly, as did Seigai in turn. However, Seigai's comments quickly moved beyond Soejima's poem to also mention what he saw as the state of the contemporary *kanshi* world: "When I look at the poetry of people these days, the poetry is not without beauty and not without skill, but all the poets are doing is garnishing old dregs; the poems have absolutely no vigor and energy to them. But Soejima's poem here in one breath turns the tide, full of spirit and replete with vigor. It will cause those who recycle old clichés and chatter away in self-satisfaction to flee thirty leagues away. I would call this enormously refreshing."[104]

Precisely whom Seigai meant by "those who recycle old clichés" was not clear at this point, but the appreciative response from Seigai in particular seems to have spurred Soejima to produce a subsequent rhyme-matching poem. This in turn was published on September 29, a little more than two weeks later, the second of five rhyme-matching poems by Soejima to appear in *Nippon* during the autumn of 1890:

又用青崖華嚴布韻有寄	*Again Using the Rhymes of Seigai's Kegon Poem, and Sending the Poem to Him*
秋風浩蕩披懷空	To autumn winds, vast and mighty, my own heart is open,
吟興乍臻肩聳從	Poetic inspiration strikes, and I raise my shoulders high in surprise.
誰令我輩至有此	Who is it that has brought us to this point?
青崖居士文騒雄	It is Master Green Cliff, acclaimed hero of letters.
久在朝市不望山	Long at court, I never gazed out at the mountains,
是日嗟嘆高碧弓	But now on this day, I gasp in amazement at the soaring blue skies.
聞説昔之韓文公	I hear tell that with Han Yu, of olden times,
無日不羨季杜風	Not a day went by when he didn't envy Li Bai's and Du Fu's style,
不剽一字渠真傑	But he never copied a single word of theirs; that was his true genius.

5

夙覺筆勢排鴻濛　He quickly learned to make his brush as
　　forceful as primeval chaos,　　　　　　10

鼎彝皷鐘藏盈肚　Sacrificial vessels carved with the achieve-
　　ments of great men, and ringing bells, they
　　filled his heart completely;[105]

賢腸猶是珍珠宮　So his spirit in this way was like a great
　　bejeweled palace.

君去今攀二荒峰[106]　Now you, too, climb your way up Mount
　　Futara,[107]

人界渺渺烟霧重　The human world left far below, under layers
　　of mist and fog,

龍潭沁洌清可鑑　Dragon pools trickle into waters so clear and
　　sparkling one can see one's reflection.　　15

玉女高擎青蓋松　The Jade Maiden raises dark-green pines in
　　offering,[108]

驅螭鞭蛟供駗駕　Driving on wyverns, whipping on dragons,
　　together they pull her chariot.

無聞塵事耳暫聾　You close your ears to worldly affairs, deaf for
　　a time,

到頭風日是明媚　But finding at last the scenery to be dazzling
　　and alluring,

脚底懸瀑鳴淙洄　Your legs hang over the edge of the falls as
　　they crash with the sound of roaring
　　water,　　　　　　　　　　　　　　20

昭回燦爛入指顧[109]　Dazzling, sparkling, as it picks up speed.

北斗低迷劍氣衝　As the North Star hangs overhead, martial
　　vigor surges in you,

彩翠晴嵐互来往　Brilliant greenery and mountain haze trade
　　places, in and out,

九霞圍繞紛盪攻　Ninefold mist enfolds, dissipates, comes
　　back.

江上廬山豈足往[110]　Mount Lu, towering over its rivers—why
　　bother going there?　　　　　　　　25

笑殺遠涉乘彼艟　I laugh at those who travel far away on their
　　boats.

好戒靁靁勿起雲　The time is right to instruct the Lord of
　　Thunder to stay his clouds,

又召雷母禁響聲	And call forth the Lady of Thunder, have her still her booming echoes.	
青天白日孤身在[111]	Under blue skies and white sun, you stand alone,	
上下四方思何窮	Thoughts free to run as they please, high and low, in all directions,	30
知君文心向誰壯	I know your literary talents shall surpass all others in grandeur;	
屈平宋玉曾稱工[112]	Qu Yuan and Song Yu were once called skilled,[113]	
降此諸子百家存	And after these men, a hundred others still,	
何人気吐萬丈虹	But which of them had a spirit that could bring forth mile-long rainbows?[114]	
自鄶以下蓋無語	All the rest are unworthy of mention, nothing to be said.[115]	35
可憐園菲抽小紅	Pity the one whose garden plants sprout the color of light mourning,[116]	
七月已去八月生	Whose seventh month has already gone, the eighth month now come.[117]	
霜露泥泥吾神恟	As it shines with frost and fallen dew, my spirit's courage fails,[118]	
焉與夫子日相從	So how could I ever follow the path of the sun with you?	
但愧才非陸士龍	To my shame, my talent is not that of Lu Shilong, the scholar-dragon.[119]	40

Soejima closely follows Seigai's original imagery of awesome natural grandeur and otherworldly spirits, albeit narrated from the point of view of another commenting on Seigai's experiences in the mountains; this change in perspective allows Soejima to repeatedly compliment Seigai by suggesting that his spirit is as forceful as the power of nature and that he himself is one of the immortals who dwell in the mountains, recognized and honored by mountain spirits such as the Jade Maiden.

The commenters for Soejima's second verse were once again Kainan and Seigai, both of them laudatory. This time, Seigai was more explicit as to whom he believed could learn from Soejima's work:

This poem's diction is surely unusually grand, intent surely fresh and wonderful; amazing talent and great verbal skill, so exalted that everything else is beneath his notice. . . . There in the midst of chaos, order and dignity naturally emerge and take shape. It is, so to speak, like gold, silver, bronze, and iron all melting together in one furnace, yet with no sense of disorder therein. . . . In our times, the only one I see [capable of doing this] is the distinguished count, and no one else at all. Those poets in our times who are men yet put on rouge and apply powder and rejoice at fashioning poems about whores; when they read this, how can they not die of shame?[120]

It is not clear whether Seigai's commentary here was intended as a direct insult to Kainan personally, but by reputation and by oeuvre Kainan was very much the kind of poet Seigai could have been referring to. The reference to "fashioning poems about whores" was, of course, unambiguous in referring to the fragrant style. Whether or not Kainan was the direct target, the terms in which Seigai's criticism was couched were withering; using the adversative 而 (Ch. *er*, J. *shikōshite*) to suggest a disjunction between being male and composing fragrant-style poetry, Seigai's implication is that real men should not be composing on this topic. In then suggesting that fragrant-style poets themselves "put on rouge and apply powder," he further calls into question their very masculinity. The fascination with the sexualized feminine so characteristic of the fragrant style is mockingly equated with the desire to look like a woman, if not actually become one.[121] Faced with the counterexample of Soejima and Seigai's hypermasculine poetry, Seigai suggests, what could an exponent of the fragrant style do but "die of shame"?

Soejima may or may not have shared Seigai's misgivings about the fragrant style,[122] but he was lavishly appreciative of the tone of Seigai's poetry, and that clearly emboldened *Nippon*'s resident *kanshi* poet. Possibly to his credit, Kainan himself refrained from addressing Seigai's comments as the two other poets went on with their exchanges. Following on from the publication of Soejima's two poems, Seigai penned a further response of his own to Soejima on October 2, accompanied by another admiring critique from Kainan that made no mention of the earlier criticism. Soejima again replied, with a third rhyme-matching poem three days later, on October 5, in which he praises Seigai for his "hero's spirit," and suggests that Japan's security as a nation was enhanced by the presence of such martially minded men:

> ...
>
> 而今未離英雄気   And you have not yet abandoned the
>   hero's spirit,
>
> 不然何至句引周郎赤壁艟   If you had, how could your verses evoke
>   Zhou Yu and the warships of Red Cliff?[123]
>
> 豈以四海邦国形勢互相雄   Is it not the stance of all nations in the
> 長互相幷吞   four seas to vie with one another in
>   domination and conquest?
>
> 神州男子亦未宜忘戰與攻   The men of the Divine Land, too, must not
>   yet forget the arts of war and strategy.[124]
>
> ...

Appearing implicitly to agree with Seigai's criticism, this section of Soejima's poem could be read to suggest that Japan might not be fully safe if weak and languid poets were an index of its overall strength; it was no less than a matter of national security to have spirited and martial poets in the land. Exaggerated praise, perhaps, but Seigai took it to heart with yet another poem, apparently intent on further emphasizing his masculine poetry as antidote to the fragrant style. This time, the specifics of his criticism leave little doubt that Kainan was indeed the intended target:

> ...
>
> 年来詩道日斯下   For years now the sun has been setting on
>   the way of poetry,
>
> 荊棘塞途雲霧濛   Thorns and thistles choke the path, 'mid
>   murky clouds and mist.
>
> 鬚眉乃學冶艷態   Those who are men, and study sensual forms,
>
> 弗異粉黛媚六宮   Are no different from painted beauties, coy
>   in the harem.[125]
>
> 小言詹詹漫自喜   Little words, shrill and quarrelsome, yet they
>   are satisfied at their ramblings,[126]
>
> 飣餖只見故紙重   Their writing so filled with needless garnish,
>   one can only view it as so many scraps of
>   waste paper,

桃李容顔若飛電	The beauty of a female face as ephemeral as a lightning flash.[127]
那似鬱鬱澗底松	These poets are like pines deep in a dark, dark ravine,[128]
蛙鳴蝉噪不耐聴	Like croaking frogs, clamoring cicadas; I cannot bear to listen,
佯道病来吾耳聾	So I shall pretend that illness has struck, my ears rendered deaf to the noise.[129]

. . .

Seigai here sustains his attack on the fragrant style and on the masculinity of its practitioners; likening them to painted beauties flattering and flirting to gain attention in the imperial harem, he again suggests they are not real men. Given that several of Seigai's interlocutors during the exchange, notably Kainan, Kinzan, and Kobai, were employed by the Meiji government in some capacity (as in fact was Ue Mukō), this again was withering criticism. Those in government who favor ornate and alluring poetry are, as Seigai has it, using their work to attract the attention of those in higher political positions, prostituting their poetry for personal gain. Both Kainan and Kinzan were in fact known to spend a lot of time in Itō Hirobumi's company, kept in attendance to comment on his poems.[130] More so than Kinzan, Kainan's relatively low formal rank in the government bureaucracy meant that he would otherwise have been highly unlikely to enjoy such privileged access. For governmental employees, the metaphor of the pine at the bottom of a ravine, one of talent never used properly, was equally pointed; in describing Kainan and his group this way, Seigai suggests that the fragrant-style poet's talent might, if used properly, actually be of service to the state. So, too, with "croaking frogs," a metaphor dating back to the poetry of Qu Yuan that refers to corrupt officials and that *Nippon* used in its pages on a regular basis for exactly the same purpose.

Kainan could hardly be expected to continue to comment on this series of uncomplimentary remarks without some kind of a rebuttal, and this duly came in the shape of an appended comment to Seigai's poem: "Kainan comments: 'Cast out the seductive and alluring, belittle and reject the ornate and beautiful'—such is Seigai's argument. 'Pretending to be deaf to the croaking of frogs and clamoring of cicadas'—this is how

Seigai himself is. He is taking up quite a lofty and exalted position here. Though Du Fu and Li Bai had a 'wall several fathoms high,'[131] yet there are still those who look askance at them. Who would not fear this!. . . It is to my deep shame that my own brush should be so weak and impotent."[132]

Considerably more restrained than Seigai, Kainan's response nevertheless contains a few subtle jabs of his own. Seigai's depiction of soaring mountain heights reflects, Kainan suggests, the author's own high and mighty view of himself and penchant for sweeping pronouncements. By way of noting that even legendary poets Du Fu and Li Bai were the subject of criticism, and that attracting criticism is no measure of a poet's quality, Kainan attempts to brush off Seigai's attacks; moreover, in alluding to the *Analects*' description of Confucius's superiority, Kainan implies that Seigai's criticism is based on his failure to fully understand the nature of Kainan's work. Yazuchi Kinzan, for his part, was rather more jocular in his responding comments to Seigai's poem: "Kinzan comments: These two regulated verses have the tone of the immortals. They spurn everyday human concerns such as food, drink, and warmth. By contrast, Kainan and I spend every night 'mid wine and meat, the smell of powder and drink permeating even to our very bones. How can we possibly bear it?"[133]

In a further comment, appended after Kinzan's, Kainan likens Seigai's work to that of Chen Bicheng. Given the latter's association in Japan with the fragrant style, this was probably not a comparison Seigai would have found particularly flattering.

Kainan continued his response to Seigai the following day, October 7, by publishing his own rhyme-matching response to the Kegon Falls poems:

贈青厓居士用其華嚴瀑詩原韻有序

Presented to Master Seigai, Using the Original Rhyme of His Poem on Kegon Falls, with Preface.[134]

| 放眼天下名山空 | He casts his eyes to the sky over the great peaks under heaven, |
| 胸中五嶽高嵂崧 | The Five Famous Mountains soaring majestically in his heart.[135] |

即今海內作長句	So now in our land, for writing lengthy verses,
意氣獨讓青厓雄	And for his spirit, who can rival Seigai in his bold manliness?
神光奕奕暘出谷	It is like divine light, flooding forth at sunrise in a valley,	5
元精耿耿星麗穹	Like the Force of the Universe sparkling in a star-resplendent sky.[136]
鬢髯戟張骨卓立	His beard broad and bristling, his bones firm and resolute,
吸噓廣莫閶闔風	His breath as vast in scale as the north and west winds.
. . .	
山巔海角盡詩料	The highest peaks, the furthest reaches of the ocean, all have been fine topics for your poetry,
敢誇一篇觀瀑工	But they pale before this single verse on viewing the falls.
華嚴百丈吾未覩	Kegon Falls a hundred feet high: I have yet to see them,[137]
想像陰壑騰霧虹	So I imagine shaded valleys and soaring rainbows.
恐將冥搜傷刻劃	I fear I must close my eyes, search my heart, as I take pains to carve out the words;[138]	35
吟苦幾剔秋燈紅	As I agonize over my song, my much-trimmed autumn lamp glows red.
不如賦君得意事	I have not your skill, Seigai, in composing on your favored topics,[139]
硬語一任兒曹恟	And so, as a swath of lesser poets cower at your mighty words,
臨風浩唱欲飛去	Wildly I chant my song into the wind; the words shall fly away,[140]
為君點破無睛龍	But you boldly put the finishing touches to pictures of dragons without pupils.[141]	40

In the face of Seigai's earlier criticism, Kainan's response reads as admiring and humble, opening by paying tribute to Seigai's manly spirit and concluding on what reads almost like an admission of inferiority, conceding that the Sendai-born poet possesses the greater skill in depicting mountain spaces. Kainan, who did not visit Kegon Falls during the trip to Sanetomi's villa, admits his poem is inferior because he must summon it entirely from his imagination; and, in the concluding two lines, Kainan contrasts his own poem, which he sees as being carried away and destroyed by the wind, to Seigai's own enduring work of art, via a reference to the legend of the painter Zhang Sengyao. Perhaps in recognition of Kainan's humility, Seigai's responding critique was rather more conciliatory than his earlier comments had been:

> Seigai comments:. . . In his youth, Kainan rejoiced in the fragrant style. In his middle years, he has made a major effort and greatly altered the path he is treading. He goes in and out of Han, Wei, and the Six Dynasties; he moves up and down through Tang, Song, Ming, and Qing. In all these various styles, there is none at which he does not excel, and as he flourishes, so people call him a master. But expectations can color what one sees, and the eyes of those of lesser intellect still see him as a Dong Lang [i.e., Han Wo] of intricate words. I find this deeply regrettable on Kainan's account. I would be remiss were I not to say something about this here. Those who doubt the truth of what I say, pray try to grasp what Kainan has written here, and chant the poem once more.[142]

Though more moderate in tone, Seigai's reference to Kainan as Han Wo of *Fragrant Toilette Collection* fame still has the feeling of a backhanded compliment, the implication being that only now, in his midtwenties, had Kainan actually succeeded in growing up. Kainan's verse in the fragrant style was thus a youthful indiscretion, the present, more manly poem evidence of his having put such follies behind him. Perhaps realizing that he had gone a little far in his criticism, Seigai's next poem offered something of an olive branch to the Mori group, the opening lines complimenting each of the main protagonists in the exchange so far and offering a jocular moment of self-deprecation: "The tiger sees the soaring dragon, and they battle for supremacy / But laughably, Seigai has not a speck of talent" (虎視龍驤互爭雄 / 可笑青厓無一藝).[143]

The exchange continued from here through an additional twelve largely cordial poems, the majority from Seigai and Soejima but also featuring verses from the more senior poet Kō Ungai 高雲外 (1833–1895), as well as Kainan's and Seigai's rough contemporary Satō Rokuseki 佐藤六石 (1864–1927), and another, obscure poet by the name of Yamayoshi Moriyoshi 山吉盛義 (dates unknown).[144] Going on through nearly two months, and summing to nineteen old-style poems of forty lines each, with at least that much again in responding commentaries, *Nippon*'s readers could have been forgiven for being exhausted by the entire experience. In fact, the conclusion of the exchange did prompt a number of the newspaper's readers to express their annoyance at what they had just witnessed:

An Admonition to *Nippon*'s Writers   Anonymous, Negishi, Hongō

I have read the sequence of various *kanshi* responses on Kegon Falls featured in *Nippon*'s Bun'en [Garden of letters] of late, finding them obscure and impenetrable, harsh and abstruse—what interest can this sort of thing possibly hold? In general, when Japanese write Sinitic poems all they do is string together a bunch of obscure characters, with none of the style and interest of poems by Chinese poets. As for the critiques, they just end up repeating the same monotonous terms over and over the whole way through. And their length! They go on and on, descending from the sky, as long and pointless as the proverbial "red rice from Nagasaki and old loincloths from India."[145] It's enough to make people nauseous. *Nippon*'s writers ought to bear this in mind.[146]

Another reader likewise found fault with the sequence's difficult and demanding language: "With the works of the poet from Changli [i.e., Han Yu], every single one of his poems has difficult and obscure words; and yet he may still be regarded as a true master. As for works these days, whether they are 'lustrous and alluring,' 'mystical,' 'free-flowing,' or 'leisurely' in style—if they are not readily comprehensible, they're bad poems. This is a fault common to poets of our land."

Printed alongside these was one last rhyme-following response to the poem Seigai had published exactly two months previously. Perhaps in sympathy with the criticism that the *kanshi* exchange was difficult for readers to understand, the final poem was glossed with the *kunten* markings that had been conspicuously absent from the earlier exchanges, making it significantly easier for nonspecialist readers to understand it. The pseudonymous authors of the poem adopted a humorous take on the motifs of soaring mountains and mystical spirits that had been a mainstay throughout:

...

彫龍畫虎惑萬重	Carving dragons, painting tigers, delusion upon delusion.
月明芝艸若有靈	If there *are* spirits in the bright moon and luxuriant grass,
叱咤喝雲松	They'll voice their grievance to the clouds and pines:
請君唱和暫可已	"Knock it off with the rhyme matching for a bit, will you?"

...

MEIJI JAPAN'S "SOFTIE" AND "ROUGHNECK" POETICS

Though it bored some of *Nippon*'s readers and nauseated others, the Kegon Falls exchange was nevertheless a significant moment for the Meiji *kanshidan*. Seigai had not been unknown as a *kanshi* poet up to this point, but the exchange with Soejima marked his full emergence as a major figure in the literary world and, perhaps just as important, highlighted his claims as a figurehead opposed to Kainan's ornate and delicate poetics. Seigai's public and full-throated criticism of fragrant-style poetics set the tone for a number of subsequent critiques. In particular, the idea that Kainan's work was inimical to a bold and manly spirit acquired further currency. An unsigned piece in 1895 commenting on the *kanshi* world in the journal *Teikoku bungaku*, for instance, carried some unflattering remarks about Kainan and his disciple Noguchi Neisai 野口寧斎 (Hajime 弌, 1867–1905): "Kainan and Neisai are major talents of our times and, as such, will do to represent Seisha; not many can measure up to their poetic works. Yet they lack spirit, lack backbone, and are deficient in grand and soaring tone. Alas, could this be because the dignity or vulgarity of a poem derives from the dignity or vulgarity of its author?"[147] The implication, of course, was that Kainan himself must be vulgar, lacking in spirit, and without backbone if he produced such poetry. Writing even in the late 1970s, the ever-abrasive Kinoshita Hyō likewise comments on one of Kainan's poems of 1880 that "it is the sort of poem where even a glance is enough to destroy one's spirit" (*ichidoku tama no kieiru yō na shi de aru*).[148]

Much of the criticism directed at the fragrant style did, therefore, depend on the assumption that a poem was a perfect mirror of the character of its composer. This assumption did not go entirely without question; in a preface to the 1912 edition of Shuntō's collected works, Yoda Gakkai addressed exactly this point: "Let us suppose that you see someone laughing and divine that they are happy, see someone cursing and infer that they are angry; that is indeed a shallow way to know someone. . . . As for the idea that one makes use of a poem to depict one's mind and character, truly, the matter extends well beyond the limits of 'laugh when happy, curse when angry.'"[149]

In like vein, Gakkai also made the point that it was wrong to claim that Shuntō was not concerned with affairs of the realm just because his poetry rarely touched on that topic, highlighting again a perceived disjunction between fragrant-style poetics and service to the nation. Suggesting that qualms about the fragrant style continued as late as 1899, another *kanshi* published in the popular journal *Taiyō* appeared to offer similar sentiments to rebut the idea that the poem was the poet:

論詩似人	*On the Proposition That a Poem Resembles Its Composer*
詩似十洲写麗妹	Poetry's like a magical land where you can portray pretty girls;
欲描神處尽工夫	If you want to depict this mystical space, push talent to the limit,
愁脂恨粉香奩体	With the rouge of regret and the powder of pain in the fragrant style,

| 即是君家没骨図 | Then that means you're more of a "boneless" painter![150] |

The "boneless style" (Ch. *mo gu*, J. *mokkotsu*) was originally a style of ink painting that did not depend on an initial ink outline; in the context of fragrant-style poetry, it recalls a criticism of the *Fragrant Toilette Collection* by Southern Song poet Xu Yi 許顗 (dates unknown), to the effect that "Yuan Zhen's alluring poems have beauty but they have backbone; Han Wo's *Fragrant Toilette Collection* has beauty but no backbone."[151] In the context of this poem, of course, being "boneless" is an insult directed at the supposedly spineless fragrant-style practitioner. Gakkai's defense of the style—that the poem was *not* the poet—actually represented a move away from its earlier, innate-inspiration-based defense as emotional truth. Defenders of the fragrant style thus seemed trapped between the two propositions that their poems were either unmanly or contained false emotion. This may explain why Kainan responded so meekly to Seigai's criticism: having already been accused early in his career of "fake passion," he could not argue that his poems were not an index of his character and was thus left with no effective rebuttal.

The studiedly masculine style that Seigai was championing seems to have found considerable favor among contemporary *kanshi* poets, not least Shiki himself. In 1892, for instance, Shiki published a sequence of poems in *Nippon* that he had composed during his travels through the central Kiso region of Japan, where he had traveled for a time after dropping out of the university. It was in fact Seigai who selected and commented on the poems that appeared in *Nippon*, marking the beginning of an amicable and productive relationship between him and Shiki at the newspaper. Seigai's influence on Shiki's poetry is clearly apparent in the first of the latter's Kiso poems:

岐蘇雑詩　其一	*Assorted Poems on Kiso: Number 1*
群峰如剣刺蒼空	Mountain peaks thrust swordlike into blue skies,
路入岐蘇形勝雄	Bold beyond measure is the road's aspect as it winds into Kiso.

古寺鐘伝層樹外	The sound of an old temple's bell carries far beyond dense ranks of trees,
絶崖路断乱雲中	The road through sheer cliffs disappears 'mid swirling clouds.
百年豪傑荒苔紫	The hero of a hundred ages is overgrown with purple lichens;[152]
万里河山落日紅	The setting sun glows scarlet over boundless rivers and mountains.
欲問虎拏龍闘跡	I ask what remains of the one who grappled with tigers and fought with dragons,
蕭蕭駅馬独嘶風	But the horse at the lonely post station just whinnies at the wind.[153]

Taken as a whole, Shiki's Kiso poems have been widely hailed by Japanese scholars as his finest achievement in the medium of *kanshi*, and this first verse follows Seigai closely in its depiction of soaring peaks, swirling clouds, and the traces of warrior heroes of old. In addition, this first poem's rhyme graphs are all to be found as rhyme graphs in Seigai's Kegon Falls poem as well, suggesting a desire to pay tribute to Seigai's earlier work. The attraction of the grand, masculine aesthetic does not seem to have faded as Shiki began his work on haiku; in his 1895 *Haikai taiyō* (Essentials of haiku), he noted the importance in haiku of a style that was "grand and bold" (*sōdai yūkon*) and gave the following as examples of what he meant:

That which is broad in expanse is "grand": the fathomless depths of lakes and oceans, the towering majesty of mountain crags, the limitless expanses of the skies; or, serried ranks of vast armies and innumerable horses upon a vast field; or, the stars of the Milky Way touching a plain—all of these are "grand." That which has force and momentum is "bold": the rustling of a great wind, the smashing and crashing of furious waves, the roaring of a flying waterfall, torrential floodwaters flowing from the heavens and rampaging through a village, two armies clashing in a hail of bullets, great warships engaging as mines churn the water; all such things are "bold."[154]

This, then, was the grand, martial—and above all masculine-gendered—aesthetic that served as an antidote to the allegedly weak, lascivious, and feminized fragrant style.

Neither Shuntō nor Kainan were, in all fairness, the poetic pornographers their critics sometimes made them out to be; both were talented and versatile poets who could and did compose in many other styles. Shuntō in particular was a farsighted and innovative poet, especially in his use of periodical media, whose contribution to the overall Meiji *kanshi* world was considerable. Yet the fact that their oeuvres as a whole came to be overshadowed by their work in the fragrant style clearly reveals considerable fractures and anxieties in the *kanshi* world over the issue of *kanshi*'s relation to the feminine. Though direct correspondences are difficult to establish, it is worth noting that Suzuki Shōtō's promise in the 1880 foreword to *Nihon keien ginsō* to survey all of Japan's female poets was not fulfilled; no such additional collection of exclusively female poets would be published. As it developed from the mid-1880s, the national-poetic community of *kanshi* poets in Meiji Japan was characterized by an emphasis on poetic masculinity as a strategy of internal differentiation and hierarchy.

Whether one criticized it on the grounds of immorality, emotional insincerity, or perceived potential for wholesale feminization of Japanese men, the problems with the fragrant style were serious enough that certain sections of the *kanshi* world considered it necessary to remain on guard well after Seigai's Kegon Falls poems had provided an aggressive performance of his version of poetic masculinity. A truly masculine poet projected strength, not languid weakness; he had "spirit" and "backbone." His compositions were sweeping and soaring, not intricate, ornate, and clichéd; his subject matter was the martial and the awe-inspiring, not the vulgar and trivial realm of the boudoir, cosmetics, and frustrated desire.

Discussing the development of Seisha, the poetic society featuring Seigai and Kainan that had been formed in September of 1890, just prior to the Kegon Falls exchanges, Miura Kanō has noted that after the society's formation, relations between Seigai and Kainan grew gradually worse, to the extent that Kainan tried to get Seigai to step down from his leadership position; although Seigai remained in situ for a while, he eventually walked away from the society and entered a period of semiretirement, remaining aloof from the daily affairs of the *kanshi-dan*.[155] One imagines that the Kegon Falls exchange and its aftermath, if not a major contributor to this rift between the two, certainly cannot have improved matters, and, judging by the vehemence with which Seigai's disciple Kinoshita Hyō laid into Kainan in his discussion of Seigai's career even as late as the 1970s, their dispute did much to divide and polarize *kanshi* for some time thereafter, even as the tectonics of the practice of *kanshi* shifted in the early twentieth century.

CHAPTER THREE

Clamorous Frogs and Verminous Insects

Nippon *and Political Haiku, 1890–1900*

To say that the newspaper *Nippon* had a difficult relationship with the Meiji government would be dramatically understating the case. For most of its first decade after dropping the name *Tōkyō denpō* to become *Nippon* under the guidance of Kuga Katsunan, the newspaper had made a point of strenuously opposing government policy in almost every area. Its editorial and reporting pages were filled with accounts of what it saw as governmental corruption, incompetence, and weakness. Among the most glaring of the Meiji government's perceived failures was its taking an insufficiently aggressive stance toward the Western powers in pursuing treaty reform; renegotiating the unequal treaties that Japan had been forced to sign in 1858 was a major long-term goal of the Meiji administration and, for *Nippon*, a matter of national pride. The Meiji government, for its part, did not always take a laissez-faire approach to regulation of the press, and *Nippon*'s hard line made it a prime target. On occasions where it was perceived that *Nippon* had gone too far, the usual official sanction was an order to suspend publication (*hakkō teishi rei*), which prevented the newspaper from publishing for a specified period. *Nippon* was not the only Meiji newspaper to suffer this punishment, but it was one of the more frequently targeted ones; and although Katsunan and his staff apparently took pride in this state of affairs, plastering suspend-publication notices on the walls of their newsroom as badges of honor, the loss of sales and advertising revenue was very damaging to their business.[1]

While *Nippon* is frequently described as nationalistic, its conception of nationalism understood the nation, as a community, to be fundamentally distinct from the institutions and mechanisms of the Japanese state. So, too, for the people who ran those institutions; much of *Nippon*'s news and editorial copy adopted a consistent line that the people in power were corrupt, incompetent, or otherwise unworthy to represent the country and argued implicitly or explicitly that the project of national advancement could be achieved only by their removal or exclusion. What, then, did this mean for Shiki's incipient haiku project, which really took off only once he was ensconced at *Nippon*? The precise nature of the media platform from which Shiki began his work has rarely been considered in depth, and this chapter argues that, as went news and editorial, so too went literary content: much of *Nippon*'s poetry was highly political in nature, casting the institutional structures of the Meiji government as unpatriotic and unworthy. This poetry was underpinned by a tacit understanding among *Nippon*'s readers and poets that they themselves were the true patriots, the ones who really had the nation's interests at heart. Though it has not generally been remarked upon, such divisively partisan poetry was an important part of Shiki's early work at *Nippon* in haiku. It was, as I show, through its use as political commentary that haiku became established as a respectable literary genre at *Nippon* and through such verse that Shiki attracted an initial audience. The communities that emerged around the mission of what we now think of as the modern haiku were thus defined in large part by political affiliation, gathering around a highly politicized form of the genre.

The following discussion centers on what were known at the time as topical haiku (*jiji haiku*), verses that referred to political and social issues of the day such as treaty reform, official corruption, censorship, and foreign affairs. One example from a haiku column under Shiki's control is the following verse, written possibly by the man himself:

衆議院解散　　　　*On the Dissolution of the Diet*

natsukusa ya　　　the summer grass—
giin monzen　　　　the Diet gate, out in front,

hito mo nashi   there's no one there.[2]

夏草や議院門前人もなし

In June 1894, after facing intractable opposition from the Diet, Itō Hiro-bumi elected to dissolve it, even though it had at that point been in session for only around two weeks. The haiku portrays the Imperial Diet, nor-mally a hub of activity, as oddly still and calm. The first line of the verse adds an ironic note to the scene; it is a verbatim quote from one of Bashō's most famous *hokku*, which he composed on seeing the deserted ruins left by the northern branch of the Fujiwara family in the far north of Japan.[3] The juxtaposition suggests the poet believes that, like the once-powerful northern Fujiwara, Japan's politicians are closer to their ruin than they realize, the empty Diet an eerie foreshadowing of the day to come.

This chapter, then, makes two main arguments. The first is that, at the point at which it began to appear in Japanese newspapers during the early 1890s, haiku was quite far from a vehicle for a vision of a homoge-neous, united national-poetic community; rather, it frequently expressed rancorous political divisions and polarization. Second, this chapter's pre-sentation of haiku as explicitly engaged in political discourse aims to challenge the conventional understanding of both modern haiku and the *haikai* tradition as concerned primarily with the seasons and the natu-ral world. For the most part, commentary on human and political affairs has generally been understood as the domain of haiku's satiric and comic counterpart, *senryū*, not haiku proper. Although it follows the same basic 5-7-5 syllable pattern, *senryū* differs from haiku in both subject matter and form: it tends to favor vernacular rather than classical language, does not use a seasonal word or a cutting word, and is usually anonymous.

It might therefore be argued that virtually all Meiji topical haiku should be regarded as *senryū* on account of their subject matter. Meiji newspapers did indeed feature *senryū* on a regular basis, but, as I show, dismissing topical haiku as simply another form of *senryū* would be a considerable oversimplification of the realities of mid-Meiji haiku prac-tice.[4] Meiji newspaper poets were fully aware of the distinction between haiku and *senryū* and took pains to compose formally correct haiku that also engaged with contemporary social and cultural issues. Particularly in the case of the highly political *Nippon*, for instance, topical haiku did not necessarily feature the (occasionally scatological) humor character-istic of *senryū*. Topical verses were often intended as serious political commentary by serious political men, and humor would have lessened their impact. Further, as in the following verses commenting on the Ashio Copper Mine pollution incident, in some cases haiku's traditional connection to the natural world actually made it a more effective vehi-cle for protest:

足尾銅山鉱毒春十句

Ten Spring Verses on the Toxic Pollution at Ashio Copper Mine

dokutsuka ni	on a mound of toxins
nogitsune shishite ari	a wild fox lies dead—
haru no tsuki	the spring moon.

毒塚に野狐死してあり春の月

haru no mizu	spring waters
dōshū o obite	take on the stink of copper—
uo sumazu	fish do not live therein.[5]

春の水銅臭を帯びて魚住まず

Spring should be a time for life and new growth, but these poems show the Ashio valley to be dead, its wildlife fled or poisoned by the toxic runoff from the mine. The second verse plays on a double meaning for "stink of copper" (*dōshū*); read literally, it is a description of the devasta-tion resulting from heavy-metal pollution. But "stink of copper" can also mean "greed" or "avarice," and so the verse also condemns mine owner Furukawa Ichibei's 古河市兵衛 (1832–1903) ruthless pursuit of profits and the Meiji government's growth-at-all-costs industrial policies, all at the expense of the livelihood of the residents of Ashio.

Topical haiku were, then, a common sight in Japanese newspapers during the 1890s, and their popularity would seem to indicate that most newspaper readers considered them to be an acceptable use of the genre. Plenty of newspapers apart from *Nippon* carried such verses; in a call toward the end of 1895 for readers to send in haiku, the *Tōkyō Mainichi shinbun* advised that "either topical verses or just plain verses [*tada no ku*] are fine" (*jiji mondai nite mo tada no ku nite mo yoshi*). Later that year, the same newspaper encouraged its readers to expand the range of subject matter addressed in their poems, noting that "topical compositions need not be limited to political questions; societal matters are also interesting" (*jijiei wa kanarazu shimo seijimondai ni kagirazu, shakai no dekigoto omoshirokaru beshi*).[6] Japan's two most widely read newspapers after the Sino-Japanese War, the Tokyo-based *Yorozu chōhō* and the *Ōsaka Asahi shinbun*, also featured such verses in abundance, seemingly to the exclusion of "literary" haiku. The *Ōsaka Asahi* ran a semiregular column called Haiku Commentary on Current Affairs (Jiji haihyō),[7] and the *Yorozu* ran topical poetry in all major genres on a virtually daily basis. Neither newspaper, though, carried a regular column featuring nontopical haiku until around the turn of the twentieth century.[8]

In terms of what was actually being read in Japan's daily newspapers, topical haiku may even have been in the majority for a sizable part of the 1890s. Though topical haiku were clearly popular with a broad audience, this should not be taken to mean that Shiki or his fellow haiku poets necessarily approved of this use of the genre; all indications are that Shiki wrote such poems somewhat reluctantly and distanced himself from them as soon as he was able. As this might suggest, there was in the background to a lot of newspaper poetry, especially at *Nippon* (which featured Seigai's *kanshi*), a broader debate about whether poetry could be adapted to political criticism. This was not because Shiki or Katsunan had any particular aversion to confronting authority figures in general. Katsunan's fiery editorials were well known, and, though he had not openly been politically active while in the capital,[9] Shiki had been well versed in the rhetoric of the FPRM while in Matsuyama. Just before he entered Matsuyama Middle School in 1881, it had been under the custodianship of the charismatic FPRM activist Kusama Jifuku 草間時福 (1853–1932). Kusama's FPRM activity was not exactly a secret; in fact, just before joining the school he had earned himself a fine of fifty yen and a two-month spell under house arrest after having a letter published in the *Chōya shinbun* arguing that it was necessary to topple an oppressive government.[10] The day after Kusama's house arrest was lifted, he officially took up his position at Matsuyama Middle School. Unsurprisingly,

Shiki's friend and classmate Yanagihara Kyokudō noted that such exploits gave Kusama hero status among his students, even to the extent of wishing that they themselves could be imprisoned so as to emulate him.[11] During his earlier days in Matsuyama, Shiki had also composed poetry and given speeches that suggested broad sympathy for the FPRM.

Having thus little compunction in speaking truth to power, Katsunan's and Shiki's ambivalence to explicitly political poetry was grounded largely in artistic criteria. Yet for all that, politically engaged poetry was extremely popular among *Nippon*'s readers, and so long as that was the case, it was to the newspaper's benefit to produce it. Whereas Shiki moved away from topical haiku once he had established himself in his column at *Nippon* and begun to get *Hototogisu* off the ground after 1897, topical haiku at *Nippon* unquestionably played a major role in launching the activities of what would later be called the *Nippon* Group, from which Shiki's haiku movement would proceed. Topical haiku thus deserves attention as a point of origin, later largely forgotten, for the foundations of the modern haiku.

SHIKI AND SEIGAI AT *NIPPON*: HYŌRIN, FOREST OF CRITICISM

Shiki's formal hiring at *Nippon*, formalized on December 1, 1892, did not come a moment too soon. At the time, he had just moved out of the dormitory run by the Evergreen Society, a mutual-aid group for students from Matsuyama, and taken lodgings on his own in the Hongō area of Tokyo. Though apparently made for reasons of health, as a way of providing a more sanitary environment in which to manage his now-chronic tuberculosis, the decision placed additional strain on Shiki's already limited budget. Shiki received a small student stipend from the Evergreen Society, which was adequate but hardly generous, and the situation became tighter when his sister Ritsu 正岡律 (1870–1941) divorced her husband and returned to the family in the spring of 1890. This raised the possibility that Shiki, as the titular head of the Masaoka household, might have to relocate his sister and mother to Tokyo and find a way to provide for them.[12]

Under these circumstances, Shiki's decision to leave the relatively inexpensive Evergreen Society dormitory for private lodgings must have seemed ill-advised; but his decision, in June of 1892, to withdraw entirely from his studies at Tokyo University would have appeared nothing short of suicidal. As Kuga Katsunan later recalled, it had been clear for some time that Shiki was not happy in his studies and was looking for alternative paths to pursue. Katsunan knew the Masaoka family through Shiki's uncle Katō Takusen, alongside whom he had studied at (and been expelled from) the Ministry of Justice Law School. Through this family connection, it was Katsunan who was ultimately responsible for giving Shiki his job at *Nippon*. Prior to formally hiring him at the newspaper, Katsunan had had Shiki submit a few literary pieces, although in his own recollections Katsunan admits that he knew nothing about haiku and had little idea how he might actually use Shiki:

> In the autumn of 1891 Shiki visited me in my home in Negishi. He said that he was supposed to graduate the following year, but that on account of ill health he planned to give up his studies. I didn't know what kind of health problems he was having, but though I suggested to him that he ought to stick it out and graduate, he would not be swayed from his decision. He said that of late he had begun to get into studying haiku and had found it rather interesting, so he was thinking of quitting the university and doing only that. . . . At this time I had absolutely no idea what haiku was about. . . . When he said that he wanted to make a contribution to literature through this I worried to myself that he might not really have thought the matter through. . . .
>
> At that time the only people putting seventeen-syllable verse in the papers were people like Kikakudō Eiki, or if not he Kakuta Chikurei and his ilk, and even then there weren't very many of them. When I asked Shiki whether he wanted to try putting something in *Nippon*, he said that he would give me a travelogue he had already written, and then produced a travelogue with haiku in it. That was how Masaoka Shiki got his start.[13]

If Katsunan's recollections were accurate, *Nippon* was probably not the venue that an aspiring haiku poet would have chosen if given a completely free hand. Katsunan's comments suggest he personally had little knowledge of (or interest in) haiku and held a low opinion of the major poets of the day, Kakuta Chikurei 角田竹冷 (Shinpei 真平, 1857–1920) and old-school master Kikakudō Eiki 其角堂永機 (1823–1904). *Nippon* was also not the kind of newspaper to go in for popular entertainment, since unlike most of its competitors, it did not carry serialized prose fiction, which it maintained was frivolous and immoral. Among a series of caricatures published on New Year's Day 1890 depicting things of which the newspaper did not approve, for instance, was a "novelist" (*shōsetsuka*). Shown asleep at his desk, the novelist's thoughts were revealed in three large graphs appearing above his head, which read, "Beautiful nude women!" (*rabijin*).[14] *Nippon*'s copy was also relatively difficult, deliberately aimed at an educated audience. Katsunan once remarked that if readers couldn't understand *Nippon*'s heavily Sinicized text without the

FIGURE 3.1 Caricature of a "novelist," *Nippon*, January 1, 1890. The large graphs above his head read, "Beautiful nude women!"; other things in his thoughts include "selling his name by writing for newspapers" and "going to the Yoshiwara [licensed quarters] for research purposes."

aid of additional glosses, he didn't want them reading his paper anyway (*yonde moraitakunai*).[15]

Nobody, then, would have picked up *Nippon* in the hopes of finding a popular genre such as haiku being executed in serious fashion; not only was there no regular haiku column but also haiku were not featured in the newspaper's main poetry column, Garden of Letters (Bun'en). Short-form verse did appear occasionally in *Nippon* prior to Shiki's hiring, usu-ally under the catch-all rubric "seventeen-syllable poetry" (*jūnana moji*) and usually providing a little levity amid the otherwise heavy diet of edi-torials. At times, the newspaper displayed a streak of silliness that belied its rather staid reputation, as in the case of a series of twenty plant-based puns commenting on procedural problems at the Diet:

> *hito mina iu kondo no gichō wa yari*　　*sugi*
> 人皆云ふ今度の議長は遣り　　　　　　杉

> "Everyone's saying, this time the speaker's really ex-*cedar*-ed
>   his authority."

> *hitori Kaishintō kaisan no unmei o*　　*matsu*
> 獨り改進黨解散の運命を　　　　　　松

> "Just the Reform Party, left alone *pine*-ing for the dissolution."

> *yonhyakuen dake de kaisan to kite wa tsuma*　　*ran*
> 四百圓丈で解散と来ては妻　　　　　　蘭

> "The Diet dissolved over just four hundred yen, now that's an
>   *orchid* situation!"[16]

Without question, however, Katsunan's star poetic performer at *Nippon* was Kokubu Seigai, seen in the previous chapter sparring with Mori Kainan through the newspaper's pages. Even before the Kegon Falls exchanges, Seigai was widely known as a forceful and publicly engaged poet. Virtually from the first, while working with Katsunan at what had been *Tōkyō denpō*, Seigai had used his *kanshi* to wade into the polit-ical issues of the day. In August 1888, he had written in protest at the miserable conditions and financial exploitation of miners employed by the Mitsubishi Corporation on islands off the coast of Nagasaki:

泣孤島	*Tears on the Lonely Islands*
仰告皇天天不答	They look up and lament to the gods of Heaven, but Heaven does not answer,
俯訴后土地不納	They look down and appeal to the gods of the Earth; Earth refuses them.
三千坑夫苦倒懸	Three thousand miners, fit to collapse from their suffering;
帝澤所及何偏狭	Narrow indeed is the span of imperial munificence![17]
. . .	

The blessings of the emperor's rule should, if the realm is being governed correctly, spread to all, and so the suffering of the miners suggests the absence of correct government. In this instance, the criticism directed by Seigai and other public intellectuals was indeed effective, embarrassing the Meiji government into conducting an investigation and working to improve the miners' conditions. Seigai continued his work in this vein through *Tōkyō denpō*'s reinvention as *Nippon* and for much of the subsequent decade, and although his constant antigovernment invective made him immensely popular, it was not without cost to the newspaper. Precise correspondences are difficult to establish, but it seems that on at least one occasion, in early 1893, one of Seigai's poems may have been enough to trigger a suspend-publication order. When the ban was lifted, Seigai responded by fulminating as follows:

十回多	*As Many as Ten Times*
敢劾私心逞揣摩	I dare to follow my own thoughts, boldly striving for truth;
忠言每每觸形科	My loyal words meet with punishment each and every time.
蝉蛙喧擾斯民已	Cicadas, frogs, their clamor has vexed the people;

蠧賊猖狂如国何	What to make of such a country, where verminous insects rampage unchecked?
発兌纔経四年久	Only four years have passed since we began to print,
停刊已到十回多	And our publishing bans number already as many as ten.
縦然毀硯折毫蓋	Let them, in their willfulness, smash my inkstone and break my brush cover,
独我丹心不可磨	But my loyal thoughts alone, those they can never erase.[18]

The columnist says: In the morning we speak of the national interest, in the evening of harmony among the people. Ah! our loyal pronouncements have many times met with harsh punishment. Four years is not a long stretch of time, but already we have accumulated ten bans. What can we say of such a country where one's brush and inkstone may be smashed?

The implication of the commentary to the poem is not hard to understand: since Seigai's only concern is for the welfare of the nation, villainous indeed must be the government that would wish to censor him. As this vehemence might suggest, although he was clearly valuable to the newspaper, Seigai was not an easy character to handle. Initially assigned to run the newspaper's Garden of Letters poetry column, Seigai seems to have grown to dislike soliciting and editing verses from readers, and particularly to dislike interacting with poets such as Mori Kainan and Yazuchi Kinzan, on account of their political leanings and close association with the cabinet of Itō Hirobumi. As we saw in the previous chapter, Kainan and Seigai's poetics and politics were very much at odds, and though *Nippon*'s editor in chief (*henshū shunin*), Kojima Kazuo 古島一雄 (1865–1952), organized a meeting between Seigai and Kainan and Kinzan to attempt to clear the air, Kojima apparently came away convinced that Seigai was right in disliking them and that the two government employees were, in using their poetry to ingratiate themselves with their superiors, little more than "a sort of high-class male geisha" (*isshu no kōtō hōkan*).[19]

Over Katsunan's objections, then, Seigai ultimately walked away from the Garden of Letters, the running of the column being handed over to fellow *kanshi* and tanka poet Katsura Koson 桂湖村 (1838–1938), with Seigai devoting himself to writing his political commentary on a full-time basis in his column Forest of Criticism (Hyōrin). Katsunan seems to have been annoyed by Seigai's move not only on the grounds of insubordination but also because he had reservations as to whether political poetry was even literature at all and felt Seigai was not properly applying his considerable talent. Trying unsuccessfully to reassert control over his star poet through Kojima's good offices, Katsunan complained to Kojima that "Seigai is at fault here, but you're to blame, too, because you egg him on" (*Seigai mo warui ga kimi ga odateru kara warui*).[20] Katsunan's annoyance also comes through in an undated letter he sent to Kojima, quoted in the latter's autobiography:

> Reading over yesterday's poems [in Forest of Criticism], all [Seigai] is doing is taking the language of the newspaper editorial page and adding rhyme and tonal prosody, and on top of that, his language is stale in the extreme. This is not poetry, it's prose. . . .
>
> I've been warned by people several times that Forest of Criticism isn't interesting anymore, but Seigai, the heart and soul of the whole operation, is entirely unconcerned, so what can I do? This is all because you ignore my views on the matter and give him special treatment.
>
> You know, I read yesterday's Forest of Criticism again this morning, and it brought me out in a cold sweat. As a poet's work goes, it is far too shallow and insipid; it has the odor of a work by some rustic bumbler from the sticks. There has to be something you can say to Seigai. Look, at least for the moment, will you just stop giving Forest of Criticism special treatment?[21]

By his own recollections, Kojima comes across as an agent provocateur, the one largely responsible for ensuring a political slant to much of *Nippon*'s poetic content even against Katsunan's own wishes. Kojima, a remarkable character who was still active in politics even after the Pacific War, had been interested in the uses of poetry as political commentary almost from the very start at *Nippon*. This interest had seemingly been sparked by a reader's sending in a *senryū* commenting on the assassination of Education Minister Mori Arinori 森有礼 (1847–1889), which had happened February 11, 1889, the same day *Nippon* published its inaugural issue:

廃刀論者包丁をわきにさし

The "No-Sword" Guy Wears a Kitchen Knife—through the Chest

yūrei ga	our well-mannered ghost
burei no mono ni	gets got by someone
shite yarare	with no manners at all.[22]

有礼が無礼のものにしてやられ

Back in 1876, Mori had been involved in the passing of a law forbidding the wearing of swords by the now-defunct warrior class and had only barely escaped assassination at the time. Though the banning of swords does not seem to have been the motivation for his actual assassination, the author of this particular verse, signed as Nishimatsu Jirō 西松二郎 (dates unknown), likely would not have known that. Inspired by this verse, Kojima subsequently scoured Tokyo to find someone who could write politically focused works for the newspaper, but though he contacted several *senryū* masters, he was ultimately unsuccessful.[23]

Given this background, and the fact that Shiki had, as a junior employee, to do more or less what his superiors instructed him to do, it is not surprising to find Kojima behind Shiki's production of topical haiku at *Nippon*. Kojima recalls explaining as much to Shiki early on in his career:

On the way home from the newspaper offices, I dragged Shiki into a certain yakitori shop, and in the manner of a senior colleague I explained to him what special efforts you needed to make when applying haiku to newspapers and that there was a certain sort of knack to newspaper-based literature [*shinbun bungaku*]. He listened with an expression on his face that said, "I know all this, you don't need to tell me," but he didn't say anything much. The look on his face at the time rather got on my nerves, and I thought, "Ugh, this guy's really full of himself." A month later, on precisely the two hundred and tenth day of the year, *Nippon* found itself the subject of a ban order. As a kind of test, I asked Shiki if he could come up with anything, and almost before I had finished speaking he had grabbed his brush and written,

kimigayo mo	even in Thy Glorious Reign—
nihyakutōka wa	September storms
arenikeri	are just as fierce.

. . . So I was delighted, as if my point had been proved by this one verse, and right away I thought that we could put haiku on current events on the page along with Seigai's Forest of Criticism column, and I asked Shiki to compose some more topical haiku.[24]

Though Kojima may not have realized it—he, like Katsunan, claimed to know almost nothing about haiku at the time[25]—the verse Shiki produced was probably an inversion of an earlier poem by Edo-period poet Ōshima Ryōta 大島蓼太 (1718–1787):

kimigayo ya	Thy Glorious Reign!
nihyakutōka mo	even September storms
monowasure	completely forgotten.[26]

君が代や二百十日も物忘れ

By folk tradition, the two hundred and tenth day of the year was a dangerous time, when violent storms were likely to occur. In the traditional cosmological view of the world and its government, good rule should prevent natural disasters. Ryōta's verse thus celebrates peace in the realm, whereas Shiki implies the opposite: the realm is being governed by the unworthy, and their rule thus does nothing to pacify the elements.

SHIKI AND TOPICAL HAIKU

Although Kojima worked to skew *Nippon*'s poetry toward the topical, his efforts do not seem to have been particularly unusual in the newspaper world as a whole. At the *Yomiuri* and *Kokumin shinbun* newspapers,

Kakuta Chikurei, another esteemed haiku poet who would later become a rival to Shiki in haiku reform, became known for his own topical haiku through the early 1890s. Writing under various pen names that all incorporated the graph for "leisure" (*hima*), Chikurei also ran contests to solicit topical haiku from readers as well.[27] In one of the *Yomiuri*'s haiku competitions, announced toward the end of 1893, Chikurei specified the set topics, which should contain either of the phrases "this spring morning" (*kesa no haru*) or "nice and leisurely" (*nodoka*). "This spring morning" should, he instructed, relate to newspapers in some way, whereas "nice and leisurely" should make reference to the Diet.[28] One set among the verses received, published in the *Yomiuri* on March 31, 1894, provided a topically relevant spin on newspapers by pairing two haiku about *Nippon* being banned yet again.

Shiki's own work in topical haiku, in which he had dabbled before being formally hired and which he would continue sporadically over the subsequent four years, took a variety of different forms. On occasion, he composed original verses to order, as in the following sequence on the machinations of the Diet and foreign affairs published in *Nippon* December 20, 1893:

議長星隕	*The Speaker of the House: A Fallen Star*

saeru yo ya   a freezing night—
ōboshi hitotsu   a single large star
nagareyuku   comes falling to earth.

冴る夜や大星一つ流れゆく

官紀振粛上奏案

On a Bill to Enforce Official Discipline among Bureaucrats[29]

shukushuku to   in dignified manner,
uma ni muchiutsu   giving a horse a good whipping—
shimoyo kana   a frosty night!

粛々と馬に鞭うつ霜夜かな

停會   *On the Suspension of the Diet*

kogarashi no	bitter winter winds,
tōka bakari wa	for ten days or so
yasumikeri	giving it a rest.[30]

凩の十日許りは休みけり

These three verses express irritation and amusement at the machinations of the Diet, all couched in seasonal imagery of coldness befitting the winter month of December. The first verse refers to an upcoming no-confidence motion in the speaker of the house (*gichō*), Hoshi Tōru 星亨 (1850–1901). Hoshi's surname is also the Japanese word for "star," and so the verse likens the speaker's fall to that of a shooting star falling to earth. The implicit contrast between the celestial image of the shooting star and the earthly machinations of party politics, a juxtaposition Shiki used in other satirical poetry, adds an extra note of irony to the poem. Other verses from the same day discuss foreign affairs, implicitly urging Japan's politicians to take a more aggressive stance in protecting the nation's interests:

千島艦事件   *On the* Chishima *Incident*[31]

rikimu hodo	the harder you fight
nao hanekaesu	the better you can turn it back—
arare kana	a hailstorm!

りきむ程猶はね返す霰かな

条約厲行案

On the Bill to Enact Strict Enforcement of the Treaties[32]

hatsuyuki ya	first snowfall—
kutsu monnai e	boots shall not pass
iru bekarazu	through the gate.

初雪や靴門内へ入るべからず

The first verse urges the Japanese government to more aggressively pursue redress for the loss of life involved in the *Chishima* incident; the second likewise urges that the terms of the 1858 unequal treaties, which allowed non-Japanese to reside and conduct commercial activities only in specifically designated areas, be strictly enforced. Boots, and by implication the Westerners who wear them, cannot be allowed to tread unchecked on Japanese soil. The ensuing debate over the "strict enforcement question" became so heated that the Diet was once again dissolved shortly after, a situation alluded to in the "bitter winter winds" verse earlier in the same sequence.

FIGURE 3.2 Caricature of a corrupt politician as a frog, *Nippon*, January 1, 1890. The larger graphs at the right of the picture read, "Bribery."

On occasion, Shiki also found ways to reinvent existing works to give them a topical spin. As we have seen in Seigai's poetry, a common insult directed at officials perceived as unworthy or corrupt was to liken them to clamoring frogs; established practice among the *shishi* of the late Edo period, this was something *Nippon* did fairly frequently. Among the same set of caricatures depicting the novelist on New Year's Day 1890, for instance, was a picture of a fat frog dressed in formal robes sitting in front of a low table filled with promissory notes and land deeds; with the frog presumably intended to represent a politician, the caption read, simply, "Bribery" (*wairo*).[33] Given the prominence of frogs in both *haikai* and contemporary political discourse, Shiki elected to bring the two together in a heavily ironic piece of March 1, 1893, titled "A Frog's Travels":

A Frog's Travels[34]

Born in a watery ditch and going out to visit the muddy fields—this isn't very elegant, but could it be because he fears that if he is in clear, pure water everyone will be able to see him? [Ki no] Tsurayuki listed him along with the warbler and counted him among the great *waka* poets, and [Ono no] Tōfū saw him and became a master of calligraphy for the ages.[35] Seen by Bashō jumping into a pond, he showed everyone the *sabi* of *haikai*;[36] one would think that this would be an unparalleled honor, but since he sits from morning to night croaking in his old well everyone laughs at him on account of the narrowness of his world—what shabby treatment![37] He may not be that bright, but he's feted for his valor in the frog wars.[38] And not only that but he unintentionally acquires all kinds of nicknames; Hibiya is famous as a place to hear his recitals, and when he comes out at Tamagawa in Ide he is surely guilty of the sin of loquaciousness.[39] Of course, the point of these frog wars is after all to gain possession of the rice field:

ta ichi mai	a frog croaking—
moteba haru zo to	"if I can get just one paddy field
naku kawazu	then it'll be my spring!"
—KATORI[40]	

田一枚もてば春ぞと鳴く蛙　可都里

And then one fights an election:

iku suberi   giving his all,
hone oru kishi no   slipping down, over and over—
kawazu kana   ah, the riverbank frog!
—KYORAI[41]

いくすべり骨折る岸の蛙かな　　去来

And if you win, you'll be renowned throughout the realm:

kaerugo ya   a baby frog—
rikō ni naru to   once he figures out what he's doing
yakamashiki   he's really annoying.
—KEIKA[42]

蛙子や利口になるとやかましき　　渓花

And then when the Diet opened they all charged for the capital, hoping to be first:

tobigao ni   on his face, as he's jumping,
funbetsu mienu   you can't see the clever expression—
kawazu kana   ah, the frog!
—CHŌSUI[43]

飛顔に分別見えぬ蛙かな　　鳥酔

ichi shian   he's got a plan
dekite tobikomu   and so he jumps right in—
kawazu kana   ah, the frog!
—KEIZAN[44]

一思案出来て飛び込む蛙かな　　鶏山

The play on frogs as politicians continued the next day, with Shiki producing another piece titled "The Frog's Defeat" (Kaeru no haiboku), in which the unfortunate amphibian was called to account and forced to beg for forgiveness for his financial improprieties.

TOPICAL VERSE AND POETIC EXCHANGE: *SHŌ NIPPON*'S CENSORSHIP PROBLEMS

The poetry column in a Meiji newspaper was to a great extent an open space, a published poem always understandable as an invitation to readers to respond. In the case of poetry with an explicitly partisan slant, the incentive to engage in exchange was perhaps even greater, the exchange of poetry functioning as an expression of both shared poetic bonds and shared political views. In this case, the process of poetic exchange through print media takes on an additional political aspect, verse exchange becoming a dialogue between reader and columnist on the issues of the day. One such example of poetic exchange with an explicitly political aspect comes in a sequence from early in Shiki's career, from late 1892, with another sequence of poems lampooning the lavish spending and dissolute habits of the country's politicians.

The origins of the sequence appear to have been a pseudonymous reader's set of eight *kanshi* that played on the Eight Famous Views of Xiao and Xiang (Ch. *xiaoxiang bajing*, J. *shōshō hakkei*). This was a group of famous sights in the vicinity of the Xiao and Xiang Rivers in southeastern China, such as Night Rain on the Xiao and Xiang Rivers and Autumn Moon over Lake Dongting. First codified in Song China, this group of eight views also became popular as an inspiration for poetry and painting in Japan beginning in the fifteenth century.[45] The iteration published in *Nippon* retains the central motifs, such as "night rain" and "autumn moon," but in place of Chinese landscapes substitutes parts of contemporary Tokyo. In the following quoted poems, the locations in question are Shinbashi and Akasaka, both of which were known as prime spots for politicians and government employees to drink and carouse, often in the company of female entertainers.[46] Two of the eight poems, along with a headnote written by Shiki, are discussed in the following:

The Eight Famous Views of Hibiya[47]
>   With the great battles between the two factions of those in government and those who are not, things have gotten rather noisy these

days, but even so there are some people who don't seem to mind. The following work came in purporting to describe the Eight Views of Hibiya. Far away there are the Eight Famous Views around China's Xiao and Xiang Rivers; nearer to home are the Eight Famous Views of Ōmi. What was old is now become new. An interesting twist, so we have printed it here.

赤坂夜雨	*Night Rain in Akasaka*
山王祠畔小繁華	A lively little gathering at the bank by Hie Shrine,[48]
幾処紅桜残柳斜	Here, there, scarlet *sakura*, a neglected willow drooping.
秋雨蕭蕭燭甚剪	Dank autumn drizzle, the lamp wicks trimmed low;
夜深猶駐議員車	Late grows the hour, and the Diet man's carriage is still there.

新橋秋月	*Autumn Moon at Shinbashi*
民選其名実宦遊	The people chose them, and rightly they're called public em-*play*-ees,[49]
新橋楽事属渠侪	Joining their fellows to indulge in Shinbashi's delights.
定知政費竟難減	For surely you know, after all, public money can never run out.
明月美人同一楼	A bright moon and a beautiful girl, right there in the same room.

In addition to the headnote, Shiki also produced matching haiku responses to each of the eight *kanshi*, the "night rain" and "autumn moon" verses being as follows:

赤坂夜雨	*Night Rain in Akasaka*

Deep within the drinking house a beautiful woman is sad and downcast. Her samisen sounds as if it were half-asleep, its tone melancholy, and there is little in the way of vigor to her playing of finger games, so the house loses most of the time. He didn't go to Shinbashi, but rather to Akasaka; I guess it's because he's the sort of man who can spend vast sums of money and still have plenty left over.[50]

horoyoi no	just a little tipsy
hauta namaru ya	her song falters—
sayo shigure	in the night, autumn showers.

ほろ酔の端唄なまるや小夜時雨

新橋秋月　　　　*Autumn Moon at Shinbashi*

Green wines and red lanterns: drinking house after drinking house is like this. Those drinking like cows and eating like horses within them—are they officials? Commoners? Samurai? Farmers? When you have to deal with getting your long beard matted with drool, and when you get called a fool in an undignified manner by a voice from somewhere while you're giving a long, pointless speech, then retreating into your own pointless little reality must be quite fun.

tsuki to sake	wine, and the moon.
teki mo mikata mo	neither enemy nor ally
nakarikeri	do they possess.[51]

月と酒敵も味方もなかりけり

Each of the original *kanshi* and haiku responses present mocking vignettes of the Diet men's activities in the licensed quarters. The first verse is a relatively subtle lampoon of the politician as a wealthy arriviste, throwing around large sums of (likely improperly acquired) money in the refined venue of Akasaka.[52] The second verse is openly contemptuous of the lavish and vulgar consumption habits of the politician, suggesting the classically simple pairing of wine and the moon as a celestial contrast to the Diet man's earthly scheming. Their behavior, the verse suggests, stems from a need to put aside for a time the opprobrium that comes with their boorish and unpopular public behavior and to retreat into the world of the licensed quarters. Taken together, the *kanshi* and haiku verses thus heap scorn on the carousing Diet men in a number of ways. Aside from the basic moral failing of spending public money in the licensed quarters, they also make fools of themselves there; they spend huge sums of public money on entertainers, are undignified in their eating and drinking, and do not merit their airs of superiority to other social classes.

The following day, *Nippon* published a set of responding *kyōka* by a reader signing himself Aoyama Hattenshi 青山秡天士 (dates unknown), who was a regular contributor to *Nippon*'s pages throughout 1892 and 1893. This contribution continued the parodic adaptation of the eight famous sights along the lines Shiki had suggested:

赤坂夜雨	*Night Rain in Akasaka*

okane kara	"before you play,
saki ni nedarare	you have to pay," she insisted,
nurekanete	so he failed to get wet,
furare furareshi	got rained on *and* brushed off—
akagaeru kana	*ah*, the red-backed frog!

お金からさきにねだられぬれかねてふられふられし赤蛙かな

新橋秋月	*Autumn Moon at Shinbashi*

kawazu naku	frogs croaking,
atarashi hashi wa	the hour grows late
sayofukete	at the new bridge.
hisoka ni noboru	the moon at Shinbashi
Shinbashi no tsuki	shiftily sneaks into the sky.[53]

かはつ鳴く新橋はさよふけてひそかにのぼり新橋の月

Aoyama develops Shiki's idea that Tokyo's courtesans dislike the carousing politicians. Where the courtesan in Shiki's Akasaka poem had been weak and yielding, Aoyama's is outright hostile, humiliating the

Diet man by requesting payment up front for her services.[54] *Nurekanete* (failed to get wet), a fairly obvious sexual reference, is ironically juxtaposed with the following line's double play on *furare*, meaning both "to be rejected" and "to get rained on." Despite the bawdy twist it adopts, Aoyama's response is not entirely devoid of subtlety: the first two lines contain a play on the poetic epithet (*utamakura*) Karasaki, a promontory on the shores of Lake Biwa that, when seen amid the evening rain, was also famous as one of the Eight Views of Ōmi. Aoyama's "autumn moon" poem combines elements of both previous works; the reveling politicians are, yet again, seen as frogs croaking out their song once night falls. Where Shiki's poem suggests the moon as innocent and apart from earthly scheming, the closing lines of Aoyama's poem have the moon rise shiftily (*hisoka ni*). Perhaps, having spent so long in the company of so many untrustworthy characters, even the moon is now engaging in unethical activities and trying to avoid scrutiny.

Underpinning the exchange of this kind of political poetry was more than simply the idea of a newspaper as shared sociopoetic space; rather, we can detect a solidarity and sense of unity based on antipathy toward a shared enemy—namely, the Meiji government and its representatives. The practices of poetic sociality, in this context, take on an entirely new and partisan aspect. The bonds of political community were made all the stronger by the Meiji government's direct efforts to put a stop to this kind of open mockery and criticism, in the shape of its censorship protocols. One case study here is *Shō Nippon*, a short-lived sister publication to *Nippon* that appeared during the spring and summer of 1894, just as the nation was preparing for the imminent prospect of the First Sino-Japanese War. *Shō Nippon*'s genesis lies in various tactics employed by the *Nippon* staff to counter the impact of cease-publication orders. In 1891, the newspaper had tried creating a stand-in publication (*migawari*) that could be published as a substitute for the main newspaper whenever it was banned. A common strategy at the time, *Nippon* had created *Dai Nippon*, which first appeared on November 23, 1891. Registered to the same parent company as *Nippon*, *Dai Nippon* mostly (though not always) appeared when its parent newspaper was subject to a ban order. The *Dai Nippon* strategy proved unsuccessful, however: the Meiji government was not fooled by the substitute publication, and despite *Nippon*'s protests that the two were entirely separate, *Dai Nippon* was banned on several occasions. In its September 10, 1892, edition, not coincidentally around the time that Shiki was composing his earlier haiku on the two hundred tenth day of the year, the substitute paper lamented that "whenever *Nippon* is banned, *Dai Nippon* also follows a day later" (*Nippon wa teishi serare ichinichi o koete Dai Nippon mo mata teishi seraru*).[55]

Nippon's response was to modify the stand-in strategy and try again. The new paper, *Shō Nippon*, would be registered as a separate company with a separate address (in fact the second floor of a local soba-noodle shop) and would publish six days a week, later rising to seven, regardless of whether *Nippon* was subject to a ban order. Katsunan appointed Shiki as editor in chief, though not without reservations. For one, he was not convinced that Shiki was ready for the responsibility, although Kojima felt that Shiki's literary talents would prove useful, and as Kojima also pointed out, they had no one else on staff who was really suited for the job.[56] In terms of content, Katsunan and his editorial staff, especially Kojima, took the decision to break with the parent paper and develop *Shō Nippon* along the lines of a small newspaper (*koshinbun*) featuring illustrations, glossed copy, serialized fiction, and columns carrying social news and gossip.[57]

In practice, and in terms of its content, readership, and general tone, *Shō Nippon* might be viewed as somewhere between a *koshinbun* and an *ōshinbun*, carrying popular content such as gossip and serialized fiction while at the same time maintaining a relatively educated audience and a sense of moral respectability, steering clear of the salacious excesses of other small newspapers. From the first, *Shō Nippon* strove to maintain the highbrow tone of its parent publication, noting on the front page of the inaugural issue on February 11, 1894, that it had been created as a "family-oriented" (*kateimuki*) publication. The reason given for this approach was that "seventy to eighty percent of the content of contemporary *koshinbun* consists of immoral relations between men and women, and so they are not fit to be read in any scene of familial coziness in a respectable home." In contrast, it declared, *Shō Nippon* would focus on moral education (*fūkyō*).[58] In terms of literary content, it carried serialized novels and in fact seemed to have a special emphasis on the literary arts, carrying haiku, *waka*, and *kyōka*, as well as reviews of *rakugo* comic monologue and kabuki theater performances. It did not carry *kanshi*, likely wishing both to reach as broad an audience as possible and to steer clear of any lingering controversy attached to Seigai's poems. The sense that *Shō Nippon* was designed first and foremost to stay out of trouble was heightened by the absence, initially at least, of any editorial or overtly political content, although the newspaper did carry national and international news stories.

As might have been expected from the preferences of its editor, haiku was probably *Shō Nippon*'s most vibrant genre. Shiki had been entrusted with the running of *Shō Nippon* just as he was beginning to spread his wings in literary criticism as well as haiku, and even Kojima had come to realize that Shiki was happier pursuing his own interests in haiku; in allocating Shiki space for a permanent haiku column in the newspaper beginning in the spring of 1893, Kojima had joked that the column would be allowed "extraterritoriality" (*chigai hōken*) and that he would not interfere in its running.[59] At around this time, Shiki had had some success in linking up his small and primarily student-based group of poets with another reform-minded group, the Friends of the Pasania Tree (Shii no Tomo Kai).[60] Impressed by Shiki's first major critical work, *Dassai shooku haiwa* (Talks on haiku from the otter's den), which had been serialized in *Nippon* from June 26 to October 20, 1892, Itō Shōu 伊藤松宇 (1859–1943), the leader of the group, asked Takatsu Kuwasaburō, one of the authors of the influential *Nihon bungakushi* (A literary history of Japan, 1890), to put him in touch with Shiki, since the latter had been Takatsu's student.

When haiku made their first appearance in *Nippon*'s Garden of Letters literary column on March 5, 1893, four of the poems were by Shiki's student friends and four by the older members of the Shii no Tomo group.[61] Over the course of the next year or so, the combined group seems to have grown considerably in number, with thirty-three new names appearing in Shiki's column at *Nippon*. Being given control of *Shō Nippon* was thus an important moment in Shiki's career; with a burgeoning group of followers and growing reputation in the literary world, he now had a chance at expansion. *Shō Nippon* did this in one main way: it ran a haiku competition every month of its existence, with increasing numbers of participants each time. From the very first issue, *Shō Nippon* solicited haiku from its readers, to be judged and selected by Shiki and his cohorts. In itself, a newspaper-based haiku competition was nothing particularly new, since Chikurei and popular novelist Ozaki Kōyō 尾崎 紅葉 (Tokutarō 徳太郎, 1868–1903) had already run similar projects at the *Yomiuri* to considerable success.[62] One significant difference, however, was frequency: the *Yomiuri*'s competition was held only once per year, whereas *Shō Nippon* ran its competition every month. In contrast to the *Yomiuri*'s cash prizes, no financial incentive was offered, although the winners of each month's competition would receive a month's free subscription to the newspaper.

Held every month, with the deadline on the twenty-fifth and the winners published during the opening days of the following month, the haiku competition proved enormously successful, garnering participation from all around the country in rapidly increasing numbers. In the five months during which it was in existence, *Shō Nippon*'s haiku competition featured poems from around 1,650 separate pen names, the numbers of participants increasing exponentially as the competition went on.[63] Exact circulation figures for *Shō Nippon* are not recorded, but given the relatively small circulations of the time, clearly a large proportion of the paper's readers were sending in their work, even if the numbers remained small in absolute terms compared with other contemporary competitions.[64] The majority of entries came from locations in Tokyo, but there were also strong showings from Kyoto, Nagano, Matsuyama, and even as far away as Aomori and Okinawa.[65] Several of those featured in the collection would in fact go on to play active roles in their own provincial haiku groups under the umbrella of *Hototogisu* beginning in 1897.[66] Shiki also began to provide his critique of the best three poems from each month's competition from June 30 onward and had illustrator Nakamura Fusetsu provide an illustration for each of the three that he felt best captured the poem's qualities. Recruited through Kojima's offices, Fusetsu had been recommended by the Western-style artist Asai Chū 浅井忠 (1856–1907), and he and Shiki made fast friends; as is well known, Fusetsu would play a key role in helping Shiki to develop his concept of "sketching from life" (*shasei*) in haiku.[67]

Much of the success of the competition at *Shō Nippon* had to do with its being very narrowly targeted to a specific demographic—namely, students and educators, who seem to have responded to Shiki's haiku work with particular enthusiasm. The paper had, for instance, a regular column titled Local Educational News (Chihō gakuji han), carrying not only news items but also local gossip, details of scholarships available, teaching vacancies, and dates and places of entrance exams, all of which served to attract student readers.[68] In a similar vein, Shiki's later disciple and successor, Kawahigashi Hekigotō, recalled that Shiki had sent him five hundred copies of *Shō Nippon* out of the blue while he was studying at the Third Higher School in Kyoto; unsure of what to do with so many copies, he left them in the student lounge for his fellow students, which was probably exactly what Shiki had envisioned.[69] From an economic point of view it made sense for *Shō Nippon* to target the student demographic, for the numbers of male students receiving a middle school education had roughly quadrupled over the previous ten years and would break the one hundred thousand mark during the next ten, in 1904.[70] Given the still relatively small numbers in which newspapers circulated prior to the Sino-Japanese War, gaining the loyalties of such a demographic could make a huge difference to a newspaper's commercial viability, and, as we shall see in the next chapter, the particular tastes and views of the elite student and educator demographic did much to influence the formation of modern haiku.

Shō Nippon had, then, been an open space for readers to submit and publish their haiku from the start, and this proved important when it, too, fell afoul of governmental censorship. Although it had initially avoided opinion or editorial pieces, these, too, began to appear in *Shō Nippon* beginning on March 13, written by Kojima. The pressure to feature opinion pieces resulted in part from the continued censorship directed toward its parent publication, so it came perhaps as no surprise that *Shō Nippon* was also served with a ban order exactly one month after it had begun to feature Kojima's editorials. Imposed on April 13 and lasting for four days, the ban order was likely for an opinion piece the previous day that had criticized the government's handling of the treaty issue. Once the paper was able to resume printing on April 19, Kojima's next editorial denounced the ban as an abuse of government power, comparing the Meiji government to the villainous Qin dynasty (221–207 B.C.E.) of ancient China. The Qin rule lasted a mere fourteen years, its

FIGURE 3.3 Political cartoon protesting censorship of the newspaper *Shō Nippon*, April 26, 1894. The cartoon puns on the homonyms *hakkō*, "radiance," and *hakkō*, "publication." The text to the right explains that the woman is trying to extinguish the lamp so nobody will see how ugly she is.

downfall traditionally attributed to its burning of books and persecution of scholars, and *Shō Nippon*'s highly educated readership would surely have understood the reference.

Coming thus under attack from the government, a hitherto studiedly nonpolitical *Shō Nippon* began to introduce topical haiku into its pages. Since the newspaper was again banned in early May and on July 6, haiku addressing the issue of censorship were particularly prevalent:

発行停止   *On Suspend-Publication Orders*

yuku haru o   the passing spring—
mugon no hito no   ah, the sadness of a man
aware nari   who has no voice.[71]

行く春を無言の人のあわれなり

号外の発行停止	*On the Banning of the Extra Edition*

hototogisu	there are some men who
naku na to mōsu	would even tell the cuckoo
hito mo ari	that it should not sing.[72]

時鳥啼くなと申す人もあり

On April 26, one week after the first ban to be imposed upon *Shō Nippon* was lifted, Fusetsu also added his own protest in the shape of a satirical cartoon called "A Picture of Someone Extinguishing Radiance" (Hakkō o teishi suru zu). Punning on two possible readings of *hakkō* ("publication" and "radiance"), this drawing depicted an unattractive woman trying unsuccessfully to blow out a glass-shielded gas lamp so that the light would not reveal her ugliness to onlookers.[73] A few days later, a reader responded to Fusetsu's illustration and the themes it raised by sending in his own satirical haiku, and others followed, addressing censorship in terms of light and darkness:

題発光停止図	*In Response to the Ban Order Picture*

hi o keseba	they put out the fire,
mata kagerō no	but the shimmering has simply
moenikeri	flared back up again.[74]
—GOKYŌ	

火を消せば又陽炎の燃えにけり　　五狂

発行停止	*The Ban Order*

hitorimushi	as insects gather to the flame—
yo wa tokoyami to	the world has become swathed
narinikeri	in eternal darkness.[75]
—SEKKYŌ	

灯取虫世は常闇となりにけり　　石狂生

In addition to ongoing censorship, *Shō Nippon*'s readers also weighed in on matters of international concern, such as the assassination in Shanghai in March 1894 of the pro-Japanese Korean politician Kim Ok-gyun 金玉均 (J. Kimu Oku Kyun, 1851–1894) and the mutilation and dismemberment of his body after it was returned to Korea:

金玉均の惨刑   *Kim Ok-gyun's Harsh Punishment*

nakigara mo   even his corpse
kuzurete haru no   now broken apart—
tadon kana   charcoal in the spring.
—MUCHŌ

亡き骸もくづれて春の炭団かな   無腸生

Muchō's gruesome imagery likens Kim's blackened and broken body to crumbling blocks of charcoal; normally associated with winter, the sight of charcoal in spring is, for the poet, a jarring incongruity that serves to highlight the injustice of Kim's treatment.

As the summer of 1894 approached, the prospect of war overshadowed much of *Shō Nippon*'s activities. More and more space in the newspaper was devoted to accounts of events in China and on the Korean Peninsula, as well as to maps, illustrations, and discussions of the Korean people and their customs. The buildup to war also meant an increasingly paranoid government, and on June 7 *Shō Nippon* was once again ordered to suspend publication. Unusually, the ban was not for "disturbing public order" (*chian bōgai*) under Article 19 of the 1887 Newspaper Ordinance, as it usually was, but rather came under Article 22, which permitted the ministers of the army and navy to embargo articles relating to troop movements. *Shō Nippon* had reported the previous day that the Japanese government had notified the Qing government of the dispatch of troops, as had several other newspapers, but nevertheless the Meiji government elected to take the unusual step of prosecuting *Shō Nippon* and four other newspapers for this offense.

The trial was held at the Tokyo District Court on June 28, and the verdict returned the following day. Somewhat surprisingly, *Shō Nippon* was found not guilty on the grounds that it had not reported troop movements per se but on the fact that the Japanese government had notified the Qing of these movements.[76] This was a hollow victory, since the courts did not have the power to overturn a ban imposed at the ministerial level, and the damage had already been done in lost sales and advertising revenue. Furthermore, though the trial was quickly concluded, legal expenses would have been an unwelcome additional cost for *Nippon*, *Shō Nippon*'s parent publication, since the former had at times over the past few years struggled to pay its employees' salaries. *Nippon itself* had lost out on a substantial amount of revenue as a result of ban orders summing to nineteen days during May and June, and so it needed to economize further. *Shō Nippon* was therefore shut down on July 15, to Shiki and his companions' understandable disappointment, although all the staff were absorbed back into the parent publication rather than being deprived of their jobs. There was time for one final insult from the government: *Shō Nippon* was once again prosecuted on July 16, the day after it had ceased publication, with a guilty verdict being handed down on July 18 and the nominal editor and distributor sentenced, respectively, to four and three months in prison without hard labor.[77]

WHITHER POLITICAL POETRY?

On February 12, 1901, the *Yomiuri shinbun* put out a call to its readers asking them for "haiku on topical issues" (*jiji mondai haiku*), seemingly discerning no particular contradiction in terms in the idea of "topical haiku." More than a hundred years later, the same newspaper's website indicates that readers wishing to engage in verse-based social commentary should write "topical *senryū*" (*jiji senryū*).[78] What happened in the intervening hundred years?

The use of topical haiku as commentary on political matters is most noticeable during the 1890s, although it did not completely disappear after this time. In addition to *Nippon*, other newspapers such as the *Mainichi shinbun* and the *Yorozu chōhō* continued to feature topical verse sporadically into the early years of the twentieth century, and between 1913 and 1920 the popular-interest journal *Taiyō* ran a column specializing in topical haiku authored by the pseudonymous Kurohōshi. Nevertheless, the vision of haiku that Shiki and the *Nippon* Group later promoted and that became in large part the mainstream of "literary" haiku did not include its use as political commentary. In the first issue of its influential journal *Hototogisu* in January of 1897, *Nippon* Group elder statesman Naitō Meisetsu laid out a manifesto detailing the group's vision of haiku. Noting that many contemporary haiku exponents used the genre to satirize and point out flaws in human affairs (*jinji no ugachi o nasu*), Meisetsu argued that "if this is as far as haiku is going to go, then how is it different from *senryū*? No—actually, *senryū* would be rather better than haiku for this purpose."[79] Rather than run the risk of lapsing into vulgarity, Meisetsu argued, the poet would do better to stick to depicting the natural world. Meisetsu's manifesto in *Hototogisu*'s inaugural issue thus attempted to reimpose clear boundaries between haiku and *senryū* in the process of explaining why the *Nippon* Group was different.

Two months later, Shiki himself argued, in reviewing the work of his friend Seigai, that poems on political affairs such as governmental corruption were necessarily vulgar and could not therefore be literary. Discussing Seigai's recently published book *Dong Hu Poems* (*Shi Tōko*, 1897), a collection of verses from Forest of Criticism,[80] Shiki argued in *Nippon* that "the materials it addresses are almost all vulgar, coarse, unclean, and ugly. This is extremely unliterary. Therefore for the most part Forest of Criticism is not literature, and we should not judge it by the standards of literature."[81] Shiki did not say that Seigai's work was without merit or that he was a poor poet but that whatever else it might be, poetic political commentary was not literature.

Particularly after Shiki's death, with Takahama Kyoshi at the helm of *Hototogisu*, topical haiku were marginalized in favor of a vision of the genre focused on the natural world and on objective description. Yet as this chapter has shown, the practice of writing haiku to address political topics during the early 1890s played a major role in establishing the genre in the newspaper world and bringing it to the attention of the educated elite, who would later become Shiki's main constituency. Topical haiku was the means by which haiku made space for itself in the elite newspapers in particular and by which it first came on the radar of people such as Kojima and Katsunan, who, it will be recalled, both claimed to have no prior knowledge of the genre. In other words, the prevalence of topical haiku was a necessary first step to its being widely known and accepted as a serious poetic genre alongside *kanshi* and tanka.

The view that topical haiku helped launch the *Nippon* Group was also shared at the time by one contemporary critic, Okano Chijū 岡野知十 (Noritane 敬胤, 1860–1932). Chijū, who wrote for the *Mainichi shinbun* newspaper and was nominally affiliated with the rival Shūseikai group but who moved with relative ease among all the major groups, wrote in late 1895 of what he saw as the main reasons for the *Nippon* Group's recent success. Among them were the group's "momentum among students" (*shoseikan ni okeru seiryoku*), a "high and elegant tone" (*kakuchō no kōga*), and, crucially, "that their work contains a satirical element" (*fūshi no i o gūseshi*). Of these reasons, Chijū felt that the latter two were the most important, and that the verses produced in response to censorship had been among the most powerful; as he wrote, "They do not hold back from interjecting haiku into current affairs, and they have carried over the best parts of the style of poems in [Seigai's] Forest of Criticism; that they have applied this to haiku must, without a doubt, be the reason why they have gained so many plaudits from Meiji haiku exponents, and why the *Nippon* Group's style has such momentum."[82] Chijū's term "Meiji haiku exponents" (*Meiji haikyaku*) was intended to distinguish between the newer generation of educated haiku poets, of whom Shiki, Chikurei, and Kōyō were part, and the so-called old-school masters, many of whom had been born before the Meiji Restoration and of whom Chijū and most other newspaper haiku columnists did not approve. These old-school masters generally did not write topical haiku or engage with overtly political issues. One of the most prominent of these masters, Mimori Mikio, used his journal *Meirin zasshi* somewhat later, in 1901, to scold one of his disciples, who had taken to writing haiku criticizing political corruption. Mimori argued that such haiku "slandered the government" (*goseitai o hiki suru mono*) and were not in accordance with the idea of "being in harmony with others" (*hito to taishite wa waseshime[ru]*), which should be found in the work of one who professed to follow Bashō.[83]

It bears repeating that topical haiku were not at all unusual in the Meiji newspaper world of the 1890s, nor were they confined to Shiki, and they continued to be read and written even after Shiki's group had established a media foothold and could downplay the importance of such verse. Topical haiku had been, as Chijū suggested, an important part of what put the *Nippon* Group in a position to be able to think about the idea of the modern haiku in the first place, and in terms of attracting an audience, it also skewed the *Nippon* Group's demographics in such a way as to favor those of similar political persuasion to *Nippon*'s readers, most notably students and educators. As such, topical haiku had a notable effect on how the group continued to operate even after *Hototogisu* was inaugurated. Topical haiku were thus, almost by their nature, doubly exclusive; assuming a specific factional political allegiance, they advocated a view of contemporary Japanese nationalism in which the nation and the state were not necessarily the same thing and indeed were often at odds. A further divide was whether it was appropriate or not to use haiku to comment on matters political. This remained an unsettled question; even though the *Nippon* Group turned against such poetry, it continued to be practiced, suggesting the continued resilience of conflicting ideas of what exactly the genre could and could not do. As Meiji Japan's national literature project began to turn its attention toward poetry beginning in the mid-1890s, Shiki's *Nippon* Group entered the discussion of people, state, and national essence with considerable aplomb. Having arisen from a venue that was staunchly antigovernment, though, the *Nippon* Group, for all that it is widely credited with laying the foundations for the modern haiku, was generally minded to adopt a contrarian stance as to the validity of the entire national poetry project. This topic is the subject of the next chapter.

CHAPTER FOUR

Shiki's Plebeian Poetry

Haiku as "Commoner Literature," 1890–1900

In November 1946, shortly after Japan's defeat in the Pacific War, the critic and scholar of French literature Kuwabara Takeo 桑原武雄 (1904–1988) published a famous polemic in which he assailed haiku as, per the title of his piece, "A Second-Class Art" (Daini geijutsu). Developing a wide-ranging critique of haiku as it was practiced in contemporary Japan, Kuwabara asked whether haiku could be considered a truly modern art form, and his answer was emphatic—it could not. One of his key arguments for disqualifying haiku as true art was that it was too easy to compose, and so too many people practiced it. As he wrote, the effect on the Japanese public of "a genre like haiku, which is easily produced by anyone," was that "proper respect for art is not possible, nor will any great art ever come into being."[1] Contrasting this with the French public, which he noted had great respect for the writer and "did not regard art as something that one can create casually," Kuwabara argued that haiku must therefore be classed as a pastime or amusement, in a similar vein to flower arranging or growing bonsai trees. "I don't think anyone would criticize . . . the elderly for devoting themselves to chrysanthemum arranging or bonsai in their spare time," Kuwabara wrote, yet "one hesitates to call the cultivation of chrysanthemums art."[2]

Had Shiki been alive to read Kuwabara's piece, he might well have found himself agreeing with many of his arguments, while at the same time being infuriated by Kuwabara's conclusion. It has often been suggested that one of Shiki's more important critical contributions was to declare haiku to be literature;[3] yet, as this chapter shows, when Shiki declared something to be "literature," his understanding of that term had as much to do with social class as with aesthetics. For Shiki's reform-minded *Nippon* Group (*Nippon*-ha), as well as for a number of its competitors, part of the process of making haiku into literature was grappling with ideas of elite versus popular art and of poetry as serious literature versus as a form of amusement. Modern haiku had to be serious literature, not word games; it needed to be sublime in nature and removed from financial concerns; and it would have to be well-read literary men who were writing it, not ill-educated commoners. As Shiki and other contemporary groups interested in the "reform" of *haikai*, notably Ozaki Kōyō and Kakuta Chikurei's Autumn Winds Society (Shūseikai) and Tokyo Imperial University's University Group (Daigaku-ha, also known as the Tsukubakai, or "Tsukuba Society"), carved out their vision of what the modern haiku was—and more important, what it was *not*—their major concerns stretched not only to what should be composed but also to who should do the composing.

Shiki in particular directed a great deal of vitriol toward so-called old-school (*kyūha*) *haikai* masters such as Kikakudō Eiki, Mimori Mikio, and Ashin'an Setsujin 阿心庵雪人 (1872–1958), whom he painted as incompetent, venal, and ill educated in the process of his project of haiku reform. By the late 1890s, Shiki's project had begun to bear fruit, his disciples around the country slowly shutting old-school masters out of Japan's media spaces and finally marginalizing them entirely. Though Mimori Mikio had apparently had ten thousand members in his poetry society in early Meiji, after his death in 1910 at the age of eighty it took his disciples six years to locate a publisher willing to publish a posthumous collection of his works.[4] The narrative of modern haiku is in many ways a victor's history, almost always narrated from the point of view of Shiki and his disciples and framed in terms of the superior literary quality of their verse. By contrast, this chapter aims to reexamine established narratives of haiku reform by highlighting the way in which divides of social class and educational background were crucial to the formation of the "new haiku," and to rebalance the picture by giving something of a voice to the old-school masters themselves.

The picture this chapter paints is of modern haiku emerging not only as a literary genre but also as an elite and exclusive literary genre, the ideal practitioner envisioned as a highly educated man who had reached the highest echelons of the state education system. Haiku, Shiki contended, was harmed by the presence of too many "commoners" within its boundaries. Although later narratives both scholarly and popular after Shiki's death may have attached a positive significance to the idea of *haikai* and haiku as "commoner literature" and posited the boundaries of the *haikai* community as being coterminous with the national community, this was emphatically not the goal of Shiki's haiku reform movement.

"A UNIVERSAL POETRY, A JAPANESE POETRY": ORIGINS OF HAIKU AS "COMMONER LITERATURE"

One major point of poetic debate in the early 1890s, and in some ways a point of origin for later haiku reform movements, was the contention that *haikai* could be understood as "commoner literature" (*heimin bungaku*). This term first saw the light of day in a series of articles in the *Yomiuri shinbun* newspaper in the summer of 1890, in which the poet Maeda Ringai 前田林外 (Gisaku 儀作, 1864–1946) advanced the idea that Japan needed a national poetry that all members of society could compose. *Haikai*, he felt, would be ideal for that purpose; it was more suitable than *kanshi* or *waka* because "the natural societal need for *waka* and *kanshi* has now faded away";[5] not only that, but *haikai* itself had the positive virtues of being "a commoner poetry, a universal poetry, a Japanese poetry, a uniquely Oriental poetry" (*haikai wa heiminteki shifu nari, futsūteki shifu nari, Nihonteki shifu nari, Tōyō koyū no shifu nari*). *Haikai* had a special connection with the Japanese people, since "everyone among the people of our land, even at the lowest levels of society, possesses a certain amount of artistic spirit" (*waga hōjin wa katō shakai no mono sura tashō bijutsushin o yūsezaru wa nashi*).[6] In this vision of what Ringai called a national poetry (*kokushi*), poetic community and national community were essentially synonymous; the act of composing *haikai* could be a focal point for national unity, since all Japanese subjects possessed the potential to be a poet.

Other critics over the next couple of years further explored the idea of *haikai* as commoner literature. Novelist Aeba Kōson 饗庭篁村

(1855–1922), writing sporadically in the literary journal *Waseda bungaku* from October 1891 to September 1892, broadly concurred with Ringai in stating that "what I believe to be the essence of *haikai* is that *it is, in contemporary parlance, a kind of 'commonerist' literature, and thus of great interest.*"[7] The term "commonerist" (*heiminshugi*) had strong political overtones, since it had been used during the 1880s by the FPRM and in the writings of its leaders such as Tokutomo Sohō, publisher of the *Kokumin shinbun* newspaper.[8]

In using the term "commonerist" in his largely positive discussion of *haikai*, Kōson seemed to be gesturing toward the idea of *haikai* as a democratic literature in the sense that it was practiced by, and thus representative of, a majority of the Japanese people. The FPRM resonances of the idea of "commoner literature" were not lost on other critics: two former activists in that movement, poet Kitamura Tōkoku 北村透谷 (Montarō 門太郎, 1868–1894) and journalist Yamaji Aizan 山路愛山 (Yakichi 弥吉, 1864–1917), published their own pieces on this topic at the same time as Kōson's work was being serialized. Writing in *Jogaku zasshi* in July 1892, Tōkoku argued that *haikai* came from the very "heart and soul of commoner society" (*heimin shakai no shinkotsu yori idetaru mono*); yet he was much more ambivalent about this fact than Kōson, also contending that the genre reflected what he termed the commoner nihilism (*heiminteki kyomu shisō*) of the Tokugawa period.[9] In Tōkoku's view, *haikai* had indeed been a poetry of the common people, but as such it also reflected the fact that those same common people had been passive and politically apathetic under Tokugawa rule. Yamaji Aizan struck a similar note; writing in Sohō's journal *Kokumin no tomo* in September 1892, Aizan held that *haikai* had come to reflect the docility and pessimism of the common people under Tokugawa feudalism. He pondered, as a representative case, a teacher of popular linked verse in central Shizuoka Prefecture who was still venerated to the present day, three hundred years after his death. Aizan could not understand why this poet was revered thus, for he "did not fight for the people, did not appeal the suffering of commoners tilling fields in their sedge hats amid the rain to the officials at the levers of power, and never ran water through an irrigation channel to this waterless plain."[10] Aizan concluded that "*hokku* was a commoner poetry well suited to old Japan," for it "had not within it the vigor to struggle for freedom and equality, nor the spirit of accomplishment" (*sono naka ni wa jiyū byōdō no tame ni arasou no genki naku, yūi no seishin nashi*).[11]

Although they disagreed about the precise significance of the fact, these four commentators all shared the view that *haikai* was, for better or worse, a genre with a special connection to the common people of Japan. By contrast, and perhaps slightly surprisingly given his reputation as the founder of the modern haiku, Shiki had little time for the idea of *haikai* as commoner literature. Denying at first that *haikai* was commoner literature, Shiki later conceded that perhaps it was, but that if the "commoner" elements could be excised, then it need not remain so. Shiki made no mention of "commoner literature" in his first extended critical piece, "Talks on Haiku from the Otter's Den," which finished its serialization as Aizan's piece came out in October of 1892. He had clearly been paying attention to the ongoing discussion, however, since in one of his next major critical pieces, "Lashing Out at the Literary World" ("Bunkai yattsu atari," serialized in *Nippon* during March 1893), he made his thoughts on commoner literature abundantly clear:

> For the twin reasons that it is easy to compose and uses vernacular language, *haikai* of late has acquired the nickname of "commoner literature." This is a new entry in the Meiji dictionary, to be sure, but nobody seems able to say for certain whether this is meant as praise or mockery; in fact, many people's judgment is that it can be meant only as a slur. . . . True literature is sublime and elegant [*kōshō yūbi*] and does not necessarily gain the approval of large numbers of people, and this is because if anything in many respects "commoner" and "literature" are almost completely incompatible. If the world really wants to call *haikai* commoner literature, then for my part I obviously have no reason to stand in the way, but one should always bear in mind that this term "commoner literature" ceases to be a part of literature; rather, it is a new, extraliterary concept. Just take a look at the people who make up *haikai* society. As we all know, while nativist scholars, nobles, and various other kinds of people may become *waka* poets, wealthy recluses, local fixers, low-class entertainers, uneducated farmers, idle lawyers, and useless officials all love *haikai*. If these can be called men of literature, then Japanese literature has become no better than a group of women gathered around the

village well, or something to keep one amused on the way back from daily prayers.[12]

For Shiki, the notion of "commoner literature" was a contradiction in terms; if everyone could compose and appreciate haiku, then it would become diluted to the point where it ceased to be literature. Ease of composition and a broad social base were essentially synonymous with vulgarity and a status as nonliterary. It followed that the modern haiku could not encompass the entire national community, or even a majority of it. Rather, its status as truly literary depended on excluding a large proportion of its potential practitioner base, lest it descend to the level of a "group of women gathered around the village well."

LINKED VERSE, LITERARY PLAY, AND "MAD MEN": SHIKI AND *TEIKOKU BUNGAKU*

Shiki's well-deserved reputation for provocative polemic means that it is often wise to take his more extreme critical pronouncements with a grain of salt, yet his antipathy toward the idea of *haikai* as commoner literature remained entirely consistent, and the idea of truly literary haiku as the domain of an educated elite remained a keynote in the *Nippon* Group for the remainder of Shiki's life. Writing in early December 1902, three months after Shiki's death, *Nippon* Group member Ueno Sansen 上野三川 (Ryōzaburō 良三郎, 1866–1907) stressed to an audience of potential poets in Nagano Prefecture that haiku was not an easy form of poetry that anyone could do. Much like *kanshi* and *waka*, Sansen argued, one needed the right kind of background and training; *haikai* may have been commoner literature under the old masters, but the new school's haiku definitely was not.[13]

Shiki was far from the only haiku critic who found *haikai*'s apparent status as commoner literature to be problematic. Similar themes are evident in discussions on linked verse among the members of another competing new haiku group, the so-called University Group, and can be traced through the pages of its influential literary journal *Teikoku bungaku*. Inaugurated in January of 1895, *Teikoku bungaku* aimed to define a "literature of the nation's people" (*kokumin bungaku*) that lost nothing in comparison with English, French, or German literature. This focus earned them a critical broadside from Shiki, who apparently felt that "literature of the nation's people" would be the same thing as commoner literature:

> I've noticed the term "literature of the nation's people" here and there in journals and so forth, but I haven't the slightest idea what that's supposed to mean. If it is to be a literature large numbers of citizens can appreciate, then for the most part it will be literature of the very lowest rank, entirely unworthy of the term. If by "literature of the nation's people" they mean something extraliterary, then that's fine, but if not then I simply can't understand what they mean by the term. (I wonder if it means the same thing as commoner literature?)[14]

Presented once more with the proposition that a literary and national community might be the same, Shiki emphatically rejects the idea in much the same terms as he had done in 1892. To extend the franchise of literature to everyone in the nation would be to devalue literature as a whole.

Though Shiki disapproved of it, the University Group's conceptual framework of exploring the "literature of the nation's people" led the group to take *haikai* seriously as part of Japan's literary heritage. This was particularly true in the case of linked verse, an area of premodern literary practice to which the University Group devoted a great deal of attention. During 1895, Shiki for his part had already made his sweeping and often-quoted statement that "hokku *is literature, linked verse is not literature*" (*hokku wa bungaku nari, renpai wa bungaku ni arazu*).[15] Although sometimes interpreted as sounding the death knell for linked verse in Japan, in reality this statement did nothing of the sort; even as late as 1895, Shiki did not yet have the level of influence with which he is often credited, and in fact from the end of 1895 and beginning of 1896, Japan's literary journals, among them *Teikoku bungaku*, began to speak in terms of a revival of linked verse. Writing in the *Mainichi shinbun* in October 1895, haiku critic Okano Chijū noted that a number of newspapers, in particular the *Yamato shinbun, Yomiuri shinbun*, the *E-iri nippō*, and the *Mainichi* itself, had started carrying linked verse sequences in their literary columns.[16] Chijū voiced optimism that this would lead to "what might be termed a 'new linked verse'" (*iwayuru "shin renpai"*) to accompany the "new haiku";[17] likewise, discussing the same phenomenon a month later in November 1895, *Teikoku bungaku* noted what it called the birth cries (*koko no koe*) of a new linked verse.[18] Even the *Nippon* Group started to get in on the act, with the eighth chapter of Shiki's 1895 instructional manual *Haikai taiyō* going into considerable detail on how to compose linked verse, and Shiki, along with other members of the *Nippon* Group, published linked-verse sequences as part of a series of essays titled "Yōa zakki" (Various notes while recuperating) in *Nippon* during the autumn and winter of 1895.[19] The *Nippon* Group's main rivals found this apparent inconsistency puzzling; *Teikoku bungaku* wondered in November 1896 why Takahama Kyoshi was publishing linked-verse sequences in the literary magazine *Mesamashigusa* when the *Nippon* Group had declared such practices worthless,[20] and Chijū noted that Shiki's inclusion of linked verse in "Yōa zakki" was "a very strange thing to do given he's the main promoter of the notion that linked verse isn't literature" (*renpai hibungaku no shushōsha ni shite kore o nasu sukoburu ishō nari*).[21]

Moving with this tide of renewed interest in linked verse, in January of 1896 *Teikoku bungaku* published a piece that argued for more research on the topic: "Even if we were to accept that linked verse is superfluous [*muyō no chōbutsu*] to today's literary world, it is nevertheless a fact that a major part of Tokugawa literature is the domain of *haikai* practitioners. The need for historical research cannot stop simply with historical research into Western literature." Moreover, since both Bashō and Buson had seen linked verse as an important part of their activities, perhaps this new focus on linked verse would lead to increased study of both master poets, which could only be a good thing for the literary world.[22]

Yet even as it argued for increased attention to linked verse, *Teikoku bungaku*'s writers displayed a profound ambivalence about *haikai* in general, with many of them seemingly unable to view the *haikai* tradition as serious literature. Back in 1895, before the discussion turned to the possibility of a new linked verse, one commentator in *Teikoku bungaku* voiced skepticism that either *waka* or *hokku* were capable of expressing "a fully rounded poetic imagination" (*enman naru shisō*), although he also argued that *haikai* might have some value if retained as a "purely subjective form of poetry" (*shukanshi*), with which "those other than men of letters might broadly amuse themselves, and which I believe it would be good to preserve as an example of so-called 'commoner literature'" (*iwayuru heimin bungaku*).[23] *Haikai* was thus worth preserving as part of Japan's literary history but not something that those who held the privileged position of "men of letters" should actually practice themselves. In much the same way as Shiki had found the notion of commoner literature to be a contradiction in terms, this article posited a conceptual chasm between the playful literature of the commoner and the more serious work of the educated poet.

As 1896 wore on, the writers of the *Teikoku bungaku* group seemingly began to lose whatever enthusiasm they may have had for linked verse as a modern form of poetry. From its inaugural issue and throughout the whole of 1896, the journal serialized Sassa Seisetsu's 佐々醒雪 (1872–1917) *A Short History of Classical Linked Verse* (*Renga shōshi*) in more than a dozen installments.[24] Tracing the history of both classical and popular linked-verse practices from the earliest use of *waka*, Seisetsu's history in many ways provided the coup de grâce to the idea of linked verse as modern poetry. His history, for one, stopped at the Tenpō period (1831–1845), thereby conveying the impression that the death of linked verse in the present day was a historical fait accompli. Describing how classical linked verse had arisen from a desire among court nobles to devise a word game in response to *waka*'s narrowing confines of subject matter, Seisetsu documented its spread among commoners, monks, and warriors and its assumption of an increasingly plebeian quality. Diverging from the *waka*, which stood alone as the expression of an individual consciousness, linked verse for Seisetsu was and always had been essentially a word game:

> Classical linked verse was thus born under these circumstances, arising in response to the demand for a new word game. Its objective was not to express one's very own individual poetic emotion but to link up with someone else's poetry. Thus opportunities to express one's poetic emotion were far fewer than those in late-era *waka*; contests of skill and intricacy played out for the main part in artifice on the level of language, and for this reason classical linked verse in terms of its essence is in fact a pure word game.[25]

Seisetsu's conclusion was even more damning; linked verse may have been an important part of Japanese literary history, but its day was done:

As for linked verse in the future, since it is simply a word game, aside from the hope that it may become something that may afford one greater pleasure than *go*, card games, or other similar diversions, I have no expectations for it . . . long forms of linked verse, which lack unity, and thirty-six-stanza and one-hundred-stanza linked verse, which depend on variation, cannot possibly compare with drama, prose fiction, or the perfect lyrical and descriptive capacities of other forms of poetry, in much the same way as a bow and arrow cannot compare with a perfected firearm. If there exist in the world perfected firearms, then what should we call one who would yet stand on the battlefield playing with bow and arrow but a lunatic? I thus have no hesitation in saying of *haikai* in the Meiji era that where not practiced for amusement, it is the province of the madman.[26]

Seisetsu's overall point was clear: linked verse was fundamentally unserious, of value only as light amusement, and possessed no future as modern literature. Writing in September of 1896, while Seisetsu was serializing his piece, another University Group writer, Ōmachi Keigetsu 大町桂月 (1869–1925), echoed these terms of serious and unserious literature and the qualitative difference between the activities of the commoner and the man of letters. For Keigetsu, neither linked verse nor premodern *haikai* was worth the time of the serious poet. Keigetsu laid out a historical narrative in which *haikai* and linked verse were only an intermediate stage in the evolution of Japanese verse, bridging the gap between classical *waka* and modern haiku. Although Keigetsu conceded that both classical *waka* and *haikai* were unique in world literature for their ability to express intricate beauty in spite of their short form, in his view Shiki's progress toward a modern haiku meant that this intermediate stage of *haikai* and linked verse had become obsolete. *Haikai* and linked verse had arisen during "the Ashikaga period, Japanese literature's most obsolete age" (*kokubungaku no mottomo sutaretaru Ashikaga jidai*), and were "not poetry, just as *go* and *shōgi* are not *Kunst* [i.e., art]" (*haikai no shi ni arazaru wa nao go shōgi no kunsuto ni arazaru ga gotoshi*).[27] Keigetsu's rhetoric, borrowing the language of German artistic criticism, articulates the link between the commoner-literature discourse and the notion of art as play, placing linked verse firmly in the latter category. Modern haiku could become *Kunst* if written and appreciated by educated specialists, but *haikai*, which was a vulgar and frivolous pursuit enjoyed primarily by ill-educated commoners, could not.

Keigetsu's use of the German term *Kunst* points to one of the *Teikoku bungaku* group's subsequent contributions to Japanese literary scholarship—namely, their work on the Nara-period (710–784) collection of native Japanese poetry *Man'yōshū* (Collection of ten thousand leaves, compiled ca. 785). As Shinada Yoshikazu has shown, beginning around the turn of the twentieth century the *Teikoku bungaku* group reenvisioned the *Man'yōshū* in a positive sense, as a "poetry anthology of the people" (*kokumin kashū*), whose attraction was that many of its poems were written by "the common people" (*shomin*).[28] Strongly influenced by German notions of the *Volkslied* (folk song), *Teikoku bungaku*'s understanding of the *Man'yōshū* was underpinned by "the German distinction between *Volkspoesie*, the folk compositions of ordinary men and women, and *Kunstpoesie*, the more artistically conceived and crafted works by professional poets."[29] The basic terms of analysis used in *Teikoku bungaku*'s discussions of *haikai* thus seem to anticipate this German-influenced schema, with the crucial difference that at this stage *haikai*'s status as *Volkspoesie*, or rather as "commoner literature," was in no way a positive aspect.

The University Group's ambivalence on the topic of *haikai* and its unserious, plebeian nature followed less than a decade later by the embrace of the *Manyōshū* on the grounds that it was the "people's poetry" highlights the unstable and frequently conflicted nature of the idea of national-poetic community and provides a good example of the processes of differentiation and hierarchy that I have argued shaped the discursive creation of a national poetry in Japan. If anything, the *Teikoku bungaku* group was actually relatively mild in its criticisms of *haikai*; other literary journals around the same time were openly derisive of the proposition that there was any point in reforming *haikai* at all. In January of 1896, for example, the popular-interest journal *Taiyō* called haiku's newfound popularity "a disaster for the literary world" (*bundan no kyōji*),[30] while *Waseda bungaku* derided haiku as "cheap literature" (*anchoku bungaku*) and lamented the "depredations" (*shōketsu*) of the "*hokku* bacillus" (*hokku bachiruren*). Among the objections raised to *haikai* was that it lacked a fully developed framework of critical vocabulary and writings; as *Waseda bungaku* went on to ask, "What shall we say about the value of *haikai* literature? Just as there is no set of scales that measures the most infinitesimal differences in decimal place, I say that no standard can ever have existed anywhere by which one might critique such a small literature."[31]

While far more dismissive than either Shiki or the University Group had been, the rhetoric in which *Waseda bungaku*'s criticism was couched, of cheap, low-quality literature spreading like a disease among the populace, seems equally calculated to appeal to concerns of class and intellectual prestige. Both Shiki and the *Teikoku bungaku* group agreed that *haikai* and linked verse, if left in its unreformed plebeian state, was little more than a form of a low-class game that did not deserve to be called literature. As Seisetsu's contrasting of linked verse with what he termed the perfected generic categories of prose fiction and theater suggests, the dominant idea of what literature actually was in these discussions was a largely European-influenced one, one that had been disseminated and discussed by men of letters, who, almost by definition, had gone through the highest reaches of the Japanese educational system. The man of letters thus assumed the privilege of defining what literature was; the *hokku*, if construed as individual expression rather than the first link in a chain of discourse, could be relatively easily assimilated within European ideas of poetry, but as Akio Bin has pointed out, the rules and practice of linked verse could not.[32]

AUTUMN WINDS OF CHANGE? CHIKUREI AND THE SHŪSEIKAI

To further contextualize the importance of social class in the haiku-reform discourse of the University and *Nippon* Groups, it is helpful to examine the third major reform group, Kakuta Chikurei and Ozaki Kōyō's Shūseikai. Although the group has been largely overlooked in extant scholarship, many critics during the mid-1890s saw the Shūseikai not only as credible rivals to Shiki and his followers but also as Tokyo's premiere *haikai* reform group. One month after the Shūseikai's formation, *Teikoku bungaku* remarked that "if many of the fine talents in Kōyō and [Iwaya] Sazanami's Ken'yūsha are incorporated into this newly formed haiku society, then we shall have great hopes for this group."[33] Likewise, when *Teikoku bungaku*'s commentators learned of the *Nippon*

Group's plans to move its newly founded journal *Hototogisu* to Tokyo from Matsuyama in 1897, they expressed concern that the publication would end up playing second fiddle (*ni no mai o enjiru*) to the Shūseikai, rather than the other way around.[34]

On the face of it, there was good reason to expect great things from the Shūseikai. Its two leading lights, Chikurei and Kōyō, were respected, wealthy, and well connected. The leader of the influential Ken'yūsha literary group, Kōyō was one of the preeminent novelists in the country, whose masterpiece *The Golden Demon* (*Konjiki yasha*, 1897) would come out at the height of the Shūseikai's haiku activities. Kōyō had acquired an interest in *haikai* through his readings of the Edo-era prose author Ihara Saikaku 井原西鶴 (1642–1693), who was himself a prominent *haikai* poet, and Kōyō encouraged the aspiring prose authors of the Ken'yūsha to practice *haikai* themselves. Chikurei, for his part, was a Diet member and successful lawyer, who had been admitted to the bar in 1880 and had a colorful legal career before turning his interest to haiku. Elected first as a Tokyo city assemblyman in 1884, Chikurei had worked initially with a number of old-school *haikai* poets, both in literary and nonliterary venues. Not only had Chikurei contributed verses to Mimori Mikio's *Meirin zasshi* but also Mikio had even retained him as counsel while he contemplated suing the *Tōkai shinpō* newspaper in Chiba Prefecture; the newspaper had, apparently, published remarks about Mikio's performance at a *haikai* gathering that were so unflattering as to be legally actionable.[35] Three years later, Chikurei hit the headlines on a larger legal stage, acting as defense counsel in a so-called poison woman (*dokufu*) case for an entertainer named Hanai Oume 花井お梅 (1863–1916), who was accused of the murder of her male assistant.[36] Rumor had it that throughout these cases, Chikurei claimed that he always had *haikai* books on him whenever he went to court.[37]

At the time of its formation in October of 1895, the Shūseikai therefore seemed as if it was poised to dominate Tokyo's haiku world. In practice, however, over the next five years it completely failed to make the impact of which its supporters had believed it capable. One reason for this was likely its overall position of eclecticism; in announcing its formation in the *Tōkyō Mainichi* on October 9, 1895, the group stressed that "we do not inquire as to whether one's poetic diction is old or new, nor whether one's group or lineage is the same or different; it is desirable that we have ever greater numbers."[38] What this meant in practice was that unlike the University and *Nippon* Groups, the Shūseikai rarely attacked the old-school masters in print and actually welcomed them to its poetry gatherings. Though there were plenty who were willing to argue with the old-school masters—Shūseikai member and novelist Iwaya Sazanami 巌谷小波 (Sueo 季雄, 1870–1933) recalls arguments with Mikio's adopted son, Shunjūan Shōkō 春秋庵松江 (1859–1899), that were heated enough to "knock the dust off the shelves"—overtly, at least, the Shūseikai showed none of the direct hostility of the other two groups.[39]

In fact, at times the Shūsekai seemed to be more interested in enjoying the social experience of haiku than seriously contemplating the pathways for its reform; in some ways, its members proved the point about the divide between play and serious literature that the other two groups had made. Iwaya Sazanami's recollections of the group's gatherings, which were usually held at Chikurei's home in Sarugaku-chō in the Kanda area of Tokyo, stress the high quality of the food and drink and the unhurried service guests received from Chikurei's wife and daughters; it was easy, he wrote, to forget that one was in the city when the surroundings were so "rich in haiku flavor" (*haimi yutakana mono de atta*).[40] This indulgent atmosphere prompted a certain amount of derision from the *Nippon* Group, which portrayed the Shūseikai as a group of dilettantes interested mostly in what the *Nippon* Group termed play haiku (*yūhai*) or leisure haiku (*kanpai*).[41]

The Shūseikai did not help itself in this respect by going to great lengths to organize extravagant entertainment at its gatherings. As an example, among the various modes of composition enjoyed at Shūseikai gatherings was a practice called haiku sumo (*kuzumō*), wherein those present would divide into two teams and have individuals face off against one another to compose a verse on a set topic within a set period. The judge for the competition would then read out the verses thus composed and ask for votes via a show of hands. To this extent, haiku sumo seems similar to practices of competitive communal *hokku* composition such as *ku-awase*, which likewise featured two teams of competing poets and a judge. However, the Shūseikai seems to have carried this practice to extremes, with Kōyō and Chikurei going so far as to have a full-scale sumo ring (*dohyō*) constructed in the lane outside Chikurei's home, complete with drapes, roof, and an ornate fan for the referee.[42]

Another major problem for the Shūseikai was of an entirely nonliterary nature, specifically Chikurei's involvement in a damaging public scandal early in 1896. On January 14 of that year, the *Yorozu chōhō* newspaper published a series of allegations accusing Chikurei of rape and adultery (*gōkan kantsū*). As befitting a paper that was making a name for itself with scandal journalism, the *Yorozu*'s first installment of reporting on the fourteenth whetted readers' appetites by fulminating against Chikurei's immorality and unfitness for high office, reserving the details of what he had allegedly done until the following day. As it transpired, the *Yorozu*'s allegations were that in July 1893 Chikurei had raped Seshimo Kaoru 瀬下かほる (dates unknown), the wife of fellow bar association member Seshimo Kiyomichi 瀬下清通 (dates unknown), at a restaurant in Hamamachi in Tokyo. Subsequently, the allegations ran, Chikurei had met Kaoru at the same restaurant in order to apologize and had been so persuasive that the two had conducted a two-year affair up until the summer of 1895. After Kiyomichi discovered their affair, Chikurei wrote a formal letter of apology to him, after which both had considered the matter closed.[43]

The *Yorozu* painted itself throughout the 1890s as the voice of the underdog against a morally suspect political elite, and the Chikurei affair fit that narrative perfectly. The newspaper took pleasure in providing as much lurid detail as possible, its coverage of the affair extending over two months and more than thirty numbered installments into March of 1896. The *Yorozu*'s satirical poetry column found the scandal to be a rich vein of material, publishing the following pair of ironic poems on the same page as the original allegations on January 15:

角田真平姦通事件

The Tsunoda [sic] *Shinpei Adultery Incident*[44]

itou beki	you despicable
itazuramono yo	good-for-nothing cheat—
yome ga kimi	says the wife's husband
—KAORU	

厭ふべきいたづらものよ嫁が君　　かほる

sono kokoro	that heart
inu ni mo hajiyo	would shame even a dog—
neko no koi	a cat's tryst.[45]

—SHINPAI

其こころ犬にもはぢよ猫のこひ　　心配

It is unclear whether the allegations were true, although subsequent events suggest that the *Yorozu* was probably not far off the mark. Chikurei resigned as a Diet member on February 15 (after which the *Yorozu* pointedly referred to him as *former* Diet member Tsunoda Shinpei), and he was also later disbarred by the Tokyo Bar Association.[46] As for Seshimo Kaoru and Kiyomichi, the effect on them was equally unpleasant, the *Yorozu* reporting on February 16 that Kiyomichi had left his wife and was planning to divorce her.

The distasteful nature of the episode seems to have prompted at least two Shūseikai members to defect to the *Nippon* Group, Ueno Sansen and Naono Hekireirō 直野碧玲瓏 (Ryōnoshin 了之晋, 1875–1905), who both helped establish the Shōseikai haiku group in Nagano.[47] Hekireirō and Sansen were not alone in defecting to the *Nippon* Group from the Shūseikai; others included Noda Bettenrō 野田別天楼 (Yōkichi 要吉, 1869–1944) and Wakao Ransui 若尾瀾水 (Shōgo 圧吾, 1877–1961), who would each be instrumental in creating "new haiku" groups in Kansai and Tōhoku, respectively. With the exception of Itō Shōu and Mori Saruo, formerly of the Shii no Tomo Kai, the process did not work the other way; as far as can be determined, no one ever left the *Nippon* Group in favor of the Shūseikai. It is hard to imagine the breaking of the scandal doing much for Shūseikai cohesion, and it is likely that other members also left, especially since the group's meetings were usually held at Chikurei's house with his wife and daughters in attendance.

For all its troubles, however, the Shūseikai put social class at the core of the modern haiku just as the other groups did. In contrast to the University and *Nippon* Groups, which were made up in large part of students, the Shūseikai consisted of established and often quite well-heeled professionals. A report carried in the group's journal *Aki no koe* (1896–1897) lists twenty-seven men as participating in one gathering, among whom were three lawyers, two judges, two journalists, two civil servants, one city assemblyman, and one city councilman[48] Likewise, in a subsequent issue of *Aki no koe* the following year, the Shūseikai gave some hint of its desired target audience, with a list of members of the nobility and political elite rumored to practice haiku. Included were several former daimyo and members of the House of Peers, including Hachisuka Mochiaki 蜂須賀茂韶 (1846–1918), then speaker of the house, and diplomat and member of the House of Peers Moriyama Shigeru 森山茂 (1842–1919).[49] Writing in the same issue, Shūseikai founding member Mori Mukō 森無黄 (Teijirō 貞二郎, 1864–1942) made the case that the group's mission was to introduce haiku to the middle and upper classes:

> There are some people who, because they go so far as to term *haikai* commoner literature and think that it is something that even the illiterate workman class can appreciate, sneer at Shiki's advocacy of abstruse ideas such as "subjective," "objective," "space," "time," "impression," and so on and his expounding on haiku as if it were very hard indeed to master; these people say that in so doing Shiki is wasting his time as surely as if he were carrying a boat to the top of a mountain. But if they do not have haiku explained to them in such terms, educated society will have trouble understanding it, and so this is surely a necessary method in order to have the middle and upper classes of society learn about the way of haiku.[50]

Mukō's approval of Shiki's efforts to apply the language of academic literary criticism to develop a conceptual framework for the modern haiku echo *Waseda bungaku*'s earlier dismissal of *haikai* as having no coherent critical standards; developing an intellectually respectable critical vocabulary would, Mukō suggests, be necessary in order to have haiku appeal to "educated society."

Some years later, in a discussion of why the Shūseikai had not performed as expected, haiku critic and founding member of the group Okano Chijū pointed once again to the importance of social class and educational background. The group's syncretic attitudes had, he felt, made it a "Unitarian-like group" (*yuniteriyanteki dantai*) that had succeeded in pleasing no one; in particular, he emphasized the failure to exclude the ignorant and ill-educated old-school *haikai* masters: "Thinking about it now, Chikurei's first idea, which was to gather a lot of people together and experiment in blending the old and new styles, was misguided. Simply gathering a lot of people together didn't mean anything much other than that it all got very crowded; there was no way they would come into agreement, and it was only asking for discord. There was no chance that the ignorant and ill-educated old-school masters would understand what syncretism was, nor its essence."[51]

In Chijū's view, then, one of the major flaws of the Shūseikai had been that it had not been sufficiently exclusive in terms of social class and educational background. Revealingly, Chijū writes elsewhere of a case in which two old-school masters had actually acquired a formal education; noting that two prominent old-school masters had graduated from a trade school and from the highly respected Keiō Gijuku (later to become Keiō University), Chijū remarked that this made clear the nature of commoner literature. These masters' acquisition of a formal education was, he wrote, a decision taken to improve their business as professional *haikai* poets (*gyōhai to shite wa isshu no eigyōteki mono naru ni chūi sezaru bekarazu*).[52] Thus even where an old-school master had acquired the requisite education, it was still possible to disqualify him on the grounds that he had done so for the wrong reasons.

"YOU'VE COMPOSED BARELY FIFTY VERSES IN YOUR LIFE": THE OLD-SCHOOL AND NEW HAIKU

One may wonder what the old-school masters themselves made of the appearance of these new-haiku groups and the vitriol that was directed toward them. In discussing the term "commoner literature," it is worth noting that even into the 1890s, the disciples of the old-school haiku poets vastly outnumbered those gathering under the banner of the new haiku. Reflecting this numerical advantage, a number of prominent *haikai* masters deployed the rhetoric of commoner literature in a positive sense, the large numbers of practitioners under their umbrella evidence of the broad appeal of the genre. The copy for an advertisement in *Teikoku bungaku* of September 1897 promoting a collected edition of works titled *Haikai bunko* edited by Kikakudō Eiki and Ashin'an Setsujin, for instance, describes *haikai* as erasing social distinctions, a genre that "was held in common by society as a whole" (*ippan shakai ni tsūji*) and in which "the voices of town and country, high and low, forever chant together" (*tohi kisen tomo ni ginga no koe taezu*).[53] Likewise the journal *Bungei kurabu*, which since its inauguration in 1895 had proved to be one of the few media redoubts for the old school, employed similar rhetoric to promote its *haikai* competitions, calling on readers in June 1897 to submit their haiku for publication and describing the genre as "the commoner literature of our country" (*wagakuni heimin bungaku*).[54]

Aside from featuring old-school masters as judges for its *haikai* competitions, *Bungei kurabu* was also one of the relatively few print media venues that afforded them space to expound on their own views of *haikai* and attempt to rebut some of the criticisms of the new-haiku groups. Writing in the journal in October of 1898, Mimori Mikio took aim at the "scholars" (*gakusha*) he claimed were confusing those new to *haikai* and ultimately driving them away:

> Let not confusion arise from the empty theories in newspapers and magazines. In today's scholarly world there is a tendency to use one's own theories in order to tear down the past. . . . The *Greater Learning* says, "Contemplate and study the illustrious decrees of Heaven." But these scholars believe that learning is obtained solely from books, and those who are self-satisfied on account of having studied a lot must be eight or nine of every ten. Therefore there are many who for all their studies are not well versed in the Great Way [of *haikai*].[55]

Mikio's comments show a clear understanding of the class divide in haiku reform; for him, the enemy is overeducated scholars who use their erudition as a badge of authority while knowing nothing of *haikai*. Later in the same piece, Mikio singles out Sassa Seisetsu, in particular the latter's criticism of a verse by Edo-era poet Narita Sōkyū 成田蒼虬 (1761–1842) in his *A Short History of Linked Verse*. On reading Sassa's work, Mikio states, "we must lament that one who holds a degree in literature should be so fixated on points of grammar and have no understanding of the deeper meaning."[56] That Mikio should again point disparagingly to his adversary's academic qualifications as meaningless in a *haikai* context makes clear his sense of frustration at coming under attack from scholars who believe their formal education qualifies them to comment on *haikai*.

A similar sense of resentment can be detected in another piece in *Bungei kurabu* two years later by the Osaka-based master Ōtei Kinshō

鶯亭金升 (1868–1954), who also acted occasionally as a judge for the *Yorozu chōhō* and *Miyako shinbun* newspapers. Kinshō's humorous piece, "Pointless Discussions on *Haikai*" (Haikai mizukake ron), posits a conversation between the old school's Master Self-Proclaimed Elegance (Jishōga Sensei) and the new haiku's Commoner with a Lit Degree (Heimin Bungakushi). Set on a veranda in the summer humidity, the conversation quickly turns into an exchange of insults:

> "Look, listen here. When it comes down to it, your so-called new school is just a handful of beginners, and it's a bit much for them to go around attacking *haikai* at large."
>
> "That's enough out of you! That's not at all true!"
>
> "What's not true about it?. . . You go and become *haikai* critics on the spot, even though the fact of the matter is that you've composed barely fifty verses in your life, and start talking about 'commoner literature' and '*haikai* is Sinitic poetry in seventeen syllables' and all sorts of serious stuff like that."[57]

The conversation ends with the two exchanging insulting *hokku* before cutting back to reveal an old man watching the scene who sums up with a verse of his own:

gojippo no	six of one laughs
hyappo warau ya	at half a dozen of the other—
suzumidai	a cool veranda.[58]

五十歩の百歩笑ふやすずみ台

Amid the humor, Kinshō nevertheless makes a serious criticism of the haiku reform movement: the so-called reformers apparently believe that the academic study of literature in general qualifies them to lead a movement to reshape *haikai*, even though they have no real training or experience in the genre. Kinshō suggests in the closing lines that even the "commoner literature" label itself is the product of rarified academic theories, developed and attached to the genre by outsiders.

Kinshō makes another significant point in the opening lines—namely, that in terms of numbers the new-haiku movements were actually a tiny minority, a "handful of beginners," and that the old school itself had a better claim to represent *haikai* as a whole (*ippan*). The idea of the new-haiku groups as a tiny minority of pretentious upstarts is somewhat borne out by the differences in the scale of audience for the publications in which they tended to work. As one example, in 1897 the main redoubt for the old school, *Bungei kurabu*, outsold the University Group's primary vehicle, *Teikoku bungaku*, by a ratio of nearly twenty to one.[59] Shiki's *Nippon*, a major metropolitan daily with considerable reach, began to decline rapidly after the Sino-Japanese War and entered a slump from which it never really recovered, losing more than a quarter of its readers between 1895 and 1898.[60] By 1900, Shiki wrote to Natsume Sōseki 夏目漱石 (1867–1916) that *"Nippon* isn't selling . . . to be honest, sales right now are below ten thousand [daily] copies (but do me a favor and don't tell anyone that)."[61] Part of the reason for this was a steadfast refusal to adopt the style of rapid news reporting made popular by the war in favor of continuing to focus on political discussion and opinion. In its roundup of daily newspapers, the popular-interest journal *Taiyō* noted in 1900 that *"Nippon* is the same old *Nippon*; one who wished to know about society would have trouble using this paper alone."[62]

HOTOTOGISU AND THE DEMOGRAPHICS OF THE NEW HAIKU

Viewed in the broad perspective of *haikai* as a whole in Japan during the 1890s, the *Nippon* Group seemed to have something of an uphill battle on its hands. It was, as the old-school masters themselves noted, tiny in terms of its overall numbers, and its rhetoric of exclusivity was a double-edged sword, working to limit its potential membership even as it provided the group with a claim to intellectual authority. As obstinate as ever, Shiki emphasized in 1896 that the social limits of the new haiku would be maintained even if it were to expand further, writing that "even if our new-style haiku should gain more widespread popularity, those ill-educated barbers, fishmongers, grocers, store clerks, and young apprentices will never come within its bounds. . . . Some people today say that haiku is plebeian, but the new faction will never allow itself to become plebeian in the same way as the old school."[63]

The ultimate success of Shiki and the *Nippon* Group had much to do with their access to and position in Japan's daily newspapers and other periodical print media, the best example of this being the inauguration in 1897 of the new haiku journal *Hototogisu*. Still publishing to this day, *Hototogisu* would go on to become one of Japan's leading literary journals and had a major impact on the careers of Shiki and Takahama Kyoshi in particular. The concluding part of this chapter focuses on the role of *Hototogisu* as a central venue in the expansion of the *Nippon* Group beyond Tokyo and Matsuyama to encompass virtually the entire country, while also noting the prominent role that the concept of haiku as commoner literature continued to play in the group's discourse.

One of the main reasons that haiku practitioners of both the old and new schools tended to publish their work in daily newspapers and general-interest journals was that specialist haiku publications were extremely difficult to run as a going concern. Shiki had tried to launch a specialist publication of his own, called simply *Haikai*, during the spring of 1893, but the journal lasted a mere two issues before folding.[64] *Haikai*'s failure was perhaps not surprising given the fledgling status of Shiki's reform group, but even much larger groups had trouble running their publications in a sustainable manner. Mimori Mikio's *haikai* publication *Meirin zasshi*, probably early Meiji's most widely read *haikai* journal, was launched in 1880 with three hundred yen in funding from around sixty benefactors. However, it ate through those funds within six months, and even though its circulation was relatively healthy, at one point reaching a peak of two thousand one hundred copies a month, Mikio himself needed to provide frequent injections of cash from additional investors and from his own *haikai* practice in order to keep the publication solvent.[65]

Some specialist *haikai* journals did carry advertising, but many supported themselves through charging readers a grading fee (*irebana*, also *nyūka*) for publishing their verses; Shiki's *Haikai*, for instance, explicitly stated that it did not charge readers to publish their work. By contrast, *Meirin zasshi* provided a number of examples of the ways in which *haikai* could be monetized, with the old-school poet using the journal to solicit marking fees, to raise funds for erecting statues to Bashō, and to advertise his own made-to-order paintings and calligraphic pieces.[66] The widely criticized "point-scoring" *haikai* was perpetuated for quite some time into Meiji largely through this and other such publications; one group, the Osaka-based Society for Promoting the National Essence (Kokusui Shinkōkai), stripped point-scoring *haikai* down to its most basic elements and made substantial sums of money by publishing nothing other than verses selected via a voting process that involved all subscribers to its journal and that took advantage of the nationwide postal system.[67] The best three hundred verses would win monetary prizes, and having readers themselves rather than a central master select verses, they were thus placed in the position of both judge and participant, reading and critiquing other entrants' verses as a necessary part of the process.

That it was undesirable to monetize haiku in this fashion was one point on which the new-haiku groups were more or less unanimous. In the first issue of the Shūseikai's *Aki no koe*, Chikurei had criticized "fee-garnering *haikai* masters" (*ryō haika*),[68] and a year earlier, in his 1895 instructional manual *Haikai taiyō* (Essentials of haiku), Shiki had admonished his followers to steer well clear of anything that might seem mercenary: "It is good to compete with other people in the *unza* format or through point scoring, but if the best verses are awarded material prizes, then it is vulgar and unworthy of a gentleman . . . and you should not engage in *mikasa-zuke*, haiku competitions with prizes, and everything else that is of the nature of gambling and has to do with personal enrichment."[69]

Shiki's mention of "haiku competitions with prizes" was in some ways prescient, since around the turn of the twentieth century both Chikurei and Kōyō of the Shūseikai frequently presided as judges over haiku competitions in the pages of the *Yomiuri* newspaper. The *Yomiuri* ran three such competitions between June 1901 and January 1902, offering as much as 236 yen as prize money and receiving in the high tens of thousands of submissions.[70] In 1904, after Shiki's death, Chikurei acted as a judge for a haiku competition that *Bungei kurabu* ran to mark its tenth anniversary. The prize money for this competition was a massive 500 yen, equivalent to well over a year's salary for Shiki at *Nippon*, and the journal was rewarded for its generosity with nearly one hundred thousand entries. Since many of its members were students who undoubtedly could have done with the money, the *Nippon* Group's principled refusal to engage in such activities was a source of considerable amusement to certain members of the Shūseikai. As one correspondent noted archly in the group's later journal *Haisei* (1901–1902), "It is indeed admirable that they keep to the spirit of the [*Haikai*] *taiyō* their godfather has laid down and avert their eyes from two-hundred-yen prizes. Or maybe they do enter, just under false names? [*sore demo henmei de dete iru kashira*]."[71]

The Shūseikai's semiserious jab at the *Nippon* Group highlighted a potential problem for the latter, which was that its principled and high-minded rhetoric did not allow it to take advantage of most of the possible streams of revenue by which haiku publications conventionally sustained themselves. It could not get involved in running haiku competitions for prize money, practices such as point-scoring *haikai*, or charging readers to mark their verses. For his part, Shiki could support himself with his salary as a journalist at *Nippon*, but his two main disciples, Takahama Kyoshi and Kawahigashi Hekigotō, both of whom had recently dropped out of the elite higher schools they had been attending, needed to find some way to support themselves.

Financially at least, the inauguration of *Hototogisu* in 1897 was thus something of a gamble, and the decision to move it to Tokyo, after a relatively stable first year in Matsuyama, even more so. Writing to Kyoshi shortly before Kyoshi assumed editorship of the Tokyo version of *Hototogisu* in 1898, Shiki laid out the economics of the enterprise; he estimated that a journal would need a capital base of three hundred to four hundred yen simply in order to sustain itself, and that even if at the same time one cut costs to the bare minimum, one was unlikely to see any kind of profit (*betsu ni rijun to iu koto wa nai yō ja*). A specialist haiku journal, in his estimation, would be unlikely to sell more than five hundred copies, "even if you adopt the vulgar methods of the old-school masters." Particularly if Kyoshi were to make the journal as highbrow as possible, it would be no small task to make it sell (*uridasō to iu ni wa taitei no koto ja nai*).[72]

Echoing Shiki's rhetoric that the "gentleman" should spurn monetary gain in haiku, *Nippon* Group elder statesman Naitō Meisetsu's preface to the January 1897 inaugural issue of *Hototogisu* revisited the idea of haiku as commoner literature, arguing, "Some say that haiku is plebeian, and therefore it should be something that everyone can understand. I say that the plebeian is indeed one part of haiku, but other than that there is also 'scholarly' haiku and 'superior gentleman' haiku, and the finest part of haiku is most often to be found therein."[73] *Hototogisu*'s sales while it was still in Matsuyama, under the direction of Shiki's child-hood friend and journalist, Yanagihara Kyokudō, were solid if not spectacular. Unable to rely on verse-marking fees or other revenue-generating models common to *haikai* publications, *Hototogisu* was instead seen through its first year partly by member donations. Reported monthly in its pages, some donations were only a few sen, but as the *Nippon* Group's network grew, so the effect came to be magnified. During the first year of *Hototogisu*'s publishing in Tokyo, from October 1898 to October 1899, the donations reported in the journal's pages came to a total of just under fifty yen, a significant portion of the three to four hundred yen Shiki had estimated the journal would need. This included five yen from one haiku group in Vladivostok and one yen from another in Incheon, and those who could not send money found other ways to contribute, such as sending consignments of writing brushes.[74]

Though undoubtedly welcome, this direct financial support was not ultimately crucial to *Hototogisu*'s survival, since the journal proved an immediate success upon launch in the capital. As noted, Shiki had expressed pessimism that the new *Hototogisu* would sell even five hundred copies and, more bluntly, had also told his junior associate in the same letter that "I do not believe you have the skills to produce a journal that will sell."[75] In the event, Shiki was completely wrong; on its launch day in October 1898, the Tokyo *Hototogisu* sold out its entire print run of one thousand copies in a matter of hours, obliging Kyoshi to telephone the printer and order an additional five hundred. This favorable reception was no flash in the pan; *Hototogisu*'s February 1898 edition announced that the December edition had sold out in less than a week and that although they had increased the print run for the January edition, those, too, had sold out in a matter of days. Not missing a sales opportunity, the same announcement stated that *Hototogisu* was now accepting orders for back issues.[76]

Probably the main reason why *Hototogisu* was able to achieve such sustained success after its move to Tokyo was its deliberate cultivation of a network of affiliated groups throughout the rest of the country. Here, comparisons with the Shūseikai's haiku journal, *Aki no koe*, are instructive, since the latter group seems to have made almost no effort to develop a readership outside the capital. Launched in November 1896, *Aki no koe* lasted a mere ten issues and folded in September 1897, just before the launch of the Tokyo *Hototogisu*. By contrast, from its earliest issues, *Hototogisu* featured updates from its regional affiliates; when *Aki no koe* published a list of active members in its second issue, it added a note to the roster to the effect that both women and those who lived outside Tokyo had not been included.[77] In October 1896, a few months before *Hototogisu*'s inauguration, the Kansai-based Mangetsukai was introduced in the pages of *Nippon* as the group's main affiliate in western Japan, and in June 1897 the Hyakubunkai in Sendai and the Hokuseikai in Kanazawa also made themselves known through the pages of *Hototogisu*.

That the first groups declaring themselves to be under the *Hototogisu* umbrella appeared in Sendai, Kyoto, and Kanazawa was no coincidence, since these cities were home to the elite Second, Third, and Fourth Higher Schools, respectively. Underlining the importance of the *Nippon* Group's emphasis on highly educated "superior gentlemen" as the antidote to "commoner literature," the Hokuseikai's correspondent from Kanazawa in June 1897 reported that the majority of its members were either teachers or students at the Fourth Higher School. In Sendai, home to the Second Higher School, the ranks of new-style haiku poets had been bolstered by Sassa Seisetsu, formerly of the University Group, who had graduated in September 1896 and taken a job teaching at the school. This school subsequently proved a fertile recruiting ground, with the Hyakubunkai reporting in June 1897 that all but one of the six new members it had recently gained were students at the school.[78] Likewise in Nagano, a prefecture that took pride in its tradition of scholarly learning and in which the *Nippon* Group did particularly well, the majority of members of the new-haiku groups were educators, including Ueno Sansen, who studied at Nagano Teacher's College and taught in Tokyo before returning home after a bout of illness.[79] *Teikoku bungaku* in March 1897 noted the burst of activity at the schools in Kanazawa and Sendai and suggested that since Shiki's friend and fellow poet Natsume Sōseki was currently teaching at the Fifth Higher School in Kumamoto, the *Nippon* Group would presently gain a foothold there, too.[80] These new groups sprang up with startling speed, "like bamboo shoots after a rain shower" (*ugo no takenoko no gotoshi*), as Shiki had put it.[81] By October 1899, one year after *Hototogisu*'s move to Tokyo, 134 separate groups had announced themselves in its pages. Some were even located outside Japan, such as the Taihokukai in recently colonized Taiwan, the Ryūsakai in Vladivostok, and the Incheon Shinseikai in Korea.[82]

If the elite institutions of Japan's state educational system, particularly the provincial higher schools, had been essential to the initial spread of the *Nippon* Group's regional affiliates, the institutions of the print media proved equally essential to its subsequent efforts at consolidation. In August 1898, the Hekiunkai of Matsue in Shimane Prefecture reported through *Hototogisu* that it had been successful in swaying the local *Matsue nippō* newspaper to its cause. Although the competing *San'in shinbun* was still in the hands of an "obstinate blockhead" (*wakarazuya*) of an old-school master, the Hekiunkai stated, "the day is not far off when we will force the surrender of the old school."[83]

That the Hekiunkai should use the language of military campaigning was not entirely inappropriate given that the *Nippon* Group was embarked on a program of conquest aimed at supplanting the old school's vision of haiku with its own. The case of another regional group, the Shizuoka Fuyōkai, is instructive; in a similar vein to the Hekiunkai, this group reported in October 1897 that it had used its contacts at the local *Min'yū shinbun* to get the newspaper to institute a moratorium on verses from the old school in its pages.[84] But where most of the *Hototogisu* groups had been founded afresh and attempted to carve their own path, the Fuyōkai had also attempted to amalgamate with a local old-school group. As it first announced itself in *Hototogisu* on October 30, 1897, the Fuyōkai claimed a respectable twenty-three members;[85] in May 1899, those numbers had shot up to nearly seventy, an exceptionally large membership among *Hototogisu*-affiliated groups. This surge in membership seems to have been the result of a merger with the local Commoner Literature Society, an avowedly old-school group whose name, as well as that of the journal it published, *Commoner Literature* (*Heimin bungaku*), could hardly have been more at odds with the *Nippon* Group's overall rhetoric. The latter journal was duly renamed *Fuyō*, although in its new incarnation the journal lasted only around a year and folded after the tenth issue in June 1900, something that was noted with some surprise by Shiki in *Hototogisu* at the time.[86] The group seems to have become far less active after this, and although precise details are hard to come by, it seems likely that internal divisions between those favoring the *Nippon* Group and those still well disposed to the old school played a part. As had been the case with the Shūseikai's attempts at eclecticism, it seemed that the most successful new-haiku groups were those that opted to marginalize, rather than incorporate, the old school.

In the Kansai region, which boasted the largest newspaper market in Japan, the *Nippon* Group's basic tactics were the same, although the outcome was rather different. Noda Bettenrō of the Kansai Mangetsukai complained in June 1898 that the *Ōsaka Asahi shinbun* newspaper was uninterested in publishing work by the members of his group, and that the *Ōsaka Mainichi* was mostly lukewarm, having featured only a handful of their verses to date. This he attributed to the inability of the notoriously avaricious citizens of Osaka to grasp the notion of haiku as cultural rather than economic capital; both main Osaka newspapers he described as "completely indifferent to literature" (*tomo ni bungaku ni sukoburu reitan ni sōrō*) and complained that "Osaka is a venal place where money makes the world go round . . . sublime literary import is not something that the residents here are capable of understanding, and the best you can expect is *mikasa-zuke* and *dodoitsu* songs."[87] A particular source of frustration to the Mangetsukai was that "not only the illiterate and ill-educated lower orders but even doctors, monks, and others who are relatively well read rarely stray from the ranks [of the old school]."[88]

LITERATURE OF THE PEOPLE, BY THE PEOPLE, FOR THE PEOPLE?

The preceding has offered a largely revisionist narrative of the processes of haiku reform; I have deliberately avoided discussing topics such as the impact of "sketch from life" haiku (*shasei*) or Shiki's arguments for the literary, formal, and aesthetic qualities of the modern haiku per se. Rather, I have tried to draw attention to the consistent rhetoric of elite identity and social distinction that undergirded the activities not just of Shiki's *Nippon* Group but also of all the major groups that took up the banner of haiku reform during the 1890s. This is, I would contend, just as crucial to understanding what haiku reform was and how it was executed as the precise literary qualities of the verse themselves. Given the consistently exclusionary vision of haiku promoted by the main reform groups, there is a certain irony to the frequently made (and entirely accurate) observation that haiku is the most widely practiced verse form in present-day Japan, with hundreds of thousands (if not millions) of amateur poets throughout the country. In Europe and North America, too, haiku's reputation as a simple and accessible verse form means that it is frequently taught to relatively young schoolchildren, making it in many cases the first form of metered poetry they encounter.

As the preceding makes clear, however, this was emphatically not the vision of haiku that Shiki, or indeed any of the major haiku reform groups, wished to promote. For Shiki in particular, a haiku-centered poetic community could come into being and acquire its true meaning only by means of the exclusion of large numbers of fellow citizens; the fundamental problem with *haikai* in his day was, in short, that there were too many commoners composing it. As should be abundantly clear, the reform groups' discourse of social hierarchy as inherent to and necessary for true literature would seem to mitigate against the idea of literary writing as a focal point for the emergence of national identity, and even more so against the idea of poetic and national communities as essentially synonymous.

Earlier in the chapter, I noted that the *Teikoku bungaku* group first found *haikai*'s connection to the commoner to be problematic, before later valorizing the *Man'yōshū* as a collection of the songs of the people and symbol of national unity. Something similar would go on to occur with the "commoner literature" label, which reappeared in the early twentieth century, deployed in a positive and unifying sense that is conspicuously absent from Shiki's writings. This was especially true after Japan's victory in the Russo-Japanese War in 1905. For instance, scholar Haga Yaichi's preface to Iwaki Juntarō's 岩城準太郎 (1878–1957) *Meiji bungakushi* (A history of Meiji literature, 1906) states that commoner literature had played an instrumental role in spreading the "warrior ethos" (*bushidō*) and "patriotism and loyalty" (*chūkun aikoku*) that had contributed to Japan's recent victory.[89] As a more striking illustration, one major figure of the late nineteenth-century haiku reform movement reappears in the early twentieth century having seemingly reversed his Meiji position on commoner literature entirely. On the occasion of the accession to the throne of the Taishō emperor in 1912, none other than Kakuta Chikurei presented the new sovereign with a collection of haiku so as to "humbly introduce His Majesty to the subtle charms of commoner literature" (*heimin bungaku no myōmi o goshōkai mōshiageru*).[90]

Rarely highlighted in narratives of haiku reform or of national literature in Japan, these shifts amply illustrate the precarious and varying nature of the narratives that work to fashion a national-poetic community and the inherently unstable boundaries of that construct. In the following chapter, I continue this line of argument. I explore how discourses of gender and masculinity, as well as factional politics, combined to give rise to strategies of differentiation that shaped the modern emergence of another poetic genre purportedly even more tightly linked to ideas of Japanese national identity. This is, of course, *waka*, and the next chapter covers the work of Shiki and Yosano Tekkan to fashion it into a modern literary genre.

CHAPTER FIVE

The Unmanly Poetry of Our Times

Shiki, Tekkan, and Waka *Reform, 1890–1900*

This final chapter of the book returns to the question of who could—or should—write poetry in the Meiji nation-state. Where the previous four chapters have focused on the boundaries of poetic community for *kanshi* and haiku, however, this concluding chapter addresses *waka*, Japan's third major traditional poetic genre.[1] On the face of it, *waka* might seem the most promising genre from which to fashion a national poetry, for it was uniquely and unarguably Japanese. It had been practiced in Japan for more than a thousand years, for much of that time the preserve of emperors and court nobles, and so had none of *kanshi*'s air of foreignness or *haikai*'s problematic associations with "commoners." *Waka* also had an impressive intellectual pedigree, boasting an extensive body of theoretical and exegetical writings produced by Edo-era National Learning scholars such as Keichū 契沖 (1640–1701), Kamo no Mabuchi 賀茂真淵 (1697–1769), and Motoori Norinaga 本居宣長 (1730–1801), one of Japan's most brilliant scholars and philologists.

These factors, in particular the strong association with the imperial institution, meant that *waka* seemed almost tailor-made as a tool with which to imagine a national community during Meiji. Among the raft of new ceremonies and (re)invented traditions centering on the imperial institution during early Meiji, for instance, was the *utakai hajime* (New Year's poetry party), a ceremony marking the New Year in which the emperor and courtiers composed *waka*, the best of which were then read aloud. There was a precedent (though by no means a continuous tradition) of emperors issuing poetic compositions to mark the new year throughout Japanese history, but the Meiji *utakai hajime* was something new in being both regular (held every year) and nationwide in scope. Revived in 1868, the Meiji *utakai hajime* initially allowed only courtiers and those close to the emperor to submit verses. In 1874, however, participation was opened to all Japanese subjects, allowing them to send in their verses for consideration. The ceremony therefore took on a modern, national-symbolic significance, presenting a spectacle of people and emperor alike joined together through the composition of an ancient and uniquely Japanese poetic medium.[2]

The *utakai hajime*, which continued throughout the twentieth century and is still practiced to the present day, has been seen as symbolic of a successful effort to link *waka* poetry and national identity in the modern Japanese nation-state. Murai Osamu, who has written extensively about the "nationalization" (*kokuminka*) of *waka*, argues that Meiji *waka* contained a "utopian discourse of 'one sovereign and myriad people'" (*ikkun banmin*) and that in the Meiji nation-state, the very act of writing *waka* came to entail a kind of "subject formation" (*shutaika*). Amplified by Japan's print media, which reported and commented on the emperor's own *utakai-hajime* verse and the selected commoner compositions, the *utakai hajime*, in Murai's view, played a critical role in Meiji state and subject formation; the ceremony, he argues, helped to create the modern imperial institution, not the other way around.[3] Other critics have drawn broadly similar conclusions. Exploring the uses of *waka* in Okinawa and in Japan's later colonies as a tool of imperialism, Suga Satoko has argued that self-expression through *waka* automatically implicated a poet as a Japanese imperial subject;[4] and Shinada Yoshikazu has described how the Meiji celebration of the Nara-period *waka* collection *Man'yōshū* was predicated on the idea that the authors of the works therein ran the gamut from emperors to commoners—a vision of national unity reflected in poetry.[5]

This modern usage of *waka* has not gone unchallenged. Both Murai and Shinada take pains to challenge the connection between *waka* and notions of Japanese national identity; Shinada has argued that the *Man'yōshū*'s supposed connection to the common people has no basis in fact, and Murai decries the long-term effects of the nationalization of *waka*. Criticizing this nationalization as rooted in "mysticism" (*shinpika*), he is particularly scathing about the Pacific War–era positing of an explicit connection between patriotism and *waka* composition, calling it "absurd" (*bakagete iru*).[6] These criticisms notwithstanding, the survival to the present day of the emperor-centered *utakai hajime*, as well as the fact that the late Meiji vision of the *Man'yōshū*'s qualities has become what Murai calls public knowledge, suggests a certain inexorable, if manufactured, logic at work in the link between *waka* and national identity in modern Japan. Certainly, the ideas that *waka* is an essential part of Japanese literary identity, and that to write *waka* is to claim membership in a national-poetic community, have proven extremely durable.

Meiji *waka* might therefore seem less-promising ground in which to search for the fault lines and discourses of exclusion that this study has argued are at work in the formation of a national-poetic community. However, despite its role as a focal point for national-subject formation through poetry, the *utakai hajime* offers a few clues as to where such an inquiry might begin. One curious fact about the *utakai hajime* is that love poetry—a major part of the historical *waka* canon—appears to have been tacitly excluded from the ceremony early on in Meiji, likely as part of an effort to recast the Meiji emperor as a modern, dynamic, and militarily inclined sovereign. This apparent anxiety, that the proximity of love poetry to the sovereign might weaken his masculine image, points toward much larger problems of gender and masculinity in Meiji *waka*. Put simply, Meiji discourse of *waka* reform was dogged by a persistent anxiety that the genre was not masculine enough and concern over what that might mean for Japan as a nation. In fact, as I show in this chapter, the question of what to do about "feminine" elements in *waka* was key to many discussions of the genre's place in the modern nation-state.

According to Meiji-era critics, the supposedly feminine nature of *waka* manifested itself in three main aspects of its history and aesthetics. The first was that a substantial number of *waka* poets, especially during the Heian period, had been women. The genre continued to be relatively widely practiced by women well into Meiji, certainly more so than haiku or *kanshi*, and Meiji critics frequently claimed that women and *waka* had a particular affinity. The second major aspect lay in the fact that poems on romantic love (*koiuta*, or *koi no uta*) made up a huge part of the historical *waka* canon; as Haruo Shirane has noted of the Heian period in particular, "the two primary topics in *waka* were the seasons and love, with love being implicit in the seasonal poems and nature being the primary expressions of love."[7] Conventionally, *koiuta* spoke of wistful or frustrated desire, longing for an absent lover, or moments of parting and sorrow and were well represented among the various imperial *waka* anthologies. As one example, slightly more than half the *waka* in the *Collection of Poems Old and New* (*Kokin wakashū*, or *Kokinshū*), an anthology that many early Meiji *waka* poets took as their touchstone, were explicitly on the topic of love. This strong representation within *waka* of both female poets and love-themed poems perhaps explains the third major criticism made of *waka* during Meiji—namely, that its predominant aesthetics encouraged weakness and effeminacy among male poets. Much as chapter 2 saw critics of fragrant-style *kanshi* alleging that a fascination with the feminine indicated an effeminate poet, so, too, *waka* about wistful love and the pathos of the changing seasons were understood as inimical to a bold, vigorous, and martial ideal of poetic masculinity.

These seemingly pervasive anxieties over *waka*'s alleged feminization complicated attempts during the 1890s to use the genre as a focal point for a national-poetic community. Some spoke positively of *waka*'s feminization as enabling the expression of emotional truth and rendering it suitable for both genders, thereby aiding the creation of a more inclusive national-poetic community. By contrast, other critics—notably, those usually credited with fashioning the modern tanka—framed their view of a poetic community in hierarchical and exclusionary terms, assailing feminized poetry and its practitioners as damaging to the national community, and as unworthy members therein.

This chapter is structured around an analysis of three main texts, all of which address issues of *waka*'s relationship to national community. The first, Yosano Tekkan's 1893 "Women and National Literature" (Joshi to kokubun), is less well known than the subsequent two texts I discuss, Tekkan's 1894 "Sounds of the Nation's Ruin" (Bōkoku no on) and Shiki's 1898 "Letters to a *Waka* Poet" (Utayomi ni atōru sho), both of which are landmarks of Japanese literary polemic. These two texts show the complicated, exclusionary processes involved in the origins of modern tanka, with Tekkan attacking the old-school *waka* poets of the officially sponsored Outadokoro (Bureau of Poetry) as not only incompetent but weak and effeminate as well. By contrast, Shiki, although he endorsed Tekkan's rhetoric of strength and manliness in *waka*, developed his critique of contemporary *waka* on more subtle grounds, electing to attack the idea that *waka* was a specifically national literature at its base. In "Letters to a *Waka* Poet" and the angry exchanges that followed, Shiki repeatedly claimed that there was nothing particularly "Japanese" about *waka*. Rather, Shiki argued, *waka* was part of a universal "literature," which was best understood by those with formal academic training. If, for Tekkan, the problem with contemporary *waka* was that the dominant poets were weak and effeminate, for Shiki it was that they were ill educated and parochial, claiming a sacred status for even clumsy and dull *waka* on the grounds that they embodied a putative national essence.

By bringing these three texts into dialogue with one another and placing them within a larger discursive framework of gender and masculine anxiety, the chapter complements previous discussions of gender and national literature by Tomi Suzuki and Tomiko Yoda, both of which focus on prose narratives and the reception of historical texts. As Suzuki has noted, although Meiji national literature scholars showed a good deal of ambivalence toward the idea, the notion of Japanese literature as essentially feminine proved enormously durable, exerting a hold even into the postwar period.[8] This ambivalence played out in various forms; Suzuki notes that as late as 1899, for instance, Haga Yaichi attacked the *Kokinshū* as "shallow" in an attempt to "de-essentialize or disentangle the ambivalent connection between the kana-based national language / literature and the feminine."[9] Later scholars, notably Fujioka Sakutarō 藤岡作太郎 (1870–1910) and Tsuda Sōkichi 津田左右吉 (1873–1961), however, attached a positive evaluation to this feminization, challenging the idea that femininity and weakness were linked. Fujioka privileged Heian literature for expressing truly human emotions, and Tsuda claimed that the expression of love and reverence for nature were crucial elements in the Japanese literary tradition.[10] Tomiko Yoda likewise has argued that the identification of Japanese literature with the feminine is "an enduring cliché in modern Japanese culturalism," often used "to assert the uniqueness of Japan," and that the deployment of gender binaries in modernizing discourses in Japanese literature enabled literature to be presented as "an essence that underwrites the national identity, integrating its diverse constituents."[11] As she notes, "specifically feminine literary aesthetics or feminine moments in literary history were typically constituted as the negativities to be overcome or sublated (both repressed and conserved) when literary discourses of the past were reconstituted in the framework of the modern national subject."[12]

The present chapter's discussion of the gendering of *waka* expands this discussion in a number of ways. One important point, not necessarily true in the case of prose works such as the *Tale of Genji*, was that *waka*'s gendering was a matter of both literary-historical interpretation and Meiji practice; as has been noted throughout this study, the idea of a national-poetic community assumed that individuals would not only read but also write poetry. Supposedly feminine aesthetics and moments in Japanese literary history were thus of importance not only for what they might say about the Japanese national character throughout history but also for how they might still influence Meiji compositional aesthetics, and what those aesthetics said about Meiji Japanese subjects. Second, I go further than either Yoda or Suzuki in characterizing the attitude toward the purported feminization of Japanese literature as not only ambivalence but also deep-rooted anxiety and, at times, vitriolic hostility. During the 1890s, critics such as Hagino Yoshiyuki and Tekkan suggested that feminized literature and feminized men imperiled Japan's national security; the exclusion of the feminine was, for them, a matter of utmost urgency.

The chapter thus examines a foundational moment for the idea of Japanese literature as feminine and also reveals the unstable terrain upon which this idea was built, with discourses of exclusion and marginalization critical to the constitution of the national-poetic subject in *waka*. *Waka* was contested territory, with competing views of what it should be and who should write it, and which poets did or did not fit into visions of national community.

THE LIGHT FRAGRANCE OF MANLINESS: TEKKAN, OCHIAI NAOBUMI, AND THE ASAKASHA

When Yosano Tekkan arrived in Tokyo in the autumn of 1892, there was as yet little to suggest that he was destined for a successful literary career, albeit one partially overshadowed by that of his third wife, Yosano Akiko.

Encouraged by his father, a Buddhist priest, Tekkan had experience in writing *kanshi* but had composed few *waka* by the time he arrived in the capital. Tekkan's father had been a priest at a temple on the outskirts of Kyoto and had been acquainted with Ōtagaki Rengetsu 太田垣蓮月 (1791–1875), one of the most famous female *waka* poets of the Edo era. It was apparently Rengetsu who suggested the given name of Hiroshi for the young man, a connection that makes Tekkan's later writings on women and *waka* rather ironic. Though scholarly and cultured, the family in which young Hiroshi grew up was one mired for the most part in poverty. For a time, Tekkan apparently prepared to take holy orders himself before electing instead to pursue a career in teaching.

Unlike most of those who pursued *waka* reform during the 1890s, such as Shiki and Ochiai Naobumi, Tekkan had little in the way of formal academic qualifications, but this did not prove an obstacle to his finding a job teaching Japanese language and literature at a girls' school in the town of Tokuyama, in Yamaguchi Prefecture, at the very western end of Honshu. Good-looking and passionate, the young Tekkan seems to have been well liked by his students, an assertion supported by the fact that he subsequently married two of them at different points in his life. While in Tokuyama, Tekkan read a number of metropolitan literary magazines, among them Mori Ōgai's *Shigarami-zōshi*, wherein he first encountered the work of his future mentor, Ochiai Naobumi. Tekkan also published a brief piece or two on literary topics in the Tokyo women's periodical *Fujo zasshi* before his departure for Tokyo toward the end of 1892.[13]

In contrast to Shiki, who had had the backing of Matsuyama's Evergreen Society when he arrived in Tokyo eight years earlier, Tekkan appears to have lacked a clear plan for supporting himself in the capital. With his family too impoverished to send him funds and no resources of his own, Tekkan spent much of his first year in Tokyo in dire poverty, bringing in a meager income by ghostwriting and copyediting, selling many of his prized possessions, and occasionally skipping meals or subsisting on a single sweet potato as his only food for the day.[14] It was, in part, these miserable living conditions that cemented the relationship between Tekkan and Ochiai. Although Tekkan had contacted him shortly after arriving in the capital and the two had previously met, it was not until Ochiai saw Tekkan's circumstances for himself that he took the young man under his wing. At the beginning of 1893, so the anecdote has it, Ochiai moved to a house near Kisshōji temple in Tokyo, where Tekkan was lodging. Taking a walk near the temple on a cold morning, Ochiai happened to see Tekkan shivering in his lodgings and was moved to invite the impoverished younger man to move in with him. This concern for the well-being of the members of his literary circle seems to have been typical of Ochiai's warm and encouraging approach to his colleagues and disciples, and he and Tekkan went on to develop a close relationship. Ochiai's admiration for the young poet's budding talent is apparent from a number of anecdotes and later recollections from Tekkan himself; in correcting Tekkan's poetry, for example, Ochiai rarely wrote anything other than "very good!" (*ito yoroshi*).[15] Likewise, when Tekkan raised the idea of enrolling in a formal course of study at the Kokugakuin academy, Ochiai apparently dissuaded him on the grounds that Tekkan was already talented enough and could progress simply by reading appropriate texts as the mood took him. Ochiai's affection for Tekkan was not necessarily shared by other members of his salon; Ochiai's younger brother Ayukai Kaien 鮎貝槐園 (Fusanoshin 房之進, 1864–1946) recalled that Tekkan alienated a number of other members of Ochiai's circle with his perceived arrogance and unsparing criticism of their work. Ayukai's assessment, at this point in Tekkan's career, was that the young poet was talented but "didn't have the ability to pull it all together" (*matomeru nōryoku wa nakatta*).[16]

By the time he had met Tekkan, Ochiai himself was already a poet and scholar of some distinction. Like Kuga Katsunan and Kokubu Seigai, he had been born in the northern Sendai domain, which had resisted the imperial forces even after the Restoration. Just south of Kesennuma, in present-day Miyagi Prefecture, Ochiai had been born as Ayukai Naobumi, a scion of the Ayukai family of retainers to the Date clan, the hereditary lords of the domain. The Ayukais were, however, not particularly wealthy or influential, with a stipend of only around one thousand *koku*. Ochiai's experience of the disturbances of the Boshin War was more direct than that of many young men his age, since his father, Ayukai Tarōhei Morifusa 鮎貝太郎平盛房 (1835–1894), had commanded Sendai domain forces against the new government in August of 1868. Morifusa led his troops ably, distinguishing himself in battle to the extent that after the hostilities the new government punished him with a year's house arrest and a reduction of the family stipend from one thousand to a mere twenty *koku*. Shortly after this, in 1874, at the age of fourteen the young Naobumi was adopted by the Ochiais, a family of hereditary Shinto priests in the coastal city of Shiogama whose surname he would use thereafter. In due course, Ochiai would find himself studying at Jingū Kyōin, a teaching academy that the Meiji government had established in the town of Ise for the education of Shinto priests. There, he met Ikebe (aka Konakamura) Yoshikata 池辺 (小中村) 義象 (1861–1923), who would also go on to play a significant role in the academic construction of a Japanese national literature, and with whom Ochiai would remain lifelong friends.[17]

Ochiai remained at Jingū Kyōin for four years, leaving Ise in 1881 to study at Nishō Gakusha before entering Tokyo University in July 1882 as part of the inaugural class for the Japanese classical literature department (*koten kōshūjo*). For reasons that remain unclear, Ochiai was called up to the military in 1884 after three years as a student and served for three years, returning to his studies in 1887.[18] After graduation, Ochiai taught at a number of public and private schools in Tokyo, including First Higher Middle School (Daiichi Chūtō Kōgakkō), Tokyo College (Tokyo Senmon Gakkō, later Waseda University), Atomi Women's School (Atomi Jogakkō), and the Japanese Language Institute (Kokugo Denshū Jo). In addition to his teaching activities, Ochiai contributed to the editing and production of a number of foundational anthologies that shaped the canon of the emerging discipline of national literature. Mikami Sanji and Takatsu Kuwasaburō's 1890 *Nihon bungakushi* credits him for "assistance" (*hojo*), and, along with his school friend Ikebe Yoshikata, Ochiai also edited the twenty-four-volume *Complete Works of Japanese Literature* (*Nihon bungaku zensho*), published by Hakubunkan between 1890 and 1892. Not content with this, Ochiai edited and produced a number of Japanese literature and history textbooks, such as the 1891 *Japanese Literary Classics for Middle School Education* (*Chūtō kyōiku Nihon bunten*), which he coauthored with Ikebe.

Ochiai's literary interests did not stop at the purely academic, for he was also an active poet. Among his early accomplishments was a well-received five-hundred-thirty-two-line *shintaishi* adaptation of an earlier *kanshi* by Inoue Tetsujirō, *The Song of the Filial Daughter Shiragiku* (*Kōjo Shiragiku no uta*), which Ochiai published in 1888 and apparently wrote while in the army. Shortly after, in 1889, one of Ochiai's students introduced him to the rising literary star Mori Ōgai, and the two struck up a long-lasting professional relationship. Ochiai collaborated with Ōgai on several translations of Western poetry that were ultimately published under the title *Vestiges* (*Omokage*) in 1889, and, apparently finding the association congenial, Ochiai also helped with the launch of Ōgai's literary journal *Shigarami-zōshi* the same year.

It was, however, in the realm of *waka* reform that Ochiai seems to have come into his own. As one of only a handful of poets and scholars explicitly aiming to reform *waka* prior to the Sino-Japanese War, Ochiai provided direct and material assistance to budding voices such as Tekkan and, indirectly, Shiki. In keeping with his background as a teacher, one of Ochiai's first publications on *waka* was a poetic lexicon, *Newly Selected Poetic Classics* (*Shinsen kaden*, 1891), which provided vocabulary and suggested topics for composition in much the same vein as the *Handbook for Beginning Learners*–type texts discussed in chapter 1. Compiled with the help of Ikebe Yoshikata, Hagino Yoshiyuki 萩野由之 (1860–1924), and other scholars, *Shinsen kaden* encouraged readers to break free of restraints on poetic vocabulary and use words reflecting new Meiji material realities, such as "mail" (*yūbin*) and "telegraph" (*denshin*), in their poetry. It met with success, going through six editions over the next eight years, and the year after its initial publication Ochiai also inaugurated a journal titled *Kagaku* in March of 1892. In his preface introducing the journal's first issue, Ochiai outlined his vision for Meiji *waka*. His concern was that *waka* was, at present, not a literature "of the nation's people as a whole" (*kokujin oshinabete*) but rather "a plaything of those highborn nobles, a pastime of those old men who have turned their back on the world; looking at such people, I will not say that our art is truly thriving." Rather, Ochiai wrote, "for this sublime thing we call *waka*, I would place my hopes in all the people of the nation [*subete no kokujin*], particularly those youth of great promise [*seinen yūi no hitobito*]." In conclusion to his short piece, Ochiai also touched on the importance of bold, masculine poems to his vision of poetic reform:

> Since the *Manyōshū*, there have been exceedingly few virile and vigorous poems; Minister of the Right [Minamoto no] Sanetomo [源実朝 (1192–1219)] and Kamo no Mabuchi are the only exceptions. All

that we call *waka* has slid into effeminacy. What is the cause of this? Does it lie in politics, religion, or education? It will be most interesting to investigate these areas. At the present time, it would appear that what we call *waka* is not well suited to our hot-blooded young men. But this surely cannot be the true essence of *waka*. In our times we must raise up a truly bold and manly, vigorous *waka*.[19]

Although it featured contributions from some of Japan's leading national literature scholars, in common with most niche poetry journals during the 1890s *Kagaku* was relatively short-lived and ceased publication after a year and a month, in April of 1893. While under Ochiai's umbrella, Tekkan had also tried to launch a poetry journal, *Hōsū*, in December of 1892, which, similarly, lasted only one issue before being abandoned. Perhaps realizing the precarious nature of contemporary poetry publications, after Ochiai formally inaugurated his Asakasha group in February of 1893, the group elected to publish its work mainly in the capital's newspapers rather than expend more effort on running its own journal.

The name of the newly formed society, meaning literally "Light Fragrance Society," was probably intended to allude to the Asaka-machi district of Tokyo, where Ochiai was living at the time and where the group tended to hold its gatherings. Ochiai's younger brother Ayukai Kaien was a founding member, as were national literature scholar and prominent critic Ōmachi Keigetsu and Shinto priest and scholar Utsumi Getsujō 内海月杖 (1872–1935). At its peak, the Asakasha was unusually large for a private *waka* group, with gatherings bringing together as many as forty participants. With the exception of Tekkan, who had approached Ochiai on his own, the majority of members were either Ochiai's own students or had studied at institutions where he taught. Notably, this included a number of women poets, including Morooka Sukako 師岡須賀子 (dates unknown) and Kazaate Sakiko 風当咲子 (dates unknown), both of whom had studied at the Japanese Language Institute, which admitted women and later counted noted feminist and Marxist Yamakawa Kikue 山川菊栄 (1890–1980) among those who passed through its halls.[20] Morooka and Kazaate were also joined as female founding members by Kokubu Misako 国分操子 (d. 1942), the poetically accomplished wife of *Nippon*'s star *kanshi* poet Kokubu Seigai. There were, apparently, enough women in the

Asakasha that it was possible to do *uta-awase* competitions featuring men against women, with Tekkan leading the men and Kokubu Misako recording the contest.

In addition to confirming Ochiai's welcoming attitude toward female poets, Kokubu Misako's membership also reflected an initial affinity between the Asakasha and the newspaper *Nippon*. Shortly after the group's founding, Ochiai published a selection of Asakasha verses in the newspaper on February 11, 1893, and Itsumi Kumi has estimated that the group published around two hundred and fifty verses in the newspaper over the subsequent four years, around half of them authored by Tekkan.[21] A significant number of the verses that the group published in *Nippon* during 1893 and 1894 were overt commentary on contemporary political events, something quite unusual in the *waka* tradition as a whole but entirely in line with *Nippon*'s antigovernment stance. An idea of the tone of the Asakasha's early topical verses can be detected in the following sequence of poems from May 4, 1893:

内地雑居 On *"Mixed Residence"*[22]

ira ōki they plan, it seems, to plant
nageki mo shirade the many-thorned demon rose
onibara o heedless of our laments
sakura no kage ni in the shade
uemu to suramu of the cherry tree.

いらおほきなげきも知らで鬼ばらをさくらのかげにうゑむとすらむ

藩閥 On the Satsuma-Chōshū Cliques

masurao ga avoiding the hunting arrows
satsuya nogarete of stalwart men
shikajimono how long will our *deer* friends
itsu made hagi ni spend blending
tachimajiru ramu with the bush clover?

ますらをがさつ矢のがれて鹿児物いつまで萩にたちまじるらむ

議会閉会	*On the Closing of the Diet*

nitari tefu	the men it's said resemble them
hito wa kaerite	go on home
Sakurada ni	and in Sakurada
ima wa makoto no	now they croak,
kawazu naku nari	a bunch of true frogs.[23]

似たりてふ人はかへりてさくら田に今はまことの蛙なくなり

The second poem likens the Satsuma and Chōshū elites to a deer hiding in bush clover to avoid a hunter's arrows—or to avoid criticism directed at their activities by "stalwart men" (*masurao*). It puns on the names of two major cities in the former domains of Satsuma and Chōshū, Kagoshima (reading the kanji literally, "Deer Child Island," in present-day Kagoshima Prefecture) and Hagi (literally, "Bush Clover" but also the name of a city in present-day Yamaguchi), as well as a poem from the *Man'yōshū*, and the overall effect is to implicitly question both the martial and political courage of Japan's political elite.[24] The third poem rehashes *Nippon*'s well-worn trope of likening corrupt politicians to clamorous frogs. Although the verses were unsigned, it is likely that Ochiai and Ayukai Kaien were behind them. Since members of their immediate family had fought against the forces of Satsuma-Chōshū during the Boshin War, it is not hard to imagine a lingering antipathy toward the new government. Moreover, Ayukai, who had studied Korean at the Tokyo Foreign Languages Academy and would later play an important role in cementing Japanese colonial rule in Korea, was also known to be a vocal member of the "hard faction" (*kōha*) urging the Meiji government to adopt a more uncompromising line in its dealings with foreign countries, and so the "demon rose" poem may well have been his work.[25]

LOVE WILL TEAR US APART: MASCULINITY IN MEIJI *WAKA* DISCOURSE

Given the direct involvement of his brother Ayukai and his star pupil, Tekkan, in advancing the interests of Japanese imperialism, as well as the ethno-nationalist tone of a number of the group's *waka*, it might be tempting to view Ochiai simply as a reactionary nationalist. Maeda Tōru, however, has noted that, like Shiki, Ochiai was part of a demographic of literarily focused men who were for the most part shut out of the corridors of power because of their domainal background and political leanings, and that in practice Ochiai "was part of the social class that, on a fundamental level, accepted Western influence."[26] In his manifesto in the short-lived journal *Kagaku*, Ochiai had been emphatic that *waka* reformers needed to study Chinese and Western poetry as well.[27] The seemingly nationalistic tone of Ochiai's work in *waka* reform can also be understood as part of a strategy, frequently used by groups opposed to the Satsuma and Chōshū groups that came to dominate the new Meiji government, of claiming righteous patriotism as a way of buttressing their own position while attacking the government. We have already seen how accusations of effeminacy in *kanshi* reflected partisan divides, and a similar subtext runs through *waka* reform. In particular, Tekkan's and Ochiai's poems and ideas for improving contemporary *waka* placed a strong emphasis on martial diction and imagery. Tekkan became famous beginning in 1895 for his so-called sword-and-tiger style of hypermasculine, martially focused poetry, and Ochiai, too, favored similar imagery. In May of 1892, for instance, Ochiai published a verse in the First Higher School magazine that ran as follows:

hiodoshi no	how fine, I think, it would be
yoroi o tsukete	to gaze on them
tachi hakite	wearing my armor with the red braid
mibaya to zo omou	and with sword strapped to my side—
yamazakurabana	mountain cherry blossoms.[28]

緋縅の鎧をつけて太刀佩きて見ばやとぞ思う山桜花

This verse earned Ochiai the soubriquet, half in jest and half in admiration, of Red-Braided Naobumi (Hiodoshi no Naobumi). In the specific context in which it appeared, the poem was perhaps intended to stir up patriotic and martial feelings in the students at the elite school, but it is also emblematic of Naobumi's part in a movement during the 1890s that aimed to restore a lost masculinity to contemporary *waka* poetics.

One of the earliest advocates of martially minded *waka* was Ochi-ai's friend and scholarly collaborator Hagino Yoshiyuki, in his 1887 manifesto *On Reforming National Learning and Waka* (*Kokugaku waka kairyō ron*). Hagino's discussion of *waka* proceeded from the premise that for much of Japanese history the genre had been harmful to the nation. As Heian aristocrats had become steeped in *waka*, so their grip on power had declined; in Hagino's view, *waka* had been a causal factor in one of the most significant changes of power in Japanese history, the decline of aristocratic power and rise of warrior rule during the late Heian period:

> Observe the state of things from the reign of Emperor Monmu [697–707] to the reign of Emperor Go-Sanjō [1068–1073]. Their greatness was such that they lost nothing in comparison with the kingly ways of the land of China. But the decline of the court came about when, beginning in the Engi era [901–923], everyone became overly concerned with *waka* and during the time of Emperor Ichijō [986–1011] the court became like women, weak and languid. Ultimately, there arose the Hōgen Disturbance [1156], and from then on through the Jōkyū War [1221] and Kenmu Restoration [1333–1336], *waka* became the plaything of noble houses, and even though it became exactly as they desired, it was risible [*okashi*]. It has been said that the reason why our Japanese *waka* corrupted our country of Japan is because the nobles and emperors forgot the rules of Emperor Monmu.[29]

Waka, as Hagino portrayed it, had distracted Heian aristocrats and sapped their masculinity, robbing them of the vigor to maintain their grip on power. Identifying specific problems in *waka*, Hagino pointed to *waka*'s concern with the depiction of love and desire, as exemplified by Motoori Norinaga's famous concept of the "pathos of things" (*mono no aware*). Writing in part against the martial ideology of the dominant warrior class of his day, Norinaga had argued for the emotional sensitivity implied by an understanding of deeply moving things as being key to the production of poetry, and also that such sensitivity was a fundamental aesthetic in the *Tale of Genji*. Moreover, in Norinaga's conception, *mono no aware* had a profound connection to the supposedly feminine characteristics of weakness and immaturity, in contrast to the warrior class's celebration of masculine steadfastness.[30] Although it does not mention Norinaga by name, Hagino's piece attacks *mono no aware*'s emotional sensitivity as simply a byword for weakness:

> **Poetic tone:** It is very bad to posit that love is fundamental to *waka* and claim that one can learn thereby of the pathos of things [*mono no aware*]. *Mono no aware* is a principle that leads to a style of timidity and weakness, and when poetic tone lacks vigor, this comes principally from viewing *mono no aware* as a fundamental element in *waka*. Look at those new-style poems [*shintaishi*]. Their poetic diction is crude and unrefined, even though they are the work of renowned scholars. Nevertheless, this crudeness has not stopped them from spreading throughout the realm in no time at all, even unto the august ears of His Majesty himself, and it is said that a number of the poems have found their way to being incorporated into military marches and music. This is surely because the poems are vigorous and good for developing a mood of martial bravery.[31]

Hagino thus rejects Norinaga's valorization of emotional truth: love poems, being rooted in *mono no aware*, encourage weakness and timidity. For a counterexample to Japan's allegedly effeminate *waka*, Hagino pointed to poems in the *Collection of New-Style Poems* (*Shintaishishō*, 1882), a compendium of experimental original poems and translations from Western-language works published by three Tokyo University professors, Toyama Masakazu 外山正一 (1848–1900), Yatabe Ryōkichi 矢田部良吉 (1851–1899), and Inoue Tetsujirō. Several of the translations in this collection were reworkings of martially themed pieces, such as Alfred, Lord Tennyson's (1809–1892), "The Charge of the Light Brigade." Though in the eyes of many *waka* practitioners the *Collection of New-Style Poems* was deeply flawed, for both its obvious Western influence and its formal clumsiness, Hagino argues that the poems are nevertheless instructive for their masculine and martial tone and subject matter, something sorely needed in *waka*: "Today's *waka* poets, even those who are solemn and imposing in their manliness, see the moon and sigh, grow melancholy on hearing chirruping insects, shed tears when moved by things such as a spring dawn or an autumn evening—and they actually regard this as a good thing! In this way the Japanese people's long-standing veneration for airs of martial glory shall gradually disappear, and so the Great Land of Eight Islands shall surely become a colony of weak and feeble women."[32]

For Hagino, the emotional sensitivity of *mono no aware* is corrosive to masculine strength, and *waka* practice leads even imposingly masculine men to be fragile and sensitive. To celebrate and encourage those who "see the moon and sigh" is, Hagino suggests, to feminize the Japanese people and erase their long-held martial traditions.

As Hagino's reference to Norinaga's aesthetics suggests, the placing of masculine martial vigor against purportedly weak and feminized emotional sensitivity in *waka* was not a new one. Hagino's framing of this question, however, was distinctively modern, since he located it in the geopolitical concerns of Japan as a modern nation-state. The precedent of *waka*-feminized Heian aristocrats losing their grip on power in this context pointed to a potentially dire future: if thoroughly feminized by *waka*, Meiji Japan risked not only internal disorder but also domination by foreign powers. The provocative term "colony" (*shokuminchi*) left no doubt as to the stakes in this scenario; where Norinaga had, as Yoda has put it, "used the inferiority of the feminine to overturn received assumptions about poetry and human nature,"[33] Hagino uses the geopolitical realities of the late nineteenth century to reassert a gendered, hierarchical view of *waka*. Emotional sensitivity led to feminization, which led to weakness; as such, reversing this trend and encouraging masculine, martial *waka* was nothing less than a matter of national security.

Hagino's rejection of *mono no aware* also entailed a negative evaluation of love-themed *waka*, despite their prominent position in the historical *waka* canon. In this, he was not alone; the sense that love-themed *waka* were not compatible with a martial and masculine Japanese identity seems to have been shared by members of the Outadokoro, the imperially affiliated Bureau of Poetry that was founded in early Meiji and that played the role of antagonist for later reformers such as Tekkan and Shiki. Both contemporary and later accounts of the activities of the Outadokoro poets note that they, too, excised love poetry from their poetic practice and ensured that all poetry associated with the emperor likewise eschewed romantic themes. The reasons for this are unclear; in an undated recollection in an anthology of essays published after his death in 1912, Outadokoro bureau chief Takasaki Masakaze 高崎正風 (1836–1912) recalls a discussion with an associate who had noticed that Takasaki did not compose love poetry. The associate praised him for shunning love poems and thereby elevating public morals, but Takasaki's response, which disappointed and enraged his interlocutor, was that he had never set out to marginalize love poetry. Rather, since the very young and very old were less moved by romantic love, his concern was to emphasize compositional topics to which all could relate. Far from calling love poetry immoral, Takasaki cites the first poem of the Chinese *Classic of Poetry*, "The Ospreys Cry," as an example of the edifying potential in the depiction of romantic love.[34]

Takasaki's explanation notwithstanding, the circumstantial evidence surrounding the Outadokoro's handling of love poems, particularly in relation to the person of the Meiji emperor, suggests there was in fact a tacit effort to marginalize love poetry, particularly where the sovereign might be concerned. This effort can be understood as part of a broader refashioning of the figure of the emperor during Meiji, spearheaded by higher-ranking officials of the new government assigned to the imperial court, many of whom traced their backgrounds to Satsuma or Chōshū. Asukai Masamichi, for instance, has characterized the refashioning of the imperial image during early Meiji as a defeminization. The young "son of heaven" (*tenshi*), before his reenvisioning as a modern "emperor," appeared distinctly feminine, since he "wore makeup, blackened his teeth, shaved his eyebrows, and was surrounded by female officials of the Rear Palace."[35] In contrast, the Meiji emperor's attire of military uniform and cavalry saber in his official portrait distanced him from the supposedly effeminate nobility and fostered the image of a martially minded, powerful sovereign. In keeping with this image, love as a topic was completely excluded from the Meiji *utakai hajime*, and no reigning emperor to the present day has ever composed a love-themed poem as part of the ceremony.[36]

A similar process of defeminization and marginalization of love poetry can be observed in the Meiji reception of the *Ogura Collection of One Hundred Poems by One Hundred Poets* (*Ogura hyakunin isshu*, hereafter simply *Hyakunin isshu*). Consisting of one hundred *waka* verses by Heian poets, the *Hyakunin isshu* collection also provided material for a popular card game, often played as part of New Year celebrations.[37] Many *Hyakunin isshu* poems explicitly address the topic of love, and during Meiji, the collection, which had been widely used in women's education during the Edo period and was one of the major avenues through which commoners might encounter Heian *waka*, was denounced for the purported immorality of its love poems. Early in Meiji, the *Hyakunin isshu* was officially deemed unsuitable for use in play at the palace, and as time went on its use among the populace in general also came under attack.[38]

Particularly active in this regard was Nishimura Shigeki 西村茂樹 (1828–1902), an influential educator and onetime tutor to the emperor on Confucian learning. Nishimura argued that the *Hyakunin isshu*'s love poems were licentious and not proper for parents to read to children, and in 1883 he went so far as to publish a *Newly Chosen "Hyakunin isshu"* (*Shinsen hyakunin isshu*), which replaced any poem that even hinted at romantic love with a different work by the same poet. In a similar vein later in Meiji, a commentary on the *Hyakunin isshu* published in the journal *Jogaku sekai* in 1908 provided both a vernacular explanation of the text of each poem and a "hygienic view" (*eiseikan*) assessing its moral aspects. For one love poem in the collection, the commenter asserted that because the love depicted in the poem was not that between husband and wife, it was not only immoral but also a form of mental illness. Those who might fall prey to such temptations should adopt a thoroughly Victorian method of dealing with them: "Scour oneself with cold water, take exercise, and then these feelings will disappear of their own accord."[39]

EVERY GIRL A PRINCESS: TEKKAN'S "WOMEN AND NATIONAL LITERATURE"

Although there had been individual poets in pre-Meiji times who had declared their opposition to love poetry on moral grounds, such as Kada no Azumamaro 荷田春満 (1669–1736), there was little precedent for a concerted attempt to eliminate love poetry from the historical canon and prohibit its contemporary composition. In the specific case of the *Hyakunin isshu*, the attacks may have had as much to do with issues of public sexual morality as with the poems' perceived ability to undermine masculinity,[40] but there was little question that for critics such as Hagino and (as we shall see) Tekkan, love poetry's prominent place in the *waka* canon was further evidence of the genre's feminized nature. Nonetheless, not everyone agreed with the idea that love poems as a whole were undesirable. In 1891, Ochiai Naobumi attempted to stake out a more nuanced position in a partial rebuttal to Nishimura Shigeki's public comments, particularly Nishimura's listing of *waka* composition among seven undesirable practices for women. Though it was true that the majority of love poetry in the Japanese *waka* canon was immoral, Ochiai wrote, if licentious topics were avoided and the poet confined herself to writing of love between husband and wife, then the worst effects could be avoided.[41]

Both Nishimura's criticism of *waka* composition and Ochiai's partial defense of it were directed primarily to an audience of educated women; Ochiai's piece appeared in the journal *Jokan* (1891–1909), for which he wrote regularly and which was among the most widely read women's journals of the 1890s.[42] In fact, a substantial portion of critical discourse on Meiji *waka* during the early 1890s appeared in journals marketed to women, notably *Jogaku zasshi* and *Fujo zasshi*, for which Tekkan wrote occasionally. One common theme in such journals was the argument by male critics, in generally positive terms, that *waka* was a desirable, polite accomplishment for women and one to which women were well suited, since they were more emotional than men.

Jogaku zasshi, a periodical founded and run by women's educator Iwamoto Yoshiharu 岩本善治 (1862–1943), was particularly keen on the idea that women should compose *waka*. As early as 1888, before Ochiai had begun his activities, *waka* poet and literary scholar Sasaki Nobutsuna 佐々木信綱 (1872–1963) had published a rebuttal to Hagino's *On Reforming National Learning and Waka* in the journal. Noting the latter's criticism of love poems and valorization of bold and masculine poetry, Sasaki countered that both kinds of poetry had a place in the *waka* tradition; to exclude love poetry was to follow the prosaic imagination of English novelist Bulwer Lytton's character Kenelm Chillingly, who argued that since hunger was a more universal experience than love, poets should write about food.[43] Rather, the essence of *waka* lay in the transcendent notion of *yūbi* (elegant beauty), and Sasaki found a close connection between *yūbi* and women: "The style of this *waka* is to sing of intricately detailed human emotions with elegant beauty [*yūbi*], and that doing so is most closely in accordance with women's natural character can be known from the presence of many great female poets both in our land and in the West."[44] Four years later in the same journal, Isogai Unpō 磯貝雲峯 (1865–1897), another male critic and poet, reprised exactly this argument using both modern psychology and Ki no Tsurayuki's preface to the *Kokinshū*. Since the writing of *waka* was based in emotion, Unpō held, and since "you, ladies, are far richer in emotion than men," it made perfect sense for women to study *waka*. Gesturing toward Hagino's arguments in *On Reforming National Learning and Waka*, Unpō noted that "those who sneer at women as delicate and yielding and laugh at them as soft and weak have yet to learn what women are."[45]

Much of the critical discourse on *waka* in women's journals during the late 1880s and 1890s thus attached a positive valuation to the purported feminization of *waka* and would seem to be largely in line with conventional analyses of *waka* as an important mechanism in Meiji subject formation. In the visions of critics such as Unpō and Sasaki, women were an important part of an incipient national-scale *waka* community, their presence justified by virtue of their greater emotional sensitivity. That women's writing of *waka* placed them in a specifically *national* poetic community is confirmed by a piece published in *Jokan* in early 1892, a couple of months after Ochiai had made his qualified defense of love poetry in the same journal. In the piece, educator Seki Iyū 關以雄 (dates unknown) argued that all Japanese subjects, men and women alike, should compose *waka*. Seki's vision of *waka* practice made it largely coterminous with national community, a literature that "knows not high or low, wise or foolish, young or old, male or female."[46] *Waka* held a privileged place in Japan, a land with a "unique emotional composition" (*tokushu no kanjōteki seiritsu naru waga Nihonkoku*);[47] as such, the genre was closely related to the sacred concept of the national polity (*kokutai*): "Truly, the art of *waka* composition has a close and meritorious relationship to our national polity, and the study of *waka* has persisted along with the unbroken line of our imperial house; from the poem 'Many Clouds Rising' by Susanoo of high antiquity and Emperor Jinmu's poem on Mount Inasa, through generations of great and heroic leaders and on to the sagely sovereign of the present, all have dedicated their heart to this Way."[48]

It followed that composing *waka* was to participate in a national tradition as ancient and venerable as the imperial house itself, an act that identified one as a modern imperial subject. Study of *waka* could even help with the "clarification of all aspects of the *kokutai*," a paramount goal for nationalist ideologues throughout much of the late nineteenth and early twentieth centuries. As if to reinforce this point, in closing Seki quoted a famous patriotic poem by Motoori Norinaga, seemingly as an example of the link between the *kokutai* and this form of poetry:

shikishima no	if someone were to ask
Yamato gokoro o	of the Japanese spirit
hito towaba	in the land of Shikishima—
asahi ni niou	it is mountain cherry blossoms,
yamazakurabana	fragrant in the morning sun.[49]

敷島のやまと心を人間はゞ朝日に匂ふ山桜ばな

In the same month that Seki published his piece, however, Tekkan made his critical debut with an explosive piece that sought to dismantle these positive associations between national subjectivity, women, and *waka*. Rarely discussed in studies of Meiji *waka* or of Tekkan's career as a whole, his "Women and National Literature" appeared in *Fujo zasshi* in four installments between March and June of 1893. Considering Tekkan's background as a teacher in a women's school and his later career, in which he not only published passionate love poems but also provided considerable support to his wife, superstar poet Yosano Akiko, "Women and National Literature" is remarkable for what appears to be its naked misogyny.

Tekkan's first installment, in March 1893, laid out the context and premises for the argument that was to come. Noting that his mentor, Ochiai Naobumi, had recently authored a piece in the journal encouraging women to study Japanese literature, Tekkan agreed with Ochiai's premise that since Japanese national literature was "elegantly graceful" (*yūbi*), it made sense for women to study it. Ochiai's encouragement, along with what Tekkan called "the momentum of the times" (*jisei*), had indeed brought impressive results in promoting literary studies for women; Tekkan claimed to "gasp in amazement at the surge in the practice of national literature in women's society [*joshi shakai*] and, moreover, at how quickly it has progressed."[50] And yet, he wrote in concluding his first installment, "I find myself obliged to maintain at this point that the popularity of Japanese literature in women's society is in one respect greatly to be lamented."[51]

In beginning the second installment of his article, Tekkan offered an anecdote to explain why he found women's study of national literature to be problematic. The anecdote centered on a farmer's daughter studying at a women's school far away from her hometown:

> The national language [*kokugoka*] teacher told her of the nature of Japanese literature, and more senior students spoke to her of its charms. This was the first time the girl had ever heard of national literature. Next the teacher instructed her in classical grammar, and lectured to her on *waka* and prose. The girl's interest inclines ever more toward national literature. The teacher has her write elegant prose [*gabun*] and compose *waka*. The girl gradually progresses in national literature. Now all her school friends praise her prose and poems. She becomes a little conceited. She sends the poems she has composed to a journal in the city. . . .
>
> The girl finishes her three years of schooling and returns to her home village. Not only her family, relatives, and old friends but also all the people of the village rejoice in celebrating her graduation. They want to see for themselves the knowledge and ethical grounding she has acquired at the women's school. . . .
>
> How does the girl decorate the living space? In the alcove she hangs up calligraphy in a contemporary style, on a pillar a calligraphic painting of a thirty-one-syllable *waka*. Piled high on the bookshelves are the *Bamboo Cutter's Tale*, the *Tale of Genji*, the *Man'yōshū*, and the *Kokinshū* . . . those who visit the house say that she is always leaning on her desk with brush in hand, but they have never yet seen her engaged in cooking or needlework. . . . Not six months have gone by since her return when the girl's father gives a deep sigh and in a low voice mutters, "Alas, the women's school has taken a farmer's daughter and turned her into a princess." An expression of disappointment passes across his face.

Reader—the above anecdote is *a true story, one that I myself have experienced.*[52]

The father's lamentation is misdirected, claims Tekkan, for it is not the women's school that has turned his daughter into a "princess" but rather national literature itself. The problem is not simply the girl's reading of national literature but her composition of *waka*; in fact, her success in having her compositions published by "journals in the city" is one of the key experiences in causing her to become "ever more conceited" and assume ideas above her station. Not only that, but the girl neglects the study of home economy, leaving her unable to manage the household on returning to her native village.

It was not until Tekkan's third installment, published in May, that he elaborated as to why national literature was so problematic. Tekkan began with the literary-historical argument that, until the end of the Nara period, Japanese national literature had maintained an even balance between vigorous and martial masculine literature on the one hand and languid and delicate feminine literature on the other. These two poles he characterized as follows:

The Two Elements of National Literature (Plebeian)

Masculine: strong and tough, bold and grand, vigorous, manly, and heroic. That over which one becomes excited, that causes a great manly roar. Like an eagle beating its wings against the storm, or a crane dancing in a clear blue sky . . .
  Feminine: Soft and yielding, elegantly beautiful, melancholy and despondent, intricately beautiful. That which moves one and brings tears. Like a willow blown by the wind, or a cherry tree assailed by rain.[53]

While literature had been in proper balance to this point in Japanese history, from the "regrettable, detestable, and infuriating era" (*kuchioshiku, urameshiku, haradatashiki jidai*) that was the Heian period, that balance had been disrupted, and almost all literature since had inclined exclusively toward the feminine. Post-Nara, Japan's national literature had been as follows:

Masculine: apart from a few elements of "vigor," almost nothing.

Feminine: weak and languid, sad and lamenting, calm and still, world-weary, licentious. Those who are prone to tears or fond of amorous pursuits. Lustrous like peach flowers, or like a withering maiden flower.[54]

Tekkan noted that there had been points of resistance: the rise of the warrior class in late Heian had given Japan the poet Minamoto no Sanetomo and warrior tales such as the *Tale of the Heike* and the *Rise and Fall of the Minamoto and Taira* (*Genpei seisuiki*), but these exceptions had not turned back the overall flow, and Japanese literature had continued to develop as "women's literature" (*josei bungaku*). Even during the Edo period, National Learning scholars such as Keichū, Mabuchi, and Norinaga had been able to only identify the problem, not resolve it, for "their efforts to return a tree that had grown deformed back to the time when it was a sapling came to naught."[55] Even to the present day, "many scholars of national literature revere the women's prose of the *Ise* and the *Genji*, and delight in the women's *waka* of the *Kokinshū*."[56]

Tekkan summed up as follows:

Our so-called national writing is women's literature, a beautiful woman with deformities. There may be some who defend this deformed beauty with the words "elegant beauty" [*yūbi*]. Very well, but how would it be if we termed it rather "languid weakness" [*dajaku*]? For truly one can see that languid weakness is the accumulated damage of centuries of women's literature. . . . This is not only about women; this languid weakness renders even bold and vigorous men effeminate, causing them to compose soft and elegant *waka* and prose, and, feeling absolutely no sense of shame, they publish them in journals and so forth. Look—it has even caused the emergence of the "elegant man" [*yasaotoko*], who adopts a female name [in the hope of getting published].[57]

An excessively feminized literature causes a range of harmful present-day effects; it attracts too many women, rendering them "conceited" in the manner of the farmer's daughter and distracting them from the study of suitable domestic skills. What is more, feminized national literature threatens even men, blurring gender boundaries to the point where men come to adopt feminine modes of behavior and even pretend to be women in the hope of getting their work published. Where Sasaki Nobutsuna had argued for the merits of the aesthetic of *yūbi* in *waka* and celebrated its connection to the feminine, Tekkan emphatically rejects the value of *yūbi* and feminized literature, painting it as a debilitating weakness that had pervaded Japan for centuries and had put Japanese men on the verge of catastrophe in the present.

In his fourth and final installment, published in June 1893, Tekkan laid out a manifesto for remedying this excessive feminization. Desperate times, he wrote, called for desperate measures: "My opinions on these measures are truly extreme. One should take no pleasure in that which is extreme, yet national literature to this point has drifted to an extreme of femininity. To return us from this extreme to a national literature of neutrality and balance between the two natures, one must resort to methods of extreme force."[58] Tekkan's "extreme force" consisted in large part of creating a set of canonical texts he understood as appropriately masculine, along with a kind of anticanon, a selection of works that needed to be marginalized. Startlingly, this anticanon included some of the best-known works in Japanese literary history. Tekkan stated that he did not bother with the *Tales of Ise* or *Tale of Genji*, or with the *Kokinshū* or *Hyakunin isshu*. The *Kojiki*, *Chronicle of Eight Dogs* (*Hakkenden*), and *Chronicle of Great Peace* (*Taiheiki*) were better prose models, the *Man'yōshū* and *Shin kokinshū* better for learning poetry. Under "Things One Should Eliminate" (Haiseki subeki mono), Tekkan suggested "*love poetry in its entirety*" (*koiuta to iu mono no zentai*; emphasis in original). As for "Things One Should Expand" (Kōchō subeki mono), in *waka* terms, Tekkan urged the composition of "hortatory poems (military and educational poems), lyric poems (what have hitherto been called miscellaneous), biographical poems (those that describe a historical personage or site), and topical *waka* (of a similar kind to the poems in *Nippon's Hyōrin*)."[59]

Tekkan's manifesto seems modeled on Hagino's arguments five years earlier on the need for martially themed *waka*, though it goes considerably further; in the interests of remasculinizing Japan, whole swaths of the country's literary history would be declared out of bounds. This would include not only "love poetry in its entirety" but also major works such as the *Tales of Ise* and the *Tale of Genji*, their excision balanced by the inclusion of tales of warrior deeds such as the *Chronicle of Great Peace* and *Chronicle of Eight Dogs*. In *waka*, too, Tekkan's selections are weighted toward the martial, encouraging the use of *waka* as an aid to morale for soldiers, to commemorate historical figures (as a matter of practicality, historical poems often depicted famous warriors or battles), and for political commentary. Political commentary was, of course, something that Tekkan and Ochiai were already doing with their *waka* in the pages of *Nippon*, but Tekkan's specific mention of Kokubu Seigai's *Hyōrin* further confirms his emphasis on cultivating aggressive masculinity. As we saw previously, Seigai was renowned for his forceful and vigorous style of *kanshi* and had launched a series of stinging attacks on what he saw as effeminacy in the *kanshi* world a couple of years earlier. Though not particularly active in *waka* per se, Seigai's *kanshi* showed him to be an excellent example of the kind of genuinely masculine poet the country required.

THE COUNTRY LOST FOR *WAKA*'S SAKE: "SOUNDS OF THE NATION'S RUIN"

Although he did not explicitly state it in "Women and National Literature," the corollary to Tekkan's argument for the remasculinization of Japanese literature would be the marginalization of both women and men who were insufficiently masculine. Women's widespread participation in national literature was, as Tekkan saw it, a symptom of an excessively feminized national literature; it followed that rebalancing national literature in favor of the masculine would mean fewer women (and fewer unmanly men) involved in its ongoing creation. At the center of Tekkan's literary reform, then, was a specific and exclusive ideal of the male writing subject, defined by the poetic performance of vigor and a martial spirit, as well as by the studied rejection of weakness and languidness.

Over the next year or so, Tekkan's critical writings narrow in focus to address specifically *waka* and to foreground the issue of masculinity—or lack thereof—among contemporary male *waka* poets. From late 1893 to early 1894, Tekkan continued to write for *Fujo zasshi*, penning a serialized piece called "On Defective *Waka*" (Utakizu o ronzu) that criticized specific verses by contemporary poets. Almost all were from the ranks of the Outadokoro, although at this stage Tekkan did not name the poets whose work he was attacking. While "On Defective *Waka*" was being serialized in *Fujo zasshi*, Tekkan was fortunate enough to be hired to write for the *Niroku shinpō* newspaper. The *Niroku* had been established only a few months before hiring Tekkan, in October of 1893, and was looking for staff writers. The connection here appears to have been Ochiai, since in addition to *Nippon*, the *Niroku* was another major venue where the Asakasha had published its poetry, and it was through Ochiai's good offices that Tekkan was introduced to the staff in November, leading to his formal employment.[60]

Much as would be the case with Shiki and *Nippon*, Tekkan's hiring at the *Niroku shinpō* was a significant moment in his career, one that afforded him not only a steady income but also a larger audience. Tekkan wasted little time in seizing this opportunity, publishing "Sounds of the Nation's Ruin" (hereafter "Sounds"), a short yet provocative piece that appeared in eight installments between May 10 and 18, 1894. The title of Tekkan's piece alluded to a famous passage in the Chinese *Book of Rites* (*Liji*) that held that a state's music reflected its overall social and political trajectory: "Therefore the music of a well-ruled state is peaceful and joyous and its government is orderly; that of an ill-governed state is full of resentment and anger, and its government is disordered; and that of a perishing state is mournful and pensive and its people are in distress" (是故治世之音安以樂、其政和。亂世之音怨以怒、其政乖。亡國之音哀以思、其民困).[61] The implication of Tekkan's title was that if the music—that is, the *waka*—of an age foretold the ultimate fate of the state, then contemporary *waka* spelled disaster for Meiji Japan.

How this ruin might come about was hinted at in the subtitle of Tekkan's piece, "Cursing the Unmanly *Waka* of Our Times" (Gendai no hijōbuteki waka o nonoshiru). In what followed, Tekkan located the faults of contemporary *waka* less in a general feminization of Japanese literature as a whole and more in the specific practices and attitudes of contemporary poets, primarily the Outadokoro. After recapitulating his earlier historical narrative of the feminization of national literature during the Heian period, Tekkan went on to explain why the problem was a pressing one in the present day, linking *waka* reform to other contemporary moral reform efforts:

> We have people for the abolition of prostitution and those who advocate for temperance; why is it that as yet we have not a single person advocating for the abolition of *waka* in our times? This statement is not as extreme as it seems.
>
> Wine and debauchery harm the body and its depredations are clear to see; but bohemian elegance [*fūryū*] can degrade the spirit, and its poison is not clearly visible. The one may only go so far as to result in the loss of the individual body; the other places the entire country in danger. The decay and fall of the Heian court and the destruction of the Ashikaga and Ouchi clans are truly good and appropriate examples of this.
>
> Who among men does not love wine and women? Yet there is surely no one who desires to lose his life for their sake. I love *waka* above all else, but I will not stand to see the country lost for its sake.
>
> Wine and women bring harm not in and of themselves but because a man will disregard what is proper. So, too, with *waka*; it is not harmful in and of itself but because it degrades people's morals. In degrading morals and spreading poison through *waka*, none are worse than contemporary *waka* poets. Reader, permit me to mount a full and frank exposé.[62]

Tekkan went on to assail contemporary *waka* poets as third-rate imitators, unaware of the truth that when the "great man" (*daijōbu*) composes *waka*, "with each breath in and out he inhales and exhales the very universe . . . thus do great and manly *waka* take shape. But our contemporary *waka* poets have no knowledge of this."[63] Because contemporary poets' entire frame of reference consisted of imitating minor poets such as Kagawa Kageki, standards declined over time, since *waka* poets failed to attain even the low level of those whose example they followed: "In this way does the *waka* of women and children take shape . . . effeminate it is, truly effeminate; weak it is, truly weak; where is the great shout of the vanguard that terrifies the armies of three states? Where is the single teardrop behind the screens that moves all for a thousand years? Alas, such are the 'great *waka* poets' of Meiji."[64]

Tekkan's next several installments consist of commentary on individual verses by named individuals, almost all of whom were affiliated with the Outadokoro. Among his prime targets were Outadokoro bureau chief Takasaki Masakaze, as well as other prominent members such as Fukuha Yoshishizu 福羽美静 (1831–1907), Kurokawa Mayori 黒川真頼 (1829–1906), and Koide Tsubara 小出粲 (1833–1908). Over the next few days, Tekkan assailed various works by these poets as "low in bearing and vulgar in imagination," "incredibly boring" (*zatsufūkei*), "puerile tricks" (*kodomo damashi*), and "sullying the eyes of the great man" (*daijōbu no me o yogosu mono*). Concluding with a "mediocre" (*heibon*) poem by Hayashi Mikaomi 林甕臣 (1844–1922), Tekkan summed up the overall state of affairs in his final installment:

> Their scale? Narrow and cramped. Their spirit? Weak and delicate. Their bearing low and vulgar, tone and rhythm licentious and disordered—given even a hundred days, I could not say enough insulting things about these kinds of *waka*. What places the nation in danger when "everyone at the helm of the state is a woman" is that the spirit of the great man weakens and women may even surpass him. What ultimately will be the insidious effects of everyone nowadays, high and low alike, venerating this kind of *women's waka*?
>
> And even worse, many of our *waka* poets do not reject love poetry; to not reject it is perhaps not so bad, but there are even some who encourage it, and that is quite beyond the pale. . . . I do not hesitate to place this "love poetry" first among the things that may upend social morality. . . . Alas, "the sounds of the nation's ruin"—I do not toss such insults around lightly.[65]

In its tone and frequent use of emphatic orthographic markers, Tekkan's disgust at the effects of effeminacy in *waka* is abundantly clear as he presents an apocalyptic vision of blurred gender identification leading to the downfall of the state itself. If those at the "helm of the state," most likely a reference to the officially sanctioned Outadokoro poets, were weak and effeminate, promoting licentious love poetry and a damaging style of *waka*, then it followed that their marginalization was a national imperative; the national-poetic community would not survive under such circumstances.

The degree of vitriol in Tekkan's "Sounds" shocked some of his colleagues, apparently earning him reproaches from Ikebe Yoshikata and Ochiai Naobumi after its publication.[66] It might also be noted that, among the criticisms leveled at the Outadokoro poets, the charge that they were degrading morals by *promoting* love poetry is dubious; as discussed earlier, the Outadokoro poets largely marginalized love poetry both tacitly and openly. Indeed, Hayashi Mikaomi, the final Outadokoro poet whom Tekkan criticized in "Sounds," had actually published a piece in the journal *Jokan* in September of 1892 titled "Do Not Compose Love Poems" (Koiuta wa yomu bekarazu).[67] Iwai Shigeki has suggested that in voicing this criticism, Tekkan may have been thinking of Takasaki Masakaze's qualified defense of love poetry discussed earlier.[68] If so, it is a striking testament to Tekkan's sense of the importance of masculine poetry that even a relatively halfhearted defense of love poetry should be grounds for blistering criticism.

Critical analyses of Tekkan's "Sounds" have frequently explained his emphasis on martial and vigorous masculinity as the product of its historical moment; "Sounds" appeared in the *Niroku shinpō* during May 1894, three months before the outbreak of the First Sino-Japanese War, when Japan's newspapers were filled with talk of conflict and Japan's territorial ambitions.[69] Given that Tekkan went to Korea shortly after "Sounds" and played an active role in advancing Japanese imperialism there, this explanation carries some weight. However, Tekkan's rhetoric was not simply a product of the nationalist fervor of the summer of 1894 but also a manifestation of a far larger anxiety over *waka* and national masculinity. This vein of discourse predated the Sino-Japanese War by some time, though it assumed added urgency as the conflict approached. Tekkan's objective was not to raise morale ahead of Japan's first full-scale war as an imperial power but to continue a thread from his earlier critical writings, one that Seki Reiko has characterized as "the exclusion of women from national literature, as well as the marginalization of female poets" (*kokubungaku kara no josei haijo oyobi josei kajin no shūenka*).[70] To Seki's assessment should also be added the marginalization of insufficiently masculine male poets. Once again, the national-poetic community was given shape and definition in terms of those who would *not* take part in it.

TAKING THE "NATIONAL" OUT OF "NATIONAL LITERATURE": SHIKI'S "LETTERS TO A *WAKA* POET"

One of the more extraordinary aspects of Tekkan's misogynistic rhetoric in these two articles is its apparent conflict with his professional life, particularly with the general attitude of the Asakasha, of which he was a prominent member. The actual composition of the Asakasha group in no way aligned with Tekkan's views; as noted, it featured a number of female poets, including Kokubu Misako, whose husband's poetry Tekkan had mentioned approvingly. One may wonder what the female members of the Asakasha group made of Tekkan's views on women's composition of *waka* and place in national literature. Tekkan's frank disdain for love poetry in particular also stands in stark contrast to his later career and relationship with Yosano Akiko, a poet made famous in large part by the passionate love poetry of her collection *Midaregami* (*Tangled Hair*, 1901).

As incongruous as Tekkan's strong focus on the propriety of love poetry and the need to project masculine strength through *waka* composition might appear in the context of his personal life and career, his emphasis on bold masculinity was entirely in line with a larger Meiji critical discourse that aimed to remasculinize *waka* to make it a suitable Japanese national poetry. Quite what effect Tekkan's attack actually had on the Outadokoro poets themselves is very much an open question; Chōfuku Kana has pointed out that a few years later, in 1897, the journal *Kokugakuin zasshi* reported that the Outadokoro had actually expanded.[71] It is, as Chōfuku suggests, possible that Shiki was moved to pick up Tekkan's baton by the sense that the latter's attacks had not had little effect. Shiki's contribution to the debate, published four years later, in 1898, would be his well-known series of "Letters to a *Waka* Poet" (hereafter "Letters"). Although the "Letters" themselves went through ten installments in *Nippon* between February 12 and March 4 of 1898, the ripples they caused went on for some time after that, since Shiki continued to argue with his critics in a series of pieces called "Answering Various People" (Hitobito ni kotau), which went on into May. A testament to Shiki's growing stature in the literary world, the "Letters" were still being talked about a couple of years later; in 1900, for instance, Shiki's subsequent disciple Itō Sachio 伊藤左千夫 (1864–1913) could be found continuing the fight in the pages of the popular *waka* journal *Kokoro no hana*, which had published two pieces highly critical of Shiki; and in Shizuoka, a local magazine run by Shinto priests informed the *Nippon* Group's local affiliate that it would no longer carry the group's haiku, in apparent retaliation for Shiki's "Letters."

Having noted that both Shiki and Tekkan devoted considerable time to attacking the old-school poets of the Outadokoro, it is helpful at this point to outline in more detail the people and objectives of the Outadokoro itself. The name Outadokoro dated to 1888; before that, the palace department responsible for poetic composition on ceremonial occasions had been known as the *Waka* Department (Outa Gakari) and Official Literature Department (Bungaku Goyō Gakari). The existence of a dedicated imperial office for *waka* afforded the genre a state sanction that neither *haikai* nor *kanshi* possessed, and in keeping with the nature of the new government, the majority of Outadokoro staff came from the Satsuma and Chōshū domains.[72] Initially headed up by the nobleman Sanjō-Nishi Suetomo 三条西季知 (1811–1880), in 1886 Takasaki Masakaze assumed the position of Outadokoro bureau chief after the office was renamed. By the time Shiki wrote his pieces in 1898, Takasaki was still in situ.

Takasaki himself was hardly the effete poet Tekkan's criticism suggested. A warrior of the Satsuma clan, he had been involved in putting down anti-*bakufu* violence instigated by other Satsuma warriors in the so-called Teradaya Incident of 1862[73] and had been part of the general staff that had mopped up the remains of the pro-*bakufu* forces after the Restoration. Appointed as a counselor of the left (*sain*) in the early configuration of the Meiji government, he had been dispatched on an official tour of Europe and America as part of his duties. This experience apparently prompted him to compose the following *waka*:

kuni to iu	having passed through
kuni o megurite	all countries worthy of the name,
hi no moto no	I have come to know
hito to umareshi	how blessed I am
sachi wa shiriniki	to be born a man of the Sun Root.[74]

国という国をめぐりて日の本の人と生まれし幸は知りにき

Takasaki was, therefore, more than simply a poet; he was a high-ranking official with a good understanding of, and considerable investment in, the aims of the new government. In his role as bureau chief, Takasaki personally tutored the emperor and empress in *waka* composition, and virtually all imperial compositions that were made public passed through his hands. It was, therefore, a position of considerable influence, and well into the 1890s Takasaki and his fellow Outadokoro poets enjoyed a privileged position in Japan's *waka* world. In 1891, *Waseda bungaku* listed Takasaki and his colleagues Fukuda Yoshishizu and Koide Tsubara as among the leading lights of Japan's *waka* world, and another specialist *waka* journal, *Kokoro no hana*, ran a popularity poll of its readers shortly after in which Outadokoro poets took all the top five spots.[75]

Although there were a number of factions therein, the dominant group within the Outadokoro was the Keien group, which followed the lineage and teachings of late Edo *waka* poet Kagawa Kageki (aka Kagawa Keien), whom we saw earlier singled out by Tekkan. The lineage connection was more than simply intellectual, since Kageki's grandson, Kagawa Kagetoshi 香川景敏 (1861–1887), had also worked for the Outadokoro before his untimely death at the age of sixteen. Kageki had been one of the most influential *waka* poets of the early nineteenth century, with a wide network of followers throughout the country. An admirer of Ki no Tsurayuki and advocate of the style of the *Kokinshū* in his poetry, in his critical writings Kageki had argued for *waka* as an inclusive national-poetic community. Kageki had criticized the aristocratic Dōjō school of *waka*, arguing that *waka* composition should not discriminate in social class and, with more nuance than Shiki and Tekkan would show, had also questioned the rationale for associating a forceful poetic style with masculinity and weakness with femininity, finding the distinction between rustic and metropolitan styles to be more important.[76]

With admirers of Kageki well represented among the Outadokoro staff, his poetry and critical writings continued to circulate well into mid-Meiji; at around the time the Asakasha poets were making their debut in *Nippon*, for instance, the newspaper was also carrying advertisements for the text *The True Meaning of the Kokinshū* (*Kokinshū seigi*), a commentary on Ki no Tsurayuki's collection authored by what the advertisement referred to as "the great Kagawa Kageki" (*Kagawa Kageki ushi*).[77] A reader of *Nippon* who went out and bought the advertised text would have found in Kageki's preface to the work a number of statements advocating a chauvinistic understanding of *waka*'s importance to Japan, such as "One who would know the heart of the songs of Yamato [i.e., *waka*] must realize that its wellspring is in the awesome nature of the Japanese spirit," or "That the sounds of all foreign countries are muddled and impure arises from the improper nature of their emotions."[78]

When Shiki and Tekkan took on the Outadokoro poets, then, they were assailing a group whose explicit, government-sanctioned purpose was to articulate a link between *waka* practice and Japanese national identity. Although Shiki's colleagues at *Nippon* had a generally hostile attitude to organs of the Meiji government, the Outadokoro's explicitly nationalistic understanding of *waka* found a sympathetic reception in the newspaper, and Outadokoro poets appeared in *Nippon*'s pages on a semiregular basis throughout the early 1890s. On one occasion in April of 1893, for example, *waka* by Takasaki and two other Outadokoro mainstays, Kurokawa Mayori and Kuroda Kiyotsuna 黒田清綱 (1830–1917), appeared side by side with haiku by Shiki, Kyoshi, and other *Nippon* Group members in the newspaper's Bun'en column. In fact, Outadokoro poets continued to place their verse in *Nippon* right up until Shiki published the first of his "Letters" in February of 1898, something that apparently annoyed Shiki and may have spurred him to write his famous polemic.

While they share a common, largely vitriolic tone, Shiki's "Letters" are only a partial continuation of Tekkan's "Sounds." Shiki does articulate, as Tekkan had, the importance of a strong and martial tone in *waka* poetry, echoing Tekkan's praise of the warrior-poet Minamoto no Sanetomo in the first of the "Letters." However, neither masculinity nor femininity are major themes throughout the "Letters," nor did Shiki attempt anything resembling Tekkan's attacks on the masculinity of the Outadokoro poets. In fact, the Outadokoro is not mentioned explicitly until the tenth and final of the "Letters," where Shiki dismisses its poets in what are, by his usual standards, relatively restrained terms:

> Country bumpkins and the like think that the Outadokoro is a collection of great poets and that the Outadokoro bureau chief is the best poet in the country, and so when they hear that a given work is

one of their compositions, they will judge it superior without ever having read it. I, too, was once among the ranks of people who thought like that. . . . But it's not the case that the Outadokoro is a collection of great men, and the holder of the position of bureau chief isn't necessarily going to be a first-class poet. We live in an age where there are no real *waka* poets to be had, but even so, if you are looking for better poets than the Outadokoro bunch, you'll likely find them among the population at large.[79]

In a similar vein, at no point in the "Letters" does Shiki cite any Outadokoro poet by name, or their actual poetry. Rather, the "Letters" challenged the Outadokoro poets more indirectly, through two main arguments. One was to deny, as Tekkan had, the poetic competence of the lineage of Ki no Tsurayuki, the *Kokinshū*, and Kagawa Kageki, on which much of the Outadokoro activities were built. The other, and perhaps the most powerful in the context of mid-1890s Japan, was Shiki's attempt to sever the notion of a particularistic connection between *waka* and Japanese national identity. Throughout the "Letters," Shiki consistently argues that *waka* must be understood and judged as "literature" (*bungaku*) in a universal, cross-cultural sense; there was, he asserted, nothing particularly special, or particularly Japanese, about *waka* itself, the way in which it was composed, or its critical apparatus. As had been the case with haiku, Shiki laid out an argument in which *waka* would have to be rescued from its "decay" (*fuhai*) by the "man of letters" (*bungakusha*), those members of the intellectual elite with training and background in not only Japanese but also Western and Chinese literary traditions. In order to support his proposition that *waka* was a form of literature, therefore, it was necessary for Shiki to denaturalize the genre's apparent connection with the Japanese people and with any putative national essence.

Given the status of both the Outadokoro poets and the utility to the Meiji government of the national-poetic mythos that they were promoting, Shiki correctly perceived that he was taking quite a risk in launching his sequence of attacks. Unusually, given his propensity for gleefully abusing his poetic enemies, in the case of the "Letters" he proceeded with caution, clearing his project with *Nippon*'s editor, Kuga Katsunan, before publication. Once Katsunan had given him the green light, however,

Shiki quickly built up a head of steam. After a relatively restrained first piece on February 12, Shiki deployed his characteristic venom in a second installment two days later:

> Tsurayuki was an awful poet and the *Kokinshū* is a collection of garbage . . . those clowns of later ages whose skill lies in only imitating it are truly the most clueless of the lot. One has to wonder at their lack of discernment in continually sucking on the dregs—not for ten or twenty years but for two or three hundred years at a time. They talk of this and that imperial collection, but it's all just the dregs of the dregs of the dregs of the dregs of the *Kokinshū*. . . .
>
> Needless to say, Kagawa Kageki was a *Kokinshū* worshipper and completely clueless. It goes without saying that he had plenty of vulgar poems, though he does have some good ones as well, rather more in fact than the Tsurayuki he so worshipped. . . . If you want to learn from Kageki, you have to learn from his good poems, otherwise you'll go completely off the rails; those who call themselves Kageki's followers these days read only his vulgar poems and so they carry on as worse poets than Kageki was.[80]

Having maligned their intellectual patron thus, Shiki shifted four days later to the topic of contemporary *waka* poets:

> There can't be many people as blithely stupid as *waka* poets. If you listen to what they say, they're always boasting that there is nothing as fine as *waka*, but the fact of the matter is that this self-satisfied belief in *waka* as the best of all things results from a total lack of knowledge about anything else. Since they're so blithely ignorant that they don't even know the slightest thing about haiku, the closest genre to *waka*, and think that haiku and *senryū* are the same thing because they're both in seventeen syllables, then you can't really expect that they'd bother learning about Chinese poetry, and they're so illiterate and ill learned that they couldn't even tell you whether such a thing as "poetry" exists in the West. If they were to hear that prose fiction and *jōruri* librettos belong to the category of literature in the same way as *waka*, their eyes would surely bulge wide in astonishment.[81]

This passage marks the beginning of Shiki's use of the term "literature" throughout the "Letters" as both argumentative cudgel and source of authority. The problem with contemporary *waka* poets is, Shiki asserts, that they are completely ignorant of any literary genre besides their own; this situation prevails because they do not grasp that *waka* is a part of a much broader conceptual category of "literature," encompassing not only other Japanese poetic genres but the traditions of the West and China as well. From this point on and throughout the "Letters," as well as the subsequent (often furious) exchanges that ensued with his readers, Shiki insists that *waka* poets are fundamentally mistaken in viewing *waka* solely within its own cultural tradition.

An excellent example of what was at stake here can be seen in an exchange, midway through the "Letters," with Chiba Inaki 千葉稲城 (1873–1934), an educator and later journalist who had studied Japanese literature at Tokyo Imperial University under noted scholar Mozume Takami 物集高見 (1847–1920). Chiba took issue with Shiki's criticism in the fourth of his "Letters" of verses by a number of Japanese poets, ranging from Kakinomoto no Hitomaro 柿本人麻呂 (660–724) and Ōe no Chisato 大江千里 (fl. early Heian) to the nearly contemporary Hatta Tomonori 八田知紀 (1799–1873). Among the criticisms Shiki had leveled at the various poems were that they were overly governed by "logical thought" (*rikutsu*) and that they went too far in the direction of being "subjective" (*shukanteki*) over being "objective" (*kyakkanteki*). One example was his criticism of a verse by the Edo-era poet Hatta Tomonori:

utsusemi no	within the limits
wagayo no kagiri	of this hollow-shell world of ours,
miru beki wa	I now know that what one must see
arashi no yama no	are the cherry blossoms
sakura narikeri	of Mount Arashi.[82]

うつせみのわが世のかぎり見るべきは嵐の山のさくらなりけり

Shiki's criticism was that the poet had taken something that ought to be described in an objective manner—namely, the cherry blossoms and their beauty—and injected a logical, intellectual operation ("what one must see") where it did not belong; this was, he wrote, an "extremely vulgar technique" (*daizoku no shiwaza*). Moreover, the idea behind the poem, that one should look one's whole life at the cherry blossoms of Mount Arashi, was "weird and stupid in its conceit" (*hen na kudaranu shukō*), and the poem as a whole "not worth one's time" (*toru tokoro kore naku sōrō*).[83]

Chiba's objections, which were to Shiki's specific criticisms as well as the way in which he had phrased them, appeared in *Nippon* the next day, February 22. Chiba did not necessarily disagree with Shiki's call for objective composition, but he noted that "the poems of the Divine Land [i.e., *waka*] take emotion as their root. . . . I do not think that one should compose in a purely objective mode. If one looks at psychological phenomena, then obviously it is true that the objective precedes the subjective, but to get to the point of composing a poem it takes a while for the emotions to mature, and so I do not think it is necessary to propose these two concepts [of subjective and objective]."

As the letter went on, Chiba's tone became far more strident: "It seems to me rather boorish that those of later generations should borrow various scholarly terms in trying to dissect the ideals of the ancients and analyze their feelings. . . . Your intent, in loosing such destructive arguments upon the national poetry, which one may term the ramparts of Japanese literature, is absolutely incomprehensible to me. . . . Do you mean, after all, sir, to destroy the national poetry?"[84]

Shiki responded to this missive two days later in uncompromising terms:

> You say, "The poems of the Divine Land take emotion as their root"—what are you talking about? Not only poetry in general but also all literature takes emotion as its root, and this has always been the same, now and in the past, east or west. . . . And also, this phrasing "the poems of the Divine Land are such and such"—I can't help but think that this is exactly what a *waka* poet who knows nothing other than *waka* would say. And then you say, "Which man in what age decided that to compose using logical thought is not poetry?," a startling question. That logic is not literature is a point on which all people in all times and places have agreed upon, and if there is anyone who says that logic can be literature, then I think it would most likely be our own Japanese *waka* poets.[85]

Shiki's reply singles out a common claim for *waka*, that it is rooted in human emotions, and flatly denies that this makes *waka* special, noting that all literature "now and in the past, east or west" is also based on emotion. Likewise, Shiki defends his dismissal of "logical thought" by appealing to a transtemporal, transcultural conception of literature, one that, needless to say, he claims to understand in a way that contemporary *waka* poets do not. Later in the same piece, Shiki further confirms his intent to departicularize *waka*, noting that "it is not necessary to know the minds of the ancients; all I am doing here is judging literature by literary standards that are common to all places and all times (or what I believe that standard to be) . . . my objective is to assess *waka* in terms of literature."[86]

"Literature" here, then, was a far more loaded term than it might initially have appeared, since Shiki was using it as a way of telling Chiba that *waka*'s distinctive critical framework was invalid. Rather, universal "literature," as defined and understood by Shiki, was the correct frame within which to understand *waka*, and Chiba failed to understand this only because of his lack of experience of other genres. Chiba's initial criticism and Shiki's response echo certain points of conflict between Shiki and the old-school *haikai* poets; as we saw in the "commoner literature" discourse discussed in the previous chapter, Shiki made frequent reference to his academic training and understanding of literature, while old-school masters pushed back on this as the posturing of the overeducated. Chiba's criticism of Shiki's "scholarly terms" (*gakujutsugo*), for example, recalls Mimori Mikio's objections (explored in the previous chapter) to the "empty theories" of various "scholars" who attacked *haikai*. As had been the case with haiku, the academic study of literature and its deployment to further the aims of the nation-state seemed to be at odds with each other.

Chiba did not let the discussion rest at this point, sending in a response that was also published in *Nippon* a little more than a month later. In this subsequent entry, Chiba continues to criticize Shiki for his assumption of scholarly airs and for mocking Chiba's use of the term "poems of the Divine Land" (*mikuni no uta*). Chiba's main objection this second time around, however, is to Shiki's classification of *waka* as "literature." In Chiba's view, to categorize *waka* as "literature" in this sense was to denature it, rendering it subservient to the dictates of foreign literary traditions. Knowledge of *waka* alone was sufficient, he wrote: "In a world where there are men of literature who do not even know our country's *waka*, there is no shame in not knowing the poetry of other lands."[87] Chiba's use of the specific term "our country's *waka*" (*kokka*), a term that Shiki eschewed in his "Letters" except to mock it, reveals his understanding of *waka* as intertwined with an essentialized Japanese national identity. Not only was knowledge of other literary traditions unnecessary but also, Chiba fired back, if anything opprobrium should properly be directed toward those Japanese men of letters who were ignorant of this most characteristically Japanese poetry. Chiba went on to point out that though Shiki had spoken of a standard of literature "common to all places and times," no such thing actually existed, "even among the literary men of England, France, and Germany, whom you lead me to believe you admire so much." Having dealt a well-aimed blow to a shaky element in Shiki's argument, however, the second half of Chiba's lengthy letter moved on to more emotive terrain, suggesting that Shiki's lack of respect for the links between *waka* and national identity was evidence of malicious intent, even lack of patriotism:

> Thus our country's *waka* inspires men and fills them with absolute loyalty, it stirs them to strive for filial piety and virtue, thereby planting deep in people's hearts respect for the national polity and the imperial house. . . . How can you call it "flimsy literature"? Did not our country's *waka* stand apart as national poetry even in early Meiji, when the depredations of European thought were at their height?. . . Ultimately, by doing nothing more than recapitulating foreign ideas, you would have Japanese literature be the slave of foreign lands, dying of starvation as it chews on Western thought for all eternity to come.[88]

Shiki's subsequent comments confirm that Chiba's reading of Shiki as trying to sever the particularistic link between *waka* and Japanese national identity was not far off the mark. As was his wont, Shiki took to arguing with Chiba with considerable enthusiasm, spreading his rebuttals to Chiba's criticism across several days in *Nippon*. To begin with, Shiki admitted, in sarcastic terms, that maybe he was one of those "men of literature who do not even know the *waka* of our land." If so, he wrote, this was because "a fair few times I've opened up a *waka* collection with the intent of finding out more about the *waka* of our land, but every time I get four or five pages in I start nodding off, so I can't go on—that's how boring they are."[89] In similar terms a few days later, Shiki rejected the idea that early Meiji *waka* had "stood apart" from foreign influence as something specifically Japanese; this assertion was, he argued, to ignore the influence on *waka* of Chinese studies and Buddhism: "Even so, maybe you meant that there is still something uniquely Japanese there, but if so, those parts that may be 'uniquely Japanese' are of little or no value and are so embarrassing that you really have no business saying that they 'stand apart.' I believe that the 'distinctively Japanese' parts in *waka* that were still left by around the time of the Restoration were likely the parts of least value."[90]

Shiki's point, by this time, was abundantly clear: *waka* was literature in a universal sense, not anything that was particularly distinctive to Japan or that had any kind of significant connection to national identity. If there was anything distinctively Japanese in *waka*, moreover, such elements were worthless. As literature, it was not the common property or birthright of all Japanese subjects; rather, it should properly be read and understood by literary men who had the training and background to appreciate and guide it.

As if to hammer home his point, as the conclusion of his "Answering Various People" series in May 1898, Shiki criticized the very same patriotic *waka* by Motoori Norinaga that Seki Iyū had cited as evidence of the connection between the *kokutai* and *waka* five years earlier:

> Quite often, when looking at a poem that is capable of moving anyone at any time, I find myself forced to admit that the poem in question is shallow and vapid. As an example, a poem that I believe has the power to move the greatest numbers of Japanese people:

shikishima no	if someone were to ask
Yamato gokoro o	of the Japanese spirit
hito towaba	in the land of Shikishima—
asahi ni niou	it is mountain cherry blossoms,
yamazakurabana	fragrant in the morning sun.

Not only am I not at all moved on reading this poem but also I find it shallow, vapid, and clumsy. . . . There was a time when I was moved by this poem. But as a result of my having specialized in literary studies over several years, I believe I have, through many small and halting steps, remedied my lack of discernment. One who has a modicum of learning will view *dodoitsu* popular songs as unrefined and beneath contempt. But it is *dodoitsu* at which the vulgar masses clap their hands and sigh in admiration. . . . If there is such a thing as a work endowed with literary import that gains broad approval, then truly it is the duty of the *waka* poet to have it take the place of all these nonliterary works.[91]

Patriotic *waka*, such as Norinaga's famous verse, had to appeal to large numbers of people, and by that very fact their status as true literature—in Shiki's understanding of the term—was called into question. As he had done in the early stages of his haiku reform movement, Shiki here makes the argument that proper *waka* is composed and appreciated by educated specialists very much like himself; he has, through "having specialized in literary studies," come to view even the most famous of patriotic *waka* as shallow and insipid, of little to no interest when viewed as universal literature. That Shiki should single out a widely known *waka* featuring an apparent celebration of Japanese national identity as an example of what would be discarded as a reader acquired greater appreciation of literature was entirely fitting, since much of the "Letters" and the subsequent debate revolved around questioning whether *waka* did in fact have any particular connection to Japanese national identity. Shiki had argued in 1895, it will be recalled, against the idea of national literature, holding that it was a contradiction in terms; anything that the vulgar masses might favor should be disqualified as true literature, and three years later his views of what *waka* was and who should be composing it seem to be cut from largely the same cloth. To make *waka* a focus for national subject formation—a verse form all Japanese subjects could and should write, one that had a unique place in Japanese culture—was incompatible with its being true literature. Throughout the "Letters," Shiki's argument is that the proper guardians of *waka* are men of letters who understand literature, not Japan's contemporary government-sponsored *waka* poets and certainly not its population as a whole. Where Tekkan had excluded women and insufficiently manly men from his vision of a poetic community, Shiki moved to exclude virtually everyone who had not been educated as he had.

THE POETRY OF WHOSE DIVINE LAND?

Even Shiki's allies and colleagues at *Nippon* were startled at the vehemence of his arguments as he developed them in the "Letters" and continued them with other poets in the newspaper's pages for several months thereafter. Amada Guan 天田愚庵 (1854–1904), a Buddhist monk who was a friend of Shiki's and who published his own *waka* in *Nippon*, was so shocked by the "Letters" that midway through their publication, on March 24, 1898, he wrote to Kuga Katsunan, suggesting that Shiki was getting in over his head and that Katsunan ought perhaps to rein him in. Using a Buddhist term, Guan observed that Shiki was on the point of "bringing misfortune upon himself via speech" (*kugō*).[92]

In the long term, neither Shiki's nor Tekkan's remarks did their careers any lasting harm. Shortly after his "Letters," Shiki founded the Negishi Tanka Group (Negishi Tanka Kai), from which would emerge such luminaries as Itō Sachio, who would assume leadership of the group after Shiki died and, in that capacity, oversee the emergence of other major tanka poets such as Saitō Mokichi 斉藤茂吉 (1882–1953). Tekkan, for his part, went to Korea in 1895, the year after his "Sounds," where he fell ill and composed the following verse, part of a sequence of ten that all began with the line "How can I die in Korea?" (*Kara ni shite / ika de ka shinan*):

Kara ni shite	Here in Korea
ika de ka shinan	How can I possibly die?
ware shinaba	If I should die,
onoko no uta zo	The poetry of real men
mata sutarenan	Would again be abandoned.[93]

韓にしていかでか死なむわれ死なばをのこの歌ぞまた廃れなむ

These verses were included in a well-received collection of verse, *North, South, East, and West* (*Tōzai nanboku*), which Tekkan published in 1896 and which featured not only forewords by Shiki and Ochiai but also a dedicatory *kanshi* by Kokubu Seigai, that most quintessentially manly of Japanese poets. In November 1899, a little more than a year after Shiki's "Letters," Tekkan founded Shinshisha (New Poetic Society), and April of 1900 would see the inaugural issue of Shinshisha's journal, *Myōjō*, which proved enormously influential in the Japanese poetry world and helped launch the career of Yosano Akiko.

In this sense, both Shiki and Tekkan did much to establish the groups, ideas, and media outlets that shaped the emergence of the modern tanka from *waka*. Yet as we have seen, both poets shared a view of *waka* that was substantially at odds with the idea that it could or should be a focal point for a national-poetic community. Neither Shiki nor Tekkan viewed a *waka* community as coterminous with a national community; rather, their ideas for the role that *waka* would play in the modern nation-state were inextricably bound up with hierarchies of education, gender, and masculinity. This is, of course, not to deny the power of the idea of *waka* in national subject formation, which scholars such as Murai Osamu and Shinada Yoshikazu have attempted to problematize; unquestionably, this conception was at work in the discussions I have surveyed in the preceding. Rather, I have attempted to expand and supplement Murai's and Shinada's criticisms of *waka* as "invented tradition" by noting that its role as a vector for national subject formation was by no means as solidly established as it might have appeared, even up to the dawn of the twentieth century.

Conclusion

Shiki died in the early hours of September 19, 1902, at the age of thirty-five. In some sense, perhaps, death came as a relief; his physical condition had been deteriorating gradually ever since his return from the Sino-Japanese War and had taken a noticeable turn for the worse in the beginning of the new century. By the very end of his life he could neither stand nor digest his food; in constant pain, he also could neither concentrate nor read, a state alleviated for short intervals by taking morphine. Though barely able to hold his writing brush—Hekigotō placed it in his hand just before his death—he remained a haiku poet to the last, marking his departure from this world with three deathbed poems, following the precedent set by his predecessors Bashō and Buson. Among them was the following:

hechima saite	the gourd flowers bloom,
tan no tsumarishi	see the Buddha
hotoke kana	choked with phlegm.[1]

糸瓜咲て痰のつまりし佛かな

Shiki's description of himself as a Buddha—that is, already dead—in this poem is striking, even gruesome, but more or less in line with the practices of objective description in haiku that would come to define a substantial part of his legacy. In fact, a couple of years earlier in his career, in the context of an essay about "sketch from life" (*shasei*) haiku, Shiki had tried depicting his own death and funeral service as an imaginative exercise in objective description; now, life presented him with one final opportunity to put his ideas into practice.[2]

The idea of *shasei* in haiku, left largely untouched in this book, is but one part of Shiki's substantial literary and cultural legacy. Much of this legacy was assured by his two main disciples, Takahama Kyoshi and Kawahigashi Hekigotō, both of whom drew much of their authority in their subsequent careers from their association with him and who had, as a result, a strong incentive to frame their teacher and friend in something of a "great man" mold, as a true genius whose presence and forceful personality were needed to break open the moribund Meiji haiku world and fashion a truly modern haiku. In Shiki's subsequent reception, particularly in the reminiscences of his friends and direct disciples, there is definitely what might be termed a Shiki mythos, one that celebrates his unquestionably extraordinary range of achievements but that also advances a number of claims about Shiki's actions and importance that are a little questionable. It is often asserted, for instance, that Shiki was the first to use the term "haiku," which he was not;[3] or, along similar lines, that he was the first to use the translation *yakyū* to render the term "baseball" into Japanese. Although Shiki was extremely fond of baseball, wrote numerous poems about it, and was inducted into the Japanese Baseball Hall of Fame in 2002, the honor of coining the term is not actually his.[4]

In a somewhat similar vein, one of the conclusions of this book is that Shiki's legacy for modern Japanese poetry was indeed formidable, but in a rather different sense than what is commonly accepted. Throughout, this book has taken as its central concern the contours of an emerging national-poetic community and repeatedly highlighted the instability and contested nature of these contours, arguing that discourses of exclusion and hierarchy are critical to its constitution. Shiki's writings, especially those examined in the preceding two chapters, are excellent examples of the ways in which this national-poetic community was discussed and defined by those generally hailed as the shapers of modern Japanese poetry. In particular, Shiki's work shows the fundamental importance of discourses of hierarchy and exclusion; as should be clear by now, Shiki emphatically rejected the idea that haiku was a literature that all Japanese could or should compose and did not believe that there was anything particularly Japanese about *waka*. He would not, one imagines, have had much time for later nationalistic claims of a close identification between poetry and national identity, such as, "To compose a *waka* is itself a patriotic act" (*waka o yomu koto ga hitotsu no aikokuteki kōdō*).[5] One of Shiki's major concerns was that those he viewed as serious, educated people should be at the vanguard of his new literature; as such, a significant part of his efforts to place haiku and *waka* in this category had to do with questions of who should *not* compose in each respective genre.

This is not to deny that Shiki was "nationalistic," a label attached to Shiki by Michael Bourdaghs and a number of other scholars. There is little question that Shiki, along with most other poets in Meiji Japan, understood his poetic activities within an explicitly nation-centered framework; his "Letters to a *Waka* Poet," for example, speak of "strengthening the flimsy ramparts of Japanese literature," and in the background of what he was doing was a strong awareness of the connection between Japan's literature and its national prestige. Shiki's understanding of what should be done to raise the standards of haiku and *waka* was, however, consciously at odds with the close identification between poetic practice and Japanese national identity that a number of critics active at the same time as him sought to promote. It was also, slightly ironically, at considerable variance with the poetic visions of a number of his later disciples, notably Kyoshi, Hekigotō, and Saitō Mokichi. As this book has made clear, when one examines Meiji discourse on the modernization of poetic genres, those most frequently credited with achieving this modernization—Tekkan and Shiki in particular—were usually the ones policing the boundaries of poetic community by excluding other poets. Those who explicitly advocated an inclusive, national-level poetic community were more often groups such as the Outadokoro or the old-school haiku poets, the very ones whom conventional narratives hold were "defeated" and relegated to the status of historical footnotes.

As several of the preceding chapters have shown, the early twentieth century saw more of an intellectual consensus emerge that haiku and *waka*—reenvisioned in its modern form of tanka—were indeed the common intellectual property of all Japanese and possessed a close connection to Japanese national identity. Natsume Sōseki, one of Shiki's closest friends, recalls meeting a fellow Japanese national during his unhappy stay in London from 1900 to 1902; on seeing that Sōseki was reading Shiki's journal *Hototogisu*, Sōseki relates, the man immediately asked him, "Do you practice the way of Emperor Tenji?" (*kimi wa Tenji tennō no hō wa yareru ka*), or, in other words, "Do you compose *waka*?" That poetry should be envisioned as a point of common cultural identity between otherwise unacquainted Japanese nationals living in a foreign land speaks to the power of the idea of a national-poetic community.

Yet even so, the idea of a national-poetic community never became entirely stable; in much the same way as notions of nation *tout court*, it was continually redefined and reenvisioned as internal hierarchies and notions of nation, ideas of literature, and media technologies shifted and reconfigured themselves. Prasenjit Duara has characterized the boundaries of national community as shifting from "hard," implying suspicion of the other, or "soft" (suggesting cultural practices held in common) on an almost continual basis.[6] Certain points in the twentieth-century history of haiku—often seen as a genre that is studiedly apolitical, concerned primarily with the natural world, and strongly "Japanese"—provide plenty of examples. We have already seen, in chapters 3 and 4, the fault lines of class and political affiliation at work as the modern haiku came into being, as well as strikingly similar concerns more than one hundred years later, as in the introduction's discussion of certain recent haiku poets and their views on the impact of the internet on haiku. One further example of the shifting boundaries of a haiku community, as well as the discourses of exclusion that are necessary to the constitution of a national-poetic community, is also worth mentioning here as a concluding note.

The incident in question is one that became known as the haiku-suppression incident (*haiku dan'atsu jiken*), actually a string of incidents lasting from the spring of 1940 until 1943 in which a number of so-called newly arisen haiku (*shinkō haiku*) groups were targeted for investigation by the Japanese secret police on the grounds that their literary activities were potentially subversive. Among the most prominent newly arisen groups was Kyōdai Haiku, the Kyoto University haiku club, which published a literary journal, also called *Kyōdai haiku*. In broad outline, these haiku groups, which flourished from around 1930 to 1940, opposed themselves to the more (allegedly) traditional and conservative view of haiku as focusing on nature and the seasons, as advanced primarily by Kyoshi's *Hototogisu*. Made up mostly of educated university graduates, such groups tried to produce a haiku that they saw as more suited to the realities of contemporary urban existence. On the one hand opposed to Kyoshi's vision of haiku, these groups also rejected Hekigotō's more free-verse approach, generally maintaining the basic 5-7-5 format for their work and electing to include seasonal words. One favorite theme was the depiction of industrial urban life for the working poor, as suggested by the cover art for *Kyōdai haiku* throughout 1939, which depicts not an idyllic rural scene but a ramshackle urban rooftop bedecked with telephone wires. This concern with urban existence also came to incorporate an overt antiwar stance after Japan's opening of hostilities with China in 1931, as in this 1937 verse by poet Sasaki Tatsumi 佐々木巽 (1880–1938), originally published in the haiku journal *Amanogawa*:[7]

mibōjin   will the reporter
nakanu to kisha wa   once again write
mata kaku ka   "the widow did not cry"?[8]

未亡人泣かぬと記者はまた書くか

The openly antiwar stance in these poets' haiku and their focus on the war's effect on the urban poor attracted the attentions of the Japanese secret police, which believed that at least some of the newer haiku poets were inspired by notions of proletarian realism, or that they were perhaps even Communist agents. One of the main figures in the Kyoto haiku school, Hirabatake Seitō 平畑静塔 (1905–1997), addressed, somewhat naively, rumors of secret police interest in their activities in *Kyōdai haiku*'s October 1936 issue by stating that he did not believe that any newly arisen haiku had been composed under the influence of left-wing ideology (*genzai no shinkō haiku ni sayoku ideorogī no moto ni seisaku sareta sakuhin wa nai*) and that "it was impossible for such pieces to directly express or convey dangerous thought or tendencies" such as socialism or Communism.[9]

Hirabatake thus argued that the very form of haiku itself was incompatible with any kind of thought that might be understood as unpatriotic; there was a complete overlap between haiku as a genre and expressing one's identity as a patriotic Japanese subject. Unfortunately, the secret police did not share this view. For some time before the eventual series of crackdowns were carried out, the police had gone to considerable lengths to gather information on their targets and their activities. In some cases, they did so in a fashion that would have been almost laughably ham-fisted had the consequences not been so serious. In a clumsy attempt at infiltration, previously unknown "members" began showing up at Kyōdai Haiku meetings, prompting regular member Nakamura Sanzan 中村三山 (1902–1967) to publish a series of thirteen verses in *Kyōdai haiku* under the title "A Tedious Visitor" (Taikutsu na hōmonsha):

> *tokkō no*　　　　　the secret policeman's
> *sarigenaki me ga*　　nonchalant eyes
> *shoka ni*　　　　　go to the bookcase.

特高のさりげなき目が書架に

> *asobi ni kitamae to*　"Drop by my place sometime!"
> *tokkō kun samo*　　says Mr. Secret Policeman
> *shitashige ni*　　　so nice and friendly.[10]

遊びに来給へと特高君さも親しげに

The second verse humorously juxtaposes poetic sociality and state suppression; in order to maintain his cover, the secret policeman (here given the male familiar suffix *kun*) feels obliged to participate in the rituals of reciprocal social obligation after a haiku gathering by offering to host the Kyōdai Haiku poets in return. The verse gains a subtle sense of menace from the poet's knowledge of the policeman's identity; the "place" to which the poet is being invited might well be the police station, where he may face beating and torture—or worse. As if these examples were not farcical enough, according to an anecdote from another Kyōdai poet, Saitō Sanki 西東三鬼 (1900–1962), the secret police knew so little about haiku in general and newly arisen haiku in particular that in preparation for their raids they pressed an unnamed newly arisen haiku member into service to lecture them on the finer points of haiku appreciation.[11]

One of the largest such crackdowns was carried out in the early hours of February 14, 1940. A total of forty-four poets from the various newly arisen groups, including fifteen members of Kyōdai Haiku, were arrested and questioned by the police on suspicion of having violated the 1925 Peace Preservation Law (Chian Iji Hō). Three of the fifteen Kyōdai Haiku poets arrested were actually prosecuted, with the rest eventually released, and the raids had a chilling effect on the newly arisen haiku and the journals with which they were affiliated. Many journals were forced out of business; those that did survive generally did so by distancing themselves from the newly arisen haiku and electing to follow a promilitarist editorial line. As an example, the journal *Amanogawa*, which had published the haiku on the war widow, announced in October of 1940 that it would change its editorial line to accord with government policy and henceforth discard the label of "newly arisen haiku."[12]

In a report prepared after a raid on a group centered on the journal *Kirishima* in the southern city of Kagoshima, the police noted the following: "[The leaders of this group] produce a coterie journal, *Kirishima*. They shun so-called conventional, nature-based, traditional season-word-form haiku, do research into non-season-word haiku, and have been producing proletarian haiku and poems based on nothing other than socialist realism, so there are strong grounds for suspicion. For this reason we conducted a group roundup and interrogation on the third of this month at 5:00 A.M."[13]

It would be overstating the case to say that the newly arisen haiku poets attracted police attention solely because of their desire to break away from traditional haiku, but it is nonetheless striking that the secret police should cite deviance from nature-based haiku among the factors contributing to what they saw as probable cause to investigate subversive activities. Rejection of nature-based haiku and violation of poetic norms held up as traditional could, apparently, be construed as prima facie evidence of possible disloyalty. Poetic orthodoxy and political loyalty were thus construed more or less as the same thing; those who did not follow the idea of haiku as apolitical and rooted in nature must therefore be viewed as unfit members of the national community.

Notably, neither *Hototogisu* nor any of its affiliated poets were investigated by the police during the wartime period; one likely reason for this was that Kyoshi was a prominent member of the prowar Japanese Literary Patriotic Association (Nihon Bungaku Hōkokukai) and quite vocal in his support of Japanese imperialism. *Hototogisu*-affiliated poets were extremely critical of the newly arisen haiku poets' antiwar poetry in particular. One of the many criticisms leveled at antiwar poetry derived from the strictures of *shasei*, noting that since the poets writing such work had not observed battlefield conditions themselves, any such depiction they might make was inauthentic and disrespectful to the soldiers who actually were on the front line.[14] Lack of direct experience was apparently only a problem with antiwar poems, since *Hototogisu* poets such as Mizuhara Shūōshi 水原秋桜子 (Yutaka 豊, 1892–1981), Usuda Arō 臼田亜浪 (Uichirō 卯一郎, 1879–1951), and Kyoshi himself wrote and published prowar verse in fairly large quantities.

The prewar haiku-suppression incidents resonated well after the war itself had ended; a number of haiku poets, particularly those who had been imprisoned by the secret police, continued to bear a degree of animus toward Kyoshi and the *Hototogisu* poets, who had at best stood idle during their persecution and may even have been active collaborators.[15] This unease at haiku's involvement in—or at least tacit complicity with— wartime ideologies of nationalism was one of the major reasons behind the publication of the famous postwar polemic cited at the beginning of chapter 4, Kuwabara Takeo's 1946 "A Second-Class Art." Questioning whether haiku could truly be regarded as a modern literary form on the grounds of its practitioners' insularity and what he saw as its feudal, "guildlike" social structures, Kuwabara pointedly remarked on haiku's status during the war and the activities of its main proponents:

> The moment a powerful authority appeared, [haiku poets] skillfully went along with it. And then, once the storm had blown over, they went back to "transcending the vulgar." A willow branch does not break under the weight of snow. . . . I recall that when the Literary Patriotic Association was established, the haiku department alone had an unusual number of membership applications and that that department was the only one for which the main branch of the association had to forcibly limit acceptance.[16]

The cases from the 1940s, as well as the prominent role in social and political protest of both *kanshi* and haiku during the Meiji era, suggest that the relationship between poetry, national community, and national identity has been contested at virtually every stage of haiku's existence as a modern literary genre. In arguing—and being imprisoned—for a conception of haiku in which the expression of antiwar sentiments was legitimate rather than traitorous, the Kyōdai Haiku poets were in a sense following a path already well trodden by their antigovernment poetic forebears Shiki and Kokubu Seigai.

The book's argument does not deny the power of the idea of a national literature and a national-literary community; rather, it is precisely because of its power that I have sought to make the interventions in the preceding chapters. For the most part, scholarship in English and Japanese has tended to criticize ideas of a national literature on the grounds that they are built upon "invented traditions"; rather less attention has been paid to contemporary discourses that compete with ideas of a national-literary community and through which one can problematize both the construction and naturalization of the ideas on a fundamental level. My own sense is that Anderson's model of the interrelation of language, literature, media, and community has become almost axiomatic, guiding our understanding of the role that these institutions and cultural phenomena play in modern states to the point where we tend to overlook that which does not readily fit with his enormously influential model. As has become quite apparent in the present-day English-speaking world, the effect of new forms of media is not always to unite; just as often, by bringing groups with competing interests and priorities together, as well as enabling upstarts and new voices to enter the public sphere, the effect is just as often to fragment and divide. By understanding that new forms of media both unite and fragment, and by understanding that the process of fashioning imagined national communities is unstable and fraught with problems of gender, class, and political affiliation, we perhaps gain a more nuanced understanding of the mechanisms through which modern nations and nationalisms come to be.

Notes

INTRODUCTION

1. Fukunaga Norihiro, "Gendai haiku jihyō: Intānetto no kōzai (1)," *Haiku* 55, no. 3 (February 2006): 114.
2. Fukunaga, "Intānetto no kōzai (1)," 117.
3. Fukunaga Norihiro, "Gendai haiku jihyō: Intānetto no kōzai (2)," *Haiku* 55, no. 4 (March 2006): 102.
4. Fukunaga, "Intānetto no kōzai (2)," 105; emphasis in original.
5. Takayanagi Katsuhiro, "Netto wa haiku o kaeruka," *Haiku* 59, no. 5 (April 2010): 160.
6. Takayanagi, "Netto wa haiku o kaeruka," 157.
7. The question of how to translate the term *kanshi* is a far from straightforward one; options include "Chinese-style poetry," "Sino-Japanese poetry," "Chinese poetry," and a few others. Here and throughout, I have elected to follow Matthew Fraleigh in adopting the term "Sinitic poetry" for *kanshi* poetry and "literary Sinitic" for *kanbun* prose. Fraleigh explains the rationale behind this terminology in *Plucking Chrysanthemums: Narushima Ryūhoku and Sinitic Literary Traditions in Modern Japan* (Cambridge, Mass.: Harvard University Asia Center, 2016), 20–28.
8. Maeda Ringai, "Kanshi waka shintaishi no aiirezaru jōkyō o joshite haikai ni oyobu," *Yomiuri shinbun*, August 17, 1890 (supplement). This article is discussed in more detail in chapter 4. A note on terminology is in order here. With the

exception of direct quotations, I use the term *haikai* to denote a range of poetic forms and practices, including linked verse, *senryū*, and "point-scoring" *haikai* (*tentori haikai*), as well as the masters who were its primary practitioners. The term "haiku," by contrast, I define as the consciously modern form of stand-alone 5-7-5 verse devised by Shiki and his fellow poets, primarily in contradistinction to (and through separation from) the broader *haikai* tradition. I also use the term *hokku* occasionally to refer to specific verses originating in a premodern *haikai* context. One complicating factor is that the terms "haiku" and *haikai* coexisted for some time, and even the so-called reformers were not always consistent in their terminology. As late as 1896, for instance, Shiki's manual on how to compose haiku was still titled *Haikai taiyō* (Essentials of *haikai*).

9. Ochiai Naobumi, "Sansei no yueyoshi o nobete *Kagaku* hakkō no shushi ni kau," *Kagaku*, no. 1 (March 1892), reprinted in *Ochiai Naobumi, Ueda Kazutoshi, Haga Yaichi, Fujioka Sakutarō shū*, ed. Hisamatsu Sen'ichi, Meiji bungaku zenshū 44 (Tokyo: Chikuma Shobō, 1968), 27.

10. Benedict Anderson, *Imagined Communities: Reflections on the Origin and Spread of Nationalism* (London: Verso, 2006), 7.

11. Anderson, *Imagined Communities*, 9–36.

12. Anderson paid particular attention to Filipino novelist Jose Rizal's (1861–1896) work *Noli Me Tangere* (Touch me not, 1887), which he saw as providing "hypnotic confirmation of the solidarity of a single community," a vision of an incipient Filipino nationalism while still under Spanish colonial rule; Anderson, *Imagined Communities*, 26–27.

13. James Huffman, *Creating a Public: People and Press in Meiji Japan* (Honolulu: University of Hawai`i Press, 1997).

14. John Pierre Mertz, *Novel Japan: Spaces of Nationhood in Early Meiji Narrative, 1870–88* (Ann Arbor, Mich.: Center for Japanese Studies, 2003).

15. See Ken K. Ito, *An Age of Melodrama: Family, Gender, and Social Hierarchy in the Turn-of-the-Century Japanese Novel* (Stanford, Calif.: Stanford University Press, 2008), especially chapter 1. Karatani notes the importance of novelists in propagating a unified vernacular language: "Despite the progress made toward political and economic modernization within the first two decades following the Restoration . . . something necessary to the formation of the nation was lacking. It is no exaggeration to say that it was novelists who provided this" (*Origins of Modern Japanese Literature* [Durham, N.C.: Duke University Press, 1994], 193). Saito's study of detective fiction, often in serialized form, likewise suggests that detective fiction was a site where "epistemological and moral issues regarded as central to Japan's nation building and Westernization process were explored" (*Detective Fiction and the Rise of the Japanese Novel, 1880–1930* [Cambridge, Mass.: Harvard University Asia Center, 2012], 7).

16. Suga Hidemi, *Nihon kindai bungaku no "tanjō": Genbun itchi undō to nashon-arizumu*, Hihyō kūkan sōsho 6 (Tokyo: Ōta Shuppan, 1995), 19. Suga's discussion centers on the concept of what he calls poesie (*poeshii*), which he considers a critical element in providing a notion of the sublime and eternal to the national imagination, as well as in the aestheticization of politics. Despite this, Suga's actual discussion is concerned primarily with prose fiction rather than specific poetic works.

17. Suga, *Nihon kindai bungaku no "tanjō,"* 37.

18. Although premodern *haikai*, especially poets such as Bashō and Buson, has received extensive coverage in English (as in, for example, Haruo Shirane, *Traces of Dreams: Landscape, Cultural Memory, and the Poetry of Bashō* [Stanford, Calif.: Stanford University Press, 1998], and Cheryl Crowley, *Haikai Poet Yosa Buson and the Bashō Revival* [Leiden: Brill, 2007]), the modern haiku has been comparatively neglected by contemporary scholars. In a similar fashion, with the exception of Matthew Fraleigh's recent *Plucking Chrysanthemums*, the premodern *kanshi* tradition is rather better covered than the modern one. Here, I want to acknowledge the pathbreaking work of Tim Bradstock, Judith Rabinovitch, Burton Watson, and John Timothy Wixted, as well as subsequent important studies by Wiebke Denecke and Ivo Smits.

19. An important exception here is the haiku-focused scholarship of Akio Bin, on whose works *Shiki no kindai: Kokkei, media, Nihongo* (Tokyo: Shin'yōsha, 1999) and *Kyoshi to "Hototogisu": Kindai haiku no media* (Tokyo: Hon'ami Shoten, 2006) this study draws repeatedly.

20. This observation holds especially for Japanese-language scholarship; Honda Yasuo, *Shinbun shōsetsu no tanjō* (Tokyo: Heibonsha, 1998), Maeda Ai, *Kindai dokusha no seiritsu* (Tokyo: Iwanami Shoten, 2001), Kōno Kensuke, *Tōki to shite no bungaku: Katsuji, kenshō, media* (Tokyo: Shin'yōsha, 2003), and Seki Hajime, *Shinbun shōsetsu no jidai: Media, dokusha, merodorama* (Tokyo: Shin'yōsha, 2007), all approach issues of audience, media, and readership during Meiji primarily from the point of view of prose fiction.

21. Isogai Unpō, "Joshi nanzo waka o manabazaru," *Jogaku zasshi*, no. 206 (March 29, 1893): 11.

22. See, for example, anthropologist Michael Herzfeld's critique to the effect that "national harmony displays a deceptively transparent surface; it does not reveal the underlying fissures easily. The easy option is to ignore these fissures altogether," and, specifically with reference to Anderson, that "he does not ground his account in the details of everyday life . . . that would make it convincing for each specific case or that might call for the recognition of the cultural specificity of each nationalism" (*Cultural Intimacy: Social Poetics in the Nation-State* [New York: Routledge, 1997], 2–6).

23. Murayama Kokyō, *Meiji no haiku to haijin tachi* (Tokyo: Kawade Shobō Shinsha, 1983), 27.

24. In its broadest sense, *waka* can be defined as encompassing almost all classical poetry in Japanese, particularly that written in the circles of the imperial court. For the most part, though, the term *waka* in this book should be understood more narrowly, as referring to poetry in a 5-7-5-7-7 syllable pattern, since this was the most commonly practiced form. *Waka* became known as tanka (literally, "short poems") around 1900, but, because the term "tanka" was not in consistent use during the period the book covers, and because most of the critics and poets surveyed in the book generally used the specific term *waka* or *uta*, I have elected to stick with the term *waka* throughout.

25. Among the more notable examples are the late Edo Rivers and Lakes Poetic Society (Kōko Shisha), founded by retired Confucian scholar Ichikawa Kansai 市川寛齋 (1749–1820). Many alumni of this group later became stars of the early nineteenth-century literary world, especially Kikuchi Gozan 菊池五山 (1769–1849), Ōkubo Shibutsu 大窪詩仏 (1767–1837), and Kashiwagi Jotei 柏木如亭 (1763–1819). Meiji examples include Mori Shuntō's Jasmine Poetic Society (Mari Ginsha—the Chinese pronunciation of the first two graphs, *mo li*, punned on Shuntō's surname), perhaps the most influential early Meiji group, and the later Star Society (Seisha), formed from the leading lights of the late Meiji *kanshi* world. From the early twentieth century, the Following Seagulls Society (Zuiō Ginsha) continued to be a major center for *kanshi* practice even as its overall practice declined.

26. There were various forms of this; *maeku-zuke* (adding to the first verse), which involved adding a 7-7 reply to a 5-7-5 initial verse; *kasa-zuke* (putting on a hat), with the first five syllables provided and the final twelve to be added; and *mikasa-zuke* (putting on three hats), in which three different first lines of five syllables were provided, all to be completed; see Akio, *Shiki no kindai*, 129–30.

27. Crowley, *Haikai Poet Yosa Buson*, 21–22.

28. Much of chapter 2 is taken up with an extended rhyme-matching sequence between two prominent Japanese poets. Rhyme matching was also possible across time; both Japanese and Chinese poets often composed rhyme-matching responses to much older poems, often to pay tribute to an admired historical poet. Chinese poet Su Shi 蘇軾 (1037–1101), for instance, composed rhyme-matching responses to every verse in the collected works of Six Dynasties poet Tao Yuanming 陶淵明 (365–427). Few if any English-language studies have paid much attention to rhyme matching as a mechanism of poetic writing, with the notable exception of John Timothy Wixted; see, for example, "Sociability in Poetry: An Introduction to the Matching-Rhyme *Kanshi* of Mori Ōgai," in

"Ōgai"—Mori Rintarō: Begegnungen mit dem japanischen "homme de lettres," ed. Klaus Kracht, 189–217 (Wiesbaden: Harrassowitz, 2014).

29. Ogata Tsutomu, *Za no bungaku* (Tokyo: Kadokawa Shoten, 1973), 14. Testament to this work's influence on present-day haiku poets is its citation as a key conceptual term in the debate between Fukunaga and Takayanagi discussed previously.

30. In his words, "Japan's modern literature has developed around the axis of the individual. And this is profoundly connected with the fateful circumstances of its birth, namely that Japanese literature, having come into contact with modern Western individualist thought, set out with the establishment of the individual as a key issue" (Ogata, *Za no bungaku*, 49).

31. Eiko Ikegami, *Bonds of Civility: Aesthetic Networks and the Political Origins of Japanese Culture* (New York: Cambridge University Press, 2005), 7.

32. Joshua S. Mostow, "The Revival of Poetry in Traditional Forms," in *The Columbia Companion to Modern East Asian Literature*, ed. Joshua S. Mostow (New York: Columbia University Press, 2003), 100.

33. Michael Bourdaghs, *The Dawn That Never Comes: Shimazaki Tōson and Japanese Nationalism* (New York: Columbia University Press, 2003), 7.

34. Prasenjit Duara, *Rescuing History from the Nation: Questioning Narratives of Modern China* (Chicago: University of Chicago Press, 1995), 13.

35. Partha Chatterjee, "Whose Imagined Community?," in *The Nation and Its Fragments: Colonial and Postcolonial Histories* (Princeton, N.J.: Princeton University Press, 1993), 13.

36. Tamar Mayer, "Gender Ironies of Nationalism: Setting the Stage," in *Gender Ironies of Nationalism: Sexing the Nation* (New York: Routledge, 2000), 6.

37. Bourdaghs, *Dawn That Never Comes*, 16.

38. Quoted in Richard Rubinger, *Popular Literacy in Early Modern Japan* (Honolulu: University of Hawai'i Press, 2007), 105–6.

39. Being part of a well-educated intellectual and cultural elite did not, however, imply that these poets were always well-off materially; both Shiki and Tekkan went through periods of near destitution on more than one occasion.

40. Quoted in Tomi Suzuki, "*The Tale of Genji*, National Literature, Language, and Modernism," in *Envisioning the Tale of Genji: Media, Gender, and Cultural Production*, ed. Haruo Shirane (New York: Columbia University Press, 2008), 250.

41. Known as the *haikai kyōdōshoku* (*haikai* education initiative), this project did not work very well in practice, partly because of intragroup rivalries and a lack of enthusiasm on the part of the majority of *haikai* masters. Sekine Rinkichi's series of articles on the old-school master Mimori Mikio, who was an enthusiastic participant in the *kyōdōshoku* project, provide a good overview of some

of the personalities and problems involved; Sekine Rinkichi, "Mimori Mikio hyōden," *Haiku* 27, nos. 4–12 (March–November 1978), especially parts 3 and 4.

42. Saitō Mareshi, *Kanbunmyaku no kindai: Shinmatsu-Meiji no bungakuken* (Tokyo: Nihon Hōsō Shuppan Kyōkai, 2007); Saitō Mareshi, *Kanbunmyaku to kindai Nihon: Mō hitotsu no kotoba no sekai* (Tokyo: Nihon Hōsō Shuppan Kyōkai, 2007); Matthew Fraleigh, trans., *New Chronicles of Yanagibashi and Diary of a Journey to the West: Narushima Ryūhoku Reports from Home and Abroad* (Ithaca, N.Y.: Cornell University Press, 2010); Matthew Fraleigh, "Songs of the Righteous Spirit: 'Men of High Purpose' and Their Chinese Poetry in Modern Japan," *Harvard Journal of Asiatic Studies* 69, no. 1 (June 2009): 109–71.

43. To call it a tradition is perhaps overstating the case somewhat; Ivo Smits, for instance, has argued that *kanshi* practice in Japan has historically been characterized by disjuncture and reinvention rather than any continuous lineage: "Minding the Gaps: An Early Edo History of Sino-Japanese Poetry," in *Uncharted Waters: Intellectual Life in the Edo Period; Essays in Honour of W. J. Boot*, ed. Anna Beerens and Mark Teeuwen (Leiden: Brill, 2012), 93.

44. Mikami Sanji, "Nihon rekishi bungakujō no kansatsu," *Nihon bungaku*, no. 19 (March 1890): 14.

45. Masaoka Shiki, *Shiki zenshū* (hereafter *SZ*), ed. Masaoka Chūsaburō et al., 25 vols. (Tokyo: Kōdansha, 1975–1978), 14:24.

46. "Kanshi sakka ni tsugu," *Teikoku bungaku* 2, no. 6 (June 1895): 96.

47. Fraleigh, "Songs of the Righteous Spirit," 111.

48. Saitō Mareshi has argued that the practice of *kanshi* by many government employees (who were not likely to criticize their employer) helped to temper its overtly political aspect, in the process giving shape to the modern separation between politics and literature and fashioning *kanshi* as a private, personal genre; *Kanbunmyaku to kindai Nihon*, 125–37.

49. *SZ* 4:230. In context, this statement was actually less inflammatory than it is sometimes made out to be, since Shiki also noted that the remaining one-tenth were so good that they fully justified Bashō's reputation.

50. Masaoka Shiki, "Futatabi utayomi ni atōru sho," in *SZ* 7:23.

51. Masaoka Shiki, "Bungaku," in *SZ* 14:192. As will be clear, it is from this insult that the title of the book is taken. Technically, *hyōsoku* should properly be translated as "tonal prosody" rather than "rhyme," but I think that the point of the term *hyōsokuya* is to describe one who composes poetry mechanically and with little thought, and so the English "rhymer" better captures the nuance of the intended insult.

52. Janine Beichman, *Masaoka Shiki: His Life and Works* (Boston: Cheng and Tsui, 2002); Donald Keene, *The Winter Sun Shines In: A Life of Masaoka Shiki* (New

York: Columbia University Press, 2013). Mark Morris's two articles are "Buson and Shiki: Part One" and "Buson and Shiki: Part Two," *Harvard Journal of Asiatic Studies* 44, no. 2 (December 1984): 381–425, 45, no. 1 (June 1985): 255–321. Burton Watson translates more than a hundred haiku by Shiki (as well as a handful of his tanka and *kanshi*) in *Masaoka Shiki: Selected Poems* (New York: Columbia University Press, 1997).

53. Yosano Akiko, "Atogaki," in *Yosano Akiko kashū* (Tokyo: Iwanami Shoten, 1986), 361; quoted in Janine Beichman, *Embracing the Firebird: Yosano Akiko and the Birth of the Female Voice in Modern Japanese Poetry* (Honolulu: University of Hawai`i Press, 2002), 70.

54. As one example, many former Matsuyama warriors apparently refused to humble themselves by seeking employment in a government run by their former enemies (Matsui Toshihiko, *Masaoka shiki no kenkyū*, 2 vols. [Tokyo: Meiji Shoin, 1976], 1:308). As discussed in chapters 1 and 3, Matsuyama was also a major center of Freedom and Popular Rights activity during early Meiji, in which Shiki himself seems to have been peripherally involved.

1. CLIMBING THE STAIRS OF POETRY: *KANSHI*, PRINT, AND WRITERSHIP IN NINETEENTH-CENTURY JAPAN

1. The definitive English-language study on the rise and fall of the *kangaku juku* during the nineteenth century, as well as their general curricula, is Margaret Mehl, *Private Academies of Chinese Learning in Meiji Japan: The Decline and Transformation of the Kangaku Juku* (Copenhagen: NIAS Press, 2003).

2. Katō Kuniyasu, *Kanshijin Shiki: Haiku kaigan no dojō* (Tokyo: Kenbun Shuppan, 2006), 15.

3. *SZ* 10:41–42.

4. Katō, *Kanshijin Shiki*, 25.

5. *SZ* 10:41–42. Tsuchiya seems to have been one of Kanzan's colleagues at the Meikyōkan, though little else is known about him. Some sources refer to a Tsuchiya Sanpei 土屋三平 (dates unknown) also active in Matsuyama at around the same time, who may or may not have been the same person. Shiki's friend Yanagihara Kyokudō 柳原極堂 (Masayuki 正之, 1867–1957) noted a rumor that one or other of the Tsuchiyas may even have starved to death after the commutation of warrior stipends into lump-sum payments early in Meiji; see Yanagihara Kyokudō, *Yūjin Shiki* (Tokyo: Maeda Shuppan, 1946), 46.

6. For most forms of Sinitic poetry, the tones of the graphs that make up the poem must accord to a specific sequence of level and oblique tones. This sequence varies according to the specific form in which the poet is composing.

7. Despite the important differences between the language of Sinitic poetry and both vernacular and classical Japanese, it would be unwise to infer that this meant there was anything necessarily alien about *kanshi* for Japanese poets. On this topic, John Timothy Wixted has made the point that because the rhyme and prosodic patterns used in Sinitic poetry tended to remain constant while vernacular Chinese shifted over time, for much of Chinese history the language of Sinitic poetry was not a vernacular one for poets in China either (although the gap was considerably less pronounced) (*"Kanbun, Histories of Japanese Literature, and Japanologists," Sino-Japanese Studies* 10, no. 2 [April 1998]: 23).

8. In addition to following correct tonal prosody, a formally correct Sinitic poem also has to rhyme. Usually, the rhyme graphs occur at the end of specific lines; in which lines the rhyme must occur depends on the specific form being composed. For example, in the quatrain form discussed in the following, the rhyme graphs must come at the end of the first, second, and fourth lines, and the third line is unrhymed.

9. Shimizu Fusao, *Shiki kanshi no shūhen* (Tokyo: Meiji Shoin, 1996), 98, notes that research on poetic primers shows that booksellers generally considered such manuals valueless and threw them away in large numbers. My own experience is that even manuals from the late Edo period can be obtained from antiquarian booksellers for as little as a thousand yen or so.

10. Yamamoto Hokuzan, *Sakushi shikō*, in *Kinsei bungaku ronshū*, ed. Nakamura Yukihiko, Nihon koten bungaku taikei 94 (Tokyo: Iwanami Shoten, 1967), 285.

11. Hokuzan, *Sakushi shikō*, 297–98.

12. Ibi Takashi, "Kōko shisha no shuppatsu: Shimin bungaku to shite no kanshi e," *Kokubungaku kaishaku to kanshō* 73, no. 10 (October 2008): 103.

13. Marius B. Jansen, *China in the Tokugawa World* (Cambridge, Mass.: Harvard University Press, 1992), 80.

14. Burton Watson, *Japanese Literature in Chinese*, 2 vols. (New York: Columbia University Press, 1975–1976), 2:8.

15. Judith N. Rabinovitch and Timothy R. Bradstock, *The Kanshi Poems of the Ozasa Tansaku Collection: Late Edo Life through the Eyes of Kyoto Townsmen*, Nichibunken monograph series 5 (Kyoto: International Research Center for Japanese Studies, 2002), 29.

16. Ibi Takashi, *Edo no shidan jānarizumu: "Gozandō shiwa" no sekai* (Tokyo: Kadokawa Shoten, 2001), 13.

17. For example, Rabinovitch and Bradstock, *Kanshi poems of the Ozasa Tansaku*, 29, attributes this to a "growing affluence and leisure enjoyed by these people and to the spread of literacy downward through society." Haruo Shirane, ed., *Early Modern Japanese Literature: An Anthology, 1600–1900* (New

York: Columbia University Press, 2002), 11, notes that "with the spread of literacy, both commoners and samurai had access to . . . various forms of refined or elite literature (such as *waka, renga, monogatari, kanshi,* and *kanbun,* which had earlier been the exclusive possession of the nobility, priests, and elite samurai)."

18. J. Marshall Unger, *Literacy and Script Reform in Occupation Japan: Reading between the Lines* (New York: Oxford University Press, 1996), 25.

19. Peipei Qiu, "Daoist Concepts in Bashō's Critical Thought," in *East Asian Cultural and Historical Perspectives: Histories and Society; Culture and Literatures,* ed. Steven Tötösy de Zepetnek and Jennifer W. Jay (Edmonton: Research Institute for Comparative Literature and Cross-Cultural Studies, University of Alberta, 1997), 330.

20. Quoted in Higuchi Motomi, "Edo jidai no keimōteki kanshi sakuhō sho," *Kōbe shōsen daigaku kiyō bunka ronshū* 29 (July 1980): 89.

21. The *Lianzhu shige* consists of verse by Tang- and Song-era poets, compiled first by Yu Ji 于濟 (J. U Sai, dates unknown) and then further edited and expanded by Cai Zhengsun 蔡正孫 (J. Sai Seison, fl. thirteenth century) before its completion and publication in 1300. According to various sources, including a preface to Jotei's version by Yamamoto Hokuzan, Cai had learned poetry from Xie Fangde 謝枋得 (1226–1289), a Southern Song general and poet who starved himself to death rather than surrender and serve the Yuan dynasty (1271–1368). This explains the collection's not including any poets after the Song and may also explain why it apparently did not circulate widely in China until after the end of the Yuan dynasty. The *Lianzhu shige* is known to have circulated in Japan during the Muromachi period (1392–1573), arriving in Japan probably by way of the Korean Peninsula; evidence for this comes in the fact that some editions of the text include a commentary on the text by Korean nobleman and poet Seo Geojong 徐居正 (1420–1488). See Ibi Takashi, *Yakuchū Renju shikaku* (Tokyo: Iwanami Shoten, 2008), 282–86.

22. As Ibi, *Edo shidan no jānarizumu,* 84, points out, a number of prominent nineteenth-century *kanshi* societies appeared in economically prosperous provincial areas. In addition to Bansei Ginsha, other examples include Enba Ginsha in Chōshi (in what is now Chiba Prefecture), a significant center for fishing and soy sauce brewing; Suihei Ginsha in Kiryū (modern Gunma), a hub of garment manufacturing; and Kōzansha in Fujieda in Suruga (modern Shizuoka), an important post station on the Tōkaidō highway between Edo and Kyoto.

23. Ibi, *Yakuchū Renju shikaku,* 290. In keeping with a practice known as *shūsei* among Japanese *kanshi* poets and other Sinologues, Kishiku frequently abbreviated his surname to a single graph, going by the three-graph soubriquet Ki Hyakunen 木百年.

24. Text from Ibi, *Yakuchu Renju shikaku*, 174.

25. Conveying the different tone and registers of the classical and vernacular Japanese is difficult in English, but some idea might be gained by comparing the more formal English "Wherefore do you dwell 'mid verdant peaks?" with the more colloquial "What d'you mean by living in green mountains?"

26. As Ibi, *Yakuchū Renju shikaku*, 46, 302, notes, Jotei's vernacular renderings are often quite free and sometimes include elements not present in the original poem. For instance, Jotei gives the first line of Zhao Shixiu's (1170–1219) "On Having an Engagement" (有約), which reads 黄梅時節家々雨, as *samidare no kore daremo kamo ame de komaru ni* (At the time of the spring showers, everyone is bothered by the rain), although the original does not contain any semantic element equivalent to *komaru* (be bothered by).

27. Ibi, *Yakuchū Renju shikaku*, 289–91.

28. Quoted in Ibi, *Yakuchū Renju shikaku*, 285.

29. Oblique tones are indicated via underlining; these and the following phrases are taken from Takeoka Yūsen, ed., *Shinsen yōgaku benran* (Kyoto: Hayashi Yoshibē, 1878), 1 verso.

30. The vocabulary for this "poem" is taken from that featured in Takeoka, *Shinsen yōgaku benran*, 5 verso.

31. This poem uses a variant rhyme scheme for a pentasyllabic quatrain, in which the first line's required tones are (with L indicating level, O indicating oblique, and E either) E / L / L / O / O.

32. Hattori's preface suggests that the origins of this pedagogical strategy were quite literally in "cutting and pasting": "I have heard that when Takano Rantei of the eastern city [i.e., Edo] taught Sinitic poetry to his pupils, for every topic that came up, they would cut out the preformed phrases of former poetic masters, and he would have them arrange them together, and thereby their compositions took shape" (Hattori Somon, "Shigo saikin jo," in *Shigo saikin*, ed. Nagata Kanga [Kyoto: Hayashi Gonbei, 1841], 1).

33. A "Persian shop" (*bosi di* or *bosi dian*) refers to shops operated in the Tang capital of Chang'an by merchants from Persia. The reference suggests the aspiring poet's being surrounded by all manner of wonderful and unfamiliar things.

34. Hattori, "Shigo saikin jo," 1–2.

35. Hattori, "Shigo saikin jo," 3–4. A "grass dog" (*yichen chugou*) refers to objects used in ritual sacrifice and then discarded, hence an object that has served its purpose and is of no further use.

36. Confusingly, the graphs used in "Shigo saikin" often varied by author, changing the meaning slightly. In addition to 砕金, one also finds 粋金 (finest gold)

and 砕錦 (patchwork brocade). The imagery in most cases is intended to liken the construction of a poem from discrete blocks of vocabulary to fashioning something beautiful from many small pieces.

37. The surveys in question are Suzuki Toshiyuki, "*Shigo saikin* to *Yōgaku shiin*," *Chūō daigaku bungakubu kiyō*, no. 101 (February 2008): 65–103; Suzuki Toshiyuki, "*Yōgaku benran* kō: Bakumatsu shisaku netsu to sono yukue," *Kokugo to kokubungaku* 91, no. 7 (July 2014): 3–17; and Higuchi, "Edo jidai no keimōteki kanshi."

38. Oki Osamu, ed., *Shinsen shigo katsuyō* (Tokyo: Bessho Heishichi, 1879); quoted in Suzuki, "*Shigo saikin* to *Yōgaku shiin*," 101.

39. Extant copies and library records show Kanga's *Shigo saikin* to have been reprinted in 1779, 1794, 1808, 1826, and 1841. There is also a similarly titled but textually distinct *Shigo saikin zokuhen* (Brocade pieces treasury, continued), published in 1815.

40. This conclusion is drawn on the basis of Okajima Akihiro, "Kango shiryō to shite no shigakusho: *Shigo saikin* o rei to shite," *Gobun kenkyū*, no. 86–87 (June 1999): 222.

41. Suzuki, "*Shigo saikin* to *Yōgaku shiin*," 66.

42. Per Higuchi, "Edo jidai no keimōteki kanshi," 71.

43. Per Suzuki, "*Shigo saikin* to *Yōgaku shiin*," 86–98, *Yōgaku shiin* was reprinted in 1821, 1822, 1834, 1845, 1857, and 1879. The "sequel," *Yōgaku shiin zokuhen*, was reprinted in 1834, 1845, 1856, and 1879.

44. The flyleaf of Hōzan's 1845 edition states, "An amalgamation of *Shigo saikin* and *Yōgaku shiin*, for quick reference."

45. Shimizu, *Shiki kanshi no shūhen*, 99–109.

46. Suzuki Shigemitsu, ed., *Shinsen shigaku jizai* (Tokyo: Tsuruya Kiemon, 1879); quoted in Suzuki, "*Shigo saikin* to *Yōgaku benran*," 101.

47. Suzuki, "*Yōgaku benran* kō," 11–12. The publisher maintained in his defense that the failure to credit Hōzan was an "oversight" (*sorō*), an explanation that the court apparently did not accept.

48. And even into the twentieth century: the introductory guide to producing *kanshi* Iritani Sensuke, *Kanshi nyūmon* (Tokyo: Nitchū Shuppan, 1986), 250–51, features an explanation of tonal prosody that is virtually identical to Meiji manuals in its use of colored dots to indicate tones.

49. Ōhashi Otowa, ed., *Shigaku shōkei* (Tokyo: Shōnen'en, 1895), 15–16.

50. Miura Kanō, *Meiji kanbungakushi* (Tokyo: Kyūko Shoin, 1998), 23. This may, Miura suggests, have been one of the reasons why Mori Shuntō, who was less immediately demanding as a teacher, was rather more successful in attracting and retaining disciples than Chinzan.

51. Hirose Tansō, *Tansō shiwa*, in *Nihon shiwa sōsho*, ed. Kokubu Takatane and Ikeda Shirōjirō, 10 vols. (Tokyo: Bunkaidō Shoten, 1920–1922), 4:224.

52. Examples are too numerous to list exhaustively but include *Quatrains by Seventeen Poets of the Bunsei Era* (*Bunsei jūshichika zekku*, 1829), *Quatrains by Thirty-Six Poets of the Tenpō Era* (*Tenpō sanjū rokka zekku*, 1838), *Quatrains by Twenty-Five Poets of the Kaei Era* (*Kaei nijūgoka zekku*, 1848), *Quatrains by Thirty-Two Poets of the Ansei Era* (*Ansei sanjūnika zekku*, 1859), *Quatrains by Twenty-Six Poets of the Bunkyū Era* (*Bunkyū nijūrokka zekku*, 1862), *Quatrains by Ten Poets of the Keiō Era* (*Keiō jūka zekku*, 1866), *Quatrains by Thirty-Eight Poets of the Meiji Era* (*Meiji sanjūhachika zekku*, 1869), and numerous other subsequent Meiji-era collections.

53. Rintaro Goyama, "How Traditional Literature Adapted Itself to Modern Media: Kanshibun in 19th Century Japan," *TXT: Exploring the Boundaries of the Book* 1, no. 1 (2014): 177.

54. Using L to denote a level tone, O for oblique, and E for where either can be used, the opening line to a standard pentasyllabic quatrain would require graphs with tones in the order E / O / L / L / O.

55. Seikei was the father of Shiki's later disciple Kawahigashi Hekigotō. Among Seikei's comments on the young Shiki's poetry are the following: "Tonal prosody a complete mess. Rewrite" (*hyōsoku sakugo hanahadashi, kaisaku o ka to su*) (*SZ* 9:432), and "Inappropriate tonal prosody; this is not worthy of being called a Sinitic poem" (平仄不相応不足以為詩) (*SZ* 9:443).

56. *SZ* 9:16. I have added vertical line breaks to highlight the distinct phrases that make up the poem. The second line alludes to the popular image of the cuckoo coughing up blood as it cried, which in turn was the reason Shiki adopted his best-known pen name after contracting tuberculosis. Although it might seem a little too neat for Shiki's first-ever *kanshi* to have been composed on the bird after which he would later name himself, there is no reason to suspect that the poem is inauthentic.

57. Shimizu, *Shiki kanshi no shūhen*, 76. Shimizu finds similar correspondences in another ten of Shiki's early poems; see *Shiki kanshi no shūhen*, 121.

58. Some sources suggest "Motoyuki" as the correct reading for Meisetsu's given name. I incline toward "Nariyuki" here because of a popular theory that Meisetsu chose his pen name because its two graphs can be read as *nari* 鳴り and *yuki* 雪, respectively.

59. Naitō Meisetsu, *Meisetsu jijoden* (Tokyo: Okamura Shoten, 1922), 122.

60. *SZ* 4:479.

61. Katō Kuniyasu, *Shiki zōsho to "Kanshikō" kenkyū: Kindai haiku seiritsu no katei* (Tokyo: Kenbun Shuppan, 2014), 100. Although Shiki did not copy out the

precise poem by Kan Chazan under discussion, Katō notes that he did copy out the ones immediately before and after it, so he would certainly have been aware of the poem's language.

62. Kōno Shizuko, ed., *Ōfuku shokan Gotō Shinpei Tokutomi Sohō: 1895–1929* (Tokyo: Fujiwara Shoten, 2005), 123.

63. Naruse Masakatsu, "Nagai Kafū shū kaisetsu," in *Nagai Kafū shū*, ed. Naruse Masakatsu et al., Nihon kindai bungaku taikei 29 (Tokyo: Kadokawa Shoten, 1969), 11. Yanagida Kunio, *Yanagida Kunio no kokyō nanajūnen* (Tokyo: PHP Kenkyūjo, 2014), 76, describes the poems he composed this way as "worthless stuff that anyone could compose."

64. Tayama Katai, "Tōkyō no sanjūnen," in *Tayama Katai*, ed. Sōma Tsuneo, Sakka no jiden 25 (Tokyo: Nihon Tosho Sentā, 1995), 22–24. Katai had more reason than most to check, since he was one of the journal's most prolific contributors with a little more than one hundred separate pieces appearing in print. This puts Katai among the top five most prolific contributors in the magazine's history. See Kami Shōichirō, ed., *Eisai shinshi: Kaisetsu, sōmokuji, sakuin* (Tokyo: Fuji Shuppan, 1993), 59 (index).

65. As attested to by Shiki's first cousin Minami Hajime; see *SZ bekkan* 3:180.

66. For instance, one regular advertiser during the mid-1880s was the Mōgyū Gijuku academy in Shimōsa (roughly present-day Saitama Prefecture), which charged three sen per piece of Sinitic prose corrected "regardless of length" and one sen five *ri* per poem "regardless of whether it is a quatrain, regulated verse, or old-style poem." See *Kokon shibun shōkai*, no. 90 (June 5, 1883): 24.

67. Goyama, "How Traditional Literature Adapted Itself," 178.

68. Suzuki, "*Shigo saikin* to *Yōgaku shiin*," 97.

69. Watanabe Katsumi, "Kaisetsu," in *SZ* 9:834.

70. *Kagetsu shinshi* published 967 *kanshi* poems during its seven years of publication, of which 446 were by ten poets and 250 by Shuntō, Shōtō, or Kozan.

71. Narushima Ryūhoku, "Omou mama," *Kagetsu shinshi*, no. 37 (February 26, 1878): 8 recto–9 verso.

72. Ōdate Seizai, ed., *Yōgaku hikkei konsei shisaku shinpen*, 2 vols. (Tokyo: Morimoto Taisuke, 1878), 1:17.

73. Yoshida Yōtoku, ed., *Kaika shigo saikin* (Tokyo: Fuzandō, 1878), 3–4.

74. Yoshida, *Kaika shigo saikin*, 35.

75. Lest it be thought that this lexicon might have been aimed at Tokyo-based bureaucrats themselves, it is worth noting that its colophon shows an extensive network of distributors across virtually the whole of eastern Japan, from Yamagata to Nagano.

76. Seki Toku, ed., *Shinsen shiin yōgaku benran*, 3 vols. (Osaka: Yoshioka Hōbunken, 1878), 3:28 verso.

77. Fukui Jun, ed., *Kinsei shisaku yōgaku benran* (Osaka: Hanai Unosuke, 1883), 9 recto.

78. Fukui, *Kinsei shisaku yōgaku benran*, 27 verso.

79. Seki, *Shinsen shiin yōgaku benran*, 2:9 verso and 1:29 verso, respectively. The second topic presumably refers to the 1878 Paris World's Fair, held in celebration of France's recovery from the 1870–1871 Franco-Prussian War.

80. Kamio Kazō, ed., *Yōgaku shiin, kaika shinsen: Shigo saikin, kaika shinsen; Kokon meika zekku shirei* (Tokyo: Fumie Shobō, 1881), 20 recto.

81. Seki, *Shinsen shiin yōgaku benran*, 1:13 recto.

82. Seki, *Shinsen shiin yōgaku benran*, 1:19 recto.

83. Seki, *Shinsen shiin yōgaku benran*, 2:38 recto.

84. Takeoka, *Shinsen yōgaku benran*, 4 recto and verso.

85. Ōhashi, *Shigaku shōkei*, 250.

2. NOT THE KIND OF POETRY MEN WRITE: "FRAGRANT-STYLE" *KANSHI* AND POETIC MASCULINITY IN MEIJI JAPAN

1. Mori Ōgai, *Ōgai zenshū*, 38 vols. (Tokyo: Iwanami Shoten, 1971–1975), 8:494.

2. Ōgai's recall may be a little hazy here, since *Keirin isshi* rarely published fragrant-style poems. See Gōyama Rintarō, "Bakumatsu Meijiki no entai kanshi: Mori Shuntō, Kainan ippa no shifū o megutte," *Wakan hikaku bungaku*, no. 37 (August 2006): 18.

3. Literally, a *xianglian* (*kōren*) is a case for makeup and other cosmetics. This derives from a late Tang anthology of quasi-erotic verse, the *Xianglian ji*, discussed in this chapter. *Xianglian* has been variously translated as "Fragrance Vanity" (Beth Upton), "Fragrant Toilette" (Dorothy Ko), "Scented Dress-Case" (Xiaorong Li), and "Fragrant Dressing-Case" (Nanxiu Qian). I have chosen to translate *Xianglian ji* as *Fragrant Toilette Collection* and the derived style accordingly as "fragrant style."

4. Spring or lakeside scenes were also popular; in extremis, even poems that were unusually ornate might be termed "fragrant style." See Gōyama, "Bakumatsu Meijiki no entai kanshi," 19.

5. Presumably, the woman and her lover once carved pledges to each other on a large stone or a tree, but so much time has passed since then that moss has grown over the words.

6. Mori Shuntō, *Shuntō shishō*, ed. Morikawa Kenzō, 20 vols. (Tokyo: Bunkaidō, 1912), 7:10 verso. For a *kakikudashi* version of this poem (i.e., rendered into

classical Japanese), see Ibi Takashi, "Meiji kanshi no shuppatsu: Mori Shuntō shiron," *Edo bungaku*, no. 21 (December 1999): 12.

7. In a popular tale widely circulated in Japan and originating in the Song-dynasty Zen monk Huihong's 惠洪 (1071–1128) *Remarks Made during Nights in the Cold Study* (*Lengzhai yehua*), Xuanzong praises the beauty of Yang Guifei's slightly drunken countenance at a banquet. Likening her appearance to that of a woman who has just awakened in the morning, Xuanzong announces that "the aronia tree has not yet had enough sleep!" (真海棠眠未足耳).

8. Xiaorong Li, *Women's Poetry of Late Imperial China: Transforming the Inner Chambers* (Seattle: University of Washington Press, 2012), 59.

9. Paul Rouzer, *Articulated Ladies: Gender and the Male Community in Early Chinese Texts* (Cambridge, MA: Harvard University Press, 2001), 144.

10. *Kagetsu shinshi*, no. 39 (March 17, 1878): 4 recto.

11. It also has yet older antecedents, one major one being the so-called palace-style poetry (*gongti shi*) of the Liang court. As Li, *Women's Poetry*, 21, notes, palace-style works "demonstrate a sustained interest in meticulously depicting feminine beauty, psychology, and settings." They also make up the bulk of works in the third-oldest extant Chinese poetry collection, *New Songs from the Jade Terrace* (*Yutai xinyong*, compiled ca. 530).

12. "Most likely" because throughout much of Chinese literary history Han Wo's authorship of the *Fragrant Toilette Collection* has been disputed, a number of scholars (to the present day) suggesting that the upright and moral Han Wo could not have been the author of an erotic text. The slightly later poet He Ning 和凝 (898–955) is often proposed as its putative author.

13. The "fish rhino horn" is likely a hairpin or other ornament made of rhino horn; Beth Upton, "The Poems of Han Wo" (PhD diss., University of California, Berkeley, 1980), 131–32, notes that such items were considered to provide protection against harm coming from water.

14. Chinese text from Han Wo, *Han Wo shiji jianzhu*, ed. Tao Qi (Jinan: Shandong Jiaoyu Chubanshe, 2000), 250–51. The English translation is adapted from Upton, "Poems of Han Wo," 130–35.

15. The model here is likely the story of Emperor Cheng of Han 漢成帝 (51–7 B.C.E., r. 31–7 B.C.E.), who bribed servants in order to be able to watch Zhao Hede 趙合德 (d. 7 B.C.E.), the sister of his favored consort, Zhao Feiyan 趙飛燕 (ca. 31–1 B.C.E.), as she bathed. See Upton, "Poems of Han Wo," 134.

16. Han Wo, *Kan Naikan Kōrenshū*, ed. Tate Ryūwan and Maki Ryōko (Edo: Suwaraya Ihachi, 1811), unpaginated.

17. Nanxiu Qian, *Politics, Poetics, and Gender in Late Qing China: Xue Shaohui and the Era of Reform* (Stanford, Calif.: Stanford University Press, 2015), 46.

18. Fang Hui, *Yingkui lüsui huiping*, ed. Li Qingjia, 3 vols. (Shanghai: Shanghai Guji Chubanshe, 1986), 1:279.

19. Chu Renhu, *Jianhuji*, Xuxiu Siku quanshu 1262 (Shanghai: Shanghai Guji Chubanshe, 2002), 112.

20. Kawada Ōkō, "Jugoi Niwa-kun bohimei," *Kokon shibun shōkai*, no. 91 (June 5, 1883): 6.

21. Hino Toshihiko makes this suggestion in *Mori Shuntō no kisoteki kenkyū* (Tokyo: Kyūko Shoin, 2013), 153.

22. As James Reichert, *In the Company of Men: Representations of Male-Male Sexuality in Meiji Literature* (Stanford, Calif.: Stanford University Press, 2006), 77, notes, Kiriyama, one of the main characters of Tsubouchi Shōyō's 坪内逍遥 (1859–1935) *The Character of Students in Our Times* (*Tōsei shosei katagi*, 1885–1886), is both closely associated with a "hard" dislike of women and portrayed in negative terms as a backward degenerate. As Kiriyama says, "Do you know what weakens men more than anything else? It's male-female love . . . Since associating with women is the biggest factor in making men soft, it's necessary to come up with a strategy for keeping them away."

23. Kinoshita Hyō 木下彪 (1902–1999), a personal friend and disciple of Kokubu Seigai's and a critic with an obvious dislike of Kainan, referred to Kainan and his group as "softie poets" (*nanpa shijin*), whereas Hosogai Kōtō, who studied under Kainan and had considerable respect for him, likewise noted that "there were criticisms that Kainan belonged to a school of 'softie' poets" (*nanpa shiha da nado to iu hinan mo atta mono de arimashita*). See Kinoshita Hyō, "Kokubu Seigai to Meiji Taishō Shōwa no kanshikai (8)," *Shi to tomo*, no. 325 (February 1977): 35, and Hosogai Kōtō, *To shi kanshō* (Tokyo: Teikoku Daigaku Shuppankai, 1929), 431.

24. See Gregory M. Pflugfelder, *Cartographies of Desire: Male-Male Sexuality in Japanese Discourse, 1600–1950* (Berkeley: University of California Press, 1999), 214–16.

25. Histories of Meiji *kanshi* have been highly critical of Shuntō for this; Maeda Ai has called him "officialdom's running dog" (*kanryō no sōku*), and Irokawa Daikichi has noted that Shuntō was willing to publish "works of an inferior or vulgar quality in order to flatter government officials." See Maeda Ai, "Chinzan to Shuntō: Meiji shonen no kanshidan," in *Bakumatsu, ishinki no bungaku*, ed. Maeda Ai (Tokyo: Hōsei Daigaku Shuppankyoku, 1972), 265–66, and Irokawa Daikichi, "Poetry in Revolutionary Thought," in *The Culture of the Meiji Period*, ed. Marius B. Jansen (Princeton, N.J.: Princeton University Press, 1985), 127.

26. Kinoshita Hyō, "Kokubu Seigai to Meiji Taishō Shōwa no kanshikai (16)," *Shi to tomo*, no. 335 (January 1978): 26. Maeda Ai's study of the names appearing in *Shinbunshi* shows that almost all of them held between the fourth and sixth rank in a government ministry. Many of the poems that appeared in the journal reflected

this constituency, composed on topics such as accompanying the emperor on a procession, congratulating a colleague who had just changed jobs, and on the occasion of lavish official dinners. See Maeda, "Chinzan to Shuntō," 250–52.

27. *SZ* 11:9.

28. Seigai, his future employer Kuga Katsunan, and Shiki's uncle Katō Takusen were expelled for protesting the punishment of other students who had engaged in a "culinary punitive expedition" (*makanai seibatsu*), a preplanned riot in the school cafeteria in protest of the poor quality of the food. Kinoshita has suggested that here again factional politics may have played a role, since the principal was a Satsuma man; Kinoshita Hyō, "Kokubu Seigai to Meiji Taishō Shōwa no kanshikai (2)," *Shi to tomo*, no. 319 (August 1976): 32–33.

29. Katō lists Shiki as owning this volume, in *Shiki zōsho to "Kanshikō" kenkyū: Kindai haiku seiritsu no katei* (Tokyo: Kenbun Shuppan, 2014), 557.

30. Hokuzan's major assault on Archaist poetics comes in his 1783 *Sakushi shikō*; in it, he closely paraphrases Yuan Hongdao in criticizing those who "discard the true poetry that is properly theirs and imitate and plagiarize the works of others" (*onore ni yūsuru shinshi o sutete, hoka no shi o hyōshū mogi suru*); Yamamoto Hokuzan, *Sakushi shikō*, in *Kinsei bungaku ronshū*, ed. Nakamura Yukihiko, Nihon koten bungaku taikei 94 (Tokyo: Iwanami Shoten, 1967), 285.

31. Quoted in Ibi Takashi, "Kōko shisha to yūri shi: Edo shidan no kakushin o megutte (jō)," *Kokugo to kokubungaku* 51, no. 3 (March 1974): 47.

32. As in, for example, Ryūhoku's *Pari chikushi*, composed on his experiences in Paris.

33. Meiji poetic discourse often grouped the bamboo-branch ballad with the fragrant style, but sexual relations were not necessarily integral to the former. Writing in 1908, Kubo Tenzui 久保天随 (1875–1934) suggested that this was one distinctively Meiji interpretation: "Bamboo-branch ballads began with Liu Yuxi and depicted only the emotions of the people in a locale. In later generations, it was considered sufficient to depict a narrower and more confined realm, of the heights of mist and lustrous beauty [i.e., eroticism, especially in the licensed quarters]. One has to say that this was very much a matter of confusing the branch with the root" (Kubo Tenzui, *Hyōshaku Nihon zekku sen* [Tokyo: Hongō Shoin, 1908], 65; quoted in Hino, *Mori Shuntō no kisoteki kenkyū*, 147).

34. For a detailed discussion of specific Edo-period female poets, see Mari Nagase, "Women Writers of Chinese Poetry in Late-Edo Period Japan" (PhD diss., University of British Columbia, 2007), and "'Truly, They Are a Lady's Words': Ema Saikō and the Construction of an Authentic Voice in Late Edo Period *Kanshi*," *Japanese Language and Literature* 48, no. 2 (October 2014): 279–305.

35. As early as 1791, during Yuan Mei's lifetime, a ten-volume set of his influential *Concordance Garden Poetry Talks* (Ch. *Suiyuan shihua*, J. *Zuien shiwa*), as well

as his thirty-one-volume collected works *Collected Poems from the House on Granary Hill* (*Xiaocang shanfang shiji*), became available through Nagasaki.

36. Famously, Yuan Mei's advocacy of female poets earned him a great deal of criticism from his contemporaries. Zhang Xuecheng 章學誠 (1738–1801), for instance, attacked Yuan Mei as an "immoral literatus" (*buxing wenren*) responsible for leading women astray from correct moral principles. For this debate and for a discussion of Ming and Qing women poets, see Kang-i Sun Chang, "Ming-Qing Women Poets and the Notions of 'Talent' and 'Morality,'" in *Culture and State in Chinese History: Conventions, Accommodations, and Critiques*, ed. Theodore Huters, R. Bin Wong, and Pauline Yu, 236–58 (Stanford, Calif.: Stanford University Press, 1997).

37. Shibutsu edited the text considerably, removing the poetry of nine of the twenty-eight named female disciples and changing the order in which they appeared. However, he did not include any preface or explanation in the version he chose to publish, so his intentions in doing so remain unclear.

38. Quoted in Matsushita Tadashi, "Nakajima Sōin no shiron to En Bai," *Nihon Chūgoku gakkai hō*, no. 18 (October 1966): 238–39.

39. Xiao Yanwan, "Nihon ni shōkai sareta *Zuien onna deshi shisen sen* ni tsuite," *Chūgoku bungaku ronshū*, no. 31 (December 2002): 66.

40. Kikuchi Gozan, *Gozandō shiwa*, in *Nihon shishi, Gozandō shiwa*, ed. Ibi Takashi and Shimizu Shigeru, Shin Nihon koten bungaku taikei 65 (Tokyo: Iwanami Shoten, 1991), 224.

41. For example, Matsumoto Keidō 松本奎堂 (Hitoshi 衡, 1831–1863), a member of the "Wrath of Heaven" group (Tenchugumi) that carried out an uprising against the *bakufu* in 1863. His collected poems, first published in 1869, feature a series of works under the title "Ten Poems in the Fragrant Style" (Kōren jisshu). In this specific case, though, it seems likely that Keidō was playing on the minister-ruler allegorical subtext of the style to comment on his desire for righteous government. See Matsumoto Hitoshi, *Keidō ikō*, ed. Usui Tatsuyuki and Hamada Tokuzō (Kariya, Aichi Pref.: Hamada Tokuzō, 1898), 21.

42. None of the three was completely unknown in Japan at this point, although they were far from famous. Arai Yōko has shown that Tanomura Chikuden's 1831 *Konsaichō shū* (Collection of talents for our times) contains one poem by Zhang and two by Guo. A selection of Zhang's poetry, *Senzan shisō*, appeared in 1848, and a collection of quatrains by Chen, *Hekijō zekku*, in 1862. Arai has found little or no overlap between these collections and the verses selected by Shuntō for *Quatrains by Three Qing Poets*, however. See Arai Yōko, "Mori Shuntō *Shin sanka zekku* ni tsuite," *Nishō*, no. 19 (2005): 255–65.

43. Iwaya Ichiroku, "Jo," in *Shin sanka zekku*, ed. Mori Shuntō, 3 vols. (Tokyo: Mori Taijirō, 1878), 1:1–2.

44. Mori, *Shin sanka zekku*, 3:2 recto. Perhaps colored by Shuntō's reputation for producing erotic poetry, some subsequent accounts of the influence of *Shin sanka zekku* have characterized it as containing nothing but fragrant-style poems, which is far from the case. Tsuji Kiichi, "Meiji shidan tenbō," in *Meiji kanshibun shū*, ed. Kanda Kiichirō, Meiji bungaku zenshū 62 (Tokyo: Chikuma Shobō, 1983), 367, for example, suggests that Shuntō's poems "imitated the alluring style of Qing poets such as Zhang, Chen, and Guo and changed poetic styles throughout the realm." In more disparaging terms, Kinoshita Hyō has suggested that the work of Zhang, Guo, and Chen show only "vulgarity and frivolity—this is the sort of thing that anyone who aspires to true and correct elegance should not go anywhere near" (*seiga ni kokorozasu mono no chikazuku bekazaru mono de aru*). He adds, "Dispassionately speaking, the fashion for Qing poems was in no way a good thing for the Meiji *kanshi* world" (*Meiji shikai no tame ni kō dewa nakatta*). See Kinoshita Hyō, "Kokubu Seigai to Meiji Taishō Shōwa no kanshikai (13)," *Shi to tomo*, no. 331 (August 1977): 46.

45. See *SZ* 8:22, as well as numerous examples over the next few years. Shiki's 1888 *Nanakusashū* (Seven herbs collection), an anthology of various prose and poetic genres, contains a series of bamboo-branch ballads that depict women waiting for their lovers; see *SZ* 9:210–11.

46. Takeoka Yūsen, ed., *Shinsen yōgaku benran* (Kyoto: Hayashi Yoshibē, 1878), 58.

47. Zheng Ziyu and Sanetō Keishū, eds., *Huang Zunxian yu Riben youren bitan yigao* (Tokyo: Waseda Daigaku Tōyō Bungaku Kenkyūkai, 1968), 116. Sima Qian's *Records of the Grand Historian* (*Shiji*) describes Qu Yuan's poetry in these terms: "The 'Airs of the States' [in the *Classic of Poetry*] are romantic without being licentious, the 'Lesser Odes' full of righteous anger without insubordination. A work like 'Li sao' may be said to combine the best of both of these" (Sima Qian, *Shiji*, ed. Wang Niansun, 2 vols. [Taipei: Yiwen Yinshuguan, 1955], 2:1004).

48. Yu Yue, ed., *Dongyong shixuan* (N.p., 1883), 41:16.

49. "Shogen nisoku," in *Nihon keien ginsō*, ed. Mizukami Yoshiaki, 2 vols. (Tokyo: Keibundō, 1880), 1:1 recto.

50. Ranchō, also known by her married name of Yokoyama, was the wife of Kaga domainal scholar Yokoyama Masataka 横山政孝 (1789–1836). Tragically, she died in childbirth at the age of twenty-one, though not before penning around two hundred poems. Rankō was the daughter of another Kaga domain scholar, Ōta Kinjō 太田錦城 (1765–1825).

51. Kakei's school catered predominantly to the wealthy and members of the nobility, and the poets that *Nihon keien ginsō* identifies as her students are for the most part drawn from wealthy or noble families. These include Itakura Seiko 板倉棲子 (dates unknown), daughter of a former Fukushima daimyo; Asukai

Eiko 飛鳥井栄子 (dates unknown), daughter of Meiji industrialist Asukai Kiyoshi 飛鳥井清 (1843–1884); Gotō Kozue 後藤梢 (dates unknown), daughter of politician and FPRM leader Gotō Shōjirō 後藤象二郎 (1838–1897); and two daughters of Kyoto noble families, Madenokōji Tomoko 萬里小路伴子 (dates unknown) and Anegakōji Momoko 姉小路桃子 (dates unknown).

52. Li, *Women's Poetry*, 9.

53. *Nihon keien ginsō*'s text erroneously lists Keien as the daughter of Shōtō's daughter Suzuki Sairan 鱸采蘭 (dates unknown) (采蘭之女). Keien was actually Shōtō's fourth daughter, according to Aida Hanji, *Kinsei joryū bunjin den* (Tokyo: Meiji Shoin, 1961), 54. Keien's dates of birth and death are unclear; *Kinsei joryū bunjin den*, 59, notes that she died in 1959 at the age of eighty-one. This would mean she was born in 1877 or 1878 and so would have been at most three years old at the time *Nihon keien ginsō* was published.

54. Wang Wei, "Composed at the Cold Food Festival on the River Si" (寒食汜上作): "Falling flowers so silent, birds crying out in the hills / Willows and poplars so green, a person crossing the water" (落花寂寂啼山鳥 / 楊柳青青渡水人). English translation from Stephen Owen, *Readings in Chinese Literary Thought* (Cambridge, Mass.: Harvard University Asia Center, 1992), 428; Chinese text from Wang Wei, *Wang Wei shixuan*, ed. Liu Yisheng (Hong Kong: Joint Publishing, 1984), 41.

55. Mizukami, *Nihon keien ginsō*, 2:7. The last line echoes Du Fu's "Bad Trees" (惡樹): "The shade, giving privacy, has become quite mixed / I cut the bad trees, but they grow many again / Matrimony vines are there because I planted them / But what can I do about you 'chicken-roost' shrubs?" (幽陰成頗雜 / 惡木剪還多 / 枸杞因吾有 / 雞棲奈汝何). The poem is conventionally interpreted as an allegory of a marriage gone awry. Chinese text and English translation from Stephen Owen, ed. and trans., *The Poetry of Du Fu* (Boston: de Gruyter, 2016), 24–25.

56. *Analects* 15:16: "The Master said, 'When a number of people are together, for a whole day, without their conversation turning on righteousness, and when they are fond of carrying out the suggestions of a small shrewdness;—theirs is indeed a hard case.'" (子曰、「群居終日、言不及義、好行小慧、難矣哉」). Chinese text and English translation from James Legge, trans., *The Chinese Classics*, 5 vols. (Hong Kong: Hong Kong University Press, 1960), 1:299.

57. Mizukami, *Nihon keien ginsō*, 2:18.

58. Empress Teishi 定子 (Sadako, 977–1001), gathered with her ladies-in-waiting on a winter's morning, asked Sei Shōnagon, "How is the snow on Xianglu Peak?" Sei Shōnagon raised the blinds to subtly show she had understood the reference, which is to a couplet by Bai Juyi: "Leaning on my pillow, I wait to hear Yiai Temple's bell / Pushing aside the blinds, I gaze upon the snow of Xianglu Peak" (遺愛寺鐘敧枕聽 / 香爐峰雪撥簾看). The episode is described in Sei Shōnagon's

Pillow Book; see, for example, Ivan Morris, trans., *The Pillow Book of Sei Shōnagon* (New York: Columbia University Press, 1991), 241–42, 368.

59. Narushima Ryūhoku, *Ryūhoku ikō*, ed. Narushima Matasaburō, 2 vols. (Tokyo: Hakubunkan, 1892), 2:158–59.

60. "Red tube" is conventionally an expression for a woman's writing brush. The locus classicus is the *Classic of Poetry*, "The Retiring Girl" (Jing nü 靜女), from the "Airs of the States": "How handsome is the retiring girl! / She presented to me a red tube. / Bright is the red tube;— / I delight in the beauty of the girl" (靜女其孌 / 貽我彤管 / 彤管有煒 / 說懌女美). Chinese text and English translation from Legge, *The Chinese Classics*, 4:69. Commentators on this verse disagree about the significance of the "red tube," a painted bamboo vessel, but here Kinsui seems to interpret it as a signifier of feminine literary talent.

61. This refers to an anecdote concerning Xie Daoyun, who as a child resided in the house of her uncle Xie An 謝安 (320–325), a distinguished statesman. One day it snowed, and Xie An composed the first line of a poem, hoping that the children in his house would respond. Asked, "What does the snow look like?" Xie Daoyun answered, "It is like wisps of catkin fluff, flying in the wind" (未若柳絮因風起). Thereafter, she was hailed as "a talent praising catkin fluff" (詠絮之才). See Barbara Bennett Peterson, ed., *Notable Women of China: Shang Dynasty to the Early Twentieth Century* (Armonk, N.Y.: M.E. Sharpe, 2000), 149.

62. Inoguchi Atsushi, *Josei to kanshi: Wakan joryū shishi* (Tokyo: Kasama Shoin, 1978), 331, notes that this is an adaptation of "Black Hair" (Kurokami), a similarly themed *nagauta* song. *Nagauta* is a genre of song originally developed to accompany kabuki performances.

63. The second pillow is, of course, redundant now that her lover no longer visits.

64. Mizukami, *Nihon keien ginsō*, 2:19–20.

65. Kinsui's poems in *Nihon keien ginsō* had a life span that extended beyond the collection in which they initially appeared; all three of Kinsui's verses cited in the preceding also appeared in *Dongying shixuan*. Yu Yue's headnote, introducing Kinsui's poems to a presumably Chinese readership, is highly complimentary: "Kinsui is extremely skilled in the old-style forms, which is very unusual among lady poets. We have four poems in her *Echoing Harmonies from Red Strings*, which are like songs or ballads; her sounds are wonderful" (琴水頗工古體在閨媛為難得有紅絃餘唱四首似歌似謠音節絶異) (Yu, *Dongyong shixuan*, 40:18).

66. "Gijōchi," *Chōya shinbun*, March 4, 1879, 1.

67. Although he was not mentioned by name, Kainan certainly understood this piece as being aimed at him. His collected works contain a rebuttal poem that features a headnote referring to being charged with "fake passion" and "borrowed nostalgia." See Hino, *Mori Shuntō no kisoteki kenkyū*, 156–57.

68. "Kikuchi Sankei Mori Shuntō o nonoshiru," in Ishigami Misao, ed., *Naigai kokin itsuwa bunko*, 14 vols. (Tokyo: Hakubunkan, 1893–1894), 12:51. Sankei was not above composing poems that looked very much like the fragrant style; starting from the September 5, 1883, edition of the *kanshi* learners' journal *Kokon shibun shōkai*, he published fifteen poems on "Beautiful Women," each addressing a different body part. See Kikuchi Sankei, "Bijin jūgo ei," *Kokon shibun shōkai*, no. 100 (September 5, 1883): 8–9.

69. Per Yoda Gakkai's diary, this conversation took place in June of 1880 (Meiji 13); see Yoda Gakkai, *Gakkai nichiroku*, 12 vols. (Tokyo: Iwanami Shoten, 1991–1993), 4:269–70.

70. It is unclear to whom Shuntō is referring with "nodding heads" (literally, "bowing Buddhas" [*tentō nyorai*]). Hino, *Mori Shuntō no kisoteki kenkyū*, 153–54, suggests (fairly tenuously) this may be a reference to a Chinese legend about a Buddhist monk who practiced sermons by reciting them to a rock, which one day bowed to him in admiration, and that this in turn may refer to Okamoto, whose pen name contains the graph for "rock."

71. Mori, *Shuntō shishō*, 5:9 recto. For a *kakikudashi* version of this text, see Ibi, "Meiji kanshi no shuppatsu," 12. Wang Yi 王彝 (d. 1374, courtesy name Changzong 常宗) was a Yuan-period poet and painter who achieved fame as a very young man by attacking Yang Tieya, who was one of the most prominent poets of the day. For a brief account in English of Wang Yi's argument, see Frederick W. Mote, *The Poet Kao Ch'i, 1336–1374* (Princeton, N.J.: Princeton University Press, 1962), 195.

72. Or, less messily, from a cup inside the shoe. This practice became so closely associated with Yang Tieya that it later became known as the Tieya obsession. See Dorothy Ko, *Cinderella's Sisters: A Revisionist History of Footbinding* (Berkeley: University of California Press, 2005), 93–95.

73. Kinoshita quotes Kozan as saying of Kainan that he "was worried that one so young might slide into licentiousness and dissolution" (*sono shōnen ni shite inbi ni nagaruru o osoru*); quoted in Kinoshita Hyō, "Kokubu Seigai to Meiji Taishō Shōwa no kanshikai (7)," *Shi to tomo*, no. 324 (January 1977): 42.

74. Yoda Gakkai, "Mori Kiki ni okuru jo," *Shinbunshi* (*besshū*), no. 14:1–2.

75. The reference is ambiguous; this could be either a set of ten prints of beautiful women or the name of a Chinese "scholar and beauty" story set in the Ming dynasty.

76. This was apparently a colloquial term for the Shinobazu area of Tokyo.

77. A Ruan was a singing girl in the Tang capital Chang'an, with whom Bai Juyi fell in love during his youth.

78. *Azuma shinshi*, no. 71 (March 15, 1885):12.

79. *Analects* 17:9: "The Master said, 'My children, why do you not study the Book of Poetry? *The Odes* serve to stimulate the mind. They may be used for purposes of self-contemplation. They teach the art of sociability. They show how to regulate feelings of resentment. From them you learn the more immediate duty of serving one's father, and the remoter one of serving one's prince. From them we become largely acquainted with the names of birds, beasts, and plants'" (子曰:「小子、何莫學夫詩。詩可以興。可以觀。可以群。可以怨。邇之事父,遠之事君。多識於鳥獸草木之名。」). Chinese Text and English translation from Legge, *The Chinese Classics*, 1:323.

80. Inoue Tetsujirō, *Sonken shishō*, 2 vols. (Tokyo: Sakagami Hanshichi, 1884), 1:24 verso.

81. Gōyama, "Bakumatsu Meijiki no entai kanshi," 19.

82. Noritsuke Shunkai, *Kokon kakutai sakushi kihan* (Tokyo: Eisai Shinshisha, 1893), 99.

83. Kinoshita Hyō, "Kokubu Seigai to Meiji Taishō Shōwa no kanshikai (9)," *Shi to tomo*, no. 326 (March 1977): 19.

84. Mori Kainan, *Kainan shū*, ed. Mori Kenrō, 28 vols. (Tokyo: Mori Kenrō, 1912), 12:14.

85. Per Kinoshita, "Kokubu Seigai to Meiji Taishō Shōwa no kanshikai (7)," 40.

86. The text of this poem is from *Nippon*, September 9, 1890, 1, and from *Meiji kanshibun shū*, 102–3. For this and the subsequent poems, I have also consulted Kinoshita Hyō's paraphrases in installments 10 through 12 of "Kokubu Seigai to Meiji Taishō Shōwa no kanshikai."

87. "Black-haired mountain" probably refers to Mount Kurokami (literally, "black-haired mountain"), one of a number of alternative names for Mount Futara, a peak that towers over Kegon Falls.

88. Seigai's rhyme graphs 龍嵸 (Ch. *longzong*, J. *rōshō*) echo the second verse in the opening couplet of the third section of Sima Xiangru's 司馬相如 (179–117 B.C.E.) *Rhapsody on the Imperial Gardens* (Ch. *Shanglin fu*, J. *Jōrin fu*), which describes the mountainous areas of the Imperial Park: "And then the lofty mountains spire on high / Arching aloft, tall and towering" (於是乎崇山矗矗 龍嵸崔巍). Chinese text and English translation from David R. Knechtges, "*Fu* Poetry: An Ancient-Style Rhapsody (*Gufu*)," in *How to Read Chinese Poetry: A Guided Anthology*, ed. Zong-qi Cai (New York: Columbia University Press, 2008), 63.

89. A *qing* was a unit of measurement equal to the width of a rice field. One *qing* was equivalent to very roughly 16.5 acres.

90. A "dragon pearl" (Ch. *lizhu*, J. *rishu*) was a mythical jewel that hung below the chin of a dragon in legends and artistic depictions and was thus exceptionally rare and prized. Seigai's imagining of Kegon Falls as a cascade of dragon pearls

both praises the beauty of the falls and foreshadows the mystical and fantastic elements that occur later in his poem.

91. The two lines here are linked through the imagery of pearls; line 12 refers to the legends of sharklike mermen who cry pearls when they weep, as described in Gan Bao's 干寶 (fl. 315, d. 336) *Soushenji*: "Beyond the Southern Seas there are mermen who live in the water and resemble fish, but they can weave and spin, and when they weep, their tears turn into pearls" (南海之外有鮫人、水居如魚、不廢織績。其眼泣、則能出珠) (Gan Bao, *In Search of the Supernatural: The Written Record*, trans. Kenneth J. DeWoskin and J. I. Crump Jr. [Stanford, Calif.: Stanford University Press, 1996], 150).

92. *Meiji kanshibun shū* has 礑 for 潭.

93. "True ruler" (真主) here is ambiguous. It may refer to Liu Xiu 劉秀 (6 B.C.E.–67 C.E., r. 25–57 C.E.) in volume 15 of the *Book of the Later Han* 後漢書 (Ch. *Hou Hanshu*, J. *Gokanjo*), *Biography of Wang Chang* (*Wang Chang zhuan*). In this account Wang Chang, one of the victorious generals at the Battle of Kunyang, states, "Now Liu has risen up again and is thus the true ruler [劉氏復興、即真主也]" (Fan Ye, *Hou Hanshu*, 12 vols. [Beijing: Zhonghua Shuju, 1965], 1:579). The Battle of Kunyang took place in June and July of 23 C.E. between the forces of the short-lived Xin dynasty under Wang Mang 王莽 (45 B.C.E.–23 C.E.) and rebels aiming to restore the Han dynasty, which Wang had overthrown. After a surprise attack from Han forces led by Liu Xiu had routed the numerically superior Xin forces at Kunyang, a flash flood drowned several thousand men of the retreating Xin army. The battle spelled the end for the detested Xin dynasty and the restoration of the Han dynasty under Liu Xiu, who became Emperor Guangwu 光武 of the Later Han.

94. The Battle of Red Cliff took place in late 208 to early 209 between the forces of the northern warlord Cao Cao 曹操 (J. Sō Sō, 155–220) and the allied southern warlords Sun Quan 孫權 (Son Kan, 182–252) and Liu Bei 劉備 (J. Ryū Bi, 161–223). Cao Cao's vastly larger naval force was destroyed by the use of fireships.

95. This line and the following are drawn almost verbatim from Sunzi's 孫氏 (J. Sonshi, dates unknown) famous *The Art of War* (Ch. *Sunzi bingfa*, J. *Sonshi heihō*): "In the tumult and uproar the battle seems chaotic, but there is no disorder" (紛紛紜紜鬥亂而不可亂也), and "In battle there are only the normal and extraordinary forces, but their combinations are limitless; none can comprehend them all. For these two forces are mutually reproductive; their interaction as that of interlocked rings. Who can determine where one ends and the other begins?" (戰勢不過奇正奇正之變不可勝窮之也奇正相生如環之無端孰能窮之). Chinese text from Sunzi, *Sunzi yizhu*, ed. Li Ling (Beijing: Zhonghua Shuju, 2007), 34–35; English translation from Sun Tzu, *The Art of War*, trans. Samuel B. Griffith (New York: Oxford University Press, 1971), 92.

96. *Meiji kanshibun shū* has 層 for 巖.

97. That is, Li Bai, who was occasionally known by the soubriquet Master Green Lotus (Qinglian Jushi).

98. Per Chinese legend, dragons were supposed to dwell in deep bodies of water such as mountain pools.

99. *Nippon*'s editor in chief, Kojima Kazuo, recalls that the exchange "startled the *kanshi* world, and anyone who was anyone as a poet chimed in with Seigai and the others. Thus Seigai's name resounded throughout the realm" (*Seigai no na wa tenka ni todoroita*); see Kojima Kazuo, *Ichi rōseijika no kaisō* (Tokyo: Chūō Kōronsha, 1951), 38.

100. Kinoshita has recounted that Soejima and Seigai did meet in person during the exchange, after Seigai replied to Soejima's first two responses. Apparently, Soejima's carriage could not pass down the narrow street on which Seigai lived, and the senior politician was obliged to get out and walk; see Kinoshita, "Kokubu Seigai to Meiji Taishō Shōwa no kanshikai (9)," 20.

101. For the text of this poem and the subsequent one by Soejima, I take the later versions contained in Soejima Taneomi, *Sōkai zenshū*, ed. Soejima Masamichi and Takei Yoshi, 6 vols. (Tokyo: Soejima Masamichi, 1917), 4:41–44, as definitive. There appear to be a number of misprints or textual corruptions in text as it appeared in *Nippon* on September 14 and 29. I note significant discrepancies between the two texts where they appear.

102. Soejima's "Master Green Cliff" to Seigai is one graph different from, and quite possibly a play on, Li Bai's soubriquet of Master Green Lotus; the point, of course, is that Soejima is favorably comparing Seigai to Li Bai.

103. *Nippon* has 胸 for 恦.

104. *Nippon*, September 14, 1890, 1.

105. 肚 is perhaps more accurately translated as "belly"; it is used here in the sense of the seat of Han Yu's emotions and spirit. *Dingyi* 鼎彝 refers to a sacrificial vessel engraved with the deeds of great men of the past.

106. *Nippon* has 君今去攀二荒峰.

107. Mount Futara is one of the main peaks in the Nikkō area. The mountain was (and is) also known as Mount Nantai—literally, "man's-body mountain."

108. The Jade Maiden (Yu Nü) was an immortal spirit believed to dwell on Mount Hua. According to legend, she was originally a palace lady of the first Qin emperor; after the fall of the Qin, she fled to the mountains and survived by eating pine needles. See Xiao Tong, *Wen xuan, or Selections of Refined Literature*, trans., with annotations, David R. Knechtges, 3 vols. (Princeton, N.J.: Princeton University Press, 2014), 3:126.

109. *Nippon* has 眼 for 昭.

110. *Nippon* has 之 for 往.

111. *Nippon* has 死 for 在, which changes the meaning to "die alone" and does not seem to fit with the rest of the poem.

112. *Nippon* has 言 for 稱.

113. Qu Yuan 屈原 (340?–278 B.C.E.) and Song Yu 宋玉 (ca. 319–298 B.C.E.) were both court officials in the state of Chu 楚 and are credited with authorship of the majority of the works in the early Chinese poetry collection *Songs of Chu* (*Chuci*).

114. That is, a bold and determined spirit.

115. Literally, "From Kuai on down" (*zi Kuai yixia* 自鄶以下). This refers to Li Zha's 季札 (dates unknown) dismissive assessment of part of the "Airs of the States" section of the *Classic of Poetry*, to the effect that "from the ['Airs of the] State' of Kuai onward, I shall not give my critique" (自鄶以下無譏焉).

116. I identify this as a reference to an imperial edict laying down procedures for mourning the emperor in the *Records of the Grand Historian*: "After the coffin has been lowered into the grave, deep mourning shall be worn for fifteen days, light mourning for fourteen days, and thin garments for seven days, and then all mourning clothes shall be removed" (巳下，服大紅十五日，小紅十四日，纖七日，釋服). Since Soejima refers to his relatively advanced age in the closing section of his previous rhyme-matching poem to Seigai, this would seem to be a similar lament. Chinese text from Sima, *Shiji*, 1:199.

117. That is, the calendar of Soejima's life is now turning toward the autumn months as he grows older.

118. "Frost and fallen dew" would seem to be a reference to Soejima's advanced age: *Classic of Poetry*, Liao Xiao 蓼蕭: "How high is the southernwood, / All wet with the fallen dew! / Now that I see my noble men, / Grandly we feast, delighted and complacent. / May their relations with their brothers be right! / May they be happy in their excellent virtue to old age!" (蓼彼蕭斯、零露泥泥。既見君子、孔燕豈弟。宜兄宜弟、令德壽豈). Chinese text and English translation from Legge, *The Chinese Classics*, 4:274.

119. Text from *Nippon*, September 29, 1890, 1, and Soejima, *Sōkai zenshū*, 4:42. Lu Yun 陸雲 (262–303) was a scholar and literatus of the Western Jin kingdom. The reference here may be a play on Lu Yun's epithet, Shilong 士龍 (literally, "scholar-dragon"); since he is not a dragon, Soejima suggests, he cannot fly into the sky along with Seigai.

120. *Nippon*, September 29, 1890, 1.

121. An alternative reading might be that the application of makeup refers to overly ornate composition covering up flawed poetry, in much the same way as makeup might be used to conceal as well as enhance.

122. Soejima's collected works does in fact contain a work titled "Boudoir Emotion" (Keijō), a typical example of the style; see Soejima, *Sōkai zenshū*, 2:23.

123. Zhou Yu 周瑜 (175–210) was the commander of the victorious forces at the Battle of Red Cliff.

124. *Nippon*, October 5, 1890, 1.

125. The language here echoes the *Song of Everlasting Sorrow*, l.7–8, which describes Yang Guifei in her harem: "When she turned around with smiling glance, she exuded every charm; / in the harem all who wore powder and paint of beauty then seemed barren" (迴眸一笑百媚生／六宮粉黛無顏色). Chinese text from Bai Juyi, *Bai Juyi shiji jiaozhu*, ed. Xie Siwei, 6 vols. (Beijing Shi: Zhonghua Shuju, 2006), 2:943; English translation from Stephen Owen, ed. and trans., *An Anthology of Chinese Literature: Beginnings to 1911* (New York: Norton, 1996), 442.

126. *Zhuangzi*, "Discussion on Making All Things Equal" (齊物論): "Great understanding is broad and unhurried; little understanding is cramped and busy. Great words are clear and limpid; little words are shrill and quarrelsome" (大知閑閑，小知閒閒；大言炎炎，小言詹詹). Chinese text from Wang Shumin, ed., *Zhuangzi jiao quan*, 2 vols. (Taipei: Zhongyang Yanjiuyuan Lishi Yuyan Yanjiusuo, 1988), 1:48; English translation from Burton Watson, trans., *Zhuangzi: The Basic Writings* (New York: Columbia University Press, 2003), 32.

127. From the opening lines of Li Bai, "Poems in the Old Style (No. 28)" (古風其二十八): "A human face passes as quick as flashing lightning / The seasons pass like whirlwinds / The grass, once green, has already turned white / The sun sets in the west, the moon rises again in the east" (容顏若飛電／時景如飄風／草綠相已白／日西月復東); Chinese text from Li Bai, *Li Taibai quanji*, ed. Wang Qi, 2 vols. (Beijing: Zhonghua Shuju, 1977), 1:124; English translation mine.

128. "Pines at the bottom of a ravine " is an expression for scholars whose ability goes without recognition; Bai Juyi, "The Pine at the Bottom of the Ravine" (澗底松): "There was a pine, a hundred feet tall, ten around / Grew at the bottom of a ravine, cold and lowly / Valley deep, mountains steep, far from the roads of men / Grew old and died, never met a woodcutter / Now the emperor's bright halls are missing a beam / This one sought it, that one had it, but neither ever knew" (有松百尺大十圍／生在澗底寒且卑／澗深山險人路絶／老死不逢工度之／天子明堂欠梁木／此求彼有兩不知). Chinese text from *Bai Juyi shiji jiaozhu*, 1:376; English translation mine.

129. *Nippon*, October 6, 1890, 1.

130. Kinoshita Hyō, "Kokubu Seigai to Meiji Taishō Shōwa no kanshikai (11)," *Shi to tomo*, no. 328 (May 1977): 47, reproduces a conversation noted by Yokoyama Kendō 横山健堂 (1871–1943) that suggests the nature of Kainan's and Kinzan's interactions with Itō: "As soon as his poem was finished, Itō would ring the bell and call his manservant to say, 'Get Yazuchi.' Yazuchi would arrive. Itō would show it to Yazuchi, who would look it over reverentially and hold it up and then chant it a couple of times, then bow and scrape and say in *kanbun*-esque style,

'It captures both human emotion and landscape, and it is perfect in every respect; there is not one word I could add.' . . . Itō would say, 'Good, good. Off you go, then,' and Yazuchi would depart."

131. A reference to *Analects* 19:23, usually taken to signify that most ordinary people could not understand Confucius: "Shu-sun Wu-shu observed to the great officers in the court, saying, 'Zigong is superior to Zhongni [i.e., Confucius].' Zi Fu Jingpo reported the observation to Zigong, who said, 'Let me use the comparison of a house and its encompassing wall. My wall only reaches to the shoulders. One may peep over it, and see whatever is valuable in the apartments. The wall of my Master is several fathoms high. If one do not find the door and enter by it, he cannot see the ancestral temple with its beauties, nor all the officers in their rich array. But I may assume that they are few who find the door. Was not the observation of the chief only what might have been expected?'" (叔孫武叔語大夫於朝、曰:「子貢賢於仲尼。」子服景伯以告子貢。子貢曰:「譬之宮牆, 賜之牆也及肩, 窺見室家之好。夫子之牆數仞、不得其門而入、不見宗廟之美、百官之富。得其門者或寡矣。夫子之云、不亦宜乎!」). Chinese text and English translation from Legge, *The Chinese Classics*, 1:347; proper names adapted into pinyin.

132. *Nippon*, October 6, 1890, 1.

133. *Nippon*, October 6, 1890, 1.

134. Preface omitted for reasons of space. As with the previous texts, the poem as originally printed in *Nippon* appears to be corrupt in a number of places. I have cross-referenced the poem with the version that appears in Mori, *Kainan shū*, 12:20–21, which I take to be the authoritative text.

135. Conventionally, these would be five mountains in China strongly associated with Daoism and arranged along the five cardinal directions of Chinese geomancy. They are Mounts Heng 恒山 (North, in modern-day Shanxi), Heng 衡山 (South, in Hunan), Tai 泰山 (East, in Shandong), Hua 華山 (West, also in Shanxi), and Song 嵩山 (Center, in Henan).

136. Kainan echoes lines 7 and 8 of Li He's 李賀 (J. Ri Ga, 790–816) "Passing by High Eaves" 高軒過: "Heavenly bodies line up in their hearts / And the Great Force of the Universe shines through them" (二十八宿羅心胸 / 元精耿耿貫当中). Chinese text from Li He, *Li He shixuan zhu*, ed. Zhen Huile (Shanghai: Shanghai Guji Chubanshe, 1994), 110; English translation mine.

137. *Nippon* has 吾来覘 for 吾未覘. This is likely a typographical or transcription error, since, as mentioned, Kainan had not in fact visited the falls.

138. *Nippon* renders this line with two different graphs: 欲将冥捜試刻劃, "I shall close my eyes and search my heart as I attempt to carve the words."

139. *Nippon* renders this line as 賦君平生得意事, "I compose on those topics in which you [Seigai] are naturally skilled."

140. *Nippon* renders this line as 只恐朗吟欲飛去, "I fear only that the words of my chanted song will fly away." The revised version of Kainan's poem alludes to "The Lesser Master of Fate" (Shao siming), one of the *Nine Songs* (*Jiuge*) in the *Songs of the South* (*Chuci*): "I will wash my hair with you in the Pool of Heaven; / You shall dry your hair on the Bank of Sunlight. / I watch for the Fair One, but he does not come. / Wildly I shout my song into the wind" (與女沐兮咸池，晞女髮兮陽之阿。望美人兮未來，臨風怳兮浩歌). English translation from David Hawkes, trans., *The Songs of the South: An Anthology of Ancient Chinese Poems by Qu Yuan and Other Poets* (New York: Penguin Books, 1985), 112; Chinese text from Jiang Shanguo, ed., *Chuci* (Taipei: Xinwenfeng Chuban Gongsi, 1982), 15 [*Jiuge*].

141. "Dragons without pupils" refers to a Chinese story about the painter Zhang Sengyao 張僧繇 (dates unknown) of the Southern and Northern Dynasties period (420–589). Commissioned by the emperor, Zhang painted four dragons without pupils in their eyes. When asked why he had done so, he painted in the pupils on two of the four, which promptly flew away. The modern Chinese expression *hua long dian jing* (literally, "to paint in the dragon's pupils," or to add the finishing touches) derives from this story.

142. *Nippon*, October 7, 1890, 1.

143. *Nippon*, October 8, 1890, 1.

144. Along with Kainan and Seigai, Satō Rokuseki was one of the founding members of the Seisha *kanshi* group.

145. The expressions "red rice from Nagasaki" and "old loincloths from India" (*Nagasaki kara kowameshi, Tenjiku kara furufundoshi*) are colloquial references to a long, drawn-out, and pointless story or endeavor. The general idea is that it makes little sense to travel to faraway Nagasaki in search of the Kamigata-region specialty red rice, nor to obtain something as common as an old loincloth from faraway India.

146. This and the subsequent comment and poem are from *Nippon*, November 9, 1890, 1.

147. "Meiji no kanshidan," *Teikoku bungaku* 1, no. 6 (June 1895): 95.

148. Kinoshita, "Kokubu Seigai to Meiji Taishō Shōwa no kanshikai (7)," 43.

149. Yoda Gakkai, "*Shuntō shishō* jo," in *Shuntō shishō*, by Mori Shuntō, ed. Morikawa Kenzō, vol. 1.

150. Matsumura Kinsō, "Kinsō Matsumura sensei," *Taiyō* 5, no. 5 (May 1899).

151. Xu Yi, *Yan Zhou shihua*, Siku quanshu 1478 (Shanghai: Shanghai Guji Chubanshe, 1987), 916.

152. Both this and the mention of "the one who grappled with tigers" are likely references to Kiso no Yoshinaka 木曽義仲 (1154–1184), a powerful warlord and

general of the late Heian era who achieved considerable renown during the Genpei Wars.

153. *SZ* 8:181.

154. *SZ* 4:373.

155. Miura Kanō, *Meiji kanbungakushi* (Tokyo: Kyūko Shoin, 1998), 56.

3. CLAMOROUS FROGS AND VERMINOUS INSECTS: *NIPPON* AND POLITICAL HAIKU, 1890–1900

1. Ozaki Takeshirō, "Meiji no shinbunjin: Kuga Katsunan," *Shūkan jiji*, October 5, 1968, 49; quoted in Barbara Teeters, "Press Freedom and the *26th Century* Affair in Meiji Japan," *Modern Asian Studies* 6, no. 3 (1972): 340.

2. *Shō Nippon*, June 4, 1894, 2.

3. Bashō's *hokku*, from *The Narrow Road to the North* (*Oku no hosomichi*): *natsu-kusa ya / tsuwamonodomo ga / yume no ato* (The summer grass—all that's left, of ancient warriors' dreams). Shiki may well have been the first person to try translating Bashō into English; Shiki's translation and commentary on the pre-ceding verse was " 'The summer grasses! A trace of the soldiers' dreams.' This was composed when he looked at the barren state of an ancient battle field [*sic*]." See "Baseo as a Poet," composed in mid-1892 as part of an English assignment at the university (*SZ* 4:16–22).

4. By one estimate, in 1889 as many as two-thirds of Japanese newspapers carried *senryū* from their readers; see Fujimori Fumio, "Jiji senryū no keifu to ruikei," *Shinbun kenkyū*, no. 358 (May 1981): 58. The *Yomiuri shinbun*, for instance, reg-ularly featured topical *senryū* sent in by its readers, with their popularity reaching a peak in the late 1870s. A second peak came around 1890 on the occa-sion of the hundredth anniversary of the death of the originator of the genre, Karai Senryū 柄井川柳 (1718–1790). The *Yomiuri* solicits *senryū* from readers to this day.

5. Composed by "Kotake" (古竹), *Nippon*, April 21, 1897, 5.

6. *Tōkyō Mainichi shinbun*, October 29 and December 22, 1895. In both cases the solicitation appears on the front page.

7. The *Ōsaka Asahi*'s Jiji haihyō, which always ran on page 5 of the newspaper, began in mid-February 1897 and continued for a number of subsequent years. See, for example, the *Ōsaka Asahi* for February 10, 11, 16, and 25, 1897.

8. The *Yorozu*'s topical poetry column, first called Kanfū shōei, went through sev-eral names over time. Others include Gensha muzai (those who speak are without blame) and Bunsha sokkai (those who hear are admonished), both alluding to the explanation of poetry's purpose in the "Greater Preface" to the *Classic of Poetry*.

9. The Tokiwakai (Evergreen Society) dormitory in which Shiki stayed in Tokyo until 1891 was funded by the Hisamatsu family, former daimyo of Matsuyama. The dormitory's first two wardens were under instructions to ensure that the students did not get involved in factional politics and thus jeopardize their future. Letters between the two wardens, Hattori Yoshinobu 服部嘉陳 (1834–1891) and Naitō Meisetsu in August 1890 show agreement that the students ought to be outwardly in favor of the current government and note the Hisamatsu family's desire that the students not affiliate themselves with any political party. Letters dated August 4 and 11, 1890, in Matsuyama Shiki Kinen Hakubutsukan, ed., *Shiki to Tokiwakai kishukusha no nakama tachi* (Matsuyama: Matsuyama Shiritsu Shiki Kinen Hakubutsukan, 1993), 13.

10. Kusama had powerful allies in Matsuyama, however; the day before the sentence for the offense was handed down, the wife of the prefectural governor, Iwamura Takatoshi 岩村高俊 (1845–1906), apparently made a gift to Kusama of one hundred yen for the express purpose of helping him pay any potential fine, a development that was, perhaps, not entirely unexpected given that Iwamura was known to join Kusama in his political oratory on the streets of Matsuyama. See *SZ bekkan* 3:177–78.

11. Yanagihara Kyokudō, *Yūjin Shiki* (Tokyo: Maeda Shuppan, 1946), 61.

12. The Evergreen Society scholarship for university students came to ten yen per month, which was not a particularly large sum; Shiki's starting salary at *Nippon* was thirty yen, and Naitō Meisetsu during his days at the Ministry of Education had made one hundred (Naitō Meisetsu, *Meisetsu jijoden* [Tokyo: Okamura Shoten, 1922], 265). Various anecdotes suggest that Shiki was in dire financial straits even before this, borrowing money from Naitō Meisetsu and having Sōseki buy him notebooks with which to take notes in his lectures. See Akio Bin, *Shiki no kindai: Kokkei, media, Nihongo* (Tokyo: Shin'yōsha, 1999), 40.

13. *SZ bekkan* 2:194–95. The travelogue in question was *Kakehashi no ki*, serialized in *Nippon* from May 27 to June 4, 1892.

14. *Nippon*, January 1, 1890, 1. The newspaper's stance on novels was apparently shared by its readers; one reader's letter published on July 18, 1898, asked, "What good are novels?" and criticized other newspapers for subverting public morals by publishing prose fiction.

15. Yamamoto Taketoshi, *Kindai Nippon no shinbun dokushasō* (Tokyo: Hōsei Daigaku Shuppankyoku, 1981), 141.

16. *Nippon*, May 24, 1892, 2. The "orchid" situation likely refers to the dissolution of the Diet in February of 1892 over its failure to agree on budget-related issues; elections were subsequently held and the Diet reconvened in May, just as this verse was published.

17. Published originally in *Tōkyō denpō*, August 1888; Text from Kokubu Seigai, *Shi Tōko* (Tokyo: Meiji Shoin, 1897), 27–28.

18. *Nippon*, January 16, 1893, 3.

19. Kojima Kazuo, "Kokubu Seigai no koto," *Gayū*, no. 1 (May 1950): 13.

20. Kojima, "Kokubu Seigai no koto," 13.

21. Kojima, "Kokubu Seigai no koto," 15

22. *Nippon*, February 12, 1889. Mori's assassin actually claimed that he had acted because of Mori's show of disrespect at Ise Shrine. The headnote puns on the *wakizashi*, a short sword traditionally worn as part of a pair by the warrior class. The first line also puns on Mori's given name of Arinori, the graphs for which can be read to mean "has manners" and can be pronounced as *yūrei* in the Sino-Japanese reading. *Yūrei*, in turn, is homophonous with *yūrei*, or "ghost."

23. Kojima Kazuo, *Ichi rōseijika no kaisō* (Tokyo: Chūō Kōronsha, 1951), 47. Kojima approached a writer known as Half-Face Adachi (Adachi Hangan 足立半顔) at the satirical *Marumaru chinbun* and the *senryū* master Sakai Kuraki 坂井久良岐 (1869–1945) but found that neither of them was able to produce the kind of work he wanted. Kojima's search for a specialist *senryū* poet ended in 1903 when Inoue Kenkabō 井上剣花坊 (1870–1934) joined the newspaper.

24. *SZ bekkan* 2:201–2.

25. Kojima recalled that when he first met Shiki, he knew almost nothing about haiku and had no idea whether what Shiki wrote was any good. He was, however, impressed by Shiki's *kanshi* (*SZ bekkan* 2:201). If another account is to be believed, when Shiki remarked during what was effectively his job interview for *Nippon* that he wanted to pursue haiku, Kojima's response was, "What's haiku?" (*Haikutte nan dai?*) (Kojima, *Ichi rōseijika*, 40).

26. Quoted in Okano Chijū, *Haikai fūbunki* (Tokyo: Hakukyūsha, 1902), 30–31.

27. Chikurei had been active in topical haiku as early as 1891, although most of his topical haiku were published in the *Yomiuri* and *Kokumin shinbun* over a two-month period from April 4, 1894, to June 3 of the same year. Chikurei published these haiku under the pen names Hankanjin 半閑人, Kankanjin 閑々人, Mikanjin 未閑人, and Sankanjin 三閑人 in the *Yomiuri* and Tontonbō 頓々坊 in the *Kokumin shinbun*.

28. *Yomiuri shinbun*, December 23, 1893, 3.

29. There is a pun here, with the final sound in the word for "discipline" (*shinshuku*) reproduced in *shukushuku* (quietly, in a solemn or dignified manner).

30. This and the two preceding haiku and the two following are reproduced in *SZ* 12:47.

31. On November 30, 1892, a British naval ship collided with a Japanese vessel, the *Chishima*, in Japanese waters. All the British crew were saved, whereas seventy-four of the Japanese crew were drowned. This led to a public outcry and

demands for compensation from the British government, a cause *Nippon* supported in vocal fashion. The case was finally settled for the sum of ten thousand pounds when the Japanese government took its case to the English courts.

32. The first revisions of the unequal treaties would be achieved in 1894, the following year. At this point, the question of "strict enforcement of the treaties" (*jōyaku rikō*) had become a major topic of public and political debate, since, as a matter of practicality, the treaties' restrictions on non-Japanese residence and commercial activity in Japan outlined by the 1858 treaties were apparently being routinely ignored on the ground. The position of "strict enforcement" advocates was that the Japanese government should clamp down on and restrict the activities of foreigners in Japan, and that doing so would provide leverage for Japan to renegotiate the treaties on more equal terms.

33. *Nippon*, January 1, 1890 (supplement). Using frogs to characterize corrupt or unworthy officials can be traced back potentially all the way to the *Songs of Chu*, in which the righteous official Qu Yuan 屈原 (b. 339 B.C.E.) lists various commonplace animals to symbolize the unworthy ministers who have found favor where he has not: "The geese, the chicken and the ducks / Fill the courtyards and the halls; / Farmyard ducks and frogs and toads / Swim about in the lotus pool." English translation from David Hawkes, trans., *The Songs of the South: An Ancient Chinese Anthology of Poems by Qu Yuan and Other Poets* (New York: Penguin Books, 1985), 258.

34. *SZ* 12:27–28. Published in *Nippon* March 1 and 2, 1893.

35. The references are to Ki no Tsurayuki, Heian poet and author of the preface to the *Kokin wakashū* (ca. 905), the first of the *waka* collections compiled by imperial command. In the preface, Tsurayuki lists the croaking of frogs as one of the ways that nature fashions its own poetry. Ono no Tōfū 小野道風 (894–967) was a Heian calligrapher who was supposedly inspired to master his craft after seeing a frog repeatedly trying to jump into a tree.

36. This is, of course, a reference to Bashō's most famous haiku of all: "An old pond! / frog jumps in / the sound of water" (*furuike ya / kawazu tobikomu / mizu no oto*).

37. Still in use to this day, the expression "a frog in a well" (*i no naka no kawazu*) refers to someone lacking in knowledge of the broader world.

38. A term for the gathering of frogs in the spring mating season. In this and the following lines, Shiki is likening political rallies at which politicians give speeches to a noisy assembly of frogs.

39. Hibiya was a major venue for political rallies in Tokyo. Tamagawa in Ide is near Kyoto and famous in *waka* poetry as a spot where croaking frogs would gather.

40. By Gomi Katori 五味可都里 (1742–1817).

41. By Mukai Kyorai 向井去来 (1651–1704), one of Bashō's most prominent disciples.

42. I have not been able to identify this poet.

43. By Shirai Chōsui 白井鳥酔 (1700–1769).

44. By Yoshizawa Keizan 吉沢鶏山 (1709–1777).

45. In their classical order, the eight views are Clearing Storm over a Mountain Village, Sunset over a Fishing Village, Sails Returning from Distant Shores, Night Rain on the Xiao and Xiang Rivers, Evening Bell of a Temple in the Mist, Autumn Moon over Lake Dongting, Geese Returning Home at a Sandbar, and Evening Snow on a River. Similar catalogues of eight famous views were also devised for picturesque locations around Japan, most notably the scenery of Lake Biwa in Ōmi (present-day Shiga Prefecture).

46. In his recollections of his youth during Meiji, *Meiji Taishō kenbunroku* (Tokyo: Chūō Kōronsha, 2005), the journalist Ubukata Toshirō 生方敏郎 (1882–1969) writes, "Shinbashi alone did not satisfy [the carousing politicians], so around Meiji 14 or 15 [1881 or 1882] they opened up another geisha district in Akasaka, and it was viewed pretty much as the exclusive playground of officialdom" (236).

47. *SZ* 12:598. Both the *kanshi* and Shiki's haiku responses appeared in *Nippon* on November 28, 1892. The Kōdansha *Shiki zenshū* erroneously dates this sequence as being published on November 18 and Shiki's response on December 2.

48. San'nō is an alternative name for Hie Jinja, located in present-day Nagata-chō in central Tokyo.

49. *Kan'yū* 宦遊 denotes leaving one's home in the provinces to take up an official position, but, reading the graphs *kan* 宦 and *yū* 遊 separately, they can also be understood to mean "officials at play," especially in the sense of drinking and visiting the licensed quarters.

50. Sasaki Hideaki, in his commentary on *Sore kara*, quotes a 1903 guide to Tokyo that suggests Akasaka courtesans may have been known as cultivating an aesthetic of being weak and yielding: "Compared with the entertainers of Shinbashi and other downtown areas, they have neither bones nor sinews, and a pleasing taste and texture" (*suji naku hone naku, hazawari yoki*) (Natsume Sōseki, *Sore kara*, ed. Sasaki Hideaki, Sōseki bungaku zenchūshaku 8 [Tokyo: Wakakusa Shobō, 2000], 297).

51. *SZ* 12:15–17.

52. Sasaki Hideaki suggests that Akasaka was known as rather aristocratic (*kazoku no Akasaka*), in the phrasing of a 1918 history of Tokyo's licensed quarters. Based on this, we can imagine that the point of the verse is to lampoon the politician in question as a boorish member of the nouveau riche. See Yamaguchi Koken, ed., *Tōto shin hanjōki* (Tokyo: Kyōkadō Shoten, 1918), 188; quoted in Sasaki's commentary in Sōseki, *Sore kara*, 297.

53. *Nippon*, November 29, 1892; see also *SZ* 12:599. As printed, in the second poem the graphs 新橋 are glossed in two different ways, first as *atarashi hashi* and then as *Shinbashi*.

54. Requesting payment up front was not usual practice in the licensed quarters and would likely have been understood as an obvious insult. It also suggests that the courtesan regards the Diet man as untrustworthy.

55. *Dai Nippon*, no. 12 (September 10, 1892): 1; quoted in Asaoka Kunio, *Kaisetsu: "Shō Nippon" to Masaoka Shiki* (Tokyo: Ōzorasha, 1994), 13.

56. *SZ bekkan* 2:212, and Kojima, *Ichi rōseijika*, 42

57. A rough outline of the differences between "big newspapers" (*ōshinbun*) and "small newspapers" might run as follows: small papers were physically smaller and aimed at a less-educated readership, using simpler diction as well as glosses for most graphs. They generally focused on gossip and local news at the expense of politics, serialized various forms of prose fiction, and were often illustrated. Big papers, by contrast, often used Sinicized or *kanbun* copy and generally viewed their audience as being the educated and elite classes. They used few illustrations, focused primarily on political issues, and were comparatively reluctant to serialize *shōsetsu*. *Nippon* definitely thought of itself as a big newspaper, though the clear lines between the two had increasingly come to be blurred by the mid-1890s.

58. *Shō Nippon*, February 11, 1894, 1. The rhetoric may also have been partly strategic: Kojima recollected that the *Nippon* staff had believed that the Meiji government would be less likely to ban a *koshinbun*, a calculation that proved to be mistaken. See *SZ bekkan* 2:211.

59. Kojima, *Ichi rōseijika*, 41.

60. The group's name alludes to a *hokku* by Bashō: "For now I will turn / to the large pasania tree— / a summer grove" (*mazu tanomu / shii no ki mo ari / natsukodachi*). English translation from Haruo Shirane, *Traces of Dreams: Landscape, Cultural Memory, and the Poetry of Bashō* (Stanford, Calif.: Stanford University Press, 1998), 92.

61. Of the five original members of the Shii no Tomo Kai, Mori Saruo 森猿男 (1861–1923) worked for the Yokohama post office, Shōu for the Yokohama branch of Daiichi Bank, Ishii Tokuchū 石井得中 (dates unknown) was a stockbroker, Ishiyama Keizan 石山桂山 (dates unknown) an official at the Ministry of Communications, and Katayama Tōu 片山桃雨 (dates unknown) a supervisor at the First Higher School dormitory, later taking up a post at the Bank of Japan. See Murayama Kokyō, *Meiji haidanshi* (Tokyo: Kadokawa Shoten, 1978), 94.

62. See the *Yomiuri shinbun*, December 23, 1893, 3, and subsequent issues; the results were published in early March the following year, after *Shō Nippon* had

begun publishing. As noted earlier, this first competition received over eighty thousand entries.

63. This estimate is based on the index of individual pen names featured in *Shō Nippon*'s haiku competition in Asaoka, *Kaisetsu*.

64. The first contest, concluded in March, featured 145 poems, rising to 202 in April, which then more than tripled to 629 in May and from there almost doubled to 1,145 in June. July showed a drop in participation with 784, probably explained partly by the fact that the paper closed down midway through that month and concluded its haiku competition early (figures provided in Asaoka, *Kaisetsu*, 32). Multiple entries from one person were allowed and sometimes printed, although at no stage could participants submit more than five verses, and it was very rare for more than three lines from any individual to appear. It is not clear why the Home Ministry's and the police department's statistics for newspaper circulation during 1894 do not record any circulation figures for *Shō Nippon*, but even if we hazard a guess that the paper's daily circulation was, say, roughly half that of its parent publication at around 10,000 copies daily, this still represents an impressive degree of reader participation, considering especially that the quoted numbers here reflect only the poems that were accepted for publication.

65. See, for example, the results from May 1, 1894, which feature poems by Tekisui 滴翠 from Okinawa and Nika (or Nikō) 二香 from Aomori. Tekisui's subsequent entries have his location as Iyo (Matsuyama), so this location was likely temporary.

66. Wada Shigeki, *"Shō Nippon" sōsho "Haiku futabashū": Kenkyū to sakuin* (Matsuyama: Ehime Daigaku Hōbungakubu Kokugo Kokubungaku Kenkyūkai, 1974), 10.

67. Kojima recalled that Asai had sent Fusetsu with a certain degree of weary resignation: "Doesn't listen to a word anybody says, but there's no doubt he's a genius. We have no idea what to do with him at our end, but I reckon you can make something of him" (*hito no iu koto o kikanai, shikashi tensai wa tashika ni tensai da, wareware no nakama dewa te ni oenai otoko da ga, kimi no hō nara tsukaikonaseru to omou*) (Kojima, *Ichi rōseijika*, 42).

68. The term *chihō* presumably should be taken as meaning "outside Tokyo," with particular focus on Japan's four other higher schools in Sendai, Kyoto, Kanazawa, and Kumamoto.

69. Kawahigashi Hekigōtō, *Shiki no kaisō* (Tokyo: Shōnan Shobō, 1944), 186.

70. Kōno Kensuke, *Tōki to shite no bungaku: Katsuji, kenshō, media* (Tokyo: Shin'yōsha, 2003), 94.

71. *Shō Nippon*, April 26, 1894, 2.

72. *Shō Nippon*, May 10, 1894, 2. No copy or record for the extra survives, so it is unclear exactly when the extra in question was produced or the ban order in question was issued.

73. *Shō Nippon*, April 26, 1894, 3. Yet again this use of artistic genres for political commentary seems to have been Kojima's idea, and apparently Shiki was not happy about it, scolding Kojima as follows: "Hey, stop having him do that so much. He's an artist—it doesn't do to be using him for cartoons and that sort of thing" (*oi kimi, amari anna koto ni bakari are o tsukau na, are wa geijutsuka da. Manga nanzo ni tsukatcha aisuman*) (Kojima, *Ichi rōseijika*, 44).

74. *Shō Nippon*, May 1, 1894, 2. Gokyō's location is listed as the Rikuchū (Tōhoku) region, and he or she also had some verse published in the general haiku competition; beyond that, however, nothing is known of this poet.

75. *Shō Nippon*, June 14, 1894, 2. Again, nothing is known of Sekkyō.

76. Asaoka, *Kaisetsu*, 25–26.

77. Asaoka, *Kaisetsu*, 26.

78. *Yomiuri shinbun*, February 12, 1901, 1; the *Yomiuri* solicits *senryū* through its website at https://info.yomiuri.co.jp/contact/index.html (accessed September 25, 2017).

79. Naitō Meisetsu, "Rōbaikyo manpitsu," *Hototogisu* 1, no. 1 (January 15, 1897): 1–2.

80. Dong Hu 董狐 (dates unknown) was a grand historian of the state of Jin who was not afraid to write in his annals that the powerful Zhao Dun 趙盾 (d. 601 B.C.E.) had murdered his king. The name of the collection suggests that, like Dong Hu, Seigai is not afraid to speak truth to power.

81. *SZ* 14:196; originally published in *Nippon*, March 22, 1897. Shiki and Seigai were good friends, and the overall review is not as negative as this quotation might cause it to seem; one of his main aims was to defend Seigai from the accusation that he was a vulgar and unskilled poet.

82. Okano, *Haikai fūbunki*, 29–32.

83. Mimori Mikio, *Haikai meirin zasshi*, no. 216 (December 1901); quoted in Ichikawa Kazuo, *Kindai haiku no akebono*, 2 vols. (Tokyo: Sangensha, 1975), 1:407.

4. SHIKI'S PLEBEIAN POETRY: HAIKU AS "COMMONER LITERATURE," 1890–1900

1. Kuwabara Takeo, *Daini geijutsu*, Kindai bungei hyōron sōsho 9 (Tokyo: Nihon Tosho Sentā, 1990), 87.

2. Kuwabara, *Daini geijutsu*, 85.

3. While Shiki's arguments were sustained over a longer period and more developed, he was not the first Meiji critic to argue that *haikai* was literature.

Old-school master Mimori Mikio beat Shiki by fifteen years, stating in 1880 in the inaugural issue of *Haikai meirin zasshi* that "it is wrong to say that *haikai* is not literature" (*haikai wa bungaku ni arazu to wa hi nari*), a contention that was debated over the next couple of years in the magazine. See Sekine Rinkichi, "Mimori Mikio hyōden (1)," *Haiku* 27, no. 4 (April 1978): 250. Donald Keene has noted that in 1890 the *Yomiuri* published a letter from Mori Sankei 森三渓 (1864–1942) asserting in the first line that "*haikai* is a form of literature, a form of art" (*haikai wa ichi no bungaku nari, ichi no bijutsu nari*); *Yomiuri shinbun*, August 6, 1890, 2, quoted in Donald Keene, "Poetry in Traditional Forms," in *Dawn to the West: Japanese Literature of the Modern Era*, 4 vols. (New York: Columbia University Press, 1999), 2:91. Sankei was an earlier pen name of Mori Mukō's, who later became a founding member of the Shūseikai. The entire piece, "Haikairon" (On *Haikai*), was serialized over four issues (August 7, 10, 12, and 13) and contained several arguments Shiki himself later used, including the notion that there was a mathematical limit to how many haiku and *waka* it would be possible to compose if no reform was made.

4. Ichikawa Kazuo, *Kindai haiku no akebono*, 2 vols. (Tokyo: Sangensha, 1975), 1:408.

5. Maeda Ringai, "Kanshi waka shintaishi no aiirezaru jōkyō o joshite haikai ni oyobu," *Yomiuri shinbun*, August 15, 1890 (supplement). The piece was serialized in five installments on August 7, 9, 14, 15, and 17. Ringai's pieces appeared under the pseudonym Shōryōshi.

6. Maeda Ringai, "Kanshi waka shintaishi no aiirezaru jōkyō o joshite haikai ni oyobu," *Yomiuri shinbun*, August 17, 1890 (supplement).

7. Aeba Kōson, "Haikairon," *Waseda bungaku*, no. 23 (September 15, 1892): 44–45; emphasis in original. Kōson's largely positive assessment was out of keeping with *Waseda bungaku*'s overall stance on *haikai*. In the same October 1891 issue in which Kōson began his serialized piece, *Waseda bungaku* had dismissed *haikai* on the grounds that "when compared with the electric light that is genuinely new literature, [*haikai*] is as a lamp burning vegetable oil"; see "Haidan no otozure," *Waseda bungaku*, no. 2 (October 30, 1891): 8–10.

8. Sohō's term *heiminshugi* has also been variously translated as "democratic" and "populist." Here I follow Roger Bowen's translation of "commonerism." Bowen defines *heiminshugi* as referring to "the ideological and social underpinnings of wide-scale participation in the popular rights movement; democratic populism, perhaps, no less captures the essential meaning." See Roger Bowen, *Rebellion and Democracy in Meiji Japan: A Study of Commoners in the Popular Rights Movement* (Berkeley: University of California Press, 1984), 125.

9. Kitamura Tōkoku, "Tokugawa jidai no heiminteki shisō," in *Kitamura Tōkoku, Yamaji Aizan shū*, by Kitamura Tōkoku and Yamaji Aizan, Gendai Nihon

bungaku taikei 6 (Tokyo: Chikuma Shobō, 2000), 91. Originally serialized in *Jogaku zasshi*, nos. 322–24 (July 2, 16, and 30, 1892).

10. Yamaji Aizan, "Heiminteki tanka no hattatsu (1)," *Kokumin no tomo*, no. 67 (September 23, 1892): 26. As the title suggests, Aizan views *haikai* and *waka* as substantially the same in formal and poetic terms, though with markedly different social characteristics.

11. Yamaji Aizan, "Heiminteki tanka no hattatsu (3)," *Kokumin no tomo*, no. 69 (October 13, 1892): 32.

12. *SZ* 14:25–26.

13. Ueno Sansen, "Kusagusa," *Nagano shinbun*, December 3–6, 1902; quoted in Miyazaka Shizuo, "*Nippon*-ha haiku undō no Shinano e no denpa no jōkyō: Shōseikai gaijō," *Haiku bungakukan kiyō*, no. 3 (June 1984): 36.

14. "Bō sanmai," in *SZ* 12:132. Originally published in *Nippon*, December 21, 1895.

15. *SZ* 4:258; emphasis in original.

16. Okano Chijū, "Haikai yūbunki," in *Haikai fūbunki* (Tokyo: Hakukyūsha, 1902), 74.

17. Okano, "Haikai yūbunki," 75.

18. "Renpai no ryūkō," *Teikoku bungaku* 1, no. 11 (November 1895): 101–2.

19. *SZ* 12:114–17. The entry in question appeared in *Nippon* October 13, 1895.

20. "Haidan kinkyō," *Teikoku bungaku* 3, no. 11 (November 1896): 85.

21. Okano, "Haikai yūbunki," 73.

22. "Haikai haiseki no koe," *Teikoku bungaku* 2, no. 1 (January 1896): 114–15.

23. "Tanka to haiku," *Teikoku bungaku* 1, no. 6 (June 1895): 96–97.

24. Seisetsu's series of articles was also published as a monograph with the revised title *A Short History of Linked Verse* (*Renpai shōshi*) in 1897.

25. Sassa Seisetsu, *Renpai shōshi* (Tokyo: Dai Nihon Tosho, 1897), 7.

26. Sassa, *Renpai shōshi*, 190–91.

27. Ōmachi Keigetsu, "Waka, haiku oyobi haikai ni tsuite," *Teikoku bungaku* 2, no. 9 (September 1896): 88. Keigetsu's argument against linked verse as literature was virtually identical to the one that Shiki had advanced the previous year, to the effect that it depended on variation among verses for its appeal and was thus not literature.

28. Shinada Yoshikazu, "*Man'yōshū*: The Invention of a National Poetry Anthology," in *Inventing the Classics: Modernity, National Identity, and Japanese Literature*, ed. Haruo Shirane and Tomi Suzuki (Stanford, Calif.: Stanford University Press, 2000), 41–45.

29. Shinada, "*Man'yōshū*," 46. After returning from study in Germany, in 1902 Haga Yaichi introduced these terms into Japanese poetic discourse by translating them as *kokuminshi* and *gijutsushi*, respectively.

30. "Haiku no ryūkō," *Taiyō* 2, no. 2 (January 1896): 104.

31. "Anchoku bungaku," *Waseda bungaku*, no. 1 (January 1896): 11–13. The Japanese translated as "the most infinitesimal differences in decimal place" is, literally, *rin, mō, shi, kotsu*, and *bi*. These are traditional notations for very small numbers, with *rin* designating the second decimal place (0.01) and one further decimal place being added with each step (thus, *bi* is the sixth decimal place, or 0.000001).

32. Akio Bin, *Kyoshi to "Hototogisu": Kindai haiku no media* (Tokyo: Hon'ami Shoten, 2006), 123.

33. "Renpai no ryūkō," *Teikoku bungaku* 1, no. 11 (November 1895): 101–2.

34. "Haidan shoken," *Teikoku bungaku* 3, no. 10 (October 1897): 85.

35. Ichikawa, *Kindai haiku no akebono*, 1:438. Quite possibly, the "idle lawyers" Shiki referred to in his disparaging remarks on commoner literature in *Bashō zōdan* was intended as a dig at Chikurei.

36. The term "poison woman" was applied to a series of high-profile murder cases featuring female defendants, many of whom had worked as female entertainers, during the 1880s. These were widely covered (and sensationalized) by the newspapers of the day and often adapted into heavily embellished prose narratives, which in turn were usually serialized in those same newspapers, thus blurring the boundary between fact and fiction. For an overview of the poison woman genre in early Meiji, see Matthew C. Strecher, "Who's Afraid of Takahashi O-Den? 'Poison Woman' Stories and Literary Journalism in Early Meiji Japan," *Japanese Language and Literature* 38, no. 1 (April 2004): 25–55.

37. Fujimori Masasumi, "Kakuta Chikurei hyōden," *Gakuen*, no. 253 (January 1961): 56.

38. *Mainichi shinbun*, October 9, 1895, 1.

39. Iwaya Sazanami, "Shūseikai no omoide," in *Haiku kōza: Gendai kessha hen*, ed. Yamamoto Sansei, Kaizōsha haiku kōza, no. 8 (Tokyo: Kaizōsha, 1932), 250.

40. Sazanami, "Shūseikai no omoide," 247. Murayama Kokyō, "Shūseikai no aruita michi (chū)," *Haiku* 18, no. 8 (August 1969): 124, suggests, in slightly tongue-in-cheek fashion, that Shūseikai meetings should perhaps be understood as dinner parties at which haiku happened to be composed, rather than haiku gatherings per se.

41. Murayama Kokyō, "Shūseikai no aruita michi (jō)," *Haiku* 18, no. 7 (July 1969): 132; see also Okano Chijū, "Shūseikai ron," *Haisei* 1, no. 5 (May 1901): 14.

42. Sazanami, "Shūseikai no omoide," 255.

43. "Daigishi Tsunoda [*sic*] Shinpei no gōkan kantsū jiken (2)," *Yorozu chōhō*, January 15, 1896, 2.

44. The graphs for Chikurei's surname, 角田, can also be read as Tsunoda, and Chikurei is sometimes referred to as such in both contemporary sources and later

studies. Murayama Kokyō, *Meiji haidanshi* (Tokyo: Kadokawa Shoten, 1978), 124, asserts that Chikurei himself stated that Kakuta was the correct reading.

45. *Yorozu chōhō*, January 15, 1896, 2. The first verse posits Seshimo Kiyomichi confronting his wife over her adultery. It depends on two untranslatable puns, both playing on terms for "mouse." *Itazuramono* can mean "mouse," but it can also refer to a woman who is unfaithful to her husband; *yome ga kimi* is likewise an archaic term for a mouse, although it can also be read literally as "a bride's husband." In the second verse, "a cat's tryst" (*neko no koi*) was a seasonal phrase in *haikai* referring to a male cat chasing after a female in heat. It became popular in the Edo period, and a number of *haikai* poets, including Bashō, used it in their poetry. Here "cat's love" is juxtaposed with "a dog's heart" for humorous effect. Finally, the signature for the second poem, "Shinpai," which means "worry" or "anxiety," puns on Chikurei's given name Shinpei.

46. That Chikurei did not take legal action against the *Yorozu* may also suggest that there was a considerable element of truth in the paper's allegations. In a similar incident in the same newspaper almost a year later, the named party, the prominent Jiyūtō member and minister to Korea Ōishi Masaki 大石正巳 (1855–1935) did pursue the matter through the courts. Kōno Kensuke discusses this second incident and its implications in some detail in "Sukyandaru jānarizumu to 'hō' no shihai: *Yorozu chōhō* no aru 'kantsū jiken' kiji ni tsuite," in *Media, hyōshō, ideorogī: Meiji sanjūnendai no bunka kenkyū*, ed. Komori Yōichi, Kōno Kensuke, and Takahashi Osamu (Tokyo: Ozawa Shoten, 1998), 21–49.

47. Murayama, "Shūseikai no aruita michi (chū)," 120.

48. *Aki no koe*, no. 2 (December 1896): 23. Among the other occupations listed were two novelists (presumably Kōyō and Sazanami, or other members of the Ken'yūsha), two students, one soy sauce merchant, and one member listing his occupation as unemployed.

49. *Aki no koe*, no. 6 (April 1897): 45.

50. Mori Mukō, "Haidan zasso," *Aki no koe*, no. 6 (April 1897): 18–19.

51. Okano, "Shūseikai ron," 15

52. Okano, "Haikai yūbunki," 65.

53. *Teikoku bungaku* 4, no. 9 (September 1897): 3 (advertisements at end).

54. "Dai yonkai haiku kenshō no yokoku," *Bungei kurabu* 3, no. 8 (June 10, 1897): 235. The material prizes to be awarded to the top twenty-one candidates were listed in full, including a jeweled watch as first prize, the cash value of which was stated as approximately thirteen yen.

55. Mimori Mikio, "*Haikai* wa daidō to iu setsu," *Bungei kurabu* 4, no. 12 (October 3, 1898): 108.

56. Mimori, "*Haikai* wa daidō to iu setsu," 110.

57. Ōtei Kinshō, "Haikai mizukake ron," *Bungei kurabu* 6, no. 16 (December 10, 1900): 252.

58. Ōtei, "Haikai mizukake ron," 254. The reference is to a famous anecdote concerning fleeing soldiers in Mencius's writings: "Mencius replied . . . 'Some run a hundred paces and stop; some run fifty paces and stop. What would you think if those who run fifty paces were to laugh at those who run a hundred paces?' The king said, 'They should not do so. Though they did not run a hundred paces, yet they also ran away'"; see James Legge, trans., *The Chinese Classics*, 5 vols. (Hong Kong: Hong Kong University Press, 1960), 2:130.

59. *Teikoku bungaku* during 1897 sold a miniscule 29,322 copies (on average 2,443 per month), as against 574,950 (47,912 per month) for *Bungei kurabu* during the same period. Outselling both of them was the general-interest magazine *Taiyō*, with an impressive yearly circulation of nearly 2.5 million. See Naimushō Sōmukyoku Bunshoka, ed., *Dai Nihon Naimushō tōkei hōkoku*, 53 vols. (Tokyo: Naimushō, 1898) 13:352–53.

60. Based on the figures in *Dai Nihon Naimushō tōkei hōkoku*, *Nippon*'s circulation dropped from 6,865,364 in 1895 to 4,671,352 in 1898.

61. *SZ* 19:482–83, letter dated February 12, 1900. Sales of below 10,000 copies a day in 1900 would put *Nippon*'s circulation at around 3.5 million yearly, down by nearly half from the high of 1895.

62. "Shinbunshi no hyōban," *Taiyō* 6, no. 9 (July 1900): 30. For a broader discussion of the factors behind *Nippon*'s decline, see Yamamoto Taketoshi, "Meiji sanjūnendai zenhan no shinbun *Nippon* no dokushazō: Chishikijin dokusha no 'shinbun ishiki' o megutte," *Hitotsubashi ronsō* 58, no. 4 (October 1967): 510–16.

63. *SZ* 11:44.

64. *Haikai*'s two issues were published March 23 and May 4, 1893. In both cases, three hundred copies were printed, but the journal failed to sell even that relatively small number, and although a third issue was prepared, the printer refused to take on the cost of production, and so it was never printed. For more details on *Haikai*, see Mori Saruo, "Shii no tomo to zasshi *Haikai*," *Niibari* 2, no. 6 (1912): 16–18, and Itō Shōu, "Shii no tomo shūdan yori zasshi *Haikai* o hakkan suru made," in *SZ* 1:549–51.

65. Sekine Rinkichi, "Mimori Mikio hyōden (4)," *Haiku* 27, no. 7 (July 1978): 252.

66. Ichikawa, *Kindai haiku no akebono*, 1:321.

67. See Akio Bin, *Shiki no kindai: Kokkei, media, Nihongo* (Tokyo: Shin'yōsha, 1999), 136–47, for a description of this group. Considering the charge of thirty sen for each ten verses submitted and a monthly participation of around five hundred people, Akio estimates that the group probably made the substantial sum of around one hundred fifty yen per month.

68. Kakuta Chikurei, "Chōsō mango," *Aki no koe*, no. 1 (November 1896): 14–17.

69. *SZ* 4:354. The *unza*, or "roundtable," format was a group-based model of composition that involved composing on an assigned topic. Each participant created verses that were then copied out by the other participants with the names removed and submitted to the presiding master for judgment. As Shiki suggests, neither this nor point-scoring *haikai* necessarily had to be practiced for monetary prizes, though in reality they often were.

70. The June 1901 competition offered 110 yen in prize money and attracted 87,509 entries, a subsequent competition in September 1901, 236 yen with 54,687 entries, and in January 1902, 75 yen and 78,657 entries. See Aoki Makoto, "Meiji haidan to Nichiro sensō: Kyūha, Shūseikai, *Nippon*-ha o chūshin ni," *Dōshisha kokubungaku*, no. 61 (December 2004): 392.

71. Jōnan Inshi, "*Haikai* kūdan," *Haisei* 1, no. 5 (November 20, 1901): 15; quoted in Aoki, "Meiji haidan to Nichiro sensō," 397. "Godfather" refers, of course, to Shiki.

72. *SZ* 19:298.

73. Naitō Meisetsu, "Rōbaikyo manpitsu," *Hototogisu* 1, no. 1 (January 15, 1897): 1.

74. One Ashida Shūsō 芦田秋窓 (dates unknown) in Osaka contributed a gift of twenty writing brushes, which he increased to one hundred the following year; see *Hototogisu* 3, no. 4 (January 1900): 32.

75. *SZ* 19:298.

76. *Hototogisu* 2, no. 5 (February 1898): 45.

77. *Aki no koe*, no. 2 (December 1896): 23.

78. "Ōu Hyakubunkai no haikyō" and "Kanazawa tsūshin," *Hototogisu* 1, no. 6 (June 1897): 11–13.

79. Miyazaka, "*Nippon*-ha haiku undō," 34. Miyazaka estimates that around sixty new groups formed in Nagano Prefecture in the decade 1896–1906; of these, the Shōseikai was the first and among the most prominent. See also Ichikawa, *Kindai haiku no akebono*, 1:348.

80. "Haidan kinkyō," *Teikoku bungaku* 3, no. 3 (March 1897): 111.

81. "Meiji sanjūnen no haikukai," in *SZ* 5:12; first published in *Nippon*, January 4, 1898.

82. "Chihō haikukai," *Hototogisu* 3, no. 1 (October 10, 1899): 30 (supplement). The name Ryūsakai (literally, "Sedge-Hat Society") may have been intended to sound similar to "Russia"; the sedge hat was also a well-established metaphor in *haikai* for travel to far-flung places.

83. "Matsue dayori," *Hototogisu* 1, no. 20 (August 1898): 12.

84. Seki Hyōu, "Shizuoka haikyō," *Hototogisu* 1, no. 10 (October 1897): 23.

85. Katō Setchō, "Shizuoka tsūshin," *Hototogisu* 2, no. 1 (October 1898): 44.

86. *Fuyō* seems to have sold fairly well for a provincial magazine, so its disappearance is somewhat mystifying; an advertisement for the magazine in *Hototogisu*

3, no. 5 (March 1900), states that the number of copies printed had been increased to three hundred to meet demand and that the previous issue had completely sold out. A possible additional cause for the Fuyōkai's decline was the loss of one of its venues for publishing its work, a local magazine for Shinto priests and National Learning scholars called *Konomichi*. *Konomichi* had featured the group's haiku, but their arrangement was apparently dissolved on *Konomichi*'s initiative as a result of its displeasure at Shiki's "Letters to a *Waka* Poet" (Utayomi ni atōru sho), which appeared in *Nippon* in 1898. See Hashimoto Sunao, "'*Nippon*-ha' no tenkai: Shizuoka 'Fuyōkai' ni tsuite," *Kanagawa daigaku kokusai keiei ronshū*, no. 31 (March 2006): 11.

87. Noda Bettenrō, "Ōsaka haidan kinkyō," *Hototogisu* 1, no. 17 (June 30, 1898): 26.
88. Noda, "Ōsaka haidan no kinkyō," 27–28.
89. Haga Yaichi, "Jo," in *Meiji bungakushi*, by Iwaki Juntarō (Tokyo: Ikueisha, 1909), 1.
90. Sazanami, "Shūseikai no omoide," 254. It should perhaps be noted that Sazanami also recalled that most of his fellows felt Chikurei's actions to be "unspeakably vulgar" (*sukoburu zoku na koto*).

5. THE UNMANLY POETRY OF OUR TIMES: SHIKI, TEKKAN, AND *WAKA* REFORM, 1890–1900

1. It was during the latter half of the period under discussion, 1890–1900, that the modern term "tanka" came into widespread use. Generally, the critics and scholars cited in the following use the term *waka* or occasionally *uta* as their primary referent, a term that in most cases they use in a narrow sense to denote the 5-7-5-7-7 syllable form. I have therefore retained the term *waka* throughout in the translations. The exception to this is in a handful of cases where the term "tanka" is used to designate a consciously modern and distinct form of poetry.

2. As Murai Osamu has pointed out, even after this "opening up" of the *utakai hajime* the authors of the poems that were selected tended to be those in government positions or with connections to the imperial household. It was not until Meiji 15 (1882) that the *utakai hajime* featured works by people who might be thought of as average citizens. See Murai Osamu, "Utakai hajime to shinbun kadan: Tanka ni yoru 'shinmin' to 'kokumin' no sōshutsu," in *Tanka ni okeru hihyō to wa* (Tokyo: Iwanami Shoten, 1999), 79.

3. Murai, "Utakai hajime to shinbun kadan," 80.

4. Suga Satoko, "Higuchi Ichiyō to waka," in *Teikoku no waka*, ed. Asada Tōru et al., Waka o hiraku 5 (Tokyo: Iwanami Shoten, 2006), 115–16.

5. Shinada Yoshikazu, *"Man'yōshū*: The Invention of a National Poetry Anthology,"* in *Inventing the Classics: Modernity, National Identity, and Japanese Literature*, ed. Haruo Shirane and Tomi Suzuki (Stanford, Calif.: Stanford University Press, 2000), 31–50.

6. Murai, "Utakai hajime to shinbun kadan," 66.

7. Haruo Shirane, *Japan and the Culture of the Four Seasons* (New York: Columbia University Press, 2013), 26.

8. Tomi Suzuki, "Gender and Genre: Modern Literary Histories and Women's Diary Literature," in Shirane and Suzuki, *Inventing the Classics*, 75–79.

9. Suzuki, "Gender and Genre," 80.

10. Suzuki, "Gender and Genre," 81–82. Suzuki has noted that Fujioka nevertheless held Heian *waka* in low esteem, finding it lacking in realism or direct, unmediated emotional expression.

11. Tomiko Yoda, *Gender and National Literature: Heian Texts in the Constructions of Japanese Modernity* (Durham, N.C.: Duke University Press, 2004), 2.

12. Yoda, *Gender and National Literature*, 8.

13. It is apparently not certain whether Tekkan moved to the capital in August or November of 1892. See Itsumi Kumi, *Shinpan hyōden Yosano Hiroshi Akiko Meiji hen*, 3 vols. (Tokyo: Yagi Shoten, 2007–2012), 1:65

14. Itsumi, *Shinpan hyōden*, 1:67.

15. Itsumi, *Shinpan hyōden*, 1:65–73.

16. Itsumi, *Shinpan hyōden*, 1:72.

17. Maeda Tōru, *Ochiai Naobumi: Kindai tanka no reimei* (Tokyo: Meiji Shoin, 1985), 3–41.

18. Maeda, *Ochiai Naobumi*, 131. Ochiai's call-up is something of a mystery; students were supposed to be exempted from military service, and none of the rest of his class appears to have been conscripted.

19. Ochiai Naobumi, "Sansei no yueyoshi o nobete *Kagaku* hakkō no shushi ni kau," *Kagaku*, no. 1 (March 1892), reprinted in *Ochiai Naobumi, Ueda Kazutoshi, Haga Yaichi, Fujioka Sakutarō shū*, ed. Hisamatsu Sen'ichi, Meiji bungaku zenshū 44 (Tokyo: Chikuma Shobō, 1968), 26–28.

20. Hiratsuka Raichō, *In the Beginning, Woman Was the Sun: The Autobiography of a Japanese Feminist*, trans. Teruko Craig (New York: Columbia University Press, 2006), 101–2.

21. Itsumi, *Shinpan hyōden*, 1:74.

22. *Naichi zakkyo*, or "mixed residence," was an important issue in the ongoing debate over reform of the unequal treaties imposed in 1858 (*jōyaku kaisei*), a topic *Nippon* took up almost daily. Advocates of mixed residence proposed allowing foreigners, who had hitherto mostly been confined to extraterritorial

settlements such as the Port of Yokohama, to live in and move about the country without restriction, and also to purchase land. Opponents, including many on the *Nippon* staff, argued that lifting the restrictions would jeopardize Japan's sovereignty and national security.

23. *Nippon*, May 4, 1893, 2. Part of a sequence of "Twelve Verses on Current Events" (Kin'ei jūnishū), signed as being written by the Asakasha.

24. *Man'yōshū* 61, composed by the Toneri maiden on an imperial journey: "Where the stalwart men / grasp their hunting arrows / stand, and shoot / Target Bay / how fair it is to see!" (*masurao no / satsuya tabasami / tachimukai / iru matokata wa / miru ni sayakeshi*).

25. Shortly after this, in 1894, Ayukai would in fact move to Korea and remain there until the end of the Pacific War, a period of nearly fifty years, working to advance Japanese interests and hosting Tekkan when he went to Korea after the Sino-Japanese War.

26. Maeda, *Ochiai Naobumi*, 136.

27. Ochiai, "Sansei no yueyoshi o nobete," 28.

28. Quoted in Maeda, *Ochiai Naobumi*, 147.

29. Hagino Yoshiyuki, "Waka kairyō ron," in *Kokugaku waka kairyō ron*, by Hagino Yoshiyuki and Ikebe Yoshikata (Tokyo: Yoshikawa Hanshichi, 1887), 34.

30. For instance, in his 1763 *Shibun yōryō* (An outline of Murasaki's *Tale of Genji*), Norinaga argues, "The true heart (*makoto no kokoro*) of an individual is usually like that of a woman or child: immature and weak (*oroka*). The true heart is not masculine, firm, or resolute: such attitudes are mere decoration. When one delves to the bottom of the heart, even the most resolute person is no different from a woman or child. The only difference is that one hides that true heart out of embarrassment, and the other does not." Translation from Haruo Shirane, *The Bridge of Dreams: A Poetics of the "Tale of Genji"* (Stanford, Calif.: Stanford University Press, 1987), 31.

31. Hagino, "Waka kairyō ron," 41.

32. Hagino, "Waka kairyō ron," 41–42.

33. Yoda, *Gender and National Literature*, 40.

34. Takasaki Masakaze, "Koiuta o ronjite sakka no seishin ni oyobu (I)," in *Utamonogatari* (Tokyo: Tōkyōsha, 1912), 42–49. As seen in chapter 2, the *Book of Odes* was also cited as a canonical justification for sexually themed *kanshi*.

35. Asukai Masamichi, "Meiji Tennō: 'Kōtei' to 'Tenshi' no aida; Sekai rekkyō e no chōsen," in *Bakumatsu Meijiki no kokumin kokka keisei to bunka hen'yō*, ed. Nishikawa Nagao and Matsumiya Hideharu (Tokyo: Shin'yōsha, 1995), 64.

36. On this point, see Amō Hisayoshi, "Waka no kokuminka: Teiō no uta, shinmin no uta; Outadokoro to utakai hajime," in Asada, *Teikoku no waka*, 105.

37. The game is based on knowledge of the one hundred *waka* in the *Hyakunin isshu*. The two hundred cards are divided into "reading cards" (*yomifuda*), which have the complete verse and the name and picture of the poet, and the "taking cards" (*torifuda*), which have only the second half of each verse. The taking cards are spread out on the floor, and players must compete to be the first to grab the correct card as another player reads out the reading cards.

38. Murai, "Utakai hajime to shinbun kadan," 78.

39. Quoted in Iwai Shigeki, "Koiuta no shōmetsu: *Hyakunin isshu* no kindaiteki tokuchō ni tsuite," *Nihon kenkyū* 27 (March 2003): 217.

40. Iwai, "Koiuta no shōmetsu," 224, notes that *Hyakunin isshu* parties were one of a very small number of occasions where men and women could interact without chaperones, thus providing opportunities for further, more illicit activities.

41. Ochiai Naobumi, "Koiuta to iu mono," *Jokan*, no. 4 (November 5, 1891): 17. This problem continued to be debated long into Meiji; in 1911, former Asakasha member Ōmachi Keigetsu observed that there would not be much left of the *waka* canon if one were to exclude love poems, and that the *Hyakunin isshu*'s poems were "pure, elegant, and beautiful, and sublime." He went on to observe that if these love poems were prohibited, the result would be to "cause people to read obscene novels, and the consequences would be that much worse"; quoted in Iwai, "Koiuta no shōmetsu," 218.

42. Chōfuku Kana, "Meiji Outadokoro-ha kadan saikentō: Tekkan, Shiki ni yoru hihan o megutte," *Kokubungaku kō*, no. 201 (March 2009): 25.

43. Sasaki Ken [Nobutsuna], "Uta no hanashi," *Jogaku zasshi*, no. 98 (February 25, 1888): 11. The reference is to the titular character's address to a poet: "It has been said by another poet, more reflective than Ovid, 'that the world is governed by love and hunger.' But hunger certainly has the lion's share of the government; and if a poet is really to do what he pretends to do—viz., represent nature—the greater part of his lays should be addressed to the stomach . . . if you wish to be the popular minnesinger or troubadour of the age, appeal to nature, sir, appeal to nature; drop all hackneyed rhapsodies about a rosy cheek, and strike your lyre to the theme of a beef-steak" (Edward Bulwer Lytton, *Kenelm Chillingly: His Adventures and Opinions* [New York: Harper, 1873], 85).

44. Sasaki, "Uta no hanashi," 11.

45. Isogai Unpō, "Joshi nanzo waka o manabazaru (1)," *Jogaku zasshi*, no. 206 (March 29, 1893): 12. In the issue's table of contents, this piece is given the English title "Why Do Girls Not Study 'Waka'?"

46. Seki Iyū, "Kokutai to kadō," *Jokan*, no. 6 (January 5, 1892): 9.

47. Seki, "Kokutai to kadō," 10.

48. Seki, "Kokutai to kadō," 12. "Many Clouds Rising" is a poem by the deity Susanoo that is featured in the *Kojiki* (712) and the *Nihon shoki* (720). Susanoo composes the poem on descending to earth, marrying the daughter of an earthly deity, and establishing a palace at Izumo: "The many-fenced palace of Izumo / Of the many clouds rising— / To dwell there with my spouse / Do I build a many-fenced palace: / Ah, that many-fenced palace! (*yakumo tatsu / izumo yaegaki / tsumagomi ni / yaegaki tatsuru / sono yaegaki o*)." Translation taken from Donald L. Philippi, trans., *Kojiki* (Tokyo: University of Tokyo Press, 1969), 91. Emperor Jimmu is the legendary first emperor of Japan, claimed to have ascended the throne in 660 B.C.E. His poem was composed when, after a series of victories, his forces found themselves exhausted and starving on the slopes of Mount Inasa, near present-day Nara: "Of Mount Inasa of the lined-up shields we fought, but now we are starving. O u-kai, you keepers of the cormorants of the isles—come to our aid!" (*tata namete / inasa no yama no / ko no ma mo / iyuki mamorai / tatakaeba / ware haya uenu / shima tsu tori / ukai ga tomo / ima tasuke ni kine*) (Philippi, *Kojiki*, 177).

49. Seki, "Kokutai to kadō," 13.

50. Yosano Tekkan, "Joshi to kokubun [1]," *Fujo zasshi* 3, no. 6 (March 15, 1893): 7.

51. Yosano, "Joshi to kokubun [1]," 8.

52. Yosano Tekkan, "Joshi to kokubun [2]," *Fujo zasshi* 3, no. 8 (April 15, 1893): 6–8; emphasis in original.

53. Yosano Tekkan, "Joshi to kokubun [3]," *Fujo zasshi* 3, no. 9 (May 1, 1893): 6.

54. Yosano, "Joshi to kokubun [3]," 7.

55. Yosano, "Joshi to kokubun [3]," 7.

56. Yosano, "Joshi to kokubun [3]," 8.

57. Yosano, "Joshi to kokubun [3]," 8.

58. Yosano Tekkan, "Joshi to kokubun [4]," *Fujo zasshi* 3, no. 11 (June 1, 1893): 3.

59. Yosano, "Joshi to kokubun [4]," 4–5.

60. Nagaoka Takesuke, *Yosano Tekkan den: Tōkyō Shinshisha seiritsu made* (Tokyo: Ōfūsha, 1984), 149.

61. Chinese text and English translation from Xu Chao, ed., Lao An, trans., *The Book of Rites*, Ruxue jingdian yicong (Jinan: Shandong Youyi Chubanshe, 1999), 164–65.

62. Yosano Tekkan, "Bōkoku no on: Gendai no hijōbuteki waka o nonoshiru," in *Shiron, karon, hairon*, ed. Yoshida Seiichi et al., Kindai bungaku hyōron taikei 8 (Tokyo: Kadokawa Shoten, 1973), 241.

63. Yosano, "Bōkoku no on," 242.

64. Yosano, "Bōkoku no on," 242.

65. Yosano, "Bōkoku no on," 246–47; emphasis in original.

66. Nagaoka, *Yosano Tekkan den*, 133.

67. Hayashi Mikaomi, "Koiuta wa yomu bekarazu," *Jokan*, no. 21 (August 20, 1892): 59–60. The gist of Hayashi's argument was that *waka* was a double-edged sword on account of its emotional power; it could therefore be used to instruct but also could lead people astray, and so topics relating to love should be avoided.

68. Iwai, "Koiuta no shōmetsu," 230.

69. For example, the imminent conflict is cited as an explanation for Tekkan's rhetoric in Nagaoka, *Yosano Tekkan den*, 154; Itsumi, *Shinpan hyōden*, 85; Itsumi Kumi, "Waka kakushin to 'Tora no Tekkan' kara 'Murasaki no Tekkan' e," *Kokubungaku kaishaku to kyōzai no kenkyū* 52, no. 7 (June 2007): 112; Iwai, "Koiuta no shōmetsu," 236; and Maeda, *Ochiai Naobumi*, 148.

70. Seki Reiko, "Kaho to Tekkan o meguru mondaikei: 'Bōkoku no on' zengo," *Nihon kindai bungaku*, no. 75 (November 2006): 13.

71. Chōfuku, "Meiji Outadokoro-ha kadan saikentō," 26.

72. Murai, "Utakai hajime to shinbun kadan," 72, argues, semiseriously, that if Shiki had been born in Satsuma rather than Matsuyama he might have found a way to incorporate haiku into the official structures of government and become "emperor of haiku."

73. The Teradaya Incident was an unsuccessful uprising by Satsuma warriors in early 1862, aiming to kill senior nobles and *bakufu* officials and restore imperial rule. It was put down when the de facto daimyo of Satsuma, Shimazu Hisamitsu 島津久光 (1817–1887), learned of the plot and dispatched men to stop it. The confrontation occurred at the Teradaya Inn in Kyoto, where the conspirators had gathered, and in the ensuing melee on May 21, 1862, several men were killed.

74. Quoted in Amō, "Waka no kokuminka," 110.

75. Maeda, *Ochiai Naobumi*, 145

76. Judit Árokay, "Discourse on Poetic Language in Early Modern Japan and the Awareness of Linguistic Change," in *Divided Languages? Diglossia, Translation, and the Rise of Modernity in Japan, China, and the Slavic World*, ed. Judit Árokay, Jadranka Gvozdanović, and Darja Miyajima (Cham, Switz.: Springer International, 2014), 97; see also Yoda, *Gender and National Literature*, 31.

77. *Nippon*, February 14, 1893, 6.

78. Kagawa Kageki, *Kokin wakashū seigi* (Tokyo: Shikishima Hakkōjo, 1893), 11–13. These lines are quoted in Nakamura Yukihiko, "Kageki to Shiki," in *Nakamura Yukihiko chojutsu shū*, 15 vols. (Tokyo: Chūō Kōronsha, 1989), 1:333.

79. Masaoka Shiki, "Jūtabi utayomi ni atōru sho," in *SZ* 7:48. Originally published in *Nippon*, March 4, 1898.

80. Masaoka Shiki, "Futatabi utayomi ni atōru sho," in *SZ* 7:23–25. Originally published in *Nippon*, February 14, 1898.

81. Masaoka Shiki, "Mitabi utayomi ni atōru sho," in *SZ* 7:26. Originally published in *Nippon*, February 18, 1898.

82. Masaoka Shiki, "Yotabi utayomi ni atōru sho," in *SZ* 7:31. Originally published in *Nippon*, February 21, 1898.

83. Shiki, "Yotabi utayomi ni atōru sho," in *SZ* 7:31.

84. Chiba Inaki, "Takenosatobito ni ippitsu mairase sōrō," in *SZ* 7:614. Originally published in *Nippon*, February 22. 1898.

85. Masaoka Shiki, "Rokutabi utayomi ni atōru sho," in *SZ* 7:35. Originally published in *Nippon*, February 24, 1898.

86. Shiki, "Rokutabi utayomi ni atōru sho," in *SZ* 7:36.

87. Chiba Inaki, "Futatabi Takenosatobito ni kigo su," in *SZ* 7:621. Originally published in *Nippon*, March 27, 1898.

88. Chiba Inaki, "Futatabi Takenosatobito ni kigo su," in *SZ* 7:622.

89. Masaoka Shiki, "Hitobito ni kotau [4]," in *SZ* 7:61–62. Originally published in *Nippon*, March 29, 1898.

90. Masaoka Shiki, "Hitobito ni kotau [6]," in *SZ* 7:66. Originally published in *Nippon*, April 2, 1898.

91. Masaoka Shiki, "Hitobito ni kotau [13]," in *SZ* 7:84–86. Originally published in *Nippon*, May 12, 1898.

92. *SZ* 7:620.

93. Yosano Tekkan, *Tōzai nanboku* (Tokyo: Meiji Shoin, 1896), 59. English translation from Donald Keene, *Dawn to the West: Japanese Literature of the Modern Era*, 3 vols. (New York: Columbia University Press, 1999), 2:16.

CONCLUSION

1. *SZ* 3:473.

2. The essay is "After Death" (Shigo) and was published in *Hototogisu* 4, no. 5 (February 28, 1901); see *SZ* 12:510–19. It contains the memorable line "At a certain point around about the summer of last year, I had the experience of observing my own death in an objective manner" (*kyakkanteki ni jiko no shi to iu koto o kansatsu shita koto ga atta*) (*SZ* 12:511).

3. In *Kindai haironshi*, distinguished Shiki scholar Matsui Toshihiko lists multiple figures, including Narushima Ryūhoku in 1877 and Mimori Mikio in 1880, who were using the term "haiku"; see Matsui Toshihiko, *Kindai haironshi*, Haiku shirīzu hito to sakuhin: Bekkan (Tokyo: Ōfūsha, 1973), 71–72. Both Matsui and Akio Bin note the term's use also in a number of early old-school *haikai* magazines throughout the 1880s (see Akio Bin, *Shiki no kindai: Kokkei, media, Nihongo* [Tokyo: Shin'yōsha, 1999], 153–54). The belief that Shiki (or at least the *Nippon* Group) had invented the term "haiku" was

possibly promoted by Shiki's later disciples; Akio Bin, *Kyoshi to "Hototogisu": Kindai haiku no media* (Tokyo: Hon'ami Shoten, 2006), 64–66, states that Sangawa Sokotsu 寒川鼠骨 (1875–1954) and Naitō Meisetsu claimed at various times (wrongly) to have been the first to use the term.

4. Kawahigashi Hekigōtō, *Shiki no kaisō* (Tokyo: Shōnan Shobō, 1944), 485, asserts that Shiki invented the term *yakyū* to replace the loan word *bēsubōru*. The Japanese Baseball Hall of Fame asserts rather that the honor of inventing the term falls to Chūman Kanoe 中馬庚 (1870–1932), an educator and baseball enthusiast who followed Shiki's own academic path in studying at the First Higher School and later at Tokyo Imperial University; see http://www.baseball-museum.or.jp /baseball_hallo/detail/detail_039.html (accessed September 25, 2017).

5. An idea quoted as characteristic of the 1930s by both Amō Hisayoshi and Murai Osamu; see Amō Hisayoshi, "Waka no kokuminka: Teiō no uta, shinmin no uta; Outadokoro to utakai hajime," in *Teikoku no waka*, ed. Asada Tōru et al., Waka o hiraku 5 (Tokyo: Iwanami Shoten, 2006), 105, and Murai Osamu, "Utakai hajime to shinbun kadan: Tanka ni yoru 'shinmin' to 'kokumin' no sōshutsu," in *Tanka ni okeru hihyō to wa*, ed. Fujii Sadakazu, Tanka to Nihonjin 6 (Tokyo: Iwanami Shoten, 1999), 66.

6. Prasenjit Duara, "Historicizing National Identity, or Who Imagines What and When," in *Becoming National: A Reader*, ed. Geoff Eley and Roland Grigor Suny (New York: Oxford University Press, 1996), 169.

7. This overview of the newly arisen haiku is taken from Kawana Hajime, "Shinkō haiku undō to haiku dan'atsu jiken," *Bungaku* 7, no. 1 (January 1996): 144–46.

8. Quoted in Kawana, "Shinkō haiku undō," 146.

9. Hirabatake Seitō, *Kyōdai haiku*, October 1936; quoted in Kawana Hajime, *Shinkō haiku hyōgenshi ronkō* (Tokyo: Ōfūsha, 1984), 136–37.

10. *Kyōdai haiku* 7, no. 11 (November 1939): 24–25; quoted in Kawana, *Shinkō haiku hyōgenshi ronkō*, 142.

11. Saitō Sanki, "Haiguden," in *Fuyu no momo: Kōbe, Zoku Kōbe, Haiguden* (Tokyo: Mainichi Shuppansha, 1977), 244.

12. Kawana, "Shinkō haiku undō," 146.

13. *Tokkō geppō*, June 1943; quoted in Kawana, *Shinkō haiku hyōgenshi ronkō*, 147.

14. Saitō, "Haiguden," 211–12. Saitō notes that he and fellow poets were criticized for writing their poetry "based on movie newsreels" (*nyūzu eiga ni yotte sakku shite iru*).

15. Kawana, "Shinkō haiku undō," 146, notes unconfirmed rumors at the time that certain contemporary haiku poets opposed to the newly arising haiku groups may have actively denounced certain of their rivals and assisted the secret police, although no names or hard evidence exists to prove the case one way or the other.

16. Kuwabara Takeo, *Daini geijutsu*, Kindai bungei hyōron sōsho 9 (Tokyo: Nihon Tosho Sentā, 1990), 81. The echoes of the suppression of wartime haiku extended even to the field of Japanese jurisprudence; writing in 1978–1979, author Kozakai Shōzō 小堺昭三 (1928–1995) alleged in a series of articles in the journal *Haiku* and in his monograph *Mikkoku: Shōwa haiku dan'atsu jiken* (Tokyo: Daiyamondosha, 1979) that Kyōdai haiku member Saitō Sanki had actually been a spy for the secret police, on the grounds that he had been arrested later and released earlier than any other member of the group. Incensed by this, Sanki's children successfully sued Kozakai for damaging their father's reputation, even though Sanki was already dead by this point.

Bibliography

NEWSPAPERS AND LITERARY JOURNALS

Azuma shinshi. Tokyo: Kyūshundō, 1883–1887.

Bungei kurabu. 1895–1933. Tokyo: Nihon Kindai Bungakkan; Hatsubai Yagi Shoten, 2005. CD-ROM.

Chōya shinbun. 1874–1893. 38 vols. Tokyo: Perikansha, 1981–1984.

Fujo zasshi. Tokyo: Hakubunkan, 1891–1894.

Haikai Aki no koe. Tokyo: Mankandō, 1896–1897.

Haisei. Tokyo: Haisei Hakkōjo, 1901–1902.

Hototogisu. Matsuyama: Hototogisu Hakkōjo, 1897–1898; Tokyo: Hototogisusha, 1898–.

Jogaku zasshi. Tokyo: Jogaku Zasshisha, 1885–1904.

Jokan. Tokyo: Joshi Shinbunsha, 1891–1909.

Kagetsu shinshi. Tokyo: Kagetsusha, 1877–1884.

Kokon shibun shōkai. Tokyo: Seishōsha, 1880–1887.

Kokumin shinbun. 1890–1942. Tokyo: Nihon Maikuro Shashin, 1966. Microform.

Nippon. 1889–1906. Tokyo: Yumani Shobō, 2002. Microform.

Ōsaka Asahi shinbun. Kikuzō II Visual Online Database. Tokyo: Asahi Shinbunsha, 2006. https://database.asahi.com/index.shtml.

Shinbunshi. Tokyo: Mori Shuntō, 1875–1884.

Shō Nippon. 1894. 3 vols. Tokyo: Ōzorasha, 1994.

Taiyō. 1895–1928. Tokyo: Yagi Shoten, 1999. CD-ROM.

Teikoku bungaku. Tokyo: Teikoku Bungaku Kai, 1895–1920.

Tōkyō Mainichi shinbun. Tokyo: Kokuritsu Kokkai Toshokan, 1966. Microform.

Waseda bungaku. Tokyo: Tokyo Senmon Gakkō, 1891–.

Yomiuri shinbun. Tokyo: Yomiuri Shinbunsha Media Kikakukyoku Dētabēsubu, 1999–2002. http://www.yomiuri.co.jp/database/kensaku/.

Yorozu chōhō. 1892–. Tokyo: Nihon Tosho Sentā, 1983–1993.

OTHER TEXTS CONSULTED

Aida Hanji. *Kinsei joryū bunjin den*. Tokyo: Meiji Shoin, 1961.

Akio Bin. *Kyoshi to "Hototogisu": Kindai haiku no media*. Tokyo: Hon'ami Shoten, 2006.

——. *Shiki no kindai: Kokkei, media, Nihongo*. Tokyo: Shin'yōsha, 1999.

Amō Hisayoshi. "Waka no kokuminka: Teiō no uta, shinmin no uta; Outadokoro to utakai hajime." In *Teikoku no waka*, edited by Asada Tōru et al., 93–112. Waka o hiraku 5. Tokyo: Iwanami Shoten, 2006.

Anderson, Benedict. *Imagined Communities: Reflections on the Origin and Spread of Nationalism*. London: Verso, 2006.

Aoki Makoto. "Meiji haidan to Nichiro sensō: Kyūha, Shūseikai, *Nippon*-ha o chūshin ni." *Dōshisha kokubungaku*, no. 61 (December 2004): 387–98.

Arai Yōko. "Mori Shuntō *Shin sanka zekku* ni tsuite." *Nishō*, no. 19 (2005): 253–76.

Árokay, Judit. "Discourse on Poetic Language in Early Modern Japan and the Awareness of Linguistic Change." In *Divided Languages? Diglossia, Translation, and the Rise of Modernity in Japan, China, and the Slavic World*. Edited by Judit Árokay, Jadranka Gvozdanović, and Darja Miyajima, 89–103. Cham, Switz.: Springer International, 2014.

Asaoka Kunio. *Kaisetsu: "Shō Nippon" to Masaoka Shiki*. Tokyo: Ōzorasha, 1994.

Asukai Masamichi. "Meiji tennō: 'Kōtei' to 'tenshi' no aida; Sekai rekkyō e no chōsen." In *Bakumatsu Meijiki no kokumin kokka keisei to bunka hen'yō*, edited by Nishikawa Nagao and Matsumiya Hideharu, 45–89. Tokyo: Shin'yōsha, 1995.

Bai Juyi. *Bai Juyi shiji jiaozhu*. Edited by Xie Siwei. 6 vols. Beijing: Zhonghua Shuju, 2006.

Beichman, Janine. *Embracing the Firebird: Yosano Akiko and the Birth of the Female Voice in Modern Japanese Poetry*. Honolulu: University of Hawai'i Press, 2002.

——. *Masaoka Shiki: His Life and Works*. Boston: Cheng and Tsui, 2002.

Bourdaghs, Michael. *The Dawn That Never Comes: Shimazaki Tōson and Japanese Nationalism*. New York: Columbia University Press, 2003.

Bowen, Roger. *Rebellion and Democracy in Meiji Japan: A Study of Commoners in the Popular Rights Movement*. Berkeley: University of California Press, 1984.

Bulwer Lytton, Edward. *Kenelm Chillingly: His Adventures and Opinions*. New York: Harper, 1873.

Cai, Zong-qi, ed. *How to Read Chinese Poetry: A Guided Anthology*. New York: Columbia University Press, 2008.

Chang, Kang-i Sun. "Ming-Qing Women Poets and the Notions of 'Talent' and 'Morality.'" In *Culture and State in Chinese History: Conventions, Accommodations, and Critiques*, edited by Theodore Huters, R. Bin Wong, and Pauline Yu, 236–58. Stanford, Calif.: Stanford University Press, 1997.

Chatterjee, Partha. *The Nation and Its Fragments: Colonial and Postcolonial Histories*. Princeton, N.J.: Princeton University Press, 1993.

Chōfuku Kana. "Meiji Outadokoro-ha kadan saikentō: Tekkan, Shiki ni yoru hihan o megutte." *Kokubungaku kō*, no. 201 (March 2009): 17–32.

Chu Renhu. *Jianhuji*. Xuxiu Siku quanshu 1262. Shanghai: Shanghai Guji Chubanshe, 2002.

Crowley, Cheryl. *Haikai Poet Yosa Buson and the Bashō Revival*. Leiden: Brill, 2007.

Duara, Prasenjit. "Historicizing National Identity, or Who Imagines What and When." In *Becoming National: A Reader*, edited by Geoff Eley and Roland Grigor Suny, 151–78. New York: Oxford University Press, 1996.

——. *Rescuing History from the Nation: Questioning Narratives of Modern China*. Chicago: University of Chicago Press, 1995.

Fan Ye. *Hou Hanshu*. 12 vols. Beijing: Zhonghua Shuju, 1965.

Fang Hui. *Yingkui lüsui huiping*. Edited by Li Qingjia. 3 vols. Shanghai: Shanghai Guji Chubanshe, 1986.

Fraleigh, Matthew, trans. *New Chronicles of Yanagibashi and Diary of a Journey to the West: Narushima Ryūhoku Reports from Home and Abroad*. Ithaca, N.Y.: Cornell University Press, 2010.

——. *Plucking Chrysanthemums: Narushima Ryūhoku and Sinitic Literary Traditions in Modern Japan*. Cambridge, Mass.: Harvard University Asia Center, 2016.

——. "Songs of the Righteous Spirit: 'Men of High Purpose' and Their Chinese Poetry in Modern Japan." *Harvard Journal of Asiatic Studies* 69, no. 1 (June 2009): 109–71.

Fujimori Fumio. "Jiji senryū no keifu to ruikei." *Shinbun kenkyū*, no. 358 (May 1981): 57–64.

Fujimori Masasumi. "Kakuta Chikurei hyōden." *Gakuen*, no. 253 (January 1961): 55–67.

Fukui Jun, ed. *Kinsei shisaku yōgaku benran*. Osaka: Hanai Unosuke, 1883.

Fukunaga Norihiro. "Gendai haiku jihyō: Intānetto no kōzai (1)." *Haiku* 55, no. 3 (February 2006): 114–20.

——. "Gendai haiku jihyō: Intānetto no kōzai (2)." *Haiku* 55, no. 4 (March 2006): 100–106.

Gan Bao. *In Search of the Supernatural: The Written Record.* Translated by Kenneth J. DeWoskin and J. I. Crump Jr. Stanford, Calif.: Stanford University Press, 1996.

Gotō Shinpei and Tokutomi Sohō. *Ōfuku shokan Gotō Shinpei Tokutomi Sohō: 1895–1929.* Edited by Kōno Shizuko. Tokyo: Fujiwara Shoten, 2005.

Gōyama Rintarō. "Bakumatsu Meijiki no entai kanshi: Mori Shuntō, Kainan ippa no shifū o megutte." *Wakan hikaku bungaku,* no. 37 (August 2006): 17–32.

——. "How Traditional Literature Adapted Itself to Modern Media: Kanshibun in 19th Century Japan." *TXT: Exploring the Boundaries of the Book* 1, no. 1 (2014): 175–81.

Hagino Yoshiyuki. "Waka kairyō ron." In *Kokugaku waka kairyō ron,* by Hagino Yoshiyuki and Ikebe Yoshikata, 1–58. Tokyo: Yoshikawa Hanshichi, 1887.

Han Wo. *Han Wo shiji jianzhu.* Edited by Tao Qi. Jinan: Shandong Jiaoyu Chubanshe, 2000.

——. *Kan Naikan Kōrenshū.* Edited by Tate Ryūwan and Maki Ryōko. Edo: Suwaraya Ihachi, 1811.

Hashimoto Sunao. "'Nippon-ha' no tenkai: Shizuoka 'Fuyōkai' ni tsuite." *Kanagawa daigaku kokusai keiei ronshū,* no. 31 (March 2006): 126–111.

Hattori Somon. "Shigo saikin jo." In *Shigo saikin,* edited by Nagata Kanga, 1–4. Kyoto: Hayashi Gonbei, 1841.

Hawkes, David, trans. *The Songs of the South: An Ancient Chinese Anthology of Poems by Qu Yuan and Other Poets.* New York: Penguin Books, 1985.

Herzfeld, Michael. *Cultural Intimacy: Social Poetics in the Nation-State.* New York: Routledge, 1997.

Higuchi Motomi. "Edo jidai no keimōteki kanshi sakuhō sho." *Kōbe shōsen daigaku kiyō bunka ronshū* 29 (July 1980): 69–105.

Hino Toshihiko. *Mori Shuntō no kisoteki kenkyū.* Tokyo: Kyūko Shoin, 2013.

Hirose Tansō. *Tansō shiwa.* In *Nihon shiwa sōsho,* edited by Kokubu Takatane and Ikeda Shirōjirō, 217–76. 10 vols. Tokyo: Bunkaidō Shoten, 1920–1922.

Honda Yasuo. *Shinbun shōsetsu no tanjō.* Tokyo: Heibonsha, 1998.

Hosogai Kōtō. *To shi kanshō.* Tokyo: Teikoku Daigaku Shuppankai, 1929.

Huffman, James. *Creating a Public: People and Press in Meiji Japan.* Honolulu: University of Hawai`i Press, 1997.

Ibi Takashi. *Edo no shidan jānarizumu: "Gozandō shiwa" no sekai.* Tokyo: Kadokawa Shoten, 2001.

——. "Kōko shisha no shuppatsu: Shimin bungaku to shite no kanshi e." *Kokubungaku kaishaku to kanshō* 73, no. 10 (October 2008): 98–106.

——. "Kōko shisha to yūri shi: Edo shidan no kakushin o megutte (jō)." *Kokugo to kokubungaku* 51, no. 3 (March 1974): 41–58.

——. *Yakuchū Renju shikaku.* Tokyo: Iwanami Shoten, 2008.

Ichikawa Kazuo. *Kindai haiku no akebono.* 2 vols. Tokyo: Sangensha, 1975.

Ikegami, Eiko. *Bonds of Civility: Aesthetic Networks and the Political Origins of Japanese Culture.* New York: Cambridge University Press, 2005.

Inoguchi Atsushi. *Josei to kanshi: Wakan joryū shishi.* Tokyo: Kasama Shoin, 1978.

Inoue Tetsujirō. *Sonken shishō.* 2 vols. Tokyo: Sakagami Hanshichi, 1884.

Iritani Sensuke. *Kanshi nyūmon.* Tokyo: Nitchū Shuppan, 1986.

Irokawa Daikichi. *The Culture of the Meiji Period.* Edited by Marius B. Jansen. Princeton, N.J.: Princeton University Press, 1985.

Ishigami Misao, ed. *Naigai kokin itsuwa bunko.* 14 vols. Tokyo: Hakubunkan, 1893–1894.

Ito, Ken K. *An Age of Melodrama: Family, Gender, and Social Hierarchy in the Turn-of-the-Century Japanese Novel.* Stanford, Calif.: Stanford University Press, 2008.

Itsumi Kumi. *Shinpan hyōden Yosano Hiroshi Akiko Meiji hen.* 3 vols. Tokyo: Yagi Shoten, 2007–2012.

——. "Waka kakushin to 'Tora no Tekkan' kara 'Murasaki no Tekkan' e." *Kokubungaku kaishaku to kyōzai no kenkyū* 52, no. 7 (June 2007): 109–18.

Iwai Shigeki. "Koiuta no shōmetsu: *Hyakunin isshu* no kindaiteki tokuchō ni tsuite." *Nihon kenkyū* 27 (March 2003): 215–37.

Iwaki Juntarō. *Meiji bungakushi.* Tokyo: Ikueisha, 1909.

Iwaya Sazanami. "Shūseikai no omoide." In *Haiku kōza: Gendai kessha hen,* edited by Yamamoto Sansei, 247–56. Kaizōsha haiku kōza, no. 8. Tokyo: Kaizōsha, 1932.

Jansen, Marius B. *China in the Tokugawa World.* Cambridge, Mass.: Harvard University Press, 1992.

Kagawa Kageki. *Kokin wakashū seigi.* Tokyo: Shikishima Hakkōjo, 1893.

Kamio Kazō, ed. *Yōgaku shiin, kaika shinsen: Shigo saikin, kaika shinsen; Kokon meika zekku shirei.* Tokyo: Fumie Shobō, 1881.

Kanda Kiichirō, ed. *Meiji kanshibun shū.* Meiji bungaku zenshū 62. Tokyo: Chikuma Shobō, 1983.

Katō Kuniyasu. *Kanshijin Shiki: Haiku kaigan no dōjō.* Tokyo: Kenbun Shuppan, 2006.

——. *Shiki zōsho to "Kanshikō" kenkyū: Kindai haiku seiritsu no katei.* Tokyo: Kenbun Shuppan, 2014.

Kawahigashi Hekigōtō. *Shiki no kaisō.* Tokyo: Shōnan Shobō, 1944.

Kawana Hajime. *Shinkō haiku hyōgenshi ronkō.* Tokyo: Ōfūsha, 1984.

——. "Shinkō haiku undō to haiku dan'atsu jiken." *Bungaku* 7, no. 1 (January 1996): 144–46.

Keene, Donald. *Dawn to the West: Japanese Literature of the Modern Era.* 4 vols. New York: Columbia University Press, 1999.

——. *The Winter Sun Shines In: A Life of Masaoka Shiki.* New York: Columbia University Press, 2013.

Kikuchi Gozan. *Gozandō shiwa.* In *Nihon shishi, Gozandō shiwa,* edited by Ibi Takashi and Shimizu Shigeru, 157–230. Shin Nihon koten bungaku taikei 65. Tokyo: Iwanami Shoten, 1991.

Kinoshita Hyō. "Kokubu Seigai to Meiji Taishō Shōwa kanshikai (2)." *Shi to tomo,* no. 319 (August 1976): 29–37.

——. "Kokubu Seigai to Meiji Taishō Shōwa no kanshikai (7)." *Shi to tomo,* no. 324 (January 1977): 38–44.

——. "Kokubu Seigai to Meiji Taishō Shōwa no kanshikai (8)." *Shi to tomo,* no. 325 (February 1977): 34–40.

——. "Kokubu Seigai to Meiji Taishō Shōwa no kanshikai" (9), *Shi to tomo* no. 326 (March 1977): 15–21.

——. "Kokubu Seigai to Meiji Taishō Shōwa no kanshikai (11)." *Shi to tomo,* no. 328 (May 1977): 40–47.

——. "Kokubu Seigai to Meiji Taishō Shōwa no kanshikai (13)." *Shi to tomo,* no. 331 (August 1977): 42–46.

——. "Kokubu Seigai to Meiji Taishō Shōwa no kanshikai (16)." *Shi to tomo,* no. 335 (January 1978): 26–31.

Kitamura Tōkoku and Yamaji Aizan. *Kitamura Tōkoku, Yamaji Aizan shū.* Gendai Nihon bungaku taikei 6. Tokyo: Chikuma Shobō, 2000.

Ko, Dorothy. *Cinderella's Sisters: A Revisionist History of Footbinding.* Berkeley: University of California Press, 2005.

Kojima Kazuo. *Ichi rōseijika no kaisō.* Tokyo: Chūō Kōronsha, 1951.

——. "Kokubu Seigai no koto." *Gayū,* no. 1 (May 1950): 30–34.

Kokubu Seigai. *Shi Tōko.* Tokyo: Meiji Shoin, 1897.

Kōno Kensuke. "Sukyandaru jānarizumu to 'hō' no shihai: *Yorozu chōhō* no aru 'kantsū jiken' kiji ni tsuite." In *Media, hyōshō, ideorogī: Meiji sanjūnendai no bunka kenkyū,* edited by Komori Yōichi, Kōno Kensuke, and Takahashi Osamu, 21–49. Tokyo: Ozawa Shoten, 1998.

——. *Tōki to shite no bungaku: Katsuji, kenshō, media.* Tokyo: Shin'yōsha, 2003.

Kozakai Shōzō. *Mikkoku: Shōwa haiku dan'atsu jiken.* Tokyo: Daiyamondosha, 1979.

Kubo Tenzui. *Hyōshaku Nihon zekku sen.* Tokyo: Hongō Shoin, 1908.

Kuwabara Takeo. *Daini geijutsu.* Kindai bungei hyōron sōsho 9. Tokyo: Nihon Tosho Sentā, 1990.

Legge, James, trans. *The Chinese Classics.* 5 vols. Hong Kong: Hong Kong University Press, 1960.

Li Bai. *Li Taibai quanji.* Edited by Wang Qi. 2 vols. Beijing: Zhonghua Shuju, 1977.

Li He. *Li He shixuan zhu.* Edited by Zhen Huile. Shanghai: Shanghai Guji Chubanshe, 1994.

Maeda Ai. "Chinzan to Shuntō: Meiji shonen no kanshidan." In *Bakumatsu, ishinki no bungaku*, edited by Maeda Ai, 246–68. Tokyo: Hōsei Daigaku Shuppankyoku, 1972.

———. *Kindai dokusha no seiritsu*. Tokyo: Iwanami Shoten, 2001.

Maeda Tōru. *Ochiai Naobumi: Kindai tanka no reimei*. Tokyo: Meiji Shoin, 1985.

Masaoka Shiki. *Shiki zenshū*. Edited by Masaoka Chūsaburō et al. 25 vols. Tokyo: Kōdansha, 1975–1978.

Matsui Toshihiko. *Kindai haironshi*. Haiku shirīzu hito to sakuhin: Bekkan. Tokyo: Ōfūsha, 1973.

———. *Masaoka shiki no kenkyū*. 2 vols. Tokyo: Meiji Shoin, 1976.

Matsumoto Hitoshi. *Keidō ikō*. Edited by Usui Tatsuyuki and Hamada Tokuzō. Kariya, Aichi Pref.: Hamada Tokuzō, 1898.

Matsushita Tadashi. "Nakajima Sōin no shiron to En Bai." *Nihon Chūgoku gakkai hō*, no. 18 (October 1966): 232–40.

Matsuyama Shiki Kinen Hakubutsukan, ed. *Shiki to Tokiwakai kishukusha no nakama tachi*. Matsuyama: Matsuyama Shiritsu Shiki Kinen Hakubutsukan, 1993.

Mayer, Tamar. *Gender Ironies of Nationalism: Sexing the Nation*. New York: Routledge, 2000.

Mehl, Margaret. *Private Academies of Chinese Learning in Meiji Japan: The Decline and Transformation of the Kangaku Juku*. Copenhagen: NIAS Press, 2003.

Mertz, John Pierre. *Novel Japan: Spaces of Nationhood in Early Meiji Narrative, 1870–88*. Ann Arbor, Mich.: Center for Japanese Studies, 2003.

Mikami Sanji. "Nihon rekishi bungakujō no kansatsu." *Nihon bungaku*, no. 19 (March 1890): 9–16.

Miura Kanō. *Meiji kanbungakushi*. Tokyo: Kyūko Shoin, 1998.

Miyazaka Shizuo. "*Nippon*-ha haiku undō no Shinano e no denpa no jōkyō: Shōseikai gaijō." *Haiku bungakukan kiyō*, no. 3 (June 1984): 23–53.

Mizukami Yoshiaki, ed. *Nihon keien ginsō*. 2 vols. Tokyo: Keibundō, 1880.

Mori Kainan. *Kainan shū*. Edited by Mori Kenrō. 28 vols. Tokyo: Mori Kenrō, 1912.

Mori Ōgai. *Ōgai zenshū*. 38 vols. Tokyo: Iwanami Shoten, 1971–1975.

Mori Saruo. "Shii no tomo to zasshi *Haikai*." *Niibari* 2, no. 6 (1912): 16–18.

Mori Shuntō, ed. *Shin sanka zekku*. 3 vols. Tokyo: Mori Taijirō, 1878.

———. *Shuntō shishō*. Edited by Morikawa Kenzō. 20 vols. Tokyo: Bunkaidō, 1912.

Morris, Ivan, trans. *The Pillow Book of Sei Shōnagon*. New York: Columbia University Press, 1991.

Morris, Mark. "Buson and Shiki: Part One." *Harvard Journal of Asiatic Studies* 44, no. 2 (December 1984): 381–425.

———. "Buson and Shiki: Part Two." *Harvard Journal of Asiatic Studies* 45, no. 1 (June 1985): 255–321.

Mostow, Joshua S. "The Revival of Poetry in Traditional Forms." In *The Columbia Companion to Modern East Asian Literature*, edited by Joshua S. Mostow, 99–104. New York: Columbia University Press, 2003.

Mote, Frederick W. *The Poet Kao Ch'i, 1336–1374*. Princeton, N.J.: Princeton University Press, 1962.

Murai Osamu. "Utakai hajime to shinbun kadan: Tanka ni yoru 'shinmin' to 'kokumin' no sōshutsu." In *Tanka ni okeru hihyō to wa*, edited by Fujii Sadakazu, 65–92. Tanka to Nihonjin 6. Tokyo: Iwanami Shoten, 1999.

Murayama Kokyō. *Meiji haidanshi*. Tokyo: Kadokawa Shoten, 1978.

——. *Meiji no haiku to haijin tachi*. Tokyo: Kawade Shobō Shinsha, 1983.

——. "Shūseikai no aruita michi (jō)." *Haiku* 18, no. 7 (July 1969): 126–36.

——. "Shūseikai no aruita michi (chū)." *Haiku* 18, no. 8 (August 1969): 118–31.

Nagaoka Takesuke. *Yosano Tekkan den: Tōkyō Shinshisha seiritsu made*. Tokyo: Ōfūsha, 1984.

Nagase, Mari. "'Truly, They Are a Lady's Words': Ema Saikō and the Construction of an Authentic Voice in Late Edo Period *Kanshi*." *Japanese Language and Literature* 48, no. 2 (October 2014): 279–305.

——. "Women Writers of Chinese Poetry in Late-Edo Period Japan." PhD diss., University of British Columbia, 2007.

Naimushō Sōmukyoku Bunshoka, ed. *Dai Nihon Naimushō tōkei hōkoku*. 53 vols. Tokyo: Naimushō, 1886–1942.

Naitō Meisetsu. *Meisetsu jijoden*. Tokyo: Okamura Shoten, 1922.

Nakamura Yukihiko. "Kageki to Shiki." In *Nakamura Yukihiko chojutsu shū*, 302–38. 15 vols. Tokyo: Chūō Kōronsha, 1989.

Naruse Masakatsu. "Nagai Kafū shū kaisetsu." In *Nagai Kafū shū*, edited by Naruse Masakatsu et al. Nihon kindai bungaku taikei 29. Tokyo: Kadokawa Shoten, 1969.

Natsume Sōseki. *Sore kara*. Edited by Sasaki Hideaki. Sōseki bungaku zenchūshaku 8. Tokyo: Wakakusa Shobō, 2000.

Noritsuke Shunkai. *Kokon kakutai sakushi kihan*. Tokyo: Eisai Shinshisha, 1893.

Ochiai Naobumi. "Sansei no yueyoshi o nobete *Kagaku* hakkō no shushi ni kau." *Kagaku*, no. 1 (March 1892). Reprinted in *Ochiai Naobumi, Ueda Kazutoshi, Haga Yaichi, Fujioka Sakutarō shū*, edited by Hisamatsu Shin'ichi, 26-28. Meiji bungaku zenshū 44. Tokyo: Chikuma Shobō, 1968.

Ōdate Seizai, ed. *Yōgaku hikkei konsei shisaku shinpen*. 2 vols. Tokyo: Morimoto Taisuke, 1878.

Ogata Tsutomu. *Za no bungaku*. Tokyo: Kadokawa Shoten, 1973.

Ōhashi Otowa, ed. *Shigaku shōkei*. Tokyo: Shōnen'en, 1895.

Okajima Akihiro. "Kango shiryō to shite no shigakusho: *Shigo saikin* o rei to shite." *Gobun kenkyū*, no. 86–87 (June 1999): 220–27.

Okano Chijū. *Haikai fūbunki*. Tokyo: Hakukyūsha, 1902.

———. "Shūseikai ron." *Haisei* 1, no. 5 (May 1901): 13–17.

Oki Osamu, ed. *Shinsen shigo katsuyō*. Tokyo: Bessho Heishichi, 1879.

Owen, Stephen, ed. and trans. *An Anthology of Chinese Literature: Beginnings to 1911*. New York: Norton, 1996.

———, ed. and trans. *The Poetry of Du Fu*. Boston: de Gruyter, 2016.

———. *Readings in Chinese Literary Thought*. Cambridge, Mass.: Harvard University Asia Center, 1992.

Ozaki Takeshirō. "Meiji no shinbunjin: Kuga Katsunan." *Shūkan jiji*, October 5, 1968.

Peterson, Barbara Bennett, ed. *Notable Women of China: Shang Dynasty to the Early Twentieth Century*. Armonk, N.Y.: M.E. Sharpe, 2000.

Pflugfelder, Gregory M. *Cartographies of Desire: Male-Male Sexuality in Japanese Discourse, 1600–1950*. Berkeley: University of California Press, 1999.

Philippi, Donald L., trans. *Kojiki*. Tokyo: University of Tokyo Press, 1969.

Qian, Nanxiu. *Politics, Poetics, and Gender in Late Qing China: Xue Shaohui and the Era of Reform*. Stanford, Calif.: Stanford University Press, 2015.

Qiu, Peipei. "Daoist Concepts in Bashō's Critical Thought." In *East Asian Cultural and Historical Perspectives: Histories and Society; Culture and Literatures*, edited by Steven Tötösy de Zepetnek and Jennifer W. Jay, 323–40. Edmonton: Research Institute for Comparative Literature and Cross-Cultural Studies, University of Alberta, 1997.

Rabinovitch, Judith N., and Timothy R. Bradstock. *The Kanshi Poems of the Ozasa Tansaku Collection: Late Edo Life through the Eyes of Kyoto Townsmen*. Nichibunken monograph series 5. Kyoto: International Research Center for Japanese Studies, 2002.

Reichert, James. *In the Company of Men: Representations of Male-Male Sexuality in Meiji Literature*. Stanford, Calif.: Stanford University Press, 2006.

Rouzer, Paul. *Articulated Ladies: Gender and the Male Community in Early Chinese Texts*. Cambridge, Mass.: Harvard University Press, 2001.

Rubinger, Richard. *Popular Literacy in Early Modern Japan*. Honolulu: University of Hawai`i Press, 2007.

Saitō Mareshi. *Kanbunmyaku no kindai: Shinmatsu-Meiji no bungakuken*. Tokyo: Nihon Hōsō Shuppan Kyōkai, 2007.

———. *Kanbunmyaku to kindai Nihon: Mō hitotsu no kotoba no sekai*. Tokyo: Nihon Hōsō Shuppan Kyōkai, 2007.

Saitō Sanki. "Haiguden." In *Fuyu no momo: Kōbe, Zoku Kōbe, Haiguden*, 155–266. Tokyo: Mainichi Shuppansha, 1977.

Saito, Satoru. *Detective Fiction and the Rise of the Japanese Novel, 1880–1930*. Cambridge, Mass.: Harvard University Asia Center, 2012.

Seki Hajime. *Shinbun shōsetsu no jidai: Media, dokusha, merodorama.* Tokyo: Shin'yōsha, 2007.

Seki Reiko. "Kaho to Tekkan o meguru mondaikei: 'Bōkoku no on' zengo." *Nihon kindai bungaku,* no. 75 (November 2006): 1–15.

Seki Toku, ed. *Shinsen shiin yōgaku benran.* 3 vols. Osaka: Yoshioka Hōbunken, 1878.

Sekine Rinkichi. "Mimori Mikio hyōden (1)." *Haiku* 27, no. 4 (April 1978): 246–55.

——. "Mimori Mikio hyōden (4)." *Haiku* 27, no. 7 (July 1978): 244–54.

Shimizu Fusao. *Shiki kanshi no shūhen.* Tokyo: Meiji Shoin, 1996.

Shinada Yoshikazu. "*Man'yōshū*: The Invention of a National Poetry Anthology." In *Inventing the Classics: Modernity, National Identity, and Japanese Literature,* edited by Haruo Shirane and Tomi Suzuki, 31–50. Stanford, Calif.: Stanford University Press, 2000.

Shirane, Haruo. *The Bridge of Dreams: A Poetics of the "Tale of Genji."* Stanford, Calif.: Stanford University Press, 1987.

——, ed. *Early Modern Japanese Literature: An Anthology, 1600–1900.* New York: Columbia University Press, 2002.

——. *Japan and the Culture of the Four Seasons.* New York: Columbia University Press, 2013.

——. *Traces of Dreams: Landscape, Cultural Memory, and the Poetry of Bashō.* Stanford, Calif.: Stanford University Press, 1998.

Sima Qian. *Shiji.* Edited by Wang Niansun. 2 vols. Taipei: Yiwen Yinshuguan, 1955.

Smits, Ivo. "Minding the Gaps: An Early Edo History of Sino-Japanese Poetry." In *Uncharted Waters: Intellectual Life in the Edo Period; Essays in Honour of W. J. Boot,* edited by Anna Beerens and Mark Teeuwen, 93–107. Leiden: Brill, 2012.

Soejima Taneomi. *Sōkai zenshū.* Edited by Soejima Masamichi and Takei Yoshi. 6 vols. Tokyo: Soejima Masamichi, 1917.

Strecher, Matthew C. "Who's Afraid of Takahashi O-Den? 'Poison Woman' Stories and Literary Journalism in Early Meiji Japan." *Japanese Language and Literature* 38, no. 1 (April 2004): 25–55.

Suga Hidemi. *Nihon kindai bungaku no "tanjō": Genbun itchi undō to nashonarizumu.* Hihyō kūkan sōsho 6. Tokyo: Ōta Shuppan, 1995.

Suga Satoko. "Higuchi Ichiyō to waka." In *Teikoku no waka,* edited by Asada Tōru et al., 113–33. Waka o hiraku 5. Tokyo: Iwanami Shoten, 2006.

Sun Tzu. *The Art of War.* Translated by Samuel B. Griffith. New York: Oxford University Press, 1971.

Sunzi. *Sunzi yizhu.* Edited by Li Ling. Beijing: Zhonghua Shuju, 2007.

Suzuki Shigemitsu, ed. *Shinsen shigaku jizai.* Tokyo: Tsuruya Kiemon, 1879.

Suzuki, Tomi. "Gender and Genre: Modern Literary Histories and Women's Diary Literature." In *Inventing the Classics: Modernity, National Identity, and Japanese*

Literature, edited by Haruo Shirane and Tomi Suzuki, 71–95. Stanford, Calif.: Stanford University Press, 2000.

——. "*The Tale of Genji*, National Literature, Language, and Modernism." In *Envisioning the Tale of Genji: Media, Gender, and Cultural Production*, edited by Haruo Shirane, 243–87. New York: Columbia University Press, 2008.

Suzuki Toshiyuki. "*Shigo saikin to Yōgaku shiin*." *Chūō daigaku bungakubu kiyō*, no. 101 (February 2008): 65–103.

——. "*Yōgaku benran* kō: Bakumatsu shisaku netsu to sono yukue." *Kokugo to kokubungaku* 91, no. 7 (July 2014): 3–17.

Takasaki Masakaze. *Utamonogatari*. Tokyo: Tōkyōsha, 1912.

Takayanagi Katsuhiro. "Netto wa haiku o kaeuru ka." *Haiku* 59, no. 5 (April 2010): 156–62.

Takeoka Yūsen, ed. *Shinsen yōgaku benran*. Kyoto: Hayashi Yoshibē, 1878.

Tayama Katai. "Tōkyō no sanjūnen." In *Tayama Katai*, edited by Sōma Tsuneo, 9–244. Sakka no jiden 25. Tokyo: Nihon Tosho Sentā, 1995.

Teeters, Barbara. "Press Freedom and the *26th Century* Affair in Meiji Japan." *Modern Asian Studies* 6, no. 3 (1972): 337–51.

Tsuji Kiichi. "Meiji shidan tenbō." In *Meiji kanshibun shū*, edited by Kanda Kiichirō, 355–78. Meiji bungaku zenshū 62. Tokyo: Chikuma Shobō, 1983.

Ubukata Toshirō. *Meiji Taishō kenbunroku*. Tokyo: Chūō Kōronsha, 2005.

Unger, J. Marshall. *Literacy and Script Reform in Occupation Japan: Reading between the Lines*. New York: Oxford University Press, 1996.

Upton, Beth. "The Poems of Han Wo." PhD diss., University of California, Berkeley, 1980.

Wada Shigeki. "*Shō Nippon*" *sōsho* "*Haiku futabashū*": *Kenkyū to sakuin*. Matsuyama: Ehime Daigaku Hōbungakubu Kokugo Kokubungaku Kenkyūkai, 1974.

Wang Wei. *Wang Wei shixuan*. Edited by Liu Yisheng. Hong Kong: Joint Publishing, 1984.

Watson, Burton, trans. *Japanese Literature in Chinese*. 2 vols. New York: Columbia University Press, 1975–1976.

——, trans. *Masaoka Shiki: Selected Poems*. New York: Columbia University Press, 1997.

——, trans. *Zhuangzi: The Basic Writings*. New York: Columbia University Press, 2003.

Wixted, John Timothy. "*Kanbun*, Histories of Japanese Literature, and Japanologists." *Sino-Japanese Studies* 10, no. 2 (April 1998): 23–31.

——. "Sociability in Poetry: An Introduction to the Matching-Rhyme *Kanshi* of Mori Ōgai." In "*Ōgai*"—*Mori Rintarō: Begegnungen mit dem japanischen "homme de lettres*," edited by Klaus Kracht, 189–217. Wiesbaden: Harrassowitz, 2014.

Xiao Tong. *Wen xuan, or Selections of Refined Literature.* Translated, with annotations, by David R. Knechtges. 3 vols. Princeton, N.J.: Princeton University Press, 2014.

Xiao Yanwan. "Nihon ni shōkai sareta *Zuien onna deshi shisen sen* ni tsuite." *Chūgoku bungaku ronshū,* no. 31 (December 2002): 60–77.

Xu Chao, ed., Lao An, trans. *The Book of Rites.* Ruxue jingdian yicong. Jinan: Shandong Youyi Chubanshe, 1999.

Xu Yi. *Yan Zhou shihua.* Siku quanshu 1478. Shanghai: Shanghai Guji Chubanshe, 1987.

Yamaguchi Koken, ed. *Tōto shin hanjōki.* Tokyo: Kyōkadō Shoten, 1918.

Yamamoto Hokuzan. *Sakushi shikō.* In *Kinsei bungaku ronshū,* edited by Nakamura Yukihiko, 263–347. Nihon koten bungaku taikei 94. Tokyo: Iwanami Shoten, 1967.

Yamamoto Taketoshi. *Kindai Nippon no shinbun dokushasō.* Tokyo: Hōsei Daigaku Shuppankyoku, 1981.

——. "Meiji sanjūnendai zenhan no shinbun *Nippon* no dokushazō: Chishikijin dokusha no 'shinbun ishiki' o megutte." *Hitotsubashi ronsō* 58, no. 4 (October 1967): 510–16.

Yanagida Kunio. *Yanagida Kunio no kokyō nanajūnen.* Tokyo: PHP Kenkyūjo, 2014.

Yanagihara Kyokudō. *Yūjin Shiki.* Tokyo: Maeda Shuppan, 1946.

Yoda, Tomiko. *Gender and National Literature: Heian Texts in the Constructions of Japanese Modernity.* Durham, N.C.: Duke University Press, 2004.

Yosano Tekkan. "Bōkoku no on: Gendai no hijōbuteki waka o nonoshiru." In *Shiron, karon, hairon,* edited by Yoshida Seiichi et al., 241–47. Kindai bungaku hyōron taikei 8. Tokyo: Kadokawa Shoten, 1973.

——. *Tōzai nanboku.* Tokyo: Meiji Shoin, 1896.

Yoshida Yōtoku, ed. *Kaika shigo saikin.* Tokyo: Fuzandō, 1878.

Yu Yue, ed. *Dongyong shixuan.* N.p., 1883.

Zheng Ziyu and Sanetō Keishū, eds. *Huang Zunxian yu Riben youren bitan yigao.* Tokyo: Waseda Daigaku Tōyō Bungaku Kenkyūkai, 1968.

Index

Han Wo (aka Dong Lang), 38–41, 43, 48, 50, 60, 74, 215n11. See also *Fragrant Toilette Collection*

Han Yu, 66, 75, 225n104

Hara Saihin, 45

Hatta Tomonori, 184

Hattori Nankaku, 6, 7

Hattori Somon, 15–16, 210n32

Hattori Yoshinobu, 231n9

Hayashi Mikaomi, 176, 177, 249n67

Heian period, xxviii, xxxv, 149, 150, 151, 230n151; "feminized" aristocrats and literature of, 163, 174, 175; national literature and, 170; rise of warrior class in late Heian, 161, 171; *waka* and decline of aristocratic power, 161

Hekijō zekku, 218n41

Hekiunkai, 141

He Ning, 215n11

Herzfeld, Michael, 203n22

hierarchy, xvi, xxv, 5, 194; national-poetic community and, xxxv; of poetic masculinity, 36, 150

Higuchi Motomi, 16

Hinoki Nagahiro, 18

Hint of Rain Collection [*Yiyuji*] (Wang Yanhong), 48

Hirabatake Seitō, 196, 197

Hirose Tansō, 20

hokku ("opening verse"), xxi, 84, 123, 136, 202n8; as "commoner literature," 120; competitive communal composition of, 130; European ideas of poetry and, 128; seen as "bacillus," 127

homosexuality, 41

Honda Shuchiku, xxxi

Hoshi Tōru, 97

Hōsū (poetry journal), 157

Hototogisu (literary journal), xxv, 87, 108, 116, 195, 199; demographics of new haiku and, 137–44; haiku manifesto in first issue, 114; move from Matsuyama to Tokyo, 129, 140; traditional and conservative view of, 196

Huang Zunxian, 53

Huffman, James, xvii

Huihong, 215n7

Hyakubunkai, 142

Hyakunin isshu (*One Hundred Poems*) collection, 164–65, 171, 247n37, 247nn40–41

Hydrangea Flowers [*Xiu qiu hua*] (Guo Pinqie), 47

hyōsokuya (rhymers), xxxi, 206n51

Ibi Takashi, 7–8, 9

Ichiichi Gakunin. *See* Soejima Taneomi

Ichikawa Kansai, 7, 44, 204n25

identity, national, xv, xxviii, 148, 182, 200; literature as focus for, xxxiv; political novels and, xvii; *waka* and, xxxv, 187, 189, 194–95

Ihara Saikaku, 129

Ikebe (aka Konakamura) Yoshikata, 155, 156, 177

Ikegami Eiko, xxiii

Imagined Communities (Anderson, 1983), xvi, xvii

imagined community, 41

imperialism, 148, 159, 177, 199

Imperial University, xxvi

Incheon Shinseikai (Korea), 141, 143

Inoue Kenkabō, 232n23

Inoue Tetsujirō, 58, 59, 155, 162

In Response to the Ban Order Picture (Gokyō), 111

intellectual property, 19

internet, xiii–xiv, 195

Introduction to the Study of Poetry, An [*Shigaku shōsei*] (1769), 10

Iritani Sensuke, 211n48

Irokawa Daikichi, 216n24

Ise Grand Shrine, xxviii, 232n22

Ishii Tokuchū, 235n61

Ishiyama Keizan, 235n61

Isogai Unpō, 167

Itakura Seiko, 219n50

Ito, Ken K., xvii

Itō Hirobumi, 27, 42, 71, 84, 92, 227n129

Itō Hōzan, 18–19, 22, 211n47

Itō Sachio, 178–79

Itō Shōu, 107, 132, 235n61

Iwai Shigeki, 177

Iwaki Juntarō, 145

Iwamoto Yoshiharu, 166
Iwamura Takatoshi, 231n10
Iwaya Kobai, 46, 60, 71
Iwaya Sazanami, 128, 130, 241n48
Izumi Kaname, 17

Jade Maiden (Yu Nü), 67, 68, 225n107
Jansen, Marius, 8
Japanese Literary Classics for Middle School Education [*Chūtō kyōiku Nihon bunten*] (Ochiai and Ikebe, 1891), 155
Jasmine Poetic Society (Mari Ginsha), 204n25
Jimmu, Emperor, 167, 248n48
Jin Yi, 45
Jogaku sekai (journal), 165
Jogaku zasshi (women's periodical), 120, 166
Jokan (journal), 166, 177
Jotei (Kashiwagi Jotei), 7, 11–12, 204n25, 209n21; "bamboo-branch ballad" genre and, 44; vernacular renderings of, 210n26
journals, literary, xiv, xviii, xix, xxiv, 59. See also *specific titles*

Kada no Azumamaro, 165
Kagaku (literary journal), 156, 157, 160
Kagawa Kageki (aka Kagawa Keien), 175, 180–81, 182, 183
Kagawa Kagetoshi, 180
Kagetsu shinshi (literary journal), xix, 27, 34, 213n70
Kaika shigo saikin [Gold dust treasury of poetic words for enlightened times] (1878), 28–29
Kainan (Mori Kainan), xxx–xxxi, xxxiii, 34, 46, 90, 92; allegedly effeminate style of, 64; criticized for emotional inauthenticity, 53–54, 221n66; critics of, 76–77; government employment of, 71; rebuttal to Seigai's criticism, 71–74; Seigai's criticism of, 68–69; as "softie" (*nanpa*), 42
Kakinomoto no Hitomaro, 184
Kakuta Chikurei. See Chikurei
Kamei Shōkin, 45
Kamo no Mabuchi, 147, 156, 171

kana syllabaries, 8, 151
kanbun (Sinitic prose), xxviii, 25, 227n129, 235n57
Kan Chazan, 23, 24, 27
Kanda Kiichirō, 57
Kanda Kōgan, 57–58
kanshi (Sinitic poetry), xv, xx, 59, 76, 115, 201n7; as aspirational genre in Meiji period, 24–30; "cut and paste" approach to composition, 4, 15, 22, 24, 210n32; Edo-period poetic lexicons and, 13–19; education in writing of, 1–6, 9; female poets and the feminine in, 35, 45–47, 80; gender and, xxvi–xxvii, 173; itinerant poets, 2; *kanshi* literacy, xxxii, 4, 5, 6–13; *kanshi* societies, xxi; lack of state sanction for, 179; manuals for composing, 4, 6, 208n9; as most highly esteemed poetic genre, xviii; national literature and, xxviii; rise as popular genre, xxxii. See also Sinitic poetry
Kanshi nyūmon (Iritani Sensuke, 1986), 211n48
Karai Senryū, 230n4
Karatani Kōjin, xvii, 202n15
kasa-zuke (putting on a hat), 204n26
Kashiwagi Jotei. See Jotei
Katayama Tōu, 235n61
Katō Kuniyasu, 23–24
Katō Takusen, 32, 88, 217n27
Katsunan (Kuga Katsunan), xxxii, 82, 86, 88, 154, 217n27; Shiki's "Letters to a *Waka* Poet" and, 182–83, 190; *Shō Nippon* and, 105, 106; topical haiku and, 114
Katsura Koson, 93
Kawada Ōkō, 40–41
Kawahigashi Hekigotō, xxx, 109, 140, 192; as disciple of Shiki, 193, 194; free-verse approach to haiku, 196
Kawahigashi Seikei, 22
Kazaate Sakiko, 157
Keene, Donald, xxxi
Kegon Falls poems (Seigai), 61–62, 72–74, 79, 80–81, 90
Keichū, 147, 171
Keirin isshi, 34, 214n2

Liu Yuxi, 44
Li Yuxi (Li Shangyin), 56
Li Zha, 226n114
love poetry, 173, 177; Bureau of Poetry
(Outadokoro) and, 163–64, 176; excluded
from *utakai hajime* ceremony, 149;
marginalization of, 164; prominence in
waka canon, 165–66, 247n41; Tekkan's
disdain for, 178
Lu You, 46
Lu Yun (Lu Shilong), 68, 226n118

Madenokōji Tomoko, 220n50
Maeda Ai, 216nn24–25
Maeda Ringai, 119, 238n5
Maeda Tōru, 160
maeke-zuke (adding to the first verse),
204n26
Mainichi shinbun (newspaper), 113,
115, 123
Maki Ryōko, 43
Mangetsukai, 142, 144
"Many Clouds Rising" (Susanoo), 167,
248n48
Man'yōshū (*Collection of ten thousand
leaves*, ca. 785), 145, 148–49, 156, 159,
246n24; as "poetry anthology of the
people," 127; women's study of, 169
Marumaru chinbun (satirical newspaper),
232n23
Masaoka Ritsu, 87
Masaoka Shiki. *See* Shiki
masculinity, xvi, xxvi–xxvii, 33, 146, 149;
"fragrant style" poetics and, xxxiii,
35–36; heterosexual desire as inimical
to, 36, 216n21; hypermasculine poetry,
64, 69, 160; martial ideal of, 150, 177; in
Meiji *waka* discourse, 159–65;
performance of, 35; "softie" versus
"roughneck" poetics, 41, 76–81; "spirit"
and "backbone" associated with, 80;
Tekkan's critique of insufficient
masculinity in *waka*, 173–77;
undermined by love poetry, 165, 177
Matsue nippō (newspaper), 143
Matsui Toshihiko, 250n3
Matsumoto Keidō, 218n40

Matsuyama, 2, 108, 138, 141, 207n5, 231n10;
Evergreen Society in, 153; FPRM in, 31,
86–87, 207n54; Hisamatsu family and,
231n9; *Hototogisu*'s move to Tokyo from,
129, 140; *kanshi* teachers in, 22;
opposition to Satsuma-Chōshū
coalition, xxxii; Shiki and, xxxii, 25, 27,
31, 86–87
Mayer, Tamar, xxiv
media technologies, xiv, xxv, xxxv, 195
Meiji bungakushi [A history of Meiji
literature] (Iwaki Juntarō), 145
Meiji emperor, 164
Meiji period, xiv, 5; censorship under,
105–13, *110*; nation-building project, xv,
xxiii; poetic lexicons in early Meiji
period, 19–24, *21*; politics of *kanshi*
lexicons during, 30–33; print media in,
xvii, xviii, xix, xxiii, xxiv, 6, 65;
regulation of the press and, 82. *See also*
Tokugawa government (*bakufu*)
Meiji Restoration, xxxii, 42, 48, 115, 154, 179
Meikyōkan, 2, 207n5
Meirin Kōsha, xx
Meirin zasshi (journal), 115, 129, 138
Mencius, 242n58
"men of letters" (*bungakusha*), xxxv, 44, 124,
125, 128, 182
Mertz, John Pierre, xvii
Midaregami [*Tangled Hair*] (Yosano Akiko,
1901), 178
Mikami Sanji, xxvii, xxviii, 155
mikasa-zuke (putting on three hats),
204n26
Miki Aika, 58
Mikkoku: Shōwa haiku dan'atsu jiken
(Kozakai Shōzō, 1979), 262n16
Mimori Mikio, xx, 115, 186, 205n41, 238n3,
250n3; *Meirin zasshi* (journal) of, 129,
138; as "old school" master, 118;
old-school "scholars" criticized by, 135
Minami Hajime, 2
Minamoto no Sanetomo, 156, 171, 181
Ming Archaists (Kobunji-ha), 6, 43, 217n29
Min'yū shinbun (newspaper), 143
Miura Kanō, 20, 80, 211n49
Miyako shinbun (newspaper), 136

STUDIES OF THE WEATHERHEAD EAST ASIAN INSTITUTE
COLUMBIA UNIVERSITY
Selected Titles

(Complete list at: http://www.columbia.edu/cu/weai/weatherhead-studies.html)

The Chinese Typewriter: A History, by Thomas S. Mullaney. MIT Press, 2017.

Mobilizing without the Masses: Control and Contention in China, by Diana Fu. Cambridge University Press, 2017.

Forgotten Disease: Illnesses Transformed in Chinese Medicine, by Hilary A. Smith. Stanford University Press, 2017.

Socialist Cosmopolitanism: The Chinese Literary Universe, 1945–1965, by Nicolai Volland. Columbia University Press, 2017.

The Social Life of Inkstones: Artisans and Scholars in Early Qing China, by Dorothy Ko. University of Washington Press, 2017.

The End of Japanese Cinema: Industrial Genres, National Times, and Media Ecologies, by Alexander Zahlten. Duke University Press, 2017.

Darwin, Dharma, and the Divine: Evolutionary Theory and Religion in Modern Japan, by G. Clinton Godart. University of Hawai`i Press, 2017.

Yokohama and the Silk Trade: How Eastern Japan Became the Primary Economic Region of Japan, 1843–1893, by Yasuhiro Makimura. Lexington Books, 2017.

Youth for Nation: Culture and Protest in Cold War South Korea, by Charles R. Kim. University of Hawai`i Press, 2017.

Scholars in Early Qing China, by Dorothy Ko. University of Washington Press, 2016.

Samurai to Soldier: Remaking Military Service in Nineteenth-Century Japan, by D. Colin Jaundrill. Cornell University Press, 2016.

The Red Guard Generation and Political Activism in China, by Guobin Yang. Columbia University Press, 2016.

Accidental Activists: Victim Movements and Government Accountability in Japan and South Korea, by Celeste L. Arrington. Cornell University Press, 2016.

Negotiating Rural Land Ownership in Southwest China: State, Village, Family, by Yi Wu. University of Hawai`i Press, 2016.

Ming China and Vietnam: Negotiating Borders in Early Modern Asia, by Kathlene Baldanza. Cambridge University Press, 2016.

Ethnic Conflict and Protest in Tibet and Xinjiang: Unrest in China's West, coedited by Ben Hillman and Gray Tuttle. Columbia University Press, 2016.

One Hundred Million Philosophers: Science of Thought and the Culture of Democracy in Postwar Japan, by Adam Bronson. University of Hawai`i Press, 2016.

Conflict and Commerce in Maritime East Asia: The Zheng Family and the Shaping of the Modern World, c. 1620–1720, by Xing Hang. Cambridge University Press, 2016.

Chinese Law in Imperial Eyes: Sovereignty, Justice, and Transcultural Politics, by Li Chen. Columbia University Press, 2016.

Imperial Genus: The Formation and Limits of the Human in Modern Korea and Japan, by Travis Workman. University of California Press, 2015.

Yasukuni Shrine: History, Memory, and Japan's Unending Postwar, by Akiko Takenaka. University of Hawai`i Press, 2015.

The Age of Irreverence: A New History of Laughter in China, by Christopher Rea. University of California Press, 2015.

The Nature of Knowledge and the Knowledge of Nature in Early Modern Japan, by Federico Marcon. University of Chicago Press, 2015.

The Fascist Effect: Japan and Italy, 1915–1952, by Reto Hofmann. Cornell University Press, 2015.

The International Minimum: Creativity and Contradiction in Japan's Global Engagement, 1933–1964, by Jessamyn R. Abel. University of Hawai`i Press, 2015.

Empires of Coal: Fueling China's Entry into the Modern World Order, 1860–1920, by Shellen Xiao Wu. Stanford University Press, 2015.

Casualties of History: Wounded Japanese Servicemen and the Second World War, by Lee K. Pennington. Cornell University Press, 2015.

City of Virtues: Nanjing in an Age of Utopian Visions, by Chuck Wooldridge. University of Washington Press, 2015.

The Proletarian Wave: Literature and Leftist Culture in Colonial Korea, 1910–1945, by Sunyoung Park. Harvard University Asia Center, 2015.

Neither Donkey nor Horse: Medicine in the Struggle over China's Modernity, by Sean Hsiang-lin Lei. University of Chicago Press, 2014.

When the Future Disappears: The Modernist Imagination in Late Colonial Korea, by Janet Poole. Columbia University Press, 2014.

Bad Water: Nature, Pollution, and Politics in Japan, 1870–1950, by Robert Stolz. Duke University Press, 2014.

Rise of a Japanese Chinatown: Yokohama, 1894–1972, by Eric C. Han. Harvard University Asia Center, 2014.